Place

of

No Pity

⌘

The Recapitulation Diaries

Volume 4

July-December 2003

J. E. Ketchel

Riverwalker Press

Cover design by J. E. Ketchel

Cover painting by J. E. Ketchel: *String Theory I*

Riverwalker Press
PO Box 101
Red Hook, NY 12571

www.riverwalkerpress.com

ISBN: 978-0-9800506-7-7

MEDICAL DISCLAIMER: The information in this book is not intended to replace treatment with a competent mental healthcare provider. Please seek appropriate support and put the book aside if it proves to be too disruptive. Any application of the material presented in this book is at the reader's discretion and is his or her sole responsibility. The author and publisher are in no way responsible or liable for misuse of this information.

Table of Contents

Prologue

Mad Cows

On a warm spring day, when my children were still young, I received a phone call from the woman who lived across the street.

"Don't let your kids go outside!" she said, having received a call from a nearby farmer. "The cows have gone mad!"

A dark mass was indeed weaving across the fields behind her house, cows on the loose! All the neighbors were being alerted should the cows break out of the wooden fencing surrounding the field and stampede through the village. From our front porch we had quite a view of the action.

We watched with astonishment as a dozen cowboys arrived to round up the wayward herd, trotting down the two lane highway on their hearty steeds, materializing out of nowhere, like the members of a volunteer fire squad. Where had they come from? This was rural upstate New York after all, not the wild west!

Traffic came to a standstill as the pack of wranglers powwowed in the middle of the lanes on their skittish horses, the horses' hooves clattering loudly on the pavement. From their high perches the cowboys eyed the unruly herd careening about in the distance, a black wave rippling across the bright green of the early spring field. Clearly they *had* gone mad! Nothing but a flimsy fence kept our little village from imminent danger.

One of the horses, startled by a honking car, reared up, throwing its rider onto the hard surface of the highway. It took off, empty saddle flapping, straight toward our yard. The poor rider picked himself up and ran limping after his horse, pointy cowboy boots slapping the pavement. The scared horse came up to our porch. Leaning over the railing, my daughter reached her arms out toward it and the skittish animal sidled up, pausing to put its enormous muzzle into the palms of her tiny outstretched hands. The winded cowboy snuck up behind and was just about to grab the reins when my daughter squealed a happy shrill of delight, a sound that only a six-year-old girl can emit, and in that instant the horse bolted again. It ran behind our house and into the backyard where it leaped over a fence and sped off into the field beyond. The poor cowboy took off after it, groaning and cursing. Eventually he captured his steed and rejoined the group of cowboys still mulling in the middle of the highway. Having decided upon a strategy, they jumped their horses over the fence, formed a line, and charged across the field, driving the wild herd into a corner before any damage could be done. Once surrounded the mad cows turned from whirling dervishes into a patch of docile old ladies.

Those dear cows, struck by spring fever, clearly exhibited a release of long suppressed, deeply instinctual energy. Though I was yet to be fully overtaken by what was brewing inside myself, I sensed its imminent arrival on that day as I stood on the porch and watched the action unfold. For I was as sensitive and jittery as the horse that bolted, aware that I too would soon go charging off, straight into what I knew not. I felt the fear and excitement of something long suppressed inside myself about to burst forth too, a great energy stirring within, though I could not have explained any of it on that day, for in that moment it was no more than a whiff of intuition, a strange sense that things were going to change and that I would not be able to stop any of it.

That vibrant energy did eventually make itself more fully known and within a few years I began my inner journey. I set off to find out who I was, where I had been, and where I was headed. Just like the rider who got thrown I too got thrown, as memories emerged, as the life I had known crumbled and fell away. As I journeyed onward, deeper into myself and my past, I experienced the highs and lows of a night sea journey, one moment in the heights of incredible energetic experiences in the light, in the next thrown down into the deepest darkness, a radical shift known in psychological terms as enantiodromia.

I got used to the rollercoaster ride of my own psyche as it took me further and deeper than I could ever have imagined. And like the rider who had gotten thrown, I would remount, regroup, reassess, and return to the churning mass of energy inside myself. Without realizing it I had witnessed my own future in the scenario of the mad cows on that warm spring day, my future recapitulation process reflected in the swirling mass of energy bursting forth, in the frightened horse, and in the intrepid rider. And my lovely little daughter's squeal of delight, innocence unleashed, was another aspect of myself that I was going to have to encounter too.

It's 2016 now as I write this prologue to this fourth book in *The Recapitulation Diaries*, many years after that spring 1998 encounter with the mad cows. I am struck by how accurate that experience was at foreshadowing what was to come, just as I am by the dreams I dreamed during my recapitulation and the hints they offered at what might transpire as well. For it is fifteen years after my recapitulation began and I now clearly see how my inner work, my dreams, and the hard work I was doing to create a new reality for myself all wove seamlessly together. For I can tell you that many of the dreams I dreamed back then, and that I interpreted in ways that were meaningful for where I was and what I was doing at that time, now, upon further reflection, reveal deeper truths having to do with things I was not ready to know or embrace at the time. I can now identify many of them as accurate premonitions, as well-laid out plans for a future me. The hard work I was doing on myself really did result in a transformed self, my core sense of self really did change. It happened gradually and it happened consistently because I elected to be present with what was stirring inside myself and because I took the changing journey as it was presented, day and night, a most difficult task and a most rewarding experience.

You might notice in this volume that I have become quite adept at interpreting my own dreams, a far cry from the almost total lack of interpretation and reflection during the first year. At that time it was all I could do to document what was happening, but as the years progressed so did my ability to analyze what came from my dream world. It's a stunning and fascinating process to be engaged in, to experience how life and dreams interweave, charting a path to the unknown self, waking it up to consciousness.

Chuck Ketchel, LCSW-R, intuitive psychotherapist and shamanic practitioner, was my steady human guide throughout the recapitulation process. As my inner journey unfolded I had so many experiences I could not explain, sometimes thinking I was hallucinating, surely going crazy. And yet, as soon as I presented them to Chuck I was relieved of any such ideas, for he never judged or dismissed what came to me or through me, but taught me how to interpret my own experiences based on where I was and what I was going through. It mattered only that I find a way to accept

3

them as meaningful lessons, come to teach me, to show me what I needed to know about myself, and about the world. It wasn't until much later that I learned that many other explorers of the inner world have had similar experiences, but while undergoing the process I often felt like a lone traveler going where no human had ever gone. And in a sense that was true, for every inner journey is unique and deeply personal.

My recapitulation was largely self-initiated and self-driven. It could be described as a self-experiential soul retrieval journey, one that I took mostly alone. Yes, I was guided by an expert, but most of my journey was taken in the privacy of my own bedroom, in the course of my everyday life, and in my brimmingly alive inner world. I do my best to define and describe my experiences in *The Recapitulation Diaries*, but it is often difficult to fully describe or explain what is purely experiential, it has to be *experienced*. Yet, I attempt to bring you, my reader, into my inner world, into my dream world, and into my everyday life in as descriptive a way as possible that you might grasp how everything that unfolded during my inner journey intertwined, how it guided and transformed me as I plunged into the whirlwind of it all. I hope I have sufficiently described that whirlwind so that you are able to experience and understand, even just a little bit, the depths and the heights of a modern soul's night sea journey.

During my recapitulation I met with Chuck twice a week, but the journey was ongoing, day and night. The clashing of worlds raged constantly, the momentum catapulting me forward so fast and so far that Chuck was not privy to most of my process. He did not learn of my diaries until much later, nor did he know of my experiences with Jeanne, his deceased wife. It was not until 2004 that I finally revealed to him my personal connection with her and all that she had meant to me as I took my journey. So, in reading my books, keep in mind that you, my reader, are privy to so much more than Chuck was at the time. It would have been impossible to keep him apprised of all that was happening to me, so I kept writing things down, as much to appease my anxiety as to document what I was going through, for it felt important to do so. The idea of turning it all into a book presented itself every now and then during the journey, a frightening idea each time it arose, and yet here we are, another volume published!

I describe many of my experiences as being "energetic" experiences, for lack of a better word. Such experiences took place in non-ordinary reality and in altered states of consciousness, but my feelings and sensations were fully of this reality, taking place in my physical body. I took the journey as a sober being and yet some of the experiences may come across as "trips" induced by chemicals or drugs. I never took drugs or altered myself with substance. Though I enjoyed a few glasses of wine every now and then in the course of everyday life, the "trips" I took were experienced in full unadulterated consciousness, fantastical though they may appear to be.

The Shamans of Ancient Mexico state, and I personally experienced, that the intent and practice of recapitulation sets in motion an autonomous unfolding of experiences whose order, frequency, and quality are determined completely outside of conscious control, perhaps from some higher center of self beyond ego. All ego can do is let go and open up to the experiences that are involuntarily presented. As each new encounter is mastered, healing ensues and the building blocks to a newly reordered self are firmly set in place. I personally experienced recapitulation in this manner. Even with all the magical stuff going on, however, the intent was always the same, the achievement of a new self, fully healed and fully available to life.

In addition to Chuck I was also guided throughout my journey by beings in other realities, in other than human form, from whom I received communications of profound guidance and wisdom. Jeanne Ketchel was the most prominent and influential, but I identified others as well. Those guides were as real to me as my energetic and physical experiences were, guiding me along through many of the most difficult phases of my journey. I learned to trust their voices as the process unfolded and I was deeply comforted by and always felt that I was held in the highest esteem by them. They cared deeply about me. Even if they sometimes delivered their messages in unexpected ways, they were never malevolent nor harmful to me. Indeed, I experienced only great love and respect from them. An abundance of gratitude showered down from them as they thanked me for trusting them too, for receiving them and allowing them to become a part of my process, and my life in general, for they are with me still.

In my experience, guidance comes to us all during the course of our lives, in many different shapes and forms, perhaps in symbols and signs, perhaps in auditory communications, perhaps in the guise of those who have left this reality, showing up with what we need when we most need it. The challenge, as was my own, is to ask our rational, skeptical, judgmental, worldly self to step aside so we can understand what is being offered, and then to ask our brave warrior self, our spiritual self, to keep us focused on the path that is shown to us, our path of heart.

Like another unrecapitulated memory the idea of writing a book festered during my recapitulation, growing inside me like a pregnancy until I finally took up the task of compiling and bringing it to life. And so, *The Recapitulation Diaries* have slowly come into being, as have so many other things that were portended during my three-year-long recapitulation journey. My intention at the beginning of this opus was that *The Recapitulation Diaries* would be a three-volume set, one book for each year of my recapitulation, but it soon became clear that to do justice to the process that number would have to extend to a five-volume set. Work on the final volume is already underway as this fourth book goes to press. And yet my story does not end there. For just as Jeanne once predicted, recapitulation has come to be the focus of my life, a most meaningful process and my life's true opus.

The words I write are the truths of my life, of who I am and who I was. *The Recapitulation Diaries* describe and expound upon the experiences that shaped me. I share them with much gratitude for having had the privilege of so many experiences and so fulfilling a journey. It is not my intention to make a believer out of anyone. I am not a believer myself, but I have had undeniable experiences and that's enough for me.

In publishing the details of my recapitulation I lay myself bare before all of you, without personal attachment or personal need. I learned a long time ago that nothing outside of myself could hurt or destroy the strong spirit inside me, the eternal self, and so I take nothing personally, not even my own story or my own vulnerabilities. This highly impersonal and detached yet very deeply loving and compassionate state is what I call a place of no pity, and so I place myself upon the altar, before your eyes, that you too may experience a place of no pity.

This book, *Place of No Pity*, continues where *Into the Vast Nothingness* left off, in July of 2003. The light at the end of the tunnel was growing larger and brighter as the year unfolded, my recapitulation running full force. And I was right there with it, finding meaning in everything that happened to me, seeking balance in the changing reality I was creating and experiencing, taking the ride of a lifetime, for which I am forever grateful.

Jan Ketchel
November 8, 2016
Red Hook, NY

Chapter 1

Murky Waters

July 1, 2003

I struggle out of a tiresome dream, seeking anchoring in the darkness of my bedroom, heavy with summer heat. Throwing off the covers, I lie sweaty and inert, the rattling box fan in my window sending out meager puffs of humid air. Suddenly, I am wide awake, in the grips of a painful childhood memory, in some old place with my abuser. I toss and turn, frantic to get away, but all I can do is hang over the side of my bed and retch.

It's early, still dark, but I get up anyway. I'll never be able to sleep now. I make coffee and curl up on the living room sofa. Sloughing off the memory pain and the grogginess of the night, I contemplate my day. I'll be using words today rather than paint, interviewing people for an article I'm writing about a local arts festival, communicating in a different way, drawing myself out of my emptiness. I will be switching from inner talk to outer talk, from my inner world of private words to the outer world of focused communication. I'm ready to do this, to move on to new venues of creative expression, and new life too.

I meet with Chuck. He suggests that the pain I woke up with, and the pain in general, must be dealt with in a new way now, that I can't let it overpower me anymore or just sit there and bear it. Just as I seek to branch out in new creative ways, making room for change in my life, so does the recapitulation require change if I am to progress.

"You must do it differently now," he says, "break the chains that hold you so tightly; shift out of the old way of handling the memories. Become intentionally proactive."

I know he's right. The pain is exhausting and draining. Once in its grip I become like a fly caught in a spider's web, frantic to get away yet quickly overpowered. Numbed by the sting of the spider and wrapped tightly in its cocoon of sticky webbing, I am innocent prey, trapped once again. I only got away this morning because I leapt out of bed as fast as I could. To move the recapitulation along, however, requires that I go through each memory. Far better to have stayed in bed, to have let it ride through me, meeting it head on, releasing it, ridding myself of it once and for all. I know the procedure well enough, but my first instinct is still to run. It takes nerves of steel to let the memory go through me, to relive what my child self once went through, and yet, this is my challenge.

The kids are away at their dad's for the first weeks of summer vacation, so I could have let myself go without fear of waking anyone, without having to hold back, but I did what I usually do—I ran! This has been a major issue in the process, as I get caught and numbed by the memories before I can think clearly, before I can even remember that it's different now, that I really do have abilities and techniques to process the memories and actually free myself. Going numb has been my main protection for so long.

"Old habits don't die easily," I tell Chuck.

"See what happens to show you what to do next time," he suggests, as we end our session. "Try to stay alert to what comes."

"I'll try," I say, secretly hoping there won't be a next time.

July 2, 2003

I dream that I meet with Chuck. We sit across from each other, conversing in the usual manner, when he suddenly gets up and leaves. I wait for him to return; I wait a very long time. When he doesn't come back I get up and leave, frustrated, and a little angry too. Instead of the usual sidewalks outside his office there are muddy ditches filled with water. I have a hard time negotiating the slippery troughs, murky brown water up to my knees. My anger grows as I wonder how Chuck can ever help me when things are such a mess around his own house. But then I see that he's been making repairs, building nice sturdy concrete walls to hold the earth back, putting in drainage pipes. I realize that he's a very capable man and is doing a fine job of fixing things.

I wake up enthused by the sight of the shoring up of the walls, confident that Chuck and I are doing good work. My dream seems to indicate that I can trust him, even though he walked away and left me sitting there in his office with no explanation. He's a professional and I have to trust that he knows what he's doing. I am also vitally aware that the real work of this recapitulation, this building of a new life, is my own responsibility and I have to do it on my own. And yet I have to admit that there's a part of me that's angry with him. I can admit this now, at dawn, when things are naturally clearer.

He recently mentioned that he has often seen women leave one relationship and jump right into another, women afraid to be alone, seeking their wholeness in a man. Well, that has not been my problem! I have no interest in a new relationship at this point, except with myself. He seemed to be implying that I was headed that way when he said it, or at least I took it that way. It made me mad when he said it, and it makes me mad now, especially as it seemed as if he himself jumped right into another relationship shortly after Jeanne died, doing the exact thing he says women tend to do! I'm sure he had his reasons. But me? I'm angry!

I wonder if I still have a transference with him? Most likely it's still present, and I'll have to confront that at some point, but more pressing right now is the heavy weight of my recapitulation and the excruciating pain it has conjured, all of which have absolutely nothing to do with him. All of that belongs totally to me and it's my job to face it and fix it, not his. It's how I will one day attain my fucking wholeness. Happy 51st Birthday!

July 3, 2003

I dream all night long that the house is being bombed. My kids and I try to sleep while bombs drop all around us, the sky lighting brightly as they come screeching down, shattering and shaking the earth upon impact. We huddle together while I try to soothe the kids to sleep, assuring them that we're safe. In spite of the bombs, I'm absolutely certain about this—we are safe. Though a war rages on outside, we aren't really threatened and I know we won't get hurt.

My dream seems to indicate that I will get through this phase of the recapitulation unscathed. Like all the other phases it's not going to destroy me, and my inner children will be safe too. I am the adult, the protector, the knower of the truth. Yesterday, I was in a big slump, depressed all day. Because it was my birthday? I don't know. I never know what each day will bring; I either wake up depressed or I wake up in a good mood. I accept the instability of where I am, still on this healing journey. Today, for instance, I feel a little more hopeful, even though the night was difficult with those bombs dropping, old demons coming in the night to blast me back into depression and despair. Well, it's not working!

Home now at the end of a fairly quiet day focused on work and staying as physically and mentally relaxed as possible. Even so, feelings of panic would rush over me every now and then, much like those bombs of my dream, screeching overhead, dizzying and nauseating in their intensity. I'd duck as soon as I sensed their shadow looming over me, the insidious taste of their smoke in my mouth, the scent of old memories lingering in the air. I know I should let them strike, but nothing other than panic seemed to ride in on them, no memories, nothing more than a hint of something to come, and so I feel I handled them perfectly by dodging them all day. It was all I could think to do at the time, even though Chuck suggested that I find a new way to face the memories now.

I'm aware that this period won't last forever, this sadness and loneliness, nor the torment of bad memories. As sad as I get I feel the hint of change ahead, the scent of happier times riding in on those bombs as well, as strange as that may sound. There was a sense of calmness underlying the intensity of the situation in my dream, the hint that one day this turmoil will be over. As long as my adult self is in charge all should be fine, and so I am cheered by the prospect of better things to come.

The cats cheer me too, the three of them running and rolling around like crazy, the little kitten so cute, though the big cats loom over her, their shadows like the bombs of memories that loom constantly over me. In spite of the pain of this time in my life, in this moment I am content.

July 4, 2003

I slept for eight hours. That alone makes me feel better, though I awaken lost and sad, haunted by loneliness. As I look out the window at the warm summer day, the clear blue sky suddenly rips apart before my very eyes and a jagged black hole appears. As if torn open by the claws of a hungry wild beast, the dark hole in the brilliant blue day sends messages of doom coursing through me. I long to escape that black hole and yet I am drawn there too. What do I still expect to find in its terrible darkness?

The reality is that I was horrifically abused from the time I was small. I saved myself by running out of the darkness into the light of forgetfulness. I survived by quickly shifting, blocking out what happened to me, leaving all the pain behind in the dark woods of my childhood. Now I'm going back into the darkness to see what really happened, down into the roots of my own memory and my own body. Will I survive it a second time? So far I've been lucky.

As I've retrieved so many memories over the past few years an incredible story has unfolded. I can touch and feel it now, the real life I once lived, the mysteries at last revealed. For so many years I was separated from the truth of what had happened to me, like a blind person I was totally incapable of seeing. Reminders came often enough, letting me know that one day I would have the opportunity to find out what it was that confused me, what haunted me, and why I was so disconnected and emotionless, so out-of-body all the time. Now everything is being revealed, the confusion transforming into clear memory. Even so, I haven't had much luck curtailing the sadness and depression, major symptoms of this recapitulation process. I suppose it's inevitable that the mental condition of my youth needs to be relived along with the memories, impacting as powerfully as the memories, having been held in check equally as long.

I have no plans except to be alone today on this holiday. Although my family is having their traditional Fourth-of-July get-together I have bowed out, just as I've been bowing out of most family events lately.

I keep busy around the house, sensing my oldest demon, Fear, edging closer and closer, my stomach lurching as he grabs, as he pokes and prods, the same way my abuser once tortured me. I keep one brisk step ahead of him. Finally, remembering that I'm supposed to be doing this differently, I wheel around and face him.

"You again, you old rascal! Can't get enough of me, eh? Back for more?"

"I am your favorite of all the torments," Fear says. "Who needs outside stimulation when you have me?"

"I get a sense of something disturbing and *poof*, it's you again," I say, "grabbing my gut and twisting it, knotting me like a rope. Feels good, eh, to get your claws back into my flesh?"

I hear him laughing, an old scratchy laugh.

"Well, enjoy it while you can, because it won't always be this way. I'm studying how you sneak up on me, how all of a sudden you're there and before I know it you have me in your clutches. You bastard! But things are changing. I'm changing! I won't always be such easy prey!"

I must work, work, work, otherwise I'm stuck in the muck of depression and it becomes impossible to pull myself out; that sticky spider web again! Work creates the balance I need, matches the intensity of the inner work, though my focus is going to have to shift back to the kids again soon enough. In the meantime, I have plenty of work. I'll be starting a new job next week, painting murals at a private home, which will keep me focused and gratefully busy. Even so, no matter where I am or what I'm doing, I must wrestle with my demons, for doubtless they will hound me. At least now I know who they are and why they exist, that they're related to something real, that they aren't just some craziness in my head. As inhabitants of my psyche, embedded in my personality, they have ruled me. But now I'm using them, not to harm but to heal.

July 5, 2003

I wake up with intense pain in my legs and hips. I beg and bargain with it, trying to psych myself into a better mood, but the pain clings in gripping unwillingness to let go. I am not happy! I must shift my focus to work; it's the only way out of this pain and the overall misery of my life. If I don't focus on work I fear I will stay stuck in the muck of depression, which has, so far, been impossible to totally extricate myself from. I find that the only way to stay sane is to work insanely. I also know that in all of this frantic need to work I must provide some caring time for myself or I will destroy myself in trying to save myself.

After a pretty good day at the studio I head out to work at the artist's gallery where I have been an active member for several years. It's a quiet evening. Few people come in and so I have time to work on a writing assignment. I pick up my pen and words easily flow from it. They slide out uninhibited until an old feeling of inadequacy seizes me. Like a heavy hand pressing on my heart it smothers my creativity and I give up. Okay, forget it. I can't. I can't do anything. I put down my pen and sulk.

Why this feeling of inadequacy? Where does my faith in myself and my abilities go? Why does it fly out the door so quickly? Why must I be in such conflict with myself?

July 6, 2003

I dream that I'm collecting junk for a sculpture, filling boxes with all kinds of stuff to be used in this creative endeavor. My daughter is with me, needing me. I turn my attention to her, aware that although I'm involved in a creative process I have to be present for her too, as her mother and protector, but also as her teacher and guide.

My creative self and my maternal self, appearing side by side in my dream, are the two things that keep me nurtured and alive. And my dream is strikingly prophetic, as I spend the afternoon with my daughter, helping her through a rough hour of anger. I pick her up at her dad's and we take a walk together. She vents while I offer supportive hugs and positive affirmations. We hang out for a while after our walk too, and then I drive her back to her dad's house to spend a few more days with him.

It's a hot night now, the fans are going, and I'm tired, but not as sad as I have been. It was cathartic to be so attentive to my daughter, to her anger rather than my own. And now, as if I had tended to my own inner child, I find her quite soothed too. A day well spent!

July 7, 2003

I am curating another show at the gallery, the artists excited to have me in charge, and yet every day I must confront my inadequacies. Real or not, they come crawling forth to challenge me. They must be part of this recapitulation, here to prod and test me, to teach me, because every day I prove that I can do anything. Why don't I believe it? Why can't I believe in myself?

"You are certainly *very* capable," a friend said to me the other day, and that is so important for me to hear. I must take in the praise that people give me, learn to accept the truth of who I really am, embrace what I am capable of, and let the old low self-esteem issue become part of the recapitulated past.

While I worked on the press release for the gallery show this afternoon everything seemed easier. The writing flowed out of me without the grip of inadequacy that came over me at the gallery the other night, though my old demon, Fear, still clutched at me, whispering his messages that I am incapable of succeeding on my own, that I will fail. As much as he railed, I railed back. After a while, I noticed that the words were not my words, not spoken in my voice but in the voices of others, perhaps people who always felt inadequate themselves, taunting me with their own demons. Once I realized this, it was easier for me to imagine myself succeeding at anything I attempt.

I vow to block out those old voices now, to get my act together and not let the negativity of others destroy me. Every time I do something for the gallery, give energy to the work I do there, I intend to value myself and give my own cause and my own work equal energy.

July 8, 2003

Fear greets me upon awakening and I am weighed down by a musty lack of self-confidence, smothered by it, in spite of yesterday's positive intentions. I see Chuck today. I'm scared.

As soon as I arrive, Chuck hands me the EMDR pods. I sit with them pulsing in the palms of my hands, wondering where I am, why I'm so stuck. Chuck suggests an image. I am like a toddler, he says, out exploring the world, naturally eager for adventure, until I suddenly realize that I am completely on my own.

As he says this, I see an old black and white movie in my mind's eye, my younger sister, a two-year-old in a white dress, gamboling unsteadily across a wide expanse of lawn. She stumbles and catches herself, landing with her hands on the ground. In my memory, she stands up again and turns back to look at us, as if to say, "Don't worry, I'm okay," and takes off running, so that I have to run after her and bring her back to the picnic blanket where my parents are sitting.

Suddenly, I become that toddler in the scene, but there is no one behind me when I turn around, no one keeping an eye on me, no one coming to get me, no big sister or parents. The anchor of assurance that I extend to my little sister in my memory is lacking in my own experience, the tender voice of encouragement that says, you're okay, you'll be fine. Frantically looking around, I realize instead, "Oh My God, I *am* alone!" Panic rises and my gut reaction is to withdraw, to go deep into depression, to hide until I feel safe again, staying away in my own darkness for a long time. It's how I've always dealt with things.

"I understand I have to create the safety within myself," I tell Chuck, "and I know I have the strength to do just that, for I am spiritually grounded and strong."

"Go back and fix it; change it," he says.

I reenter the scene. In my mind's eye, I am the little girl in the white dress running across the wide expanse of grass. I am also right behind this little girl. I am my adult self, watching every step, reassuring and encouraging my child self, letting her know that she's safe. As my child self, I know I can run back to the safety of my own anchoring adult self anytime, and that I can venture out again too. By the time the exercise is over I do feel safe, for the first time in a long time.

My newly confident adventurous self and my anchoring adult self remain present and attentive as I head over to the studio. I gather supplies to start work on the mural tomorrow and pack the car. My creativity flowing, I turn to work on a large collage that I've been trying to finish. It needs something strong and meaningful to fit into a specific spot, making a statement about how I feel now, strong and guided. I shuffle through my bits and pieces of cutout paper figures. Just as I'm thinking that I need to leave the past behind, represented by the forest in the background of the collage, a cutout of a paper angel falls right off the shelf above me and floats down onto my collage, landing smack in the very spot where I need something special. I know she's a guard and a guide, blocking access to the old way of doing things, pointing in a new direction. It's perfect!

"No, don't go back there," I hear, *"and you don't need anyone else either. You just need your own strength, your own power. It is what has gotten you this far."*

I clean up, lock the studio, and head home feeling that something big has finally shifted inside me. I feel blessed, renewed, suddenly free. The kids arrive soon after, bustling in with all their things, happy to be home again. The need to return to nurturing and mothering anchors me in this world a little more firmly, another shift offered. As we settle in for the night, I admit to myself that I don't want to be afraid of anything, that I want to flow with my life as easily as that angel floated down onto my collage. But I also have to admit that I'm afraid of everything. That seems to be my biggest challenge right now, facing my fear of everything.

July 9, 2003

I dream that I'm with all sixteen of my inner girls. I line them up in a row. Each girl represents a different year, each having had different experiences of abuse. One by one, I take each girl and put her away into a coffin-like box, a time capsule that I tape up and put a label on. Each girl is a unique individual, with her own unique story, and she deserves her own unique resting place. I put the sixteen boxes away in a closet and close the door on them. The girls are not happy about what I'm doing. Angrily, they confront me, accusing me of deserting them.

"Why are you doing this? What are you doing to us?"

I hear them yelling as I pack them up, write their labels, and lovingly tuck them away in the closet. I tell them that we need to do this, that it's the right thing. I tell them they'll be fine, they'll be safe.

In another dream I am full of pain and on the verge of panic. I hear Chuck's voice telling me that everything will be okay and that I should just let go. I know he's right. I begin to let go and soon I'm falling fast, dropping at a tremendous rate of speed. And then suddenly I'm floating, as if a parachute has opened. I feel incredible relief, and yet I'm still scared.

"I can do it, I know I can do this," I tell myself.

When I hear Chuck's voice again, still telling me to let go, I feel myself falling fast through the air again, so fast that I split into six paper-thin copies of myself. As I watch from above, six black shapes float gently down to the earth, six silhouettes that land on the ground like corpses in a row. I'm aware that each dark shape represents a different emotion or issue—physical holding, fear, hopelessness, loneliness, pain and panic—the trademark issues of my traumatized self. I lie down on top of each silhouette in turn and release the emotion or issue that each shape represents, feeling each of them pass through me and seep far down into the ground. As I get to the last shape, panic, I know that it's the most difficult of all. As soon as I lie down on top of it I wake up.

Panic greets me as soon as I open my eyes. It's still alive inside me, still unreleased. Immediately the image of the toddler comes to mind again and I understand how deeply embedded this panic is. It goes back to my two-year-old self who was unable to fathom what was happening to her at the hands of her abuser. Thus it was that panic arrived and it has stayed ever since.

The image of my toddler self stays with me as I get up and prepare for work. It's the perfect metaphor. It's exactly what's happening with me now as I face my traumatized self, for I am stuck at the age of two, confused and terrified. The challenge is to deal with the panic differently now. I must remain anchored in my adult self, rest assured that she will be there if I turn around and look behind me. And so there will be no panicking and hiding this day, nor will I withdraw into my dark tunnel of safety and depression. If I am to heal, I must stay fully present and face everything that comes to challenge me.

I am beautiful. I am capable. I am smart. I am able to do what I set out to do. I must be my own support now, my own validator. I must keep in mind just how far I've come and how strong I really am. I must remember that I have never given up. This is what I tell myself as I get up and face the day.

July 10, 2003

I wake full of anxiety, my stomach in queasy knots, panic rising. I lie on my side, in excruciating pain, knowing that I have to somehow get myself into a better place if I am to function at all today, away from the vicious attack dog of panic. It is proving to be quite an opponent, not something I can easily let go through me; far better to fight it, to keep it at bay. Fear I can let go of, but panic I don't even want to go near.

I work on the mural, keeping the panic at bay. I've been enjoying the company of the house sitter, taking care of the property while the owners are away for the summer. He makes me coffee and serves me cake when I take a break. He's pleasant and thoughtful, a musician, composer, playwright. His girlfriend, a giant of a woman, pale and beautiful in a strange way, has come to stay for a few days. I meet her for the first time. She's a writer, by all accounts pretty successful. They rattle off name after name, television shows and celebrities that she has written for, but like an alien from another planet I don't know any of them. They have a childish relationship, chiding and challenging each other like two bickering siblings. Clearly they enjoy each other's company, though I also sense conflict. I like to watch how couples interact, especially ones who have been together a while, as it offers the opportunity to study relationships in action. So far my own have been lacking in any real connection, so distant have I been.

They remark on how incredibly confident I appear, how quiet I am as I go about my work with such focused discipline. I tell them that I love painting, that it's like meditation to me, and that, no, I don't need music when they offer to lend me a CD player. I prefer the quiet, I say. It offers me everything I need.

I take note of that quiet confidence as I work into the late afternoon, acknowledge that it has in fact always been there as regards my work, but that it has been growing quite steadily for months now, anchoring in a new way, as if I really am owning it. I no longer have to put it on like a garment the way I once did, an extroverted self I'd take out of the closet and wear out into the world. Now it has become part of who I naturally am, a perk of this recapitulation work. I know this because in the past, as talented as I was, my confidence was not as embedded as it now feels. It's more solid now. At a very deep level I know who I am and what I'm capable of. It's a good feeling, a new sense of solidity. I'm aware that people have long viewed me as this extremely competent person, but I have self-deprecatingly dismissed it. I have to admit it's nice to finally own it as a true aspect of my personality, no longer only a costume I wear to cope but truly a part of who I am. In the shaman's world it's called *stalking*, taking on and living a role so impeccably that no one would ever know the difference. I realize I have stalked being a confident artist very well. Now I am no longer playing a role; I have become it.

July 11, 2003

I wake in panic again. I can't even drink my morning cup of coffee. I'm scared, the panic pulsing in my veins, choking me, my confident self of yesterday only a dim memory. I feel like crawling into a cave and staying there, becoming a hermit, the solitary life of the ascetic so appealing to me. But I can't, I have to meet with Chuck.

"BREATHE!" he says, as soon as I walk in, the panic so real that it follows me right into his office and plunks me down in the chair. "Breathe, even if it's shallow breathing at first. It will help dispel the panic. Breathe! Push it out so there won't be any room for it. You can do that."

Gulping for air, taking one small breath after another, I gradually calm my racing thoughts, unclench my throat, and still my beating heart.

"When the panic arrives I don't know who I am anymore," I say. "I have to meditate, keep the panic away, try to get back to my spiritual center, empty my mind."

"Yes, find a way to keep the panic at bay," Chuck says, "but it's not a final solution. You have to face it and find out what it's trying to show you."

"Face the panic," he says, handing me the EMDR pods.

As soon as I feel the familiar bilateral pulsing in my palms, the image of the toddler in the white dress crossing the wide expanse of lawn appears, but this time I don't just see her, I become her. And she's afraid.

"I need something to latch onto," I say, in a child's voice.

I sit there for a while clutching the EMDR pods tightly, my head down, unable to speak, frightened, my mind a total blank. And then I remember that in a confident moment I had been thinking about perhaps illustrating children's books again. I tell Chuck about this idea, wondering if I'll ever feel safe enough to actually do it.

"Can you go back to the time when you first took art lessons, to the art lessons your parents sent you to?" Chuck asks. "Is that a safe place you can go to?"

"No, not at all! It was a frightening time because my father forced me out into the public eye when I wanted to be hidden. It was just after the abortion, but it was when my art abilities were becoming visible to others and my dad was getting me into county art exhibits, arranging interviews and write-ups in the papers when all I wanted to do was crawl into my hermit's cave and warm myself with my introversion. I can't go back that far, to a time when I was being raped in the woods by a madman one day and put on a pedestal the next. No, I can't go back that far, there is no safety back there."

Even so, the panic subsides enough that I am free to ponder what it would mean to take up my career as a children's book illustrator again. I'd have to venture into the city, make new connections. It's been a long time, perhaps things are done differently. I'm my twenty-year-old self again as I talk about it, afraid of rejection, afraid of failure, and equally afraid of success, which I ran from before. But it's enough of a diversion; I notice that the panic is gone.

"I need to feel my way though this, see if it feels right."

"Be calm," Chuck says. "Don't push. Remind yourself often that things will work out, that somehow the right thing will work out for you."

I head home to get the kids up and off to their summer activities. Later, while working on the mural I get a terrible pain, vaginal, anal pain. I try to ignore it. Then I try to send it away, out to a point on the horizon. Then I decide to confront it straight on, just like I'm supposed to. The house sitters are out for the day and I feel safe getting down on my hands and knees. Once on all fours, I let myself feel the pain, acknowledging how excruciating it is. I even let myself cry a little bit. I notice how tightly I clench against it, so I make an effort to release as much as I can. I let it go, incrementally, almost calmly, making sure to feel each detail of the pain as it goes through me, how it feels to hold it back and how it feels to let it go. Twenty minutes go by before I am able to stagger up to a standing position and get back to work.

I marvel that there are so many different nuances to recapitulating painful memories. Allowing myself to actually feel the pain in such detail is a new step. I have preferred to push it away, or walk it off, or yell at it to go away. This time I consciously chose to pay attention to it. I accepted it, assumed the position—on all fours—and really felt it as it went through me. It hurt like hell, but I was able to stay with it!

My horoscope today said: "Make the art and the money will follow." I have not had a good relationship with money. I've always felt unworthy of it, and so no relationship ever developed. I have preferred to disdain it as something I don't need, though when I make it I am certainly happy to have it! The dire necessity of making money hounds me though, worries me, especially as the parent of two children. Even though I ask a fair price for my work, it is by no means extravagant. I barely make ends meet. I realize I need to become better friends with money, that it's as necessary a relationship as a love relationship. I cannot live without money, nor will I be able to adequately support my children if I do not have a healthier attitude toward it. And so, I intend a new relationship.

I am open to money flowing into my life!

I open to receive it!

As soon as I write those words I immediately feel better, more optimistic. Of course things will work out! Stop worrying! Life is short enough as it is, so make the most of it. The hell with being so afraid all the time!

July 13, 2003

It's Sunday. The kids are still asleep at eleven when I wake to see that the sky has changed from the early morning clear blue that I had glimpsed when I first woke at six. Now hidden behind clouds it reflects my own spirit, leaden and grey. I toss and turn, feeling the usual panic rising, and although I long to stay curled up in bed, I know I shouldn't. I roll onto my side and pull the covers over me anyway. As soon as I do I realize that it's a grave mistake, an old place that offers nothing good.

I had dreamed about hiking along a new path, but I ended up in a bad place, in a murky lake difficult to extricate myself from. Along one shore of the lake was a brick wall topped with pots of dead rose bushes, the flowers wilted, yellowed and dried. I think my dream was telling me that I don't need to go to a new place, just stay where I am. After all, the path that led me to the lake was well-trodden, the lake and beach area crowded with too many people. It was not an energetically unique or sacred enough environment for deep work; it was not a personal path. There really is no need to look for another path. I am already on my own.

I often wish I had someone to give me advice. Chuck never tells me what I should do. His method is to let me find my way to believing in myself. I guess I should just stop worrying so much and trust that everything *will* work out fine!

July 14, 2003

I wake up each morning completely drained, pulled so strongly to go down into the depths of despair and hopelessness again. A tremendous weight, as heavy as a cinderblock, drags me down into that murky lake of my dream. I can't find the energy to pull myself away from these dark feelings, to unbind the weight. I have to be a mother, a parent, a provider; I have to swim out of the deep and be present for my children, and myself. Sometimes it feels impossible. I have to find the spark that will reconnect me with my desire to do life, the fire that will get me motivated and productive once again.

My first intention is to be fully present in my body today, but as I roll out of bed I discover that I am so tense I must move extremely slowly to avoid pulling a muscle. As I carefully move my limbs it suddenly dawns on me that when I recapitulate the pain that occurred during the abuse, I am feeling it for the first time. It's as if it hadn't happened when it actually did happen. I understand that when I dissociated—left my body during the abuse—I left the pain behind too. Now as I go back into my body I finally encounter the pain, for the first time really. As I encounter all the places in my body that ache, where the memories lie embedded still, I sense them waiting for me to come and unlock them, the keys of release and freedom in my hands alone.

It's now eleven at night. Somehow I got up and moving this morning and kept going all day. I didn't allow for time to think or let stuff bother me. I'm taking it one day at a time. Sometimes one day is good and the next devastatingly depressing, but good things are happening nonetheless. Today I felt more optimistic, once I got going that is. Things feel possible on days like today; everything seems possible. I want more days like this.

July 15, 2003

I meet with Chuck. I feel good. I'm at a new stage now, really making progress. I've learned to accept the pain, to let it go through me, rather than flat out refuse it like I used to.

Chuck points out that the water in my dream of the lake was neither cleansing nor refreshing, not symbolic of rebirth, but instead was stagnant and dead, as were the roses along the shore. It's an old world that I'm no longer interested in. I'm ready for new life, as I've consciously taken a stand to fully recapitulate in a new way now. By going through the pain I'm actually encouraging new growth inside myself.

I've discovered that the only way to get to full birth is to keep going deeper into this recapitulation, reconstructing myself as slowly as I'm dismantling myself. At times it feels like I'm just a bottomless pit, as murky as that lake in my dream, my emotions as dead as the roses, but in actuality I've been doing good work, and my emotions and feelings are beginning to push through now too. New growth is happening all the time. It just takes patience, and the intent to see it through.

July 16, 2003

In a dream I check into a hotel for a body cleansing session with a massage therapist. I'm not really sure what it entails. I become very uncomfortable when I notice a woman who has just gone through her own cleanse. She has a lot of yellow stuff, the texture and color of beaten egg yolks, pouring out of her vagina. It doesn't look good to me. When the massage therapist approaches me I blurt out that I was raped as a child and that I don't like to be touched. She immediately puts me on her table and begins working on me. I don't protest; I just go along, though I am still concerned. I see more of the disgusting yellow stuff coming out from between the legs of other women and suddenly realize that it's part of the cleansing process, that it's actually a good sign of detoxification.

I wake up disturbed, realizing that things can't stay the same, that I have to make some big changes. And that, yes, I need a cleansing, that all the stuff I'm exposing myself to has to be naturally eliminated. If I don't flush out the memories and the pain they will remain inside me, festering like bad karma. Releasing them is such a necessary part of this whole process and not to be shirked at.

It's clear that most of this deep work is now taking place in my dreams and in my body. My dreams confront me with the issues still needing attention, and in the light of day I have to figure out what I'm supposed to do when they arise, what choices are in alignment with this healing paradigm I am now engaged in. My body clenches and tenses while I sleep and dream, while I go off into dream worlds of symbol and meaning. When morning comes again I must reenter this reality and this body as best I can, slowly inch back into each stiff bone and muscle and, like the Tin Man in *The Wizard of Oz*, carefully flex and adjust my joints and limbs so I don't freeze up and injure myself.

My mood is definitely lighter today. I'm busy but staying in balance, taking time to do fun things with the kids; a little bit of work, a little bit of play, a little bit of loving attention to all of us. I almost dread the night though, for when the sun sets and darkness descends the shadowy darkness in my soul stirs, calling me to the mysterious world of sleep and dreams once again.

July 17, 2003

The first thing I think of as I wake up is how to merge my two worlds, my present reality and my past. It's quite a dilemma. Part of me would like to keep my inner girls locked away in their coffin-like boxes, where I put them during a previous dream, and just get on with things. But I'm also aware that doing that won't solve anything. My inner girls are still inside me, still needing me, going where I go, and I still hear them crying out from inside those boxes. It pains me deeply to imagine keeping them locked up. They've spent decades waiting for me to find them. And although I had no inkling of their existence, something was not right with me, some huge and mysterious ache cast a sad shadow over everything, especially my spiritual and mental wellbeing. At least now I know what it's all about.

I wonder if I'll ever be able to talk about what happened to me as a child. Will it help people understand abused children better if I do? Will it help other abused people, now grown and yet still partially stuck in childhood, to understand what happened to them? Will revealing my own deepest inner truth allow someone else to rescue themselves from their own misery, abused or not? If someone had alerted me earlier perhaps I would have been a happier, more productive person, perhaps my life might have been different. Perhaps I wouldn't have held myself back or suffered so many years of agony and depression, or been plagued by such doubt and fear. But perhaps that's not possible, as I am the only one who can rescue myself. And it could only happen when I was ready. I also sense that everything that happened to me, the good and the bad, is important. Every moment of my life has been meaningful and necessary. Who else could possibly know when I would be ready to finally face my past? And who else could possibly find the healing path that would be right for me?

I'm afraid to write my story, though I fear I am going to do just that. I'm afraid that what I have to say will hurt many people and that it may even pain me again as I write it. But I have to. I have to not only recapitulate but put the whole sad tale into words. It feels imperative that I do that, and that's frightening. I also know that if I keep it to myself I will not complete an agreement I seem to have made with myself long ago, sometime, somewhere. I really do have to do it for others too, so that others will understand what abuse does to children, how we carry the scars and burdens of it throughout our lives, how it affects every aspect of our existence.

There is no escaping what happens to any of us in our childhoods. Whether we were sexually abused or not, we all suffer some wounding that just won't go away. It is with us forever, hurting us, keeping us from owning our full maturity and achieving our full potential, until we face it and heal ourselves. The bleakness of an unfulfilled life is, unfortunately, I believe, rampant, due to our failure to deal with our deepest issues. In essence, we never quite grow up, but remain partially frozen in infancy, acting out childish behaviors that compromise and confound us our whole lives. There comes a point in life when we are given a choice, to turn and face our infantile fears or turn away from them. In fact, many such opportunities to do deep work are offered to us throughout our lives. We might elect to ignore them, those knocks on our soul, but the woundings of our lives will never leave us until we answer their knocks. Like faithful companions they will hound us forever, reminding us of what we are challenged with, until we recapture, relive, and release them once and for all. This is what I'm doing every day of my life now, as I venture deeper into this process, as I face my demons and finally rid myself of them. This recapitulation really is a cleansing process.

I've recently come to realize more fully just how those demons get into us, how they nestle in and take over, creating havoc, shifting moods and attitudes; how they physically, mentally, emotionally and spiritually rule and control us. Children are especially susceptible to such possession. As an abused child I was ripe for takeover by such entities, my psyche weakened by what was happening to me. Such entities slip in unnoticed. One day we are who we are, the next irrevocably changed, possessed.

Times of stress, illness, and trauma, whether emotional, physical, or psychological, are all opportunities for possession. We become encapsulated by our trauma; our wounds fester and feed the entity, to its great delight. Meanwhile our real self is smothering, disappearing, slipping further and further from our grasp. All we want is to get back to where we once were, who we were before "it" happened, before we transformed into someone even we don't recognize. We feel different inside and outside, and yet often we have no explanation for the changes that come over us. We simply no longer exist as we once did; we are not our self.

Such possession is noticeable in changes in behavior, in sleep disturbances, in eating habits, in psychological changes, in mental illness, emotional outbursts, in addictions, in any number of issues and changes in the normal pattern of behavior, causing us to behave in strange ways, to act out, or to withdraw from the world. Those demon entities settle in deeper and deeper, grooming us to become close allies, pitted against a world that we no longer trust, and so after a while they are all we know of ourselves; we become what they make us.

In my case, I became exceedingly fearful, painfully shy and withdrawn. On the rare occasion that my real self emerged, momentarily playful and carefree, the demon energy inside me would also show up and a battle would ensue. My happy innocent self would immediately step down, so well-trained was she to acquiesce to the demon energy. "Better not get too happy, bad things happen," she'd say. And as much as this was the pattern that ruled my life, there was another part of me that wished for it to be otherwise, who yearned for the lightness of being that had once been mine, if only very briefly.

I've learned through this process of recapitulation that no one else can rid me of my demons, that I alone must tackle them. For who else knows them the way I do? Who else knows how they speak to me, how they treat me, how I collude with them, how I let them have their way with me? We have spent our whole lives together, my demons and I, and we know each other far better than any other human being ever could. Through this process I have been disentangling myself from them, picking them out of me like lice on strands of hair, examining them, crushing them, ridding myself of them once and for all. And so, I can honestly say that my demons are noticeably fewer now.

As each one leaves, I step out into the world a little more freely. My fears are subsiding now, my darkness lifting, my shyness being replaced by confidence. The urge to hide, once so pressing, is no longer as necessary as it once was. The sanctuary of home still offers a place of refuge, though it's no longer an escape from the world, as it once was, but instead a place of rejuvenation. All of this is an indication of the being I am becoming.

I used to fight myself, hate myself, get angry at myself for all that I could not do, for my fears, my agoraphobia, for my need to stay in control, solitary and confined, for my inability to loosen up and be "normal." But now I know it was something else I was fighting, a foreign presence, something I never had any real control over. The evil predator who was my abuser delivered the first big wounding. He ripped me open, leaving me vulnerable to all kinds of energetic entities. He was the first saboteur that lived inside me, constantly trying to overpower my spirit, sucking as much of my innocence as he could. Other entities soon followed, fear and panic, distrust and depression but a few.

Though I did not have addiction demons to deal with, at least not the usual kind—alcohol, drugs, food, sex, to name a few—I was certainly addicted to control! It's funny, as I let go of my need to control everything, and my anxiety and depression too, my demons leave. It's pretty clear that I produced exactly what they desired. I see how important it is that I reestablish my own energetic presence in my body, not only taking back the terrific amount of energy that got stolen from me, but healing all the woundings, closing off access so I can channel my renewed energy into something nurturing, self-sustaining, and good.

As I enter this new stage in my recapitulation, I'm going to stop thinking about suicide. I've decided that I will not allow such thoughts to continue to pollute and steal my energy. Even if they aren't serious thoughts—I would never kill myself—they're still negative and debilitating. Fleeting as they may be, they depress me, old thoughts from old times, filled with whispers of death as a viable outlet.

I once walked onto the thin ice of a lake, daring it to break and take me with it into the chill waters. I was in my early twenties, so numb and frozen myself that I barely knew what I was doing. A man walking by called out to me and I walked back to shore where he scolded me for being stupid. "You could have gone through the ice, it's too thin!" he yelled, though I could barely hear him through the depressive veil that hung over me. I never told my young husband what I was feeling, though he often had to deal with my debilitating black moods. I didn't even know why I was so darkly depressed; something just came over me, swallowing me up, taking me away until it spit me back out again. I wrote about walking onto the thin ice in a short story that I sent off to an editor to read. She wrote back with concern for my safety. At the same time she also wrote that I had the stuff of a real writer, and to keep writing. Her words planted a kernel of hope, saved me actually.

I know my dark moods have been hard for others to tolerate, especially my children, and I don't wish to burden them any longer. Children are natural sponges; just being in the same house with me I know they are absorbing everything, moods and unseen energies alike. My own childhood was blanketed by the fears and depression and of my own parents, on top of my own demons, and so I know how debilitating such transference of energy can be to the spirit of a young child. I no longer wish to bear the fears of my parents, and I hope I will not pass my fears onto my own children.

As I continue this journey I have a real sense of being okay in the end, especially as the darkness is lightening up a lot now, as the demons leave, though I wonder if I'll always have a dark spot inside me. I sense a shift though. I'm getting excited about life and work again. I'm trying not to panic, but to do positive things for myself instead. Maybe that's the way to rid myself of this incessant threat of darkness. Think positive!

July 18, 2003

I wake up sad, my body in the usual pain, nerves on edge, feeling like I could tip into panic any second. I sense apprehension around meeting with Chuck today too, though I'm not sure why.

We talk about crossing the metaphorical bridge that Chuck envisions I now stand before. I get to the bridge, but then what? Panic sets in. How do I get across, or even onto the bridge? How do I access the courage to keep going? In the past, I would have withdrawn, not even ventured forth onto the bridge. I did this when I ran from what was good in my life, as well as when I ran from what frightened me. I was always pretty good at turning around and taking another path, no bridges for me! I liked safety.

Chuck suggests that a bridge spans worlds, offers a link to new life and an unforeseen, unplanned adventure. Could I really do it, cross that bridge and let myself be so open and vulnerable? I sense panic behind me and I anticipate panic before me.

"I have to find a calm place," I say.

"Might you find that calm place in an incident that is forcing you into shift?" Chuck asks, suggesting that something in the outer world may be offering me the catalyst I need.

31

"No," I say, resolutely. "I find it in myself. I find it in the angel that fell so synchronistically onto the collage I was working on, falling off the shelf above me, right onto the exact spot where something important was needed, telling me not to turn back but to just keep going."

I find it in Jeanne's voice, telling me I have everything I need inside me, not in the past or the future, but already and always inside me, though I don't tell Chuck this. He still doesn't know that I communicate with Jeanne, his dead wife, on a regular basis. I still have not shared that secret with him, though I have shared so many other more intimate ones.

"*The key*," Jeanne tells me, as we sit there and ponder this bridge I must cross, "*is to remember that you have the key always within. You carry it with you at all times.*"

I know how to get to that Zen place within myself where I work best, my natural creative zone where I am without fear or panic. I already know how to achieve a state of reverie.

"The calm is within," I tell Chuck. "When I meditate or do yoga, or when I do something creative I naturally arrive at a place of knowing, deep inside myself. It's an innate natural state of calmness and I know it well."

Chuck nods.

"I know I can't go back to the old way of doing things. The only place to go is inward. I carry all the creativity and calmness I need inside. I hold everything within myself."

I told Chuck this morning that I was no longer interested in death, that I'm feeling happier, more excited about life now. Even so, I'm sad tonight. I cry in the solitude of my bedroom, the kids gone for the weekend to their dad's, no one to keep quiet for. Perhaps I cry for everything I must leave as I cross that bridge into new life, the sad and depressed self, the old self whom I must leave behind forever. We have been strong and dedicated partners, she and I, intent upon our mission, but now we must part forever.

July 19, 2003

As usual, I wake in tremendous pain, tightly clenched, stiff as a board. In order to get out of bed I have to relax one muscle at a time, going slowly up my body from the tips of my toes to the top of my head. I feel sick again today, my stomach achy, and my bowels continue to be loose, like they have been for months. But the sun is shining, and it's nice and cool out at seven in the morning.

I walk before going to the studio, a cleansing method I can handle, incremental movement that I control, slowly loosening my stiff muscles. As I walk in the cool morning light, I sense how disconnected from the world I feel, a solo journeyer floating alone on a vast sea of uncertainty. My inner world is the only true reality right now, though I yearn for connection to another, to someone to talk to, but I'm not ready for intimacy yet. The only intimacy that matters now is uniting with my struggling body and taking the slow and painful journey across that metaphorical bridge, calmly, one step at a time.

I struggle all day to get myself across that bridge, but I am constantly sucked back into the murky past. It casts a wide net over me and suddenly I find that I am the catch of the day, spun up in a gooey cocoon, so familiar, so sickly safe. I have tarried here for far too long; it's time to wake up and move on, to make the crossing into the unknown. Animal instincts tell me to fight fiercely or I risk remaining caught in this sticky web for the rest of my life.

I watch some movies in the evening and then take a midnight walk, but the neighborhood is so dark I don't go far, too hard to see, a fitting analogy for the uncertainty of what lies on the other side of that bridge. I cry quietly as I walk, letting my tears drip into the darkness, letting sadness and loneliness seep out, purging myself of the old me. How good it is to cry! Back at home, tucked into bed with my three cats, I feel loved.

July 20, 2003

I sleep in a tight leg lock every night, guarding myself, protecting myself. Do I really think my abuser is going to come into my bedroom at night and rape me? Obviously not, but my body thinks so! That's how real this recapitulation is to my body.

July 21, 2003

I wake up early, a writing assignment on my mind. I know I'll do a good job and I'm excited to get to work on it, but my body just won't move! I am a solid leaden weight, steeped in depression so gloomy I can barely breathe, paralyzed with some old fear. My legs, clenched and heavy, will not budge. Perhaps I can get myself out of this slump by thinking positive thoughts. I really would like to feel good! Maybe I can intend my way to a healthier state of mind and body, but how do I help myself on a more regular, steady basis? I could get a part time job, be around new people, have a steady income, have the opportunity to use my skills—provided it's the right job.

The kids will be home later today. I miss them and I look forward to having them with me again. Just thinking about them makes me feel better and the gloom slowly dissipates.

A guy is interested in me. How do I feel about him? Am I interested? No, I am wary.

July 22, 2003

I'm afraid, afraid to get too close to another being. Is it really me who is afraid or is it my sixteen inner girls? The answer comes immediately.

"Don't! Don't even think about letting anyone else in," they say. "We're already angry about letting Chuck in, about you telling him things."

I ignore them. I go out to lunch and take a walk with the guy who's interested in me. I overhear him tell someone on his phone that he enjoys my company, that we have coffee sometimes, and that it's a nice thing. I enjoy his company too, but I'm not sure how I view him yet; more as a kindly gnome than a suitor perhaps.

July 23, 2003

I'm getting my hair done today. Maybe I can relax a little and just enjoy the pampering. I know I should do some yoga, walk, or start running again too, but I feel so shattered, so fragmented, like Humpty-Dumpty, unable to gather my parts and put them back together again.

I am involuntarily sucked back into the past, barely able to stay present while the hairdresser works on my hair. Gripping the arms of the chair, I resist the murky waters of recapitulation. I keep my eyes open, staring into the mirror in front of me, but the old world, trickster that it is, sees an opportunity. Soon the mirror no longer reflects back my own face nor the room behind me but a sinister fogginess out of which come flickering, unclear scenes from the past. Does anyone else see them? How they reflect in the mirror like lights passing in the fog? A deep sadness sweeps through me while I focus on breathing, silently telling them to go away, not now! It's more than I want to deal with in a public place, but I can't stop it. As I leave the salon I remember my college roommate asking me not long ago, after we had reconnected after many years, if I still had those "black moods," as she put it. "No one could go near you for days or weeks when you went into those black moods," she said. I told her I was working on freeing myself from them. Each time I recapitulate another memory, I get a little bit closer to freeing myself forever.

Once again, I realize that pushing this recapitulation, trying to speed it up, is not a good idea, nor is it necessary. It just creates a lot of unbearable tension. The recapitulation happens on its own; it comes without my pushing at all, when the time is right, or even not so right, like at the hair salon today. I have to trust that each phase comes when it's ready to come, which also means that it must be coming because I am ready and able to receive it.

Tomorrow, I will head back to the house where I have been painting and I will spend the morning finishing up the murals and I will be served a cup of coffee and some cake. And then there's a new gallery show to curate and the opening reception to plan. See, I'm not so down anymore!

July 24, 2003

I dream of wandering naked down narrow cobblestoned streets, worried and panicking. Men grab at me, but I push them away, angry that they think my nakedness is an open invitation, that they think it's okay to touch me. I am not here for you; I am here for me! Get away from me! Running, stumbling on the slippery stones, I try to pull myself together, try to calm myself. "You can do it," I say encouragingly. "The world is open to you."

I wake up feeling bad, but I calm myself just as I did in the dream. I'm aware that my worry and panic are related to fears that I will not be able to support myself and the kids, an old incessant worry, always there somewhere in the back of my mind, like an old record playing repeatedly, insisting that I do not have what it takes, that I am not a man. After all, men can do anything. The world accepts them as they are, expects them to be aggressive, just like they were in my dream, taking what they want. It's expected that they command a good salary and make enough money to support a family. Right? It's an old paradigm, I know, and not one I really adhere to, but I have to face that it lies at the root of my panic-inducing inadequacy; it's a big factor. It's what I grew up with and is directly related to old low self-esteem issues and a generally fragile ego, which I have really been working hard to piece into a strong, confident, and happy self. But each time the panic arises, I know I am being challenged to face this core issue once again, proving that I am not quite done with it. I must tear down the old ideas and supplant them with new strong, self-enhancing ones.

I know I am fully capable. In fact, I have already more than proven that, but something deep inside me refuses to accept it. Am I afraid to be independent, afraid it might mean I don't need anyone else after all? In the dream, in spite of being naked, I was successful at deflecting the men, really insisting that my nakedness had nothing to do with them. I was not naked and looking for sex; I was nakedly facing my own fears. And the fear that has repeatedly arisen lately has been the fear of not being a capable and reliable support. With that comes all kinds of other worries, most of them pretty farfetched, I admit, but some of them real concerns.

I didn't grow up with any sense of myself as being equal to men. In spite of having grown up during the feminist revolution of the 1960s, I still carry an underlying sense of inadequacy as far as the real world is concerned, a certainty that the real world isn't particularly interested in me, as a woman or as a citizen, and that I will only matter if I am determined to matter. It's up to me to value myself as a being on equal footing because no one else is going to do it for me or give me a pass. It's the same thing all women face, we really do have to prove ourselves much more than any man has ever had to. It's interesting that I don't have this sense of insecurity when in a creative state; it wouldn't cross my mind then. When I'm actively creating, issues of ego, personal worth or value never intrude. Then I am neither female nor male, I simply am.

I have always taken responsibility for myself, paid my way, so to speak, but the idea that I could be successful and adequately compensated for my hard work has remained a distant enigma. Even the fact that I have been successful in my chosen field of art and illustration does not sink in. I am never good enough, valuable enough, worthy enough, adequate enough when I compare myself to others in the world. Why can't I trust myself to be as strong and reliable as I expect a man to be? Why do I continue to be so scared, thinking I am incapable of doing life on my own? That's how I felt when I woke up this morning, totally afraid of the life I have embarked upon. This recapitulation journey was really a decision to go solo, but the truth is that I am also taking this changing journey with my two children in tow.

I must be fully present and attentive to their needs while simultaneously taking care of myself, often a daunting task, hard to juggle. I know I don't have to be afraid about anything. In fact, I'm pretty certain that my feelings are related to how I was raised, the times I grew up in, old ideas about men and women in general and their strictly defined roles in the world. Underneath it all, I have a strong sense that women are really the capable, strong sex, the ones who can, in fact, do it all. We don't really have to do anything to be that way, we just are, but that's been kept from us. It's time to reclaim what's been lost. If I'm really going to embrace myself as the strong, capable woman I envision, I just have to set my sights on her and keep going. As my dream said, the world belongs to me now.

"Don't be frightened," Jeanne says. *"Everything will be okay. Keep moving forward in the direction you are going. Listen to what people say about you. Don't put yourself down; accept. You will be fine. Everything will be fine."*

July 25, 2003

I am in a house full of children. We are captives, dressed in rags, forced to eat charred and blackened food. Steeped in terror, pain, and fear I wake up out of this nightmare. Time to get up and leave my demons behind. I pull the covers over them as I make the bed, preparing myself to go out and have a good day. The sun is shining, the birds are chirping, the car has a full tank of gas, and I have work waiting for me. What more could I wish for? If only I could get over the sadness.

Every morning when I wake up I wonder, who am I today? Where am I today? Fully present? My daily incremental changes, my steps into the light, are balanced by the ongoing process with my inner girls. They so easily pull me back into a dark and dirty past where feelings were numb and life had no good side. They show me how one day I was raped and tortured in the woods by a madman, the next I was the responsible girl that everyone looked up to, the budding artist, the big sister, the reliable babysitter, the quiet one, the sweet one, the shy and withdrawn one, modest to a fault, but good, good, good.

July 26, 2003

I realize that I still don't trust, but also that I simply do not really care about anything. It's a dangerous place to be. I don't care enough about anything to trust. I have to care first, don't I? I have to at least care about myself. I care about others, but I am so dead to myself. It's as if I'm in a coffin, sealed in and cut off from air, light, and sustenance. I am like my inner girls, boxed up, suffering the same fate I have imposed upon them. In spite of this not caring attitude, I am off to meet with a potential client. I have to support my family!

July 27, 2003

I know I am perfectly capable of everything I set out to accomplish, but the old fears and self-hatred still hover nearby. They take over without a moment's notice, usurping my power and before I know what's happening I am their slave. Keeping my self-confidence at a steady level and fully accessible is perhaps the most difficult and most critical task right now. But I've been here before. I know I can get beyond it. I *will* get beyond it!

July 28, 2003

I have too many days when I'm not fully present, when I can't function or communicate. How will I ever be able to live? How will I be able to carry on a life with these dark drowning days so prevalent? It's like I'm still underwater in that murky lake of my dream. I know that life is teeming on the surface, but I just can't seem to make it up there.

I have had no periods since early June. Is that it? Am I in menopause now? Hurray!

July 29, 2003

I wake full of anxiety about curating the upcoming show at the gallery. Why am I still taking on such responsibilities when I should be cutting back and spending my energy on myself? A painting by an artist in the show swirled around in my dreams all night long, an angry black central eye surrounded by furious color, depicting anger unleashed. Am I angry at myself, at the old me who just won't let go, who clings to her old world so tenaciously? I concentrate on staying calm as I head up to meet with Chuck, telling myself that everything will be okay, just as Jeanne so often reminds me.

I realize that detaching from life, retreating into my usual depressive state, and hiding in bed all day are not, in the long run, good or healing tactics. They do, however, offer quick and ready answers when things get overwhelming. When I tell Chuck this he mentions balance, that I need balance. I guess he's right because everything right now is so precarious, so completely *out of balance*. But I just can't envision it; no visual image of what balance might look like comes to me.

"I guess gaining balance means having another person in my life, someone to love me, someone to know what I'm feeling without my having to even speak," I say, and then I realize that the old me just spoke out loud.

"I know that's impossible, it's not the right answer," I say, quickly reasserting the new and changing me. "I know I don't need another person. I have to do it differently now. I have to become that someone to myself. I have to love myself unconditionally, communicate with myself on an ever-deepening level until I understand everything there is to know about myself, all that I still keep hidden, all that I still don't want to talk about. If I don't talk, even to myself, there will be no feedback, there will be no reciprocity. But sometimes I want you to give me answers. I want direction."

"I listen and give you what comes through me," Chuck says, "but I don't have the answers, you have to find those within yourself."

I accept this because I know he's right. He also suggests that I most likely have a lot of unexpressed anger, as the image of the painting swirling through my dreams all night seems to be suggesting. In the dream, I kept trying to still the central angry eye, to get it to stop spinning, frustration building when I couldn't.

"It might be time to let the anger out," Chuck says.

After the session I go over to the artist's gallery. A few people come by to help hang the show with me. I go back in the evening to work for two quiet hours, happy to be alone.

"You have to live in your physical body; you can't ignore it," Chuck said today.

"I know," I said, "I just can't be there all the time yet. It's too scary."

Do I trust yet? I'm worried about intimacy, about having sex, frustrated by not having it, worried that I won't be able to, that I'm sexually dead.

July 30, 2003

I'm awake early after a night of anxious dreaming. Tossing and turning, I try to sleep a little more, dozing on and off until I finally get up. I have too much to do to stay in bed! I feel a little weak and realize that I haven't been eating much lately. I feel a lot perkier after drinking a cup of coffee, and after eating a good breakfast I'm ready for a long day at the gallery. There are lots of loose ends to tie up and I expect to be there for most of the day.

People have been great about getting their framed artwork to me on time; they know I expect them to be professionals.

As I head out for the gallery, I admit to myself that Chuck is right. I do have anger inside me, deep down. I feel its desire to spread out into my limbs, to take over completely. Though I keep it in check, I'm tired of it, bruised and exhausted by being incessantly watchful. I don't want to live like this, always anxious and on edge, always expecting to be overtaken, yet I know I must be patient. I still need more healing time.

I'm pleased with the work submitted for the show, intricate and intense. I don't want the gallery to have a cluttered look, each piece must have space around it, air to breathe. I too need air. I need to fill my lungs with clean fresh air, get out of the deep murky lake of recapitulation and focus on the real world for a change. As Chuck suggested, I need to stay in my physical body. So I keep moving, purposely, with awareness of doing so, intent on not being dragged back down into the deep. I concentrate on staying in the present moment as much as possible, trying to not push myself to the very limits. Once I've gotten a slow and steady physical pace established, anchored by repeated mantras to stay present, I notice how effortlessly everything gets done—with no stress!

I had a premonition the other day, about a friend of mine. I was certain she had a medical problem. A few minutes later she walked into the studio and told me that she just found out she has ovarian tumors. I've had other premonitions in the past. I looked at an acquaintance once and saw cancer lurking beneath her happy glowing exterior. Within a few weeks she was being treated for a recurrent cancer, after ten years of remission. Once, at a Christmas gathering, I looked around the roomful of people. I could feel everyone's energy. As I gazed upon one woman, I felt her absence. She's not really here anymore, I thought, and she won't be here next year. There was no sign or mention of illness for nine more months. She died three days before Christmas the following year, cancer taking her quickly.

I realize I've always been able to read energy, though I never imagined it was anything special. I first learned to do this as a small girl during encounters with my abuser. At the first sighting of him I'd go inward, read his energy, and know if he was coming for me. I could feel he wouldn't be nice. And when things turned badly my skills were available to take me out-of-body until it was safe to return. Now I'm reading energy again. This time I intend to put it to good use to help me grow.

July 31, 2003

I wake up tired and clenched, the anxiety chomping to get back in. I push it away. The need to withdraw is strong. I push that away too. I need to be "on" today. I need to be present in my head, if not my whole body. I have to work and deal with people.

Eleven at night now, the house is quiet. It's a hot night. Although I've spent hours setting up the show, there are still things to be done tomorrow; make a sign, finish labels, clean the floor, meet the last straggling artist as she finally brings in her work; meet the gallery sitter there at five, and send a final email to everyone in the show. In the midst of it all, I feel like a drowning person, slowly sinking down into the murky underwater world.

Tomorrow I see Chuck again. I am driven to tell him that he's not the spiritual guru, the shaman that I thought he was. He's just a man. Am I angry because I felt he wasn't helping me the other day? Did he disappoint me when I felt so frustrated and wanted answers? He's so knowledgeable, so nonjudgmental, so deeply spiritual and open, but the truth is, he is just a human man. Perhaps I've put him on a pedestal, and that's unfair, but perhaps this signifies the end of my transference with him as well. I see him very clearly now, more grounded in this world, without the glowing aura that always bedazzled me before. It's as if I've come down to the ground myself, a good sign of that balance I seek. At the same time, I clearly accept him as the expert he is, more than capable of guiding me along on this immense journey.

I recently dreamed that he came to me and told me he couldn't be all that I want him to be, that I ask too much. He's right! I still feel angry though, like I want to tell him off, right to his face!

Chapter 2

A New Reality

August 1, 2003

A bit on edge, I head out to meet with Chuck. As soon as I step into his office I begin to dissociate, yesterday's anger at him a distant memory. My old demons pull me down into the depths of the murky lake of despair, offering escape from all that plagues me, telling me to rest in the quiet, no need to talk to anyone today.

"What's happening in your body?" Chuck asks.

I struggle to swim back up to the surface, to stay present, to open my mouth and say something, but I am dragged down into the muddy depths of the lake. Lost and drowning, I roll mutely onto the floor. Chuck jumps up, shouting.

"Move! Get up! Stand up! Make a change, make the change physically! Get out of your head! Stop thinking and just move!"

He's been telling me this for months, but have I listened?

August 2, 2003

The morning is full of struggle. I try to heed Chuck's advice to get out of my head. "What is happening in your body?" I hear him asking. I try to move, but I am immediately both sad and frightened. "Get out of your head," I hear him saying, but I find it so hard when my body is full of triggers, full of feelings I don't want to know about.

I set the intent to focus on living life above the murky waters today, to get back into my physical body. I start by doing yoga, followed by meditation, and then I set the intent to stay relaxed and present throughout the day. At the studio, I varnish some painted furniture and call a client regarding a piece she's interested in. Maybe I'll make an extra sale. I write up the final invoice for the murals that I recently completed and then write an article, getting it to the publisher just under deadline.

I notice how I'm able to get out of my head and into my physical body, into my physical life, as I set my intentions and accomplish things in the world. All of a sudden I feel pretty good and I become aware that one day this recapitulation *will* be over and that great things lie before me. I sense an expanded universe just waiting for me.

"*Don't be afraid. Go for it; see where it leads,*" says Jeanne. "*You have your whole life ahead of you.*"

I heard Maurice Sendak, the children's book author and illustrator, speaking last night on the radio. He said he draws and writes for the frightened child in all of us. There is no denying that we all have a frightened child churning in our bellies, yelling, but it's also true that many people don't listen to that frightened child self. Lucky or not, I have sixteen little girls inside me, all yelling: "Don't forget about us!"

August 3, 2003

As soon as I wake up I focus on my body, on the physical. Where am I? How am I feeling? Get moving!

The intense August heat and the tension of getting this show up and running at the artist's gallery have made eating difficult, but I try to get some food into me. I spent a long time crying last night when I got home, from frustration, exhaustion, anger, and fear, letting those sixteen little girls yell at me. They told me the truth, that being involved with the gallery really sucks right now, being in charge of the show even worse. "Why are you doing it?" they wanted to know. The artists are either bitching about having to work at the gallery or just plain not showing up when it's their turn to open for the day and do their sitting time. I had to be there on Friday night to orient a new artist. Then on Saturday no one showed up to open at noon, all my calls went unanswered, so I had to go up there and sit until five when the next sitter showed up. The girls are right—it really sucks! I hope today's gallery sitter shows up, otherwise I will be there again, and not at all happy about it!

I've put so much energy into the gallery that my own business has suffered, I've suffered. I've lost track of what I'm doing and why. Funnily enough, what I'm doing doesn't really seem so important anymore. When I'd started it was a way to recycle old furniture, giving it fresh life, but that intention has lost its import. And although my business has expanded along other avenues I have an underlying sense of something different waiting for me in the future, something much more meaningful.

Luckily, the gallery sitter did show up today and I was able to spend the day at home relaxing. In the afternoon, I received an email from one of the artists in the show. He wrote: "You are an excellent communicator." I cried when I read that and I continued to cry on and off into the night, from exhaustion and also because of the desire to feel, to let come what may, to release all that is inside me.

I want some good things to happen to me now. I need some happiness and some prosperity. I need some love too.

August 4, 2003

I dream that I'm in Chuck's office, rolled into a ball on the floor, crying. Suddenly, a tall black woman barges in followed by an angry black man. The session ends abruptly. I leave without saying anything. Unlike Chuck's real office, in a cottage on his property, this dream office is in a large building. I head toward a bathroom down the hallway and when I turn back I see Chuck poke his head out of his door. I want him to acknowledge me, but he doesn't, he just stares past me. When I come out of the bathroom I glance down the hallway again. Chuck is still standing in his doorway, and still he doesn't acknowledge me. I'm disappointed. He deserted me during a vulnerable moment. Something new was happening in the session; I was letting myself cry in front of him, which I've never done before. He didn't stop the intruders but merely watched them take a seat and then raised his hands in a gesture of surrender, and shrugged. "Oh well!" he said. It bothered me that he didn't push them out and give me the rest of the time I needed, nor did he say goodbye.

As the dream continues, I leave the building taking my pain and disappointment with me. My plan is to get run over. I leave Chuck a message on his answering machine telling him that I'm taking the easy way out, that I'm going to destroy myself. I walk down the middle of the street, right into traffic, but by the time I get to the end of the long street I feel better, not so desperate anymore. Then I see a friend walking in traffic, just as I had done. I run up and grab her, scolding her for walking in the road. She says that once you have it in your mind to kill yourself you take risks.

"But you don't want to kill yourself, do you?" I ask.

"No," she says, "not anymore."

I grab her as she veers toward the road again. She laughs and says, "Just an old habit, I guess."

The black woman and black man are shadow aspects of myself, the woman entitled and the man angry. They have come to let me know what I really have to deal with. It's not the murky water that's the issue, it's what I'm avoiding by getting drawn into it. I'm disappointed that Chuck doesn't kick them out of the office, but they represent my own problems and it's appropriate that they are there in the place where I should be facing them. I carry my disappointment with me as I leave, deciding to walk in the middle of the street, to "get run over." It's an obvious effort to get Chuck's attention, manipulative. The friend veering into the road, a part of myself, reminds me that I'm not really interested in suicide, that thoughts of it are just an old habit. I have to agree with that!

My dream produced some very interesting and helpful characters! I do have to contend with what lies in my shadow self, the demanding, entitled self that wants to be noticed and the self that is so angry, as well as the self who is evolving, pointing out how she knows how the old habits slip in uninvited. This is what Chuck was saying the other day when he yelled at me in his office, to get up and move! He was really saying, "Get out of that damn lake and do something for yourself!"

I struggle to find my footing. People need me and I need them, but I'm having a hell of a time swimming up from the deep. I'm out of that murky lake one day and back in the next. When I'm out I must struggle to stay out, which is tremendously hard to do. It's not just about self-confidence either, it's about facing the pain and fear, how I've dealt with them in the past and how to break my attachment to them now. It cannot be done overnight! It can't even be done in a year or two, but perhaps in three, as Jeanne once told me, or hopefully sometime during this lifetime!

I keep busy and moving throughout the day, wondering if this is the way I'm going to have to live, in constant motion for all the rest of my days. I don't think I'll be able to keep it up. Every position I'm in, whether it's sitting, lying, standing, or walking, is uncomfortable. I don't know how to be, how to think, or how to stop thinking. I just know that I'm not done remembering yet. I want to get beyond the past, but I can't while I'm still trying to remember it. I'm also trying to remember how to feel, or perhaps I'm learning to feel for the first time. I'm changing so much and so rapidly that I've lost all sense of myself. I'm in a crazy whirlwind now.

I spend the evening with the kids, anchored between the two of them on the couch. We watch comedy on television until eleven. It's hilarious and it sure feels good to laugh!

August 5, 2003

I dream that I'm stuck in my own collages, running all night between trees—forests constructed of sticks laid side by side, glued or nailed to the background—trying to find a way out. I keep moving. "Don't stop or he'll get you! Keep running! Don't let him get you!" These are the words I hear, promptings from the inner voices of fear, commanding that I keep moving all night long.

I wake up exhausted, my body crumpled and in pain, sweaty and unhappy. How will I make it through the day? I just want to stay in bed. Why do I keep doing this recapitulation? What will I get out of it? I'm living a nightmare! In a panic, I call Chuck.

"How am I going to get through this day?" I ask.

"I wouldn't wonder how I'm going to get through my day," he says. "I wouldn't plot my day in order to *get through it*. You need to take the focus off that struggle. It's like an addiction, the pull to go back inside, to hide from life, and you have to fight it the way an addict fights the desire for a substance that is killing him. Old habits are hard to break. Don't panic, things will be fine."

I miss my guide, my Jeanne. Where is she? I need her help, though I have to admit he sounds so much like her.

August 6, 2003

Chuck comes as a guide and healer into a dream. Clothed in a long white cotton kaftan, he leads me through one of my stick-collage artworks, calmly assuring me that everything will be okay.

"Just keep going, don't give up," he says, as we make our way through the tangled forest of sticks that make up the collage.

"You can do this," he says.

I trust him. As we slowly and calmly make our way along I experience it all without the usual fear. Then something happens to my house, devastation, and I am suddenly catapulted out of the stick collage. Now I stand in front of my destroyed house with a woman healer, Jeanne, also dressed in a long white gown. She too calms me down, letting me know that everything will be fine.

In spite of the calming advice in my dream, I wake up whirling with fear and anxiety, body and mind on a crazy carnival ride that I can't get off. Nauseous and shivering, I hide under the covers until even that becomes unbearable. Am I still dreaming? My healing guides told me everything would be okay, but my body is in agony. My dream of the night before, when I was running through my stick collages, full of anxiety, is followed by this dream, with the guides and healers in my life coming to calm me within the framework of the same artwork, reflecting the past, this process of recapitulation, and the healing that it promotes.

It's one of those days when it seems almost impossible to get out of bed, but at least I am able to breathe. "Such a simple and natural thing," I tell myself as I sit up in bed. I breathe all the time so unconsciously, but if I focus on my breath I know it will aid in my healing—the breath of life all I need. And so, breathing very slowly, I reach a good level of calmness, but I can do no more, no yoga or deeper breathing, though it gets me up, out of bed and moving, and for that I am thankful.

On the drive over to the studio I realize I need to change my thinking, but I'm not sure how to begin. Positive mantras work for a while, but I need some deeper shifts to happen, internal changes preferably, so that old thoughts and beliefs no longer gain entry or find a foothold. I intend to deliberately refuse them, even shout at them to leave, and then turn on my heel and walk away. I hope I can remember to do that when the time comes!

I work for a few hours before exhaustion and the heavy depression return, and then I just want night to come so I can go back to bed. The few hours of work are enjoyable, however, deeply calming time spent inside my creative bubble. A few calls come in while I work, new commissions lining up, and my heart lifts. This could work out after all, this life I've chosen. I intend to "just keep going," as my healers say.

Violent thunderstorms roll through the valley during the night, clashing and crashing, drawing forth the shadow self.

ANGER! ANGER! ANGER! YES, I HAVE ANGER!

Lightning flashes, thunder rattles the earth, the house, and me in my bed. BOOM! BOOM! BOOM! Like fire-breathing dragons the storms steamroll through the neighborhood, shaking me and shaking my world.

August 7, 2003

I dream that I'm clinging to the back of a wild dragon, a snakelike monster, as thick around as a man. I grip tightly while he whips me to and fro like a wild horse trying to throw its rider. Suddenly, the fiendish monster rapes me in mid-air, painfully and viciously. I scream and cling to him, afraid that if I let go I will plunge to the earth and certain death. Even though I am being brutally violated there is nothing to do but hold on. The irony is that I need him; I need this monster. He is my only hope of survival; even while he forces himself upon me most violently and against my will, I know that I need him if I am to survive.

I am shocked awake in the middle of the night by fiery, seething PAIN. REAL. INTENSE. PAIN! The thunderstorms entered my dream world and manifested in this nightmarish fire-breathing rapist of a dragon. I slow my breathing, try to get calm. I get out of bed and go over to the open window, gasping for air, willing the pain to stop, breathing it out, breathing it out, and breathing in the damp air of the dark and rainy night.

"Okay! Okay! Okay! Why do I need to keep feeling? Why, why, why? To make me angry? OKAY! I am FUCKING ANGRY!"

The irony of this dream is not to be ignored, as it clearly and cleverly underscores the dichotomy of the precarious situation I now find myself in. The recapitulation is very painful, but if I don't go through it, if I don't ride that wild dragon, I am as good as dead. It's imperative that I hang on for dear life and ride it to the end if I am to ever heal from my traumas. It was how I survived in the first place. With that point made and accepted, I slip back into bed. It's one o'clock in the morning and I hope only for sleep now.

When I woke last night to that fiery dragon pain I was full of fear and memory, but a new insight dawned on me too, along with a new acceptance of this recapitulation process, for it really is my salvation. No matter how I try to persuade myself otherwise, I am destined to take the ride, horrific and painful as it is. It's so crucial that I remember everything that happened to me and fully experience it, and the best way to do that is proving to be just as my dream implies, hang on and go along for the ride, keeping in mind that this journey will end when there is nothing left to recapitulate. Only then will I be freed of all my demons and only then will the dragon come in the night no more.

The dragon dream has delivered another message as well. It has stirred a whirling tornado of anger, though there is a part of me that feels it should still be held back. A part of me won't allow it out, fearful that it's too ferocious, far more brutal and evil than even the dragon rapist. But maybe letting it out won't hurt as much as holding it in does. I am innerly volatile, though externally I am mostly quiet. Beneath the surface, however, runs an undercurrent of powerful energy, much like that snakelike monster of my dream.

The lack of discourse in my family of origin sent me off on my journey deficient in skills of communication, lacking in trust, and fearful of everything. I was taught to be independent, that I had only myself to blame, that anything that happened to me was my fault, and so I was responsible for everything. I was taught to be polite and obedient, to be honest and respectful, and to always do my best. My parents, like many, sent me out into life with those meagre values, and yet I took them to heart. They have been the mainstay of who I am and how I operate. So, in all humility, I must turn to my parents and thank them, even as I turn away from them now too and evolve into the being I truly am, totally absent of them. I must also turn to the shadow selves inside me—the entitled woman who burst into Chuck's office in that dream and the angry man following her—and thank them for the gifts they bring me too. The woman teaches me that I am entitled to life just as much as the next person, and that angry man is making himself heard now too. That seems to be the next leg of this journey, finding the gifts among the pain and trauma, the diamonds in the coal.

What I received at birth, and from my family, was all I had to work with and the rest was up to me, not because I was deficient or denied anything, but because it was my karma, what nature gave me, what I was given to work with and work out in this lifetime. So what if I got frightened and withholding parents? So what if I got abused as a child? Sometimes things just happen to us. Sometimes things come to teach us great lessons, or to wake us up. Whatever happened to me is what got me where I am now, providing me with all that makes up who I am, and I have to be pretty okay with that.

It's now almost midnight as I write these final words for today. We just got back from the theatre production my daughter has spent the summer involved in, resulting in a final weekend of performances. It was a pleasure to watch her onstage, so confident and poised, a fine little actor with a pleasant and commanding stage presence. She is nurturing her own creativity, and I couldn't be happier for her.

I'm tired now, wanting only sleep. In spite of everything, I didn't just "get through" the day, but actually flowed well and even enjoyed parts of it. And writing things down sure helps to process and assimilate this most crazy and mysterious journey!

August 8, 2003

Once again, I dream that I'm running through the trees of my collages. I am screaming as I run, trying to find a place to hide because something is about to happen. I wake up shaking, wondering what lies ahead. I see Chuck this morning. I'm nervous.

"What lies ahead is the rest of the journey, that's what's about to happen," Chuck points out. "You are being challenged to focus on yourself, to give yourself permission to stop running and hiding, to pause and analyze and investigate yourself now in an ever-deepening way, without feeling guilty."

"Nature has a way of letting things happen without our control," Chuck goes on, "and everything that is going to happen will happen, when the time is right. It's our decision to choose to go with it."

Yes, nature happens, and it's nobody's fault. When the time is right each challenge will appear, and I'll be ready. I'm beginning to realize that I really can support myself with my studio business. The time is right for me to accept this. More commissions are coming in and this has helped greatly to boost my morale. While challenging myself to create a new outer life, I'm also doing this deep inner work, creating a new inner life as well. These parallel lives mirror each other, as one grows so does the other.

I guess when the time is right I'll find someone to share my life with too. I know I'm not there yet, but hopefully the right person will be there when I'm ready. When the time comes, I will know him. I'm sure of it.

August 9, 2003

It's a hot and muggy day. I fear the gallery will be too hot tonight for the opening, with no air conditioning and only a few meager fans. Hopefully a storm will come through and bring some relief!

Chuck is so important to me and has been for the past few years now. I fear I have become obsessed with him in an odd way; I want him there for me alone. I don't really want him to be a man, or married, or have kids, or have a life outside the consulting room. I need him to only be that guy I meet in the office, asexual, kind and understanding, in his place and in no other place, like a ship that is always anchored in the same harbor. I need to know where he is and that I can get to him. I want him to be only what I need at the moment and nothing else. It's too painful to share him. When I see him as a man, his strength, intellect, and wisdom as a healer diminish and then he is no longer my guru. He's just a man then.

I get upset when he tells me personal things. Not that he does very often, but even just hints of a personal life, a life outside of the office, are startling interferences in my process. I don't really want to know anything about him, except that he's there in his office waiting for me to speak. To picture him there makes me feel safe. It makes my story feel safe.

It's over! The opening was fabulous, but it was way too hot. People were packed into the gallery like sardines, drenched in sweat but happy to be hanging out anyway. My brother and a friend came and provided music. They were so well received and appreciated. I passed the hat for them, so grateful that in spite of the sweltering conditions they performed with gusto.

I'm exhausted now, still buzzing, trying to unwind. I have to go back to the gallery tomorrow morning to clean up. It was so hot we just locked up and left everything. It's raining now, finally, but still sticky, humid, and extremely hot. Reminds me of living down South, though it's pretty oppressive with no air conditioning. The fan in my window is of no help whatsoever!

August 10, 2003

It's been a depressing day. I tossed and turned all last night in the heat of this hot, muggy spell we've been having and woke to an equally humid morning. I never really got any energy together today. I did get the gallery cleaned up early in the morning though and then spent the rest of the day fighting my demons. Fear crept into my body and I've tried to calm it. I've wanted to walk, but it's been thundering and lightning and pouring like crazy. I've wanted to curl into a ball too, but I'm fighting it. I want to call Chuck, but I'm fighting that too. I feel hopeful one minute and devastated the next. And still no energy.

I've been thinking about the anger that boils inside me. If I let it out I might just go crazy and I'm wondering if I should just let myself do that, skip the anger part and just go crazy. I think it's a choice. Would I dare choose it?

August 11, 2003

I dream that I'm looking into a large rectangular box. Everything about my past and present life is in that box, heaped up in a huge mess, including everything that nags and worries me now, such as not having enough money, not having enough work, my responsibilities to the kids, the house, and even the cats.

Everything swirls before me in a sickening panic. I stand there alone, looking at it, taking it in, knowing that it's my life to deal with. I am the only one who can sort this mess out. Then I begin to break down the large box into smaller boxes, to sort through the mess, compartmentalizing it. I work with intent, gaining calmness as I work, though I sense the anxiety and whirlwind of panic still hovering nearby. Then a calm voice says: *You are fine for today. Today is fine. Think of it one day at a time.*

It takes a long time to come out of this dream. Even though I was able to compartmentalize and break things down into a "one day at a time" mentality I wake up feeling hopeless. I was aware of my thinking during the dream and I was able to gain control over all-out panic and so I remind myself that I am indeed okay for today, that today is fine. However, in spite of my recent good feelings about myself and the progress of my work, I have to acknowledge that I've landed back in an old place, with the panic coursing through my veins again. Fear and panic swirl inside me just as they did inside the box in my dream. I am just one big mess of tension.

Lying flat on my back, I breathe. The soft voice of my yoga teacher comes to me, quietly soothing: *"Breathe. If it hurts then only go as far as is comfortable. Breathe."* And then the panic begins to subside.

I wonder if I'll ever be able to live with abandon, safe enough in this world that nothing frightens or scares me. The truth is that I will only be able to live with true abandon when I've finished this recapitulation work. Only then will I be free enough to embrace what that really means, to have no triggers pulling me back, nothing getting in the way. First complete the breakdown, then complete the rebuilding, only then will the option to live life with abandon be truly available. Out of the ashes comes new life.

I get up, shaky and afraid, aware that I must not stop. I must keep going no matter what. I gather my breaking self together and go to the studio. I work for a few hours, but am unable to concentrate. I futz around until five when I finally emerge from the dark murky lake, the deep watery pocket of depression I've been in all day. I'm tired, totally worn out, as if I've swum a hundred miles. I barely have enough energy to make it home and cook some food for the kids. None of us slept very well last night in the oppressive heat. After dinner we head to our separate rooms, each of us yearning for quiet and eventually, hopefully, sleep.

I sit in bed with William Buhlman's *Adventures Beyond the Body*, hoping that something in his book will spark me into a different kind of dreaming tonight. Even having the book next to me offers hope, imbued as it is with the magic and mystery of out-of-body travel. I know I've reached a new plateau, but I still get dragged back into the dark underwater world of depression, into filmy hopelessness. I want to dream of progress now. I want to remain conscious of all that I have gained and learned. I want to look out from my new plateau and see another plateau, hopefully within jumping distance so I can leap onto it without falling into the endless darkness between. But what if I do fall? What will I find there? Is there a possibility that it won't be just endless darkness in between the plateaus, that it will turn out to be something else? I will try to find out. I set my intent to dream my way out of the darkness I've been in for so long. And please, give me a sign that I'm not alone.

August 12, 2003

I dream that I am down inside the deep watery pocket of the murky lake of my previous dream, alone and lonely. "Help!" I call out, lifting my hands upward. I see a light above me, shining down through the muddy water, my hands clearly illuminated. A strong masculine hand suddenly breaks through the surface of the water and firmly grasps my hand, quickly pulling me up and out of the water. I am immediately aware that this being is a conduit. As soon as he pulls me up and out of the water the light of God strikes him from above, shoots right through him, bathing him in a brightly glowing aura, a giant oval cocoon of neon white light. He floats in the air, looking very much like Chuck, smiling, with light streaming down through the top of his head, through his body, out his hands and feet directly into me. When he releases my hand, I drop easily to the ground and see that we are in the artist's gallery.

The conduit, floating above me and still streaming with white light, points out many blank rectangular canvases lining the room. I intuitively know that I am expected to create a world, that I am fully capable of creating my own world. Then, quite suddenly and magically, I see that the entire gallery is filled with artwork—many complicated assemblages incorporating tree branches and sticks, many painted canvases, and many constructions—from dark and moody pieces to a small and intricately constructed model house, painted white, with a porch on the front. I think that this being, this conduit, must have created everything because it all happens so quickly. But then I realize that I am the creator of everything. I am just finishing the construction on the house when I "come to," as it were, and wake up in the dream. Yet I still cannot fully grasp that I have actually done all the work that surrounds me. At the same time, I am certain that no one else had anything to do with it, or that anyone else pulled me up out of the murky water. I am in a quandary, trying to figure out what has just happened. I don't want to admit that I need anyone and yet I know that I am not alone.

I sit on the gallery floor, surrounded by all the artwork, the bright white figure gone now. Who was that man who helped me? Was that really Chuck? Then it all becomes clear and I realize it wasn't anyone else at all, it was me, a part of me. I pulled myself out of the murky lake. My dreaming self used the image of Chuck to prove that I am capable and strong enough to save myself, to do life on my own, that everything I need is in me. I finally used my transference with Chuck to good advantage, fully taking it back, owning it now. I am my own conduit.

As the dream continues, it finally becomes clear that the artwork is my own, things I've done in the past, current projects, and even work I haven't done yet. I become fully aware of who I really am, of my fuller potential as a human being and of my higher spiritual self. I have no doubt that I am strong and fully capable of everything I set out to do. Then I realize a deeper truth, that the human being that I am doesn't really want to do life on her own. As capable of being alone as I am, I really do want other people in my life. As a human being I need help sometimes, and it's okay to admit it and to ask for it. And so I become aware that I must prepare for a new kind of life now. I must leave the comforts of my aloneness behind and prove to my human self that other people really are trustworthy.

I awaken from this profound dream vibrating, aglow with energy, feeling as if I really have been struck by ethereal lightning from above. I am so alive! I am also stunned by the revelations that came through: I am not alone, I no longer want to be alone, and I will be okay by accepting and receiving help! I asked for a sign that I was not alone and boy did I get it!

I can now fully admit that I have indeed not been alone on this recapitulation journey. I would say to Chuck: "I know you are here, but I am still doing it alone." But that just isn't true, it never was. I've been accompanied the entire time, not only by Chuck, but by my human self and my higher self as well, my own spirit, not to mention the guidance I've received from Jeanne. I can now admit what my dreaming self recognized, what I have been refusing to accept, that I do need other people in my life and that I must not be afraid of other human beings. I cannot do life alone. That's an old idea, as this dream clearly points out, and it's no longer a viable or useful option. It's time to let it go. Indeed, reality is changing rapidly now, and so I expect that everything else I've held onto, thinking I needed it, will be going soon too. As Chuck is fond of saying: *there must be sacrifice for new life to take place.*

Chuck has been here all along, offering me a light in the darkness, daring me to move out of the old world and into the new. The choice to do so has always been mine to make. I've had enough glimpses of that new world now to know that it does indeed exist. Without his help I wouldn't be here, so why do I want to deny him? Why do I want to deny that I have relied upon and received help from others? The real truth is that I am never alone.

A few days ago, I could not imagine life without Chuck sitting in his office, forever waiting for me to show up. In that scenario he was not allowed to be anything other than my guru, eternally present for my needs alone. I did not want to see him as a man, but it wasn't a healthy position for either of us to be in. Here, in this dream, I am given the gift of the light: *I am my own guru.* And the truth is, Chuck really *is* a man. My transference is now officially dead. True reality has set in.

Over the past two nights my dreaming self has presented rectangles. First a rectangular box filled with the tangled mess of past and present, and then rectangular canvases waiting to be filled with something new, waiting for realization of my fuller potential and ownership of all that I am, as well as for the future unfolding of life as I venture into the great unknown. I am astonished, as it slowly dawns on me in the dream that the artwork is my own, that

I have produced it. The images represent not only the work of my creative self and the life I have lived thus far, but also the work of this recapitulation, spread out before me in dream reality, the story of my own life, created through me! Though I'm not sure I get the full meaning of this dream, I begin to understand that I create my life in everything I do, in every choice, and in every hard lesson I've ever had to learn. I have created my dream world too, all of it, with a lot of help of course!

I'm going to read a little more in Buhlman's book before sleep again and set a new intention! I want to dream the next step. Perhaps letting go of fear?

August 13, 2003

I have no recollection of dreams right now, except that they were full of people. Although I asked for something else, I got what I need, what I am being challenged with right now—to be a part of life, to trust others—and that means being around people!

I lie flat on my back for a long time before getting up, letting the residual sadness and anxiety of a lifetime seep out of me. I give myself this mantra: *Today will be good. Today will be good. Today will be good. Today will be good.*

I know Chuck is here, and he knows I need him. Those are facts, but what am I still so afraid of? For I cannot deny that in spite of the beauty and empowerment of that conduit dream, I am still afraid. But what do I really fear? I'm afraid of life itself. I'm afraid of the unknown. I'm afraid of all that I've never experienced before. I have long been addicted to my own lonely darkness; it has been my protection. It will be hard to give it up, but I understand that that is my challenge now, to allow myself to be vulnerable and open to what life has in store for me, whether I am fearful or not.

Today will be good. Today will be good.

Now it's late. I actually did have a good day! I felt fairly light and optimistic for the better part of it, the easiest day I've had in a long time.

August 14, 2003

I realize that I am two people at once: the frightened, panicky abused self who wants to remain isolated and alone, and the mature adult self who wants to participate in life, who is capable, confident, and competent. This is the split human self that I am confronted with at this moment, whom I must merge into one being and guide into new life by encouraging my higher spiritual self to take over now.

It's eleven at night now. There's been a blackout since four o'clock this afternoon. I'm reading and writing by candlelight and flashlight. I've been reading Buhlman's book again and will try some new ideas from it tonight. Last night I kept waking up all through the night, hearing my son awake in his room next to mine. Then I woke up suddenly at five-fifty in the morning to find him still awake. My dreams flew out the window then, never to be seen again. He's with his dad tonight so I may have better luck with tonight's sleep and dreams! And hopefully he will sleep too!

More than anything, I desire one final sign that all of this is true, that all these memories are true, that I am not making them up, that I did not read about them somewhere, or see them someplace. I envision sitting in Chuck's office with a huge board between us upon which everything I have told him is laid out, like a giant three-dimensional map, and I just want to flip the whole damn thing! Flip it into oblivion and say: "I don't believe any of it! It's too hard to believe! I'd much rather forget it, forget all of it, and get out of here! Just get out of here!"

Please help me with all of this. Please help me.

August 15, 2003

In a dream, I am with a doctor I know. We go into a hotel barroom where a lot of people are sitting at a long bar. The room is painted and draped in deep red velvet. My abuser's daughter is there, and although I don't immediately recognize her, I feel that I know her. My doctor friend has to go make a phone call. A space is made for me at the bar. As I look down the length of the bar, I see everyone lifting small glasses of alcohol and I realize I don't want a drink. I don't want to alter my perception or ability to think, move, or drive. I want to stay very sober. Just then the doctor returns. We will go up to the hotel room he has reserved for us, he says. When I hear this I feel like rolling into a ball in the dark of the bar, but I follow him upstairs anyway. I am aware that I am very depressed.

Once in the room, the doctor has to use the bathroom. I sit on the edge of the bed feeling uncertain and vulnerable. I am still intent on not altering my state of alertness or perception. I want to stay aware. When the doctor comes out of the bathroom he is no longer the doctor, but an old boyfriend of mine. I feel trapped; I cannot move or do a thing. I just sit there frozen. The situation is not good. The old boyfriend tells me that he has to go home to get something and he leaves. I'm glad he's gone, but at the same time I feel deserted. It's reminiscent of our actual relationship when he would leave me to go have liaisons with other women, telling me he had work to do and that he'd be back later. Dutifully, I sit in the hotel room waiting for him to come back, as I once did in reality, but he never returns.

The lights came back on at some point during the night. I hear on the news that the blackout was huge, spread over several states and into Canada. It included all of New York City and apparently created quite a lot of havoc. Part of the problem was the overload of electrical usage due to the oppressively hot and humid weather we've been having. The wires got too hot and successive meltdowns occurred. Not too unlike what is building up inside me right now, a grand meltdown!

I meet with Chuck. We talk about having the power to change things, to react, and be in control. In last night's dream, I remained aware of wanting to be in control but was still held back by old traumas, not able to initiate action. It was definitely an old scenario with the old boyfriend. I was my old numb and frozen self, unable to extricate myself from an uncomfortable situation, to act on my own behalf, and it was stagnating. I went into blackout mode! I just sat and waited for him to return. In spite of my intent to remain alert and aware, to remain soberly present, things didn't progress beyond that decision, as I was unable to shift out of my old behavioral pattern. So the intention I set for my dreaming self worked to a certain extent, but I guess I forgot to intend what to do after that!

"You have the power to change things. You can react. You can say no. You can walk away," Chuck says, motioning me to get out of my chair. "You want to not just say these things, but do them. It's a magical pass, turning and walking in a new direction with the intent to change."

"I have the power to change things," I say. "I can react. I can say no. I can walk away."

I repeat this over and over again as Chuck instructs me in how to turn and pivot, how to shift abruptly, how to infuse my intent with action.

"I have the power to change things. I can react. I can say no. I can walk away," I say, turning and shifting until it all feels like a part of me.

"I can do these things," I say, and by the time the session is over that's exactly how I feel.

My question to my dream world was clearly answered last night. Are the memories real? Yes, the memories are indeed real, my dream tells me. They are so deeply embedded that I act them out repeatedly, in waking and dreaming life, even when I intend otherwise. As if on cue, I freeze, I go numb. Even the fact that my abuser's daughter showed up in the dream is an obvious sign of the truth. She represents the abusive past that still has me in its grip. Even though I've set the intent to be alert to old habits, I haven't completely extricated myself from the old state of frozen numbness and inaction, a state directly related to the abuse, and which my old boyfriend was able to take advantage of so often, as the dream reminds me. During my relationship with him, blocked memories were triggered often enough, though they went no further than strange and mysterious scenarios. I realize now, of course, that my psyche was desperately trying to tell me something that I just was not ready to grasp at the time.

It isn't at all odd that my abuser's daughter and he would be in the same dream, for they were both energetically connected to the old me, for I knew them both as a deeply confused and abused person. My abuser's daughter was involved in the abuse with her father, and the relationship with my old boyfriend, twenty years older than me, was a constant trigger of that abuse. Both his age, close to that of my abuser, and his need to control were typical of my abuser's behavior as well. All very big triggers!

I have come far, but obviously not far enough yet, for the indelible impressions of the abuse are still impacting me. But I'm getting there! Every day I get a little nearer to completion as I work all of this out in dreams and in waking life. Everything is slowly but surely merging into one world. All worlds are working with me, all the time, and I'm very happy about that!

It's seven in the evening now and I'm exhausted. I tried to mow the lawn, but the mower wouldn't start and it's leaking gas. I have no energy anyway, but I feel anger building up and I want to scream! The kids are at their dad's for the weekend, so I could scream my heart out if it came to that.

This morning, when Chuck and I discussed my dream of him as a bright conduit, he said: "Don't make too much of it." In other words, he was saying, "I am not your guru." Fine, I get that. I'm not looking for a guru, but my dreams are an important part of my recapitulation and so is he. I am learning not to make too much of him, part of taking back my transference, but I have to acknowledge that he plays a significant role in my life at this point, in both waking and dreaming life. The recapitulation, a constant and ever-present process, doesn't shut down just because we are not sitting across from each other; it's ongoing, in dreams and reality. So, as far as I'm concerned, the fact that it was he who reached down and plucked me out of the murky lake of despair has to be taken seriously.

I gain deeper understanding of my transference in this dream, and the real truth that I am my own guru is clear, but the other truth is that Chuck *is* a big part of this process. He shines a light in so many different ways; in offering new perspectives that I could never see on my own, in pointing out the deeper workings of my psyche, in explanations of how the inner journey works, in his vast knowledge and experience of the psychotherapeutic process and the world of the shamans. I never even knew of such a thing as recapitulation until I met him. Don't make too much of that? Well, believe me, I am really trying hard not to make too much of it. All I want to do is flip that damn board over and walk away, but something is telling me I am not going to do that, especially since I asked for a sign that I was not alone and I got the biggest damn sign I could ever want—as clear as a white neon sign blinking right in my face!

August 16, 2003

I dream that I'm on a train. Outside the window I see my daughter. She's about nine years old, happily skipping and running alongside the train, coming to meet me. When the train pulls into the station she's there waiting. She reaches down from the platform and swiftly pulls me up to stand beside her because for some reason the platform is much higher than the train.

Another dream where someone reaches down and helps me! This time it is my little dream child, who has taken this entire journey with me in the guise of my sweet daughter, a lithe little spirit girl. It's interesting that she too pulled me up to a higher plateau, just as Chuck did in the conduit dream. I had wished to jump to new and higher plateaus and here I have two beings in my life ready and eager to help me. And they are both parts of myself!

It's hard to believe, but I'm in a good mood! My little dream daughter has imbued me with some sweet energy. I notice that for once I don't feel heavy or depressed, just thoughtful and sensitive. I head over to the studio wondering if perhaps today will be a good day, as I'd like this good feeling to last!

The guy who is interested in me comes to visit at the studio. I find him somewhat interesting too, but also predictable and slightly boring, entrenched in his own issues, his energy heavy. He is sensitive, intelligent, creative, but not spiritual. I am missing something when in his company. It could be a friendship, but I know he is looking for something more. There is nothing more I can give.

Back home, I feel like I need to take a walk, but it's too dark and I don't feel safe. I want to call Chuck, but I don't know why. I just need the contact. For the past two days I've been able to stay at the studio all day, which I haven't done in a very long time, so that's good, and I've been turning and walking, pivoting away from negative energy whenever I feel the need, but I still feel that something's wrong with me. Something isn't right, though I'm not sure what it is. My good mood of the morning has deteriorated, replaced by the taste of fear on my tongue. I need to shift!

Instead of going out into the dark and scary night, I go into the living room and do calming walking meditation. After all the turning and pivoting I've been doing all day it feels more in alignment with what I need right now. I look down at my feet as I slowly plod along, hoping that the walking might heal me, be healing. To focus downward and on the movement of walking very slowly takes focus off everything else, so that nothing else matters, nothing. Life doesn't matter, just the walking and my feet touching the floor, slowly making headway, each calm step only, nothing else. But where will such walking take me?

August 17, 2003

I dream that I enter an empty gallery. The guy who is interested in me comes in behind me wearing flowing white robes. He grabs me and gives me a big hug. I am not into it.

My dreaming self presents this guy who likes me in the same manner in which the conduit appeared, in white flowing guru robes, but this guy is comical, clumsy and overbearing. He's not here to help or guide, only to take. There is no resonance, no good energetic tingling, nothing. I guess my dreaming self just wanted to underscore what I had already determined!

At some point in the future I will meet a successful, happy person to share a life with, a real partner. But first I need to keep working on myself; I need to be successful and unafraid myself. I need to be ready.

All those terrible things, all those horrible memories really did happen to me! I have tried to pretend that this story was about someone else, not me, so that I could distance myself from the pain of what happened. If it was about some other little girl then it was easier. It's been devastating to face, too much to handle at times, so I shut down. I cut off my feelings and keep my distance from the truth, picturing another girl in my mind's eye. Now I am ripping open, discovering that it has been about me all along and not some other little girl, and the truth of it hurts like hell. On the one hand I am so sick of this recapitulation. I want nothing more than to be done with it, but on the other hand I can say that I haven't truly dealt with all of it yet. I haven't *fully* realized it. I am just beginning to feel the painful truth of it.

August 18, 2003

I dream that I'm riding that dragon monster from an earlier dream. We fly above a large city, many tall buildings spread out below. I argue with myself about whether or not I can let go. I experience a tremendous sense of freedom as I think about letting go and falling, but I'm worried about hitting one of the buildings on my way down, surmising that if I don't fall right between the buildings I might get hurt as I go down. The space between the buildings is pitch black, but that doesn't bother me. It's really quite enlightening to realize that the fall itself will be just fine, liberating in fact. I shed old fears as I dream, fear of the blackness, fear of the nothingness. It all sheds so easily from that higher perspective. As I take the dragon flyover, I get a glimpse of what I will encounter next and discover that I've changed; I'm really not afraid of letting go anymore.

Every time another emotion goes through me, it feels as if I'm releasing something, shedding some heavy dark cloak, putting down an old burden that I've carried forever, as well as unveiling something new, opening to something previously unknown about myself. I feel more real afterwards too, more present, less weighted down by my past, lighter and freer, for the sense of freedom in the wake of the unburdening is exquisite.

At the same time, I still look for signs that none of this is true, a sign that I don't have to believe it, that I can *un-believe* it instead. But all the signs point to *believe it*. My body, my emotions, everything says, *believe it!*

August 19, 2003

Inside me there is a frantic animal incessantly scratching, trying to get out, to dig a hole to let the feelings out. No flying dragon dream, no easy fall, and though my intent remains strong this is playing out in reality rather than in the ease of dreaming now. I must wander on the ground, facing the darkness of my past in this reality. My body shakes and I find that I really am afraid to let go after all. But what am I really holding onto, and why?

I meet with Chuck and the first thing I do is finally admit that it, the sexual abuse, did happen. *It happened. It happened. It happened. It happened. It happened. It fucking happened!*

"I've been holding onto the old idea that I'm perfectly fine, that nothing ever bothers me, but I can't do that anymore. It's too painful, but it's equally painful to admit to all the feelings and emotions I have pent up inside me and to let them go."

"Control can be good," Chuck says, "but letting go and seeing what happens is better. You couldn't handle the emotions and feelings before, but now you're able to cope with them. It's a sign of just how far you've come."

Maybe this really will all become a distant memory one day and I won't recall it anymore; it won't be crawling across my skin, the taste of it on my tongue, the pain of it in my bones. I won't need to recall it, as Chuck tells me, because the memories won't have the same meaning and intensity they now hold. Everything will be revealed and thus nothing will remain to create this ever-present tension, this pain that I have lived with my entire life, the incessant thought that something is wrong with me. Indeed, let the releasing begin!

It happened. It happened. All those memories, all the pain; they all happened. It happened. Believe it. I try to wrap my mind around it, but it's all too big, too unbelievable, too devastating to take in and behold in all its fullness. *It happened. It happened. It happened. It happened. It happened!*

I keep busy all day and long into the evening after work; take a walk, get the mower started and mow the lawn, shower, eat something, all these things keeping me sane. It happened. Accept it. It happened. I drink a glass of wine and think about getting drunk in order to loosen things up, in order to cry. I need to cry, but it's too hard, too painful. When I was with Chuck today and finally spoke those fateful words, "it happened," I felt the same intense reluctance to speak as when I have to talk about the memories, a strange mixture of guilt, shame, embarrassment, pain, self-hatred, all underscored by doubts and what ifs. To say it to another being makes it real, makes it true beyond a doubt. When I spoke those two simple words, "it happened," an intense pain shot through me; my body, as usual, underscoring the truth. And then, the sober voice of my spirit inside me confirmed what my body has always known.

"It happened," it solemnly said, "have no doubt."

The wine makes me drowsy and relaxed, but underneath I feel ANGER and PAIN and SADNESS. It seethes and builds until I can no longer hold it back. I SCREAM and SCREAM and SCREAM! Then I am limp and helpless. The alcohol releases my body and yes, I can cry, but it does not release my mind. My mind still whirls like an old record, spinning, endlessly playing the same old tunes. I think about standing up and shifting the way Chuck taught me, turning away and shouting that I am powerful now, but I just can't. It's not time to turn and run. Instead I must face the truth. I must fully realize what it means when I say, "it happened." I must sit in the mucky truth of it. My body hasn't forgotten a thing, even things that happened forty-eight years ago, such far distant memories still so real. It *did* happen. It *did* happen. It *did* happen.

"Relax now; sleep and dream," Jeanne tells me. *"Go to sleep, just go to sleep and forget everything. Dream about falling into peacefulness, just softly floating down."*

August 20, 2003

I dream that I'm lying in a hospital bed, recuperating from a long illness. All my energy is directed toward healing. I hear people talking about me, unaware that I can hear them. I should remember how to speak Latin, they say. I know they are referring to the fact that I learned Latin in Catholic school as a child. It bothers me that they insist I remember something so distant. "Okay, I'll remember," I try to tell them, but I am too weak to even speak. Soon I am left alone to shower and dress, my recuperation period over. Then I set out to get my daughter. On the way, I stop to visit my aunt. She is thin, young and energetic, not her usual plump and aged self. She looks like me. I tell her she looks great and then set off again to meet my daughter. I see her standing on the side of the road, waiting. She is little, about seven or eight. We wave. "I'm coming, I'm coming," I call. Along the way there are lots of other little girls and I have to stop and listen to their stories. It takes a long time and when I finally get to my daughter she has changed. She's a teenager now, wearing clothes I've never seen, tall and leggy.

"Where have you been?" she asks. "I've been waiting."

"Yes, I know," I say, "I'm here now."

My dream seems to be telling me that I will get through this, that by remembering I will be fine, but all the finer details must be recapitulated first. I must remember everything if I am to heal, even though I often feel as if I am entering foreign territory, and even if I have no idea how to handle what arises I must keep going. It's like being asked to speak a foreign language that one has not spoken in years, the dream tells me, but once the process is begun, the language, the memories all come back. I have to agree.

At the same time, I have to admit that it's a long road to fuller healing and I must allow myself the time it takes to both remember and recuperate. Eventually, I will be totally healed, that I am sure of more each day, and until then I remain unavailable for little else but this process. I am aware that every step is necessary, that all the pieces of the puzzle will fit and in the end I will be fine. I realize that my aunt in the dream is not her at all, but the future me, fully alive and with new vital energy. My daughter represents the future inner self, all my little girls matured, their stories finally accepted and fully assimilated. She offers proof that the process of recapitulation brings drastic change and I am certainly looking forward to that!

I wake feeling battered though, as if still in my dream, still recuperating. In a sense it's true, for I am still healing from a lot of old traumas, things never dealt with before. Even though it all took place decades ago my body is only now feeling the pain of it, still wounded after all these years. Pressure to remember every tiny detail increases and the frustration that arose in the dream creeps into the reality of the day, anger and sadness close behind.

I call Chuck, struggling with how best to deal with this rise of emotions. He warns me not to exhaust myself any further but remain aware that I must deal with what arises, as it arises, in a conscious and thoughtful manner. Instead of running away from it, the best new plan of action is to turn and face whatever arises. I admit that things get complicated if I resist. He tells me that I must simplify everything down into what it truly is that I'm dealing with: *emotions*. Resistance gives the emotions a lot of power, he reminds me, and the challenge is to deal with them as simply as possible, seeing them for what they are, without bringing the whole damn thing crashing down upon myself. I must simultaneously fully experience the emotions and inculcate the process of releasing them, he tells me.

"If anger arises, I will go into the garage and beat on a big empty box I have there for that very purpose," I tell him. "If I have to cry, I will cry. It's okay to cry."

"Yes, let the emotions come out in the way they need to," Chuck says. "Don't be afraid; the emotions won't hurt you."

"Holding them in hurts," I say. "I must remember that. I intend to keep my focus forward now. I don't really need to look back anymore. I already know that it happened. So now I'll focus on dealing with the emotions. I look forward to becoming that new vivacious person I met in my dream."

I hang up the phone and go right out to the garage where I beat the heck out of the big box with a stick I keep handy for just that purpose. Time to unburden, simplify, and grow. Afterwards, I step out of the cool garage into the hot summer morning. Flinging my arms skyward I proclaim my freedom.

"Let the wind take my pain, let it carry it and scatter it far beyond the atmosphere. Let it take it into darkest space, suck it into eternal storage. Gone, gone, gone... no longer accessible, only a distant memory, only a long ago dream."

I am relaxed and quiet afterwards. Suddenly, everything seems possible. I sense the need to begin moving the memories out of the present and back into the past, but into a different past, a known past. I need to create a different memory bank where I can store them away, fully explored, fully recapitulated, fully disrobed of the tight cloak of power they have held over me, the power to hurt. I have had enough hurt, enough to last a lifetime. No more hurt. Sadness too can go. Anger too. I can lay aside all these terrible burdens, leave them on the side of the road, along this recapitulation path, and walk away, fully aware of them but no longer needing to carry them.

I make it over to the studio by noon, the dream still with a hold on my body, asking me to slow down, reminding me that it really is time to recuperate. With that intent, I grow increasingly calmer and find that it's easier to work than I'd imagined. Even though my energy is low there's a consistent flow. While I work I focus on two things: one, *it happened*, and two, *time to unburden*.

The truth is, I'm eager for this recapitulation to speed up. I miss being happy. I want to get through this and get back to real life. I know it's a one-step-at-a-time thing, that it's a process and I'll have to be patient as it unfolds at its own pace. And I'm still so bowled over by the memories too, still feel their newness, their rawness still crushing me, but at the same time I want to be done. Why can't I get through this faster? Why can't it be over right now!

"Don't be angry at yourself," Jeanne says. *"It's not your fault. The anger is part of it all, but you, yourself, don't deserve anger. It wasn't your fault."*

I stay at the studio until three, enjoying my time there. As I head home I am innerly calm and quiet. I realize that I'm making good progress, feeling much more present every day. I'm shedding rapidly now. That's the way I envision this process, as if I'm shedding an old self, like a snake shedding its skin. I am gradually transforming myself by shedding the past, preparing to grow a new self. As I shed, I find that I am the person I've had glimpses of all along, that talented, confident, capable woman. I'm going to be just fine. I will be that happy woman in my dream and the little girl in me will be contented too. We will both evolve; we will be fine.

"Remember, it's the past," Jeanne says. *"It happened. Let it go. Unburden. Let it go. It happened once upon a time, but you can let it go now. Don't struggle with it anymore, let it go."*

In the evening, I call my studio partner to talk about a job we'll be working on together. She's abrupt, rude, grumpy, loud on the phone. I am immediately thrown into doubt and even though I know she's dealing with some personal issues that have nothing to do with me, the old scared me tries to take over, tries to reassert her feelings of inadequacy; it must be my fault that she's angry.

I find it's easy enough to *say* that the abuse happened, to direct myself to get over it, to unburden myself, but it's another thing to fight a lifetime of old habits. Even though I don't need them anymore they hover nearby, powerful old feelings ready to sneak in and sabotage me at a moment's notice. Even though I am in the midst of optimism and growth, they easily swoop in, grab me, and fly me right back to the land of worthlessness and hopelessness. Doesn't my studio partner like me anymore? Have I offended her in some way? Our once compatible energy all of a sudden feels so combative, and I don't even know why! Perhaps it really has nothing to do with me, as a part of me feels, but there is another part of me that senses something else is up.

Then I remember my dream of last night and I know that, yes, I *will* get through this. I *will* be happy. I *will* grow to be a new person. I shed my worries about my studio partner for the present moment. We will just have to see what, if anything, transpires.

August 21, 2003

I dream that I'm inside a dark and dirty house. It's nighttime and I'm taking care of a child. I'm not sure whom the child belongs to. Our job is to clean the house, but we end up playing games instead. Every time someone comes into the house I get my hopes up because I'm waiting for someone. Whoever it is never shows up. I'm disappointed. Then I'm on a bus. I'm alone now, having left the child behind. The bus is traveling far out into the dry desert of New Mexico. It's still dark, but I can see the silhouettes of mesas etched on the horizon. At daylight, I get off the bus and go into a small adobe house. This house is bright and clean, though there is also rebuilding going on. As the day grows lighter, I'm given tasks, for I must help with the renovations. I'm waiting for someone to show up here as well. I just don't know who it is and, once again, the person never arrives.

Suddenly I find myself sitting straight up in bed, laughing with glee, my room lit with bright and vibrant energy. A giant tree of light hovers to my right, its roots dangling to the floor, crackling white energy pulsing through it and pulsing through me too. I'm not at all surprised to see Chuck encased in the trunk of the tree with a big smile on his face. Like a man on a cross his arms are spread wide, his hands flowing into long branches that fill the room, reaching out through the walls of my house and beyond. I am aware that Chuck is a man of knowledge, that he is imparting his knowledge to me, that I too am part of this tree of knowledge, that everyone is, for it is the tree of life.

The roots and branches of this tree of life extend far beyond ordinary vision and ordinary reality, into non-ordinary reality and into the vastness of infinity. I see that it's connected to everything and that everything is connected to it, that everything is alive with vibrant luminous energy. I understand that this tree also represents the work of this recapitulation, my own journey of self-knowledge. I understand that such a journey is not to be hurried or exploited, that it goes at its own pace. I am also aware that everything is possible, that all of us are capable of accessing this tree of knowledge, that we all have the potential to change from the inside out.

The delightful energy of the tree courses through me and I am still laughing as I come to full waking consciousness. As I watch the tree fade, I become aware that this is what I've been waiting for, not for another person, as my dream implied, but for myself, the awakened being I am striving so hard to become as I take my journey. Yes, Chuck is my expert teacher and guide and I must acknowledge his guidance throughout this journey, for he has been teaching me things I never was able to access before, but this is my journey to wholeness. My dream is showing me our relationship, that of teacher and apprentice, and yet I also know that we are neither of those but equals, as we all are. We just have to wake up to this truth, just as I did during this dream vision.

Suddenly, life is full of promise! I feel so alive!

The stages I've gone through and must still encounter in the coming phases of this recapitulation are described in the first part of my dream. I must still delve into the dark past, as the part of the dream with the child suggests, but eventually I will leave the child behind. When I enter light-filled New Mexico everything is different, but I still have work to do, for I must complete the final stages of this recapitulation. Finally, I awaken in the dream and become conscious, as a profound explosion of energy, coupled with the inner realization that this is what I am working toward, courses through me. The person who never showed up in my dream is a future me, a fulfilled being of insight and knowledge. I have been waiting for myself all along! If I am to be so lucky, she will be the final outcome of this long and arduous journey of recapitulation.

August 22, 2003

It's eleven-thirty at night. Dare I admit that this was one of the best days I've had in a long time? I worked in the studio all day and then spent a nice evening with my daughter. I even cried tonight, perhaps because I drank wine again, but it was with the intention of shifting things, of loosening and opening.

Fear comes when I'm exhausted, *because* I'm exhausted, as Chuck noted when we met this morning. If I can recognize it for what it is—an entity seeking my energy, he reminded me—and remember that it tends to "get me" when my energy is depleted, then perhaps I can work with it in a different way now. The obvious answer is to not get so exhausted! Also not only the fear but the sadness and anger must be replaced with positive feelings about myself now.

I do feel real changes in myself and I really am beginning to know myself on a much deeper level! I really do want to embody my fuller potential, that strength, intelligence, and confidence that I have refused to own, shirking them for so long as if they belonged to someone else. And I really do want to achieve oneness with that vast tree of knowledge from my dream of the other night, for I see that as the ultimate goal, to merge with the higher consciousness of which we are all a part. The work of this world is to detach from all that keeps us so stuck in the personal, to let go of the ego!

Time to sleep, a little drunk, a little sad, a little scared, but oh, so hopeful!

August 23, 2003

It's a quiet Saturday morning, bright and sunny; cool at last. I set my intent to consciously shift from depressing thoughts to positive ones throughout the day, to leave my fears under the bed, and envision only a good and happy life to come!

It's ten-thirty at night. I happily cruised along through the day until suddenly the urge to flee, to withdraw, came over me with a grand urgency like I haven't felt in a long time. All I wanted to do was take all I've learned about myself and retreat into a cave, become a hermit, a recluse. No other scenario played out in my mind; I just could not get my thoughts to wrap around any other idea. All I wanted to do was what I have always dreamed of; living alone in a woodsy cabin, doing my freelance writing and drawing, isolating myself so as not to have to see or be around other people, totally disappearing into my own world, my only companions a couple of big sweet dogs. In spite of everything I know and have learned about myself, even with all the inner work I've done, I still have festering inside me that old urge to retreat, to completely withdraw from life and all interactions. It's partly a deep desire to write and create undisturbed, though the real culprit lurking behind it is an old fear that takes over, telling me I'm so much better off alone.

That fear is deeply rooted in my past, in the old needs of my damaged child self. Fear attaches to her and she calls out to me, letting me know that she's afraid, afraid of this new life I'm carving out for us. Part of me wants to simply dismiss the fear—aware of its tricky ways—but at the same time I can't just dismiss my child self because I too sense that fear, in the adult me. I have a sense that it might always be there, challenging me not to run and hide but to accept it as the signal to push through and finally move beyond fear. I know that new life waits on the other side of fear, but at the same time I must pause and wonder. Is it better to be alone? Am I better off with less interaction? Am I just exhausted, or have I really had enough? Am I done with the world? No, not by a long shot! But I see how the trickery works, how fear gets to me through the vulnerable child self. Rather than signaling retreat it signals a time to retaliate against isolation as a defense, an avoidance of life, for how could I possibly retreat when I have yet to fully realize who I am or even utilize the skills that are finally being awoken? I must note, however, the old pattern. How I find myself on the familiar verge, and all I want to do is flee. How typical!

Am I headed for success? Is it that which has me running again, as it did in the past? Even now, just the thought and I only want to run and hide, but I can't let that happen. My children are counting on me. As their mother I need to not only care for them and guide them, but show them by example that it's okay to be successful—that it's a natural consequence of honest hard work and dedication—just as I must show my inner child.

Would success really be so different from where I am now? What would change? Would I? I don't think so, except that I'd have to be out in the world. Now that would be challenging! And that is my biggest fear. Just thinking about it and I'm ready to agree with my child self. Yes, let's close the door on everything and be safe in our own space! The feeling is physical as well as emotional. It's the old feeling of my traumatized body needing to curl up and hide, to be protected and safe. This very strong desire to withdraw from life is proving to be my biggest battle at this point, but I refuse to capitulate. I will only recapitulate! And then move on!

August 24, 2003

While I slept and dreamed I lay on my back, aware that it was important to do so. My torso got cut open and lots of stuff was pulled out of me, gnarly old things that are no longer useful or necessary. That was the only way to get them out of me, I was told. I surrendered completely and participated in full awareness. I was not allowed to curl up in a ball and hold things in as I usually do, but I didn't want to either.

The weather is beautiful today. My daughter and I take a long hike in the morning. She has friends over in the afternoon and they spend the entire day outside. I feel a surge of energy after the hike, but remain calm and quiet rather than exhaust myself as I might have done in the past. I stay inside and bake brownies, read, cook dinner, not much else, a quiet afternoon, but then I have a sudden panic attack during dinner. It just creeps in when I'm not paying attention and suddenly I'm fearful of everything again.

I talk myself through it, even though all I want to do is run away. The real issue is that there is a part of me that's still a reluctant child, like a fledgling that doesn't want to leave the comforts of the nest and go out into the world on its own, but that child will no longer rule in this house!

August 25, 2003

After a string of some really good days I suddenly have no energy. I am heavy with depression. It's a struggle to just get out of bed, eat, shower, and move on to doing what needs to be done, my fledgling self protesting loudly. I dreamed frustrating dreams all night, unable to get lazy people to clean up their messes. Am I one of them?

I've been trying to figure out all day if it's really possible to survive in this world without having to deal with other people. How can I become a recluse and still support my kids? How can I retreat as far as possible and still be present when needed? My child self and I are in cahoots on this again. She has me almost convinced that it's the only thing to do. I'm trying to figure out if she's right and how we could possibly manage it.

Anger and frustration ride in with the night, kicking up the dusty past and the strong desire to run away from everything barrels in with it, stronger than ever. Suddenly, I am in the whirlwind again, blind to everything except the old fear, an old place for sure. The closer I get to stuff that's uncomfortable the harder I want to RUN! It's what I've always done. I've even run from good things, suddenly quitting and moving someplace new. The pressure is on, but I won't run this time! This time I intend to stay and face whatever's coming, because I do feel that something is coming. I don't know what it is, but I sense it approaching and it scares the hell out of me. And, yes, I'd much rather get out of here! But I acknowledge that I'm different now. I've already begun to depart from the old scared self. I've seen what the new self can do. I've had a glimpse of who I might be in the not too distant future. It's time to fight for that new me, to fight through to the end this time, though first I must deal with the child self who insists on withdrawing.

"You want to withdraw too," she tells me. "You use me as an excuse, but you really want to be like a character in a book, real on the pages of the book, but not really real."

"If you're not real," she says, "then you don't have to deal with all these torments, these strong urges to be one way or the other. But if you're not real then you can't have a future either, so you'd better decide what you really want."

She's so right! I have to stop blaming her. It's time for me to take over. I cry for her and for myself, for where we've been and what we must face as we change, as I dare to put her to rest and move on in spite of our fears.

"I must do it," I tell her, "for both of us."

And then I try to sleep, but all I can do is toss and turn. There will be no peacemaking tonight.

August 26, 2003

I dream. I'm living in New York City, in a college dorm. I intend to meet a friend who lives in the building, but I go outside instead and get lost in the dark and foggy night. I can't even find my way back to the building. A campus security guard shows me a map. My inner compass reset, I set off running. Before long I'm flying, paddling with my arms as if I'm a human canoe shooting through rapids. I cut through narrow openings, fly between tree trunks and around every obstacle in my path. I'm aware that I've been over this route many times before, but now I have a sense of purpose and I know that I will get there. I'm flying so fast, nothing can stop me. I'm aware that any obstacle merely needs to be shot past. People cheer me on. It's a joyous ride!

In spite of the thrilling night flight of my dream I awaken lost in the fog again. I push myself out of bed and head up to meet with Chuck, laden once again with my usual sadness. Can't I let myself show up happy for once? Do I always have to be so sad? Am I depressed because I think he expects it? Am I sabotaging my own process? I'm sure Chuck will have some unique perspective to blow the fog away once and for all. At least I hope so!

"You shot like a torpedo and nothing else mattered," says Chuck when I tell him my dream.

"So, why am I still so afraid?"

"I think you're wallowing in self-pity," he says, bluntly.

I'm angry when he suggests it, not what I expect or want to hear. I want to protest, but I just look at him, my thoughts racing. I want to prove him wrong.

"I am not full of self-pity! Not me!" I shout. "I'm so humble and self-effacing. It's not like I whine all the time. I never ask, why me? I never say, oh, poor me!"

I don't agree with him. All I feel is anger. But deep down inside me I do sense a shadow of something else, something else in control of this whole process, something pushing me down, deep into the old places of fear and hopelessness. Is Chuck right, is it self-pity that has me stuck? Is that what lies at my core? Self-pity? How abhorrent!

During the flying dream I had the thought that if I put my attention on what was actually happening, it would hurt. If I thought about the physical impossibility of hurtling unprotected through thickets, hedges, and trees then I would be ripped to shreds. In other words: *If I thought of reality, then the dream would end, but if I let the dream be reality then anything was possible.*

Since I chose not to think about my physical body and essentially ignored the facts of waking reality, then I suffered no pain or damage. Nothing touched me. I created my own reality by the way I chose to think! If I can do that in my dreams, I can create my own reality in this life too, by how I *decide* to think. That's the answer I've been looking for! Yes, I must create a new reality for myself in my life. I must get beyond the old pain and fear and just go for it! I must fly onward now, just like I did in my dream, outside the constraints of known reality. I must get out of the fog and think differently now!

August 27, 2003

I wake up knowing that some issues were resolved while I slept. There was building going on in my dreams, a five-gallon bucket of nails, carpenters taping and plastering walls. Repairs of derelict spaces were underway; there were new beginnings, first steps being taken, new decisions made, and new ideas were taking shape. *Just relax and let it happen*, I was told.

Running away is not the answer; letting things flow and getting to a place of release is. In accordance with all that I'm reestablishing my personal yoga and meditation practice, a new caring-for-myself routine. Hints of liberation swirl through me, the fresh smell of freedom, though a slight sadness still lingers beneath these new good feelings. Can I let it go? I'm aware of being a little afraid to feel good. Is that why the sadness lingers? Is it trying to convince me I still need it? I know I don't. In fact, it's actually inhibiting my evolution; it has slowed me down. I admit that allowing myself to feel good has always been scary, but I think it's going to be okay now. It's the next challenge. One step at a time!

I get a call to do another writing job. Great! I'm excited. I let myself feel happy and yet the old feelings are right there, ready to take me back, ready to smother me. Go away old feelings! Go away! I don't need you anymore! With a quick sweep of my arm I whack them out into the universe, envision them sailing off, being absorbed by entities, hungry little critters just waiting for tasty morsels of food. And then a sudden realization strikes along with the sound of a bell clanging loudly, saying: Self-pity! Self-pity! Self-pity! It strikes again and again and I know Chuck is right, I am *full* of self-pity! It comes disguised in so many different costumes, even I get tricked. It sneaks up as sadness, fear, doubt, and such, taking me back into old places where all I want to do is curl up and lick my wounds. What's good about that? Nothing! All it does is keep me cycling through all the old shit again and again.

A part of me refuses to feel sorry for myself, but that is exactly what happens if I give in to the sadness and depression. They take over and deliver the message of self-pity, telling me that I'm suffering, saying, "Oh, poor you! How depressed you are! Poor thing!" And then I give myself permission to wallow, repeating what they say, disguising it as inner work, as part of this recapitulation process, but really I'm holding onto an old method of coping, that of withdrawal and avoidance. It's a defensive choice rather than an offensive action. The truth is, as Chuck so aggravatingly pointed out, I really am just wallowing in self-pity! It's time to shift, though I'm aware that I had to go there, and that I had to be reprimanded by Chuck too. I had to finally realize that I was indeed stuck in self-pity and just how sticky a place it is.

As I acknowledge the presence of self-pity, I completely let it go. I understand its use, but I don't need it anymore. I feel much lighter as I release it, grateful and thankful for the way this process is unfolding. Waves of kindness and tenderness ripple through me too, for my own vulnerabilities and those of others, for the whole world in fact, as I sense that we are all on the same journey, trying to find out why we're here and where we're going, trying to get ourselves unstuck once and for all. I feel Butterfly Girl right beside me, the transformational being that I envision accompanying me on this journey from traumatized, frightened child to full-fledged mature adult. The metamorphosis is in full swing. Her wings are forming now and I am changing rapidly.

August 28, 2003

Something in a dream makes me cry out and I wake up suddenly. The weight of the kitten sleeping on my shoulder sends a wave of pain along my skin, sensitive to even the lightest and softest touch. She whimpers as I gently move her limp form aside and get up, ready for the day to begin. I will not wallow in bed today.

I take a walk, trying to slow down from a near run to a quieter pace. I don't want to be a raging river. I just want to be a quiet stream, meandering gently, trickling and flowing along, a solitary rivulet, not interfering, not taking too much or leaving too much, just calmly making my own way.

The slower pace echoes a quieter inner tone. I realize that the biggest changes lately have been happening on the inside and that I'm pretty close to becoming a full-fledged feeling being, as I've been experiencing feelings like never before. I don't push them away now; I let myself have them. I can experience dark anger in the morning and be utterly happy in the afternoon, and both are acceptable. No more numbness, no more shutting down. Instead, I'm reacting and talking and expressing and *feeling*.

The calming walk sets a good pace for the rest of the day. I spend an intensely productive stint at the studio, full of creative energy, painting all day, filling several canvases as I let feelings pour out of me through my arm and hand and onto the canvases, barely aware of what I'm doing. Nothing is rushed, but my creative juices flow steadily. Emotions arise as well, and I let them come tumbling, crumbling, and crashing out, mixing tears with paint. Happiness, sadness, and anger are followed by more tears and more paint, one abstract painting leading to another as the perfectionist in me relinquishes hold and lets things flow without thought or planning. I paint directly from an unknown part of myself, not the old controlling part but a newly accessed part, a part I never knew existed, my unconscious self finally showing me who she really is and how she operates.

Suddenly, an old thought sweeps through me: *Don't get too happy; it's dangerous.* Then I remember the flying dream and the moment I realized I was actually flying: *If I think about this, if I care, then it could really hurt.* And then I realize, that's what I have to do all the time, *not think*, because if I think too much then I get caught and it really does hurt. But if I just let it all go through me without a care, without attaching, I'll be okay.

And then everything is suddenly different. I feel different and I know I'm not only painting from a new place, I'm actually creating a new reality!

August 29, 2003

I arrive at Chuck's office in my new calmness, stable and present though still feeling a little of the old sadness.

"It may be the last of it," I say, feeling hopeful. "I'm finally getting through it, mostly by painting it out of me. I'm creating the same abstract paintings I dreamed of a few weeks ago, in the dream of you as the conduit. It's not conscious, as they are coming on their own, but I recognize them all. They are the future work I saw in the gallery. Everything that's coming out of me I dreamed about. It's been quite a week."

"Keep painting," Chuck says. "Stock up on canvases!"

I work at the studio all day again, painting, only taking a break in the middle of the day for some fresh air and lunch. Filled with the energy of my new calmness, I watch as canvases fill with what comes pouring out of me, with what flows out my hand through the brush and onto the canvas with nary a thought interfering. The only thing that interferes is the sadness, which I quickly release, painting it away, never to return. I notice, as I face the sadness directly, how quickly I return to stability and calmness. And no signs of self-pity arise.

August 30, 2003

My dreams last night dealt with the clenching pain that is my constant nighttime companion. As opposed to my calmer days I spent the entire night wandering through old derelict buildings in dreamscape after dreamscape, looking for release, in a yoga class, a meditation class, in a bathroom where I could pee.

"Calmness is important," I remind myself upon waking. With that thought in mind, I do yoga and meditate for real, then take a long walk, all the while focusing on releasing the pain that came in the night. It's cloudy and muggy and a few sprinkles fall while I walk, but I have some energy, though I still sense that underlying sadness. As much releasing as I've been doing, it's a wonder there's any left! I flick it off as I walk, leaving it behind to seep into the ground along with the raindrops.

In the evening, I work at the artist's gallery. The gray cloudiness of the day clears to a sunny coolness, a nice night for a stroll. The gallery is unusually busy and I am animated and relaxed for the first time in a long time. Tomorrow is the last day of the show. Then I can take it down at five, patch the walls, and be done! No more shows. No more giving away my energy. It's time to pull it in and finish this recapitulation journey.

August 31, 2003

I dream that my answering machine is broken, only partial messages are being recorded. I try to fix it. I put the answering machine on a shelf in a closet while I look for a wire. My three cats follow me into the closet. At first they get in my way, annoying me. Eventually they crawl up onto a tiny shelf in the top of the closet and lie there all tucked up together. I try to hook a new wire up to the machine but in so doing bump against the back wall of the closet, which just falls away like a soft foam panel. Beyond it is a room that I never knew existed. When my kids see this room they are so excited; they can't believe we never knew about it! We explore it, talking about what we'll do with it, but it just doesn't feel like the right time. I sense we aren't ready for it yet and suggest coming back another time. We leave, carefully putting the panel back in place, though now that it's been revealed I know I will never forget about this secret room. I'm equally aware that it's been there all along, just waiting to be discovered.

Am I putting my feelings aside, shelving them like the cats in my dream? Have I forced them aside because they're annoying? Am I really dealing with my deepest feelings as I release and paint them away, or am I just finding a new way to push them aside, not dealing with them at all but keeping them hidden? Is this what I'm doing as I've decided to cut back my twice weekly meetings with Chuck to only one? Is the answering machine in the dream telling me I'm making a mistake, cutting off the communication that has been going so well? Am I setting up a scenario where I'll be stuck in an old place, unable to clearly communicate, even with myself, unable to access that surprising new room? Am I afraid of what that new room might mean, perhaps representing the end, the fulfillment of this spiritual journey? What could be so frightening about that?

When I told Chuck the other day that I only wanted to meet once a week now, he said very little. I'm not sure he thinks it's a good idea, though I also know he'd never say anything. "You're in charge," he simply said. Am I just looking for a break when I should actually be pushing forward? Am I opting out? Is the fearful child still in control? Yikes!

It's nighttime now. The show is down. Hardly anyone came to get their work and buyers didn't pick up what they bought either, but the walls are patched and clean now. I enjoyed the last few hours alone there, in the quiet of taking the work down, patching and painting the walls. It was a very soothing, meditative ending to a very successful show. Of the two artists who did come to pick up their work and chat with me, one man said: "I am beginning to understand you, very quiet but very effective." And a woman responded by saying: "She gets the job done!" It made for a nice ending.

Tomorrow I will buy more canvases. I feel that I really am being guided to paint in the abstract, in the direction that my unconscious has been taking me. I've run out of canvases and ended up painting over previous paintings, the need to paint not willing to wait even a few minutes. I've used some of the canvases at least five times, layers of my unconscious spilled onto them, coats and coats of who knows what—I don't even remember.

It seems that ever since the expanding tree dream, when Chuck appeared in my room embedded in that massive tree of light, I've stepped into another world, beyond the personal into the transpersonal, into a world of expanded awareness and greater consciousness. That's what this painting frenzy is all about, as I am painting my experiences of the transpersonal universe, that which exists beyond physicality, beyond the known world. I notice that a bit of fearfulness invades my pleasure at actually doing the paintings. It's hard to look at what my unconscious produces, almost painful. I have been painting over what I have not been able to fully take in. I think my dream the other night was pointing out this transpersonal realm in that extra room I discovered in my house, so close and yet so hidden, though the wall between was soft and pliable, easy to pass through. Such a surprising find, and yet it feels too soon to fully inhabit it, too soon to take it in too, though the thrill of finding it still courses through me. Obviously my unconscious has other ideas, as it's pushing right ahead, taking me there every day now, into that mysterious realm of light and knowledge. "Paint it," it says, "paint like crazy!" And I do. Fearful or not, that's just what I'm doing.

The truth is, the transpersonal realm is such a familiar place, though I find myself going there in a new way now, freely, by choice, rather than in the dissociative manner of the past. It's all making so much more sense to me now. What's "out there" isn't as frightening as it once was because really it's all been "in here," inside me the whole time. I've become much more comfortable with the idea of infinity, the cosmos, the endless nothingness of it all, with death. It's no longer as frightening or unfathomable as it once was, in spite of my decision to close the door on that magical room in my dream and to paint over what comes out of me.

I'm not so attached to myself as a physical being anymore either, for I have become increasingly aware that I am a spiritual being. There really is so much more to life than meets the eye!

Chapter 3

Forging the Energy Body

September 1, 2003

My daughter called around eleven last night. She's at my parent's house, staying with her girl cousins who are visiting for the Labor Day weekend. She told me my mother fell down and had a fever of a hundred and two and that my brother was taking her to the hospital. I told her not to be scared, that everything would be okay and I'd see her in the morning.

I just called to find out how things are going. My dad answered the phone. He was the only one up, he said. My mother was home and everyone else was sleeping. I told him I'd be down later. The situation is sad. My parents are sad. I feel sad.

My mother has a kidney infection. I spend a good part of the day sharing the duties of her care with my sister, one of my brothers, and my sister-in-law. My parents are two pale gray ghosts. I peak in at them sleeping side by side, lying on their backs, not touching, mouths open, arms crossed on their chests like two dead people, already far gone. Then they come back to life, sit up, and speak. I sense it's almost time for them to leave this world. "It's okay," I say to them under my breath, "you can go."

Each generation has the opportunity to evolve the world a little bit more, and we do, to a certain extent, simply because we learn from the preceding generation how not to do certain things, but that's a ploddingly slow evolution. There must be some better way to speed up our progress toward a more inclusive, kind and compassionate world. Enough brilliant people have tried to get us nearer to a higher and more equal standard of existence—Gandhi, Eleanor Roosevelt, Martin Luther King, Nelson Mandela, to name a few in my own lifetime—yet for the most part we lag far behind the proposals of those great and daring beings. Perhaps our hearts are in the right place, but how do we enact the changes that are so needed? C. G. Jung said that we will never change the world if we don't change ourselves first. And yet who has taken the time to study themselves on a deeper level, such as in recapitulation? Very few, is my guess, and my family is no exception. The silent bearing of life's trials and tribulations has produced, in my parents at least, a pair of stoic beings whose expressions are so devoid of feeling and emotion as to appear to be mere shadows of human beings.

As a caring human being myself I sense it's time to make some changes in the way things are done. If everyone were to investigate themselves on a deeper level, learn to love themselves, as I am doing as I take this recapitulation journey, wouldn't the whole world be a better place, sooner rather than later? We are taught, however, to not be so concerned with the self. Obviously, intentional self-investigation and analysis are far different from narcissism. What I'm talking about here is an ego-breaking, ego-shedding process in which the outcome is a total revelation, a synthesis of self, an awareness of self as part of the greater whole, the oneness of everything. The ego has no place there, only love does, that much I've learned already.

I have always felt that my children came into this world to become who they are meant to be. I am a conduit, the chosen means by which they accessed life in this world, but they are separate and unique beings, brilliant and talented in their own ways, seeking their own fulfillment. My job is to prepare them for life in this world, to get them ready to launch into lives of their own. I do not own them, nor do they owe me anything. We are separate beings on our separate journeys, though we may travel together for a long and meaningful time.

I wish for my children to be curious and unafraid, free thinkers, perhaps open to what I've begun to comprehend as I've deepened my journey of recapitulation, if they so choose and are ready to do so. I admit they may not be, but they are the next generation and possibly far more ready for a new and changing world than my own generation ever was, though we came to adulthood in the midst of one of the most energetically charged eras of all time, the 1960s. There is no denying that those of us who lived through that time as young people were all affected in some way, and continue to be. Even if we've buried it, that wave of energy is still reverberating inside us somewhere, begging for life. The thing to realize is that it was not just youthful energy, or energy of a particular time, but energy that the world needed and still needs. It is and always was the energy of love. Such energy is not to be laughed at or dismissed as youthful naïveté, for at the core it was and is the energy of transformation and, far more poignant, the energy of nature calling us to discover the loving beings that we truly are. Such powerful energy cannot be held back indefinitely. It begs expression and it will reemerge, just as nature reemerges each spring from the dead of winter.

I seek to launch my two children into adulthood as solid citizens of the world. Hopefully they will always be as curious and alive, as thoughtful and respectful of all of life as they are now. My happiness for them will be to see them grow beyond what I, their mother, could offer them. I gave them the ride into this life, and I am still in a position to teach them and have some kind of impact, small though it may be. I hope that I am filling them with enough so that as they step out into the world and begin their separate lives they will have what it takes to go far, in alignment with what is right for them, in keeping with the loving compassionate energy of that wave of 1960s energy that I carry inside myself and surely have passed on to them.

I try not to worry about them, though as a parent that is often very difficult, but I also try to remember that just as I feel certain that I came into this life fully equipped with everything I needed, so have they. I try to keep in mind that one day their individual journeys into the greater world and the fulfillment of their own potential will begin on a larger scale, transforming them more fully into who they are meant to be in this lifetime, and that my job will be largely done then. I try to remember my own critical moments of individuation, how the last thing I wanted was my parent's thrusting themselves into my life, even when I was suffering. I trust that my children's journeys will be fulfilling, no matter what they must deal with, taking them where they need to go, just as my own individual journey has taken me where I have needed to go. We all must struggle and face what we must, yet we are all here for some definite reason, that I am sure of. It's up to each of us to figure out what that might personally be.

Even as I must one day let my children go, I see now that I must let my parents go as well. When I gently ask them if they have made plans for their future, if they think about what comes next as they grow older, they just stare at me, as if I am speaking a foreign language. They say nothing and in their silence I know they are asking me to butt out, letting me know that they have chosen how they are going to finish out their lives, much as they have lived. I drop the subject. It is not for me to judge.

I head home at the end of the day, my energy spent. My daughter stays another night with the cousins. I will return in the morning.

September 2, 2003

I meet a man in a dream. He shows me photos of an ancient statue that has my face on it, but he can't help me with what concerns me at the moment, getting directions to my college class. I wander around and end up in the right place anyway. I put my assignment down on a table, ready to be critiqued. It's a model of a tiny white house, nice and neat, sitting right smack in the middle of a large square sheet of white paper. It's perfect in every way, as far as I can see. "See, everything is fine," I tell myself as I look at it, but underneath my confident exterior I'm aware that it's only a model, not yet actualized, though it's the best I can do at the moment.

I wake up feeling queasy, in a grumpy mood. My dream, however, suggests that I not let my old physical self get in the way of my progress. I must stay focused on the newly constructed model of my dream home in the center of the white square, the unadorned mandala of the new self I'm creating. I notice that the white house in this dream is the same white house that I worked on in the conduit dream.

The man pointing out my face on the ancient statue in my dream, though he is not able to offer me direction in this world, nonetheless reminds me to consider my ancient self. This is especially helpful as I must go take care of my mother again today, this time without the support of my siblings, who will all be heading off to their own homes. I must not let the energy of my aged parents interfere with my spiritual progress, difficult though that may be!

I meet with Chuck before I leave. We do a grounding movement, a magical pass called *forging the energy body*, going over it again and again, preparing me for what the day might have in store.

"It's important that the physical be reintegrated with what is really going on in the psyche, with the changing self," Chuck tells me.

Even doing the movements for just a few minutes makes me feel remarkably better. When the session is over I arrange to meet with him on Friday and then no more Fridays, as I had previously decided. I still don't think he agrees that it's a good idea, but it's my decision.

I drive into the old neighborhood and immediately hunch over the steering wheel, a wave of sadness and memories sweeping through me. I see the barn where my abuser used to take me, now tumbling down in decay. If you know where to look, if you know it's there, you can catch a glimpse of it from the road. I am assaulted by a heavy pain in my soul as I pass by, still bruised I realize. The old me tries to imagine that it didn't happen, tries to sneak in denial, but the new me knows the truth and recognizes the feelings that sit at the heart of me still, terrible, heavy, dark, and sad—all too real.

The new me states her position, remembers all the work she's done, and immediately the pain lessens, a reconciliation of sorts reached between my two selves, the old me acquiescing to all the work I've done. As I turn off the main road I remind myself that I must not get caught in the fog of my parent's lives or that of the old neighborhood or go to the memories while I'm here. For though I have learned to navigate the fog of the past, I am here on another mission today. I must stay focused on that mandala of my dream, the pure clarity of my new home within myself, the new me. That new me is strong and tender at the same time, fully intent upon giving but not being taken advantage of, available to serve but remaining whole within herself. That is the intent I set as I drive up to my parent's cottage.

My mother is better today, still weak but more alert, eating and drinking. While I spoon feed her some hot broth she makes the comment that if she had known we would all pitch in and help her so much she would have "done this a long time ago," whatever that means. Is she implying she'd allow herself to get sick and be taken care of by her children? She just wants to be taken care of? Wow! That blows me away!

"I didn't know you were such a good, caring person," she says to me, which pisses me off.

"There's a lot you don't know about me," I hazard, looking her straight in the eyes, which are big round scared little girl eyes, but then I see the curtain fall. Her eyes grow blank, closing off quickly, and I know she can't go there.

"Don't push it; walk away," I tell myself.

I clean, do laundry, make sure there is food in the house. Later, my mother gets up and heats some soup for herself. She eats three meals. My dad sits in his corner of the sofa, not doing much of anything.

Aware of my posture and physical tension throughout the day, I constantly send messages to my body to relax and release, to let go, to simply be present without attachment. Even so, I notice how tight I am, always tense and on alert. "Work on release of the trauma from the physical body," Chuck had said this morning. Doing it here, where it all began, and amidst the stifling energy of my parents, surely offers a good challenge. I forge my energy body over and over again, as Chuck taught me this morning, sometimes in real physical movements, sometimes imagining the movements, but always striving to integrate myself as best I can.

Late in the day, more than ready to leave, the many challenges faced, my daughterly duties done with a steady measure of grace and kindness, I gather my daughter and we head home, leaving the past behind, for this moment at least.

It's the first night of the new school year. My daughter, exhausted after her weekend with the girl cousins and the drama at my parent's house, goes right to sleep. My son resists, as usual. Threats to remove his computer keyboard are to no avail, but I am not in the mood for disagreement. At eleven o'clock I take the keyboard away and stand over him like a tyrant, waiting until he gets into bed so I too can go to bed and sleep undisturbed.

September 3, 2003

I consciously turned onto my back during the night to escape the old feelings of fear and inadequacy, my body begging to curl into the fetal position, instinctively wanting to hunch against unseen threats. My body tells me it's afraid today, that fear has spread into my entire being.

"Be strong, relax," I tell myself, "let it all go."

I practice the magical pass I learned yesterday, forging my energy body, putting new energetic limbs on, accepting them as best I can. It's as if I've been disassembled, all my parts spread out on a table, and I'm slowly trying to figure out how to put myself back together again. The parts seem to have changed while they lay apart. They don't fit together anymore, and I have to find a new way to assemble them into the new person that I have become. I am not the old me anymore but someone who is aware, alert, and really living life. I no longer have a shell to surround myself with. I don't have numbness to protect me anymore and I don't have dissociation to escape to either. Instead, I have new knowledge, new techniques, new mantras, new voices, new postures, new movements and, yes, new energy. I am also more consciously aware of my place in the world and the space I inhabit, more aware of my own presence too, that I matter and how I choose to live my life matters too.

I meet with a prospective new client for lunch at her restaurant. I find it very hard to relax. I hadn't really thought about having to actually eat. I discover that I can either eat or talk, but I don't feel at ease enough to do both. In fact, I am so tense I can't eat at all. Instead, I focus on trying to stay present, explaining what I do and what she could expect from me; writing press releases and website copy, editing her books and the articles she writes for a myriad of publications she contributes to. I give her samples of my published writings and she gives me my lunch to take home in a box, which I feel somewhat chagrined about, but she insists, telling me how best to reheat it.

From there I go to the studio for a meeting with my studio partner and a reporter from a local newspaper. We had tried in vain to dissuade him from coming but he'd insisted. He's written about us plenty of other times and has grown to like us and our work, but I am of another mind. I don't like deception. The truth is we rarely work together anymore and it feels wrong to make it sound like we are something that we aren't. We spend most of the afternoon with him discussing our decorative painting business. I am mostly concerned with being as honest as possible, careful not to present ourselves as anything other than what we are, a small operation, always optimistic.

As he's leaving he informs us that we will be featured on the front page of the Sunday business section. My original feelings about the whole thing resurface and I feel bad. It just doesn't seem right for us to take up the space when we are in fact in the midst of dismantling our partnership. It still bothers me as I head home, physically spent. It feels like I ran a long road race today, having been so tense and nervous, having to smile and be "on" all day, finding it so much more exhausting and draining than expected. It makes me wonder if indeed any of it was right to be involved in.

Breathing deeply and calmly, I slowly do the magical pass, forging my energy body until I almost feel like myself again. I have to admit that overall my days are better now. I have more distance from the memories now, go for longer periods without flashbacks, enjoy longer and longer periods of relief. I never imagined I would get to this point.

September 4, 2003

In spite of yesterday's discovery that I've come pretty far I spend most of the day trying to stave off fullblown panic. Doing the magical pass that Chuck taught me I forge my energy body over and over again, breathing deeply and calmly, trying to stay present. It's not memories that plague me now, it's feelings! My old barriers have been removed and I'm totally exposed, like a turtle without its shell, feeling things intensely for the first time in my life. My new energy body may be strong and solid, but the rest of me is exceedingly soft and tender! I'm not sure what to do except keep breathing, keep forging. I'm not in my old place anymore and I'm not quite in my new place either. I'm in fucking limbo!

September 5, 2003

"From now on, when you go down to your parent's house, when you drive that road, do it differently, change something," Chuck instructs me. "Play some music, shout, scream, zigzag, spill something, breathe, cleanse. Take something back!"

"That place has tremendous power," he tells me, "and you need to dismantle that power. It can't control you anymore. You need to control it. In order to do that you have to be aware of the habitual tendencies that overtake you when you go there."

"You must learn to change the physical in order to change the habits," Chuck says.

I spend the day at the studio. My energy flows well, but I do have two cups of coffee during the day to perk me up. I work on two new paintings, prime some furniture, and plan some future work. The restaurant owner calls to let me know I got the job. I'm happy about it!

I plan on spending a relaxing evening with the kids. I'm glad tomorrow is Saturday. We can sleep late, take it slow and easy, free from the usual morning rush.

September 6, 2003

Ten in the morning, the kids still asleep. The cats wake me, the three of them lined up on the foot of the bed, staring at me, hungry. Feed me! The neighbor's dogs are barking.

I'm at a critical place once again, the point where in the past I've panicked and run, where I couldn't deal with the energy swirling toward me, the tornado of life that I felt I was not able or ready to cope with, positive though it was. As in the old days, all I want to do is run and hide. I want to disappear, be non-existent, frightened of the spotlight focusing on me, aware that something is expected and all I want to do is disappear!

On top of those old feelings, I got the school tax bill in the mail and it's twice the amount I thought it would be! I haven't saved enough! Another burden. And I have to not panic! I have to remember to stay in the present, to not let worry rule! Luckily it's not due for another month. Perhaps all I have to do is psyche myself up, rev myself into a state of positive self-confidence and stay there, assured that everything will work out just fine, as Jeanne always tells me!

Eleven at night. The house is quiet. I have time to think. Okay, no freaking out! Just stay calm, calm, calm. The large tax bill is really only a money question, perhaps indicating that it's time to make a change, give up the worrisome business of freelancing with its inconsistent income. Maybe it's time to reach out for the steadiness and security of a fulltime job. The truth is, I've been through this scenario so many times before and always rejected it. Why would I do it this time? Perhaps I'm being hasty, as actually things are going pretty well now. Should I stick with where I am, in spite of the big tax bill? Getting a job wouldn't really tackle that immediate question anyway. What should I do? Dream about it, of course!

September 7, 2003

I dream that I am sledding down an icy mountain slope, trying to avoid hitting any trees. It's a bumpy, painful ride, but I'm able to make it to the bottom of the slope safely and in one piece. Suddenly it's summer. I'm standing in a golden field at the bottom of the mountain that a second ago had been the icy snow-covered slope. I see Chuck and his wife, Jeanne, sitting at a picnic table nearby, talking and sharing a meal. I walk over to an artist friend and help him set up an easel so he can paint the vast and beautiful landscape spread out before us.

Then I dream that I'm giving haircuts in a very crowded salon. People love what I'm doing for them. A lot of them have bald spots and hair loss. They can't see what's on the backs of their heads, but I see everything. I know what's there. I don't camouflage it, just work around it. No matter who sits in my chair I make them look great. I am happy, busy, and full of vitality. Clients constantly walk away without paying me and I have to run after them and get the money they owe me. I am not shy at all but bold and assertive.

In my second dream I don't hide anything. I clearly see the reality that is in front of me and I am unabashedly bold. The first part of the dream, however, seems to imply that my business is winding down and that it will be a rough and painful ride to the very end. I gave it such a valiant effort. I really did. The burden of continuing in such a precarious day-to-day fashion feels too great, as if I am indeed always sledding down an icy slope, never knowing if I am going to make it safely and with enough money from one month to the next.

I want financial security, and that's the core issue right now, for myself and the kids. I *crave* financial security. I want to enjoy what I do without the constant hassle of having to chase down money owed or worry about whether or not I'll have enough money to pay the bills each month. Such a tiresome waste of energy! Are the decisions I make while sleeping and dreaming real decisions, feasible ones? Am I interpreting these dreams correctly? My conclusions do make a lot of sense.

In mulling everything over, I decide that if I don't see an increase in business over the next month I'll look for a fulltime job and work at the studio on the weekends. Having work, steady income and benefits, are important right now. I need to support my family. That being determined, I peruse the classified ads. I find a job to apply for, at an historic site, for a development office assistant. I decide to put together a résumé and cover letter just for the heck of it and see what happens. It's the kind of job I would hope for, to be able to use my brains and my writing and organizational skills in a useful post, "with growth potential, possibly doing research." I'd like that. I'll apply and see where things stand in a month.

With that decided, I head off to check on my parents, having promised to stop in again. Nearing the old neighborhood, I remember what Chuck suggested, that I do something to break the hold it has over me. As I pass the barn and the orchards I let loose, yelling at the top of my lungs. Something loosens and I am giddy, almost woozy, as I drive up to my parent's cottage. I stay only a short time, satisfied that they are doing well and have everything they need. My mother is so embarrassed by my visit that she can't even look at me. Feeling better, perhaps embarrassed that she has needs, her old walls quickly reconstruct, locking in all feelings; not even a "thank you" escapes her. I don't attach and am happy to be back in my car, back on the road again. Nibbling on a sandwich I'd made before I left home in the morning, I drive slowly down the road. Scanning the landscape with a softened gaze, I take it all in. I see the reality of it, the truth of it, without attachment.

"So what?" I say to myself. "It's ugly and overgrown. There are vultures circling in the sky, perching in the trees, feeding on carcasses, cleaning ancient debris, including the ancient carcasses of my own memories, the crumbling barn, the overgrown orchards. There are houses going up all over the place. Big changes are really happening. The old world has been demolished. It's being replaced and I am slowly replacing it in myself too. Let the vultures have it all! Let them have the fuckers!"

"Channel the anger into good energy," I tell myself as I drive away. "Channel the tension into work and establishing a new place in the world, into writing a résumé and applying for jobs. Channel it out of this poor tired body. Become someone new."

When I look at pictures of myself I am unrecognizable, even to myself. I appear as if perched on a branch, almost looking like those vultures, hunched, ready to spread my wings and fly, just waiting for the signal that it's time to go. I am peering into the future, looking at something only I can see.

September 8, 2003

In a dream I make sure that my sixteen inner girls have everything they need, because I am going to leave them and I want to make sure they will be safe and provided for. I put them in a large storage unit, white and bare, set up like a dormitory, with enough supplies and clothing for a long stay. While my back is turned they mess everything up; chairs are flipped, beds messed, walls and new clothing scribbled on with crayons. One of the littlest is the instigator, a mischief-maker who forces the others to partake in the destruction, but I am aware that she is the true culprit. I tell her I love her and that it's okay, that I'll bring more clothes next time I come. I don't make a big deal about it. I know she feels deserted and that she's angry about the decision I've made to lock them up, but I'm going to stick with it. Later, when I pull up in my car, returning with clean clothes, several men run from the storage unit, jump into waiting trucks and drive away. And every time after that, when I bring things to the girls, I see men run to their trucks, jump in, and speed away.

I wake from this dream shaking, full of fear. Get calm, I tell myself, calm, calm. It's only the old stuff. Fight it, fight it, fight it. Don't let it drag you down. The fear crept into my body while I slept, fear of the men and what they were doing to the little girls, old memories lingering in dreamscapes, still too real. I must let them go, detach from them. Real though they may seem, they are just memories.

I do the magical pass, constructing my stable energy body, seeking anchoring in who I am in this moment, on this day. Then, slowly and methodically, I go about preparing to send the kids off to school, striving to stay present in each moment. The same intent as in my dream, the desire to take a break from the intensity of this recapitulation process, is encapsulated in every movement of my morning preparations. I am aware that I won't have to deal with this intensity forever, but it's especially invasive right now, sparked by my realization of how vulnerable my innocent little girls are, how they always have been, how vulnerable I was as a child. In locking them up I think I'm protecting them, but they may not be safe after all and that freaks me out!

Though I try to not take the dream literally, I cannot get away from the fear that courses through my veins. Whether old or new, it's real. And so I stay focused on each moment, mindful only of the clock and the bus schedule, intent on getting my kids off on time, dressed, fed, with their backpacks, lunchboxes, and musical instruments, the mundanity of life my saving grace.

An hour goes by and I am noticeably calmer, having worked my way back from the fearful dreamscape, back into REALITY, at least what appears as reality. But what kind of calmness have I actually arrived at? It feels like exhaustion. I wish I could sleep. I wish I could sleep forever, but I know I can't. I have to stay up and go to battle against my old demons. This is my life now, hunting and driving out the demons, a phase that I know won't last forever, for soon I will cross into a new phase. Like the phases of the moon, everything changes.

For most of the day I am okay as I constantly turn my attention to the moment and nothing else, until the afternoon arrives and then I am suddenly worn thin with exhaustion. As if coming for its scheduled appointment the fear arrives too. Having slipped in unnoticed, it attacks, grabbing my gut, leaving me sick to my stomach. It's a familiar feeling, what I woke up with this morning, fear and more fear. Its return haunts me like a dream hangover. I do the magical pass, forging my energy body, and successfully release the stomach pains, returning myself to the present, to this body.

I spend part of the day working on the letter and résumé for the job I had seen advertised. It's really a secretarial job, but it could offer a step in a new direction. Am I ready for such a change? A sense of sadness washes over me at the thought, a sense of tremendous loss of something I love. I hope getting a fulltime job doesn't mean I have to give everything up, that I will still have time to do all the things I love and enjoy. As I work on my résumé, the first writing assignment for the restaurant owner arrives. And then I get a call to do a painting job and I am momentarily relieved, business picking up right before my eyes!

Have I misinterpreted my recent dreams? Am I to have smooth sailing ahead? Have I already gone down the treacherous slope of my recent dream? At the bottom of the icy winter slope it was summer and I saw Chuck and Jeanne Ketchel sitting there, happily picnicking. I stood nearby, working with a landscape artist, perhaps a reference to the future, a broader vision of what is to come. Jeanne constantly reminds me that everything will be okay. Is that why she showed up in my dream? Perhaps things will turn out okay if I stick with where I am now. But business has to pick up a lot more for me to feel secure, and sooner rather than later if I am to be relieved of my constant worry. Let's hope it does!

It's clear that I have to be more assertive about getting paid for the work I do too, as my dream in the hair salon suggests. I can't be afraid to ask for money that is long overdue. Perhaps I'll send out the application for the job anyway, just to see what kind of response it might elicit. But first I will dream and see if anything comes through. I hope to dream about my girls tonight too!

September 9, 2003

I dream that I receive an invitation to attend a function at the home of my abuser. I am invited to see their "updates." I accept, though when I arrive it's clear that no one else is coming; I am the only invitee. I walk into an old house that has not been cleaned or painted in a very long time. Clothes are strewn all over the floors, beds are unmade, but for some reason my abuser and his wife are very proud of it. They want to show it off. The invitation says that "it's an opportunity to view our renovations," but obviously it's a ruse. I soon discover that, indeed, I have been tricked. I have been lured to my abuser's house to be injected with an embryo. I am told that I am to carry a fetus and give birth for someone else, that as a woman I *should* be doing this. I know they are right, that I am not worthy of anything other than this. I'm not happy about it, but it's expected that I do as instructed. I have to pee, so I go looking for a bathroom, but none of the toilets in the old ramshackle house are functioning. The woman administering the shot with the embryo says it's important to pee *beforehand*, otherwise the injection might not take. A part of me doesn't want the injection, knows that I don't want to carry a fetus, that I am not just a baby maker. I decide I won't pee. Maybe I can foil the plan, I think. At the same time, I know I won't be able to hold out forever; at some point I will have to pee.

I wake from this dream intensely angry, angry that I was tricked, but also angry at the possibility of things unfolding in such a manner. In reality, I'm trying to move forward, but the dream suggests I'm about to veer far from my current path of detachment and freedom. It's as if my dream is warning me that I'm heading right back into an old place, to be taken advantage of and used for someone else's gain. Yikes! With the anger bubbling inside me I set out for my appointment with Chuck. I imagine him suggesting that we ask the *I Ching* for advice on what this dream means.

"I have to figure this out," I say. "Not only my dream, but everything. How does this dream reflect on my decision to seek fulltime work? Is it the wrong decision? Will it cause me to lose everything I've been working so hard for?"

"Let's ask the *I Ching*," Chuck says, not surprisingly.

I write my question on Chuck's pad: Should I take a full time job? He hands me the coins and I throw them. The answer I receive is Hexagram #59, Dispersion: wind blowing over water.

Wind is blowing the water, dissolving it. When there is a blockage within, gentleness must be used to dissolve it. Rather than be driven by ego I must be guided by spirit. Rather than barreling ahead I must use the gentle stirrings of my heart to decide what is right for me. I must resort to the calmness of my heart and listen to what it tells me. No, I take this guidance from the *I Ching* to mean, don't take a full time job, but listen to your heart for guidance.

"What is your motive for wanting a change? What is driving you?" Chuck asks.

"Fear," I say, "as usual. Fear of failure, fear that I can't do what I've set out to do, fear I won't make enough money. But I know deep in my heart that I would be unhappy if I went to work for someone else. In all of my adult years I've only spent a few years working for anyone else. I've always been a freelancer. Yes, I have a lot of abilities and yes, I could do another type of job, but what I really want to do is what I already do so well—art, writing, creative stuff. It's who I am. It gives me such pleasure, such inner peace and calmness of heart. It's my true path. I have to stop resisting my path. Why do I resist?"

"Fear is a blockage," says Chuck. "It may be what the *I Ching* is referring to."

"Yes, there's an enormous black block standing in the way, but there's a disturbance too. It was present in my dream of the girls in the storage room, especially in the little girl I call the mischief-maker."

"Okay, so there's a disturbance," Chuck says. "What is it?"

"Anger," I admit. "I am blocked by fear and entrapped in anger. I feel it when I wake up in the morning and don't want change anymore. The idea of change makes me ill, that's fear too. And then I get angry at myself for being afraid. Usually, I get the sense that the fear is challenging me to keep going, to go through and beyond it, to use it as a catalyst to change. Usually, I just tell myself to work through it. But maybe it's there for a different reason now. Maybe it really does mean, *don't go this way, there's something not right about this decision.* Maybe the blockage is a warning to turn in a different direction."

"I need to figure my way through this by listening to what my body is saying. Maybe I feel ill because it really is the wrong decision. It makes me feel sick when I think about getting a fulltime job because I know, deep down in my gut, that I shouldn't do it. My gut reaction is that I'd hate it as much as I hated being back in my abuser's house in that dream. That's the feeling in the pit of my stomach. Maybe my gut reaction is the right one. I'll have to sit with it a little longer to really find out."

"That's what the *I Ching* is suggesting," Chuck says, "sit with it a while longer and see what comes."

I realize that if I stay in alignment with what's right I'll get where I need to be, and I'll know I'm there because it will feel right. It will be a natural and easy fit, like a new shoe that fits perfectly. I won't feel like I have to force myself into some place where I don't really belong to begin with. I received an invitation to go to my abuser's house, but when I got there discovered that it was trickery. There was nothing new there. I was merely being enticed into an old place by old energy assuming that I too was still the same, but I am not the same anymore. The *I Ching* supports and substantiates that, suggesting that I must take over now and make decisions based on a new set of facts and truths: I matter, I'm in charge, I'm on a new path, a path of heart now.

My dream and the *I Ching* are both telling me to beware! Don't go the way of the false invitation; it won't be right. It will only lead down an old path to an old place. That old path is full of pain, despair, and fear while the new path is light, open, and happy. Be who I am, my dream and the *I Ching* are telling me, not who I think I should or could be. Be the naturally quiet capable artist that I am, not the outgoing office efficiency expert I could force myself to be. That would be a false persona, much like the old numb self who kept everything together in the past by being in control. She's the old me, the dutiful hard worker, but also the fearful me. I must turn and follow the new me now, in a new direction, even if I'm afraid. I must remember that fear can also be a guide, letting me know that yes, I am afraid, but it's time to face it and move on.

The path *is* clear: let go of the fear and the future will unfold as it should, naturally. If I don't rid myself of the fear I am no better than a little dung beetle pushing its great ball of dung, always taking on more, stuck in an endless loop. I *can* let it go. I can get beyond it if I just leave it and walk away, a dung beetle no more.

Suddenly, it dawns on me that the little mischief-maker of my dream was trying to get my attention. She was warning me, much as the *I Ching* does. "Really?" she was asking. "Are you going to do that again? Are you going to abandon everything we've been working so hard for?" She created havoc but was really trying to get my attention, saying, "Watch out, things are not what you think. You are about to make a big mistake!" She was waving a red flag, one that I failed to see during the dream, signaling that I was about to get tricked by another part of myself, my ego telling me I would make a great office assistant and that I should take the job! My dreaming self knew it was a bad idea and created the mischief-maker and a disturbance of fear. She knew I would react to fear, that it would shake me. She warned me in the same way the *I Ching* warns me. "No," they are both saying, "you can't go to ego, you have to stay with spirit."

I must bear all the tension of this grueling process of transformation, the simultaneous breaking down of an old self and the building up of a new one. I can't run back to an old self, no matter how great the pull or how familiar the energy, she doesn't really exist any more. Only the new self and the new path of heart matter.

At the end of the workday I go home and crawl into bed for an hour, too exhausted to even move. The need to escape for a little while is strong, but a little while is enough. Even if I still crave withdrawal, it's not as often or for as long as before, though the need still exists. In fact, today I thought, "Okay, as exhausted as I am, if I push myself for a few days and get a lot accomplished then I won't feel so guilty about withdrawing for a day or two." But that seems twisted!

I love all this stuff! The dreams, the *I Ching* reading, the asking and receiving, the messages from Jeanne, listening to my own heart. All day I calmed myself by envisioning gentle winds of calmness blowing through me, as the *I Ching* suggested. It's so true that I must be gentler with myself. If I am to progress I must stop resisting, let worry go, and let life happen. All that energy being wasted by worry needs to be re-channeled into useful energy now.

I notice that when I shift out of painful positions I feel better. When I breathe calmly and gently, with love for myself, I feel better too. When I take care of myself, I feel better. This changing process is really working. I will be okay now. I know I will be okay.

September 10, 2003

In a dream, I am sitting in a hospital lobby opposite a doctor. He's tanned, dressed all in white. I feel good around him. My daughter is with us. She's laughing and happy, four years old again, extremely comfortable around the doctor, climbing on him, totally uninhibited and without fear. The doctor tells me about having to care for so many people, running up and down the stairs all day long while he's at the hospital, yet he appears very happy. He says he goes outside and runs whenever he needs to take a break from the stress. It refreshes him so that he can give all of his energy to helping others. Eventually, I pick up his feet and begin to massage them through his white socks. After a while I massage his neck and back and arms. The word *intimacy* pops into my head. "Do I want intimacy?" I ask myself.

I wake up to find myself sleeping on my back rather than curled up on my side. The usual fear and dread in the pit of my stomach are noticeably gone. I am totally relaxed and happy!

In the dream, I too worked at the hospital. It was a place where people had bad things removed, a place of recuperation and healing, much like the phases of this recapitulation process. There was such a deep sense of calmness and real trust in the dream, not only did I experience this with the doctor but with others as well. The hospital was a place of total giving. Compassion flowed out of me for everyone I met, especially toward the people I was personally caring for. I experienced such pure, unconditional love for everyone I met. Is my dream suggesting that it's time to allow intimacy and love into my life, as part of my own caring and healing process? Is that what I need for this to be a complete healing journey?

The *I Ching* is right, I must let the fear go, the blockage that obstructs the natural flow of life. It lurks inside me, not a figment of my imagination but a real presence that inhabits and inhibits me, body and soul. It torments me. It must be replaced by relaxation, calmness, gentleness and, yes, love. This is what I gave to others in the dream. It was also what my little dream child, in the guise of my daughter, innocently experienced in the dream. She was completely relaxed and totally without fear as she flourished in the loving atmosphere of the place. Her uninhibited happiness was striking to me, for I have rarely, as a child or an adult, been so carefree.

There is certainly the possibility for all kinds of changes and new life, if I can let the fear go. And perhaps there is room for intimacy too because, yes, I would like intimacy in my life, but it would have to be with the right person, a caring, compassionate person who would understand my inner world and the work I must still do, someone to love, but also someone who truly loves me as well. Is that where I need to go next?

First, I must focus my energy on trusting myself and my own abilities. As I look over the letter I wrote for the job application I see a very capable and competent person. I need to allow myself to be that person, to accept her but also to encourage her. I must allow her to grow, not fight her or suppress her but guide her in the right direction. At the artist's gallery everyone says to me: "It's you! You make it all happen! What will we do without you?" It's time to accept that I am fully capable of making things happen, but it's time to make things happen for myself now! It's all about being selfish with my time and my energy, being kinder to myself. I must take the time I need to heal and reconstruct myself in such a way that I am better than before, be the unique person that I truly am. Trust myself. Stop fighting myself. Let new energy push the fear out. Let the anger go too. Center myself in my own heart, my own strong, calm heart.

Tonight my dream intention is to find out how to let go of the fear, the self-loathing, the self-doubt, and the gripping pain.

September 11, 2003

I got another word! It made so much sense to me when I woke up in the night, but I didn't write it down and now I'm not sure what it was. Fairness? In the dream, I was lying on a mat in a room filled with glowing candlelight. Lit candles surrounded me on the floor and one was placed on my stomach. A man dressed all in white, with white hair and a wonderful light around him too, gave me a word. He knew everything about me without my saying a thing. I received the word and it made all the sense in the world to me. I was on my back and felt so happy, satisfied, and very safe. I actually woke up and thought about writing the word down in the middle of the night. I said it over and over again, sure I would never forget it because it made so much sense to me. But I forgot it! Now I want it back. Please give it back!

On this date, two years ago, my inner work began going much deeper when I finally acknowledged that I had something wrong deep inside myself. At that time I had yet to face what it was. Now I have faced it and I am much softer now as a result. My heart is softer. I felt such sadness and grief today like I haven't ever felt before. I was so numb two years ago, though I was able to feel and acknowledge that numbness. For the first time I allowed it to exist in reality and that was what started the deepening of this whole inner journey, this slow unraveling of life as I once knew it. I must still keep unraveling everything, stay on the course of change and transformation. Whatever comes, I must let it come. It is the only way of being that I know now.

My dream last night was very compelling. Once again I dreamed a mandala, though this time, rather than the little model house at the center, I lay at the center, a circle of light surrounding me. And, at the center of the mandala, on my bellybutton, another candle illumined the very core of me. I knew exactly what I needed and when I was given the word—perhaps to be fair to myself—it was such a wonderful moment, the feeling that I had solved and resolved everything. Yes, I thought, that's it, it's all I need! I tried to remember it, but obviously I couldn't! So tonight, once again, I will try to revisit that place of light and discover what I must do if I am to release from the constant fear and self-doubt.

In last night's dream, the man in white spoke so softly to me. I recognized him from other dreams, though I don't know who he is, just that he is someone extremely familiar, someone I know and admire, someone I trust implicitly. Please come back to me again, so I can hear what you have to tell me. If the word I received *was* fairness, I remember it as being something like this: "Be fair to yourself. Treat yourself fairly, as well as others, but first of all yourself, so that you will be able to pass it on."

September 12, 2003

I got a new word! "Satisfied!" I woke myself up and wrote it down. I can't remember the dream at all, but I was determined to remember the word. I also know it wasn't the same word as the night before. This is the third dream in a row where I've received a word. What do they mean? Allow myself *intimacy*? Treat myself with *fairness*? And I will be *satisfied*? Is that what needs to happen? Perhaps.

In spite of my decision to not meet on Fridays anymore, it's Friday today and I have my usual appointment with Chuck. I just don't have the stability to do this on my own, it's not time yet. I appreciate his silence on the matter, as he let me discover on my own what I'm sure he already knew—that I'm still in the thick of it!

"You're at a point of decision," says Chuck. "No more domino effects, just letting the dominoes fall as they will, letting things happen. It's time to make choices now. You have new life ahead of you!"

"I have to deal with the anger," I say. "Once I get through that I feel like I'll be able to allow for a lot of other things, all those things in my dreams. I also have to stop being so nice to everyone else and give a little niceness to myself, be fair to myself, forgive myself. Oh! That's the second dream word: *Forgiveness*!"

"Forgive yourself. Forgive yourself, as well as others, but first of all yourself, so that you will be able to pass it on, that's what the man in my dream told me. I had asked how to let go of the fear, the self-loathing, self-doubt, and the gripping pain. He gave me the answer I've been needing: self-forgiveness!"

I've had several dreams now with men in white, the first one was Chuck coming as the conduit, more recently the doctor dressed in white, and then the man in white in the light-filled room. What does all of this white clothing and white light signify; innocence, purity? When I was lying on the mat, surrounded by candlelight, the man in white massaged my feet just as I had massaged the doctor's. That was intimacy, closeness and trust, coming into my dreamworld again, but he also whispered the word forgiveness to me. I woke up satisfied.

He was telling me to forgive myself so I can forgive others and so I will be able to pass it on. Pass on forgiveness? Pass on what it means to forgive? Perhaps I am learning to forgive myself as I do this recapitulation. Perhaps that's the real healing crux of this journey. Maybe it's not about having to forgive anyone else, but only about finding a way to forgive myself.

It's almost ten at night. I'm a little drunk. I had three big glasses of wine and I'm feeling very sad. Self-pity? I don't know, but I cried. I actually cried. And it felt so good! Crying is good. As Chuck always says, "it's a release."

September 13, 2003

I wake up early not feeling well, stuffy from my wine binge and the crying jag that followed. My mind, however, is focused. I have to finish writing a press release!

I get to the studio early and stay there all day. Not much energy, but I finish the press release and paint a little. I'm tired at night and don't do much, waste time in front of the TV. I need it, I guess—time to do nothing, not even think.

September 14, 2003

3 a.m. Awoken by shouting. Car doors slamming. A girl cries out. "Oh god, Daddy! Oh my god! Daddy! No Daddy!" This is followed by screams, the sounds of fists hitting flesh, followed by more screams. A young child cries uncontrollably. There is more yelling, attempts to break it up. I'm so glad that my kids are with their dad for the weekend!

The screams and shouts ricochet off the walls of my bedroom. It sounds so much like my abuser hitting his children with the big spanking board they kept at the ready, their screams like nothing I had ever heard. I am dragged right back into my abuser's house, once again cringing at the top of their cellar stairs, waiting for the beatings to be over. I hear their screams coming up from the cellar and across the decades. "No Daddy! No Daddy! No Daddy!" The world collapses. Time is all time. They are in my bedroom. I am in their house. I am a child. I am an adult. I am frozen in my bed, shaking violently.

Eventually, quiet returns to the neighborhood, but I am stuck in a time warp, terrorized by nightmares for the rest of the night. Every now and then I wake up, try to get calm by envisioning winds of calmness blowing in through the open window, try to settle my beating heart, remembering the advice of the *I Ching* to find stillness this way.

Lying awake in the morning, I have a brief moment of clarity, that "it's" all happening, the recapitulation process, the business, everything progressing at every turn, even as I worry, even as I shake in my bed in terror, even as I pull myself out of the time warp and back into reality. *Change is happening.*

The nighttime episode in the neighborhood stays with me, my anxiety level rising as the day progresses and by evening I am visibly shaking. It's as if I've been locked up in the storage unit with my little girls all day, traumatized by the men outside hankering to get in. I keep busy with things around the house, seeking calmness in the mundane tasks of living, eventually concentrating on the words in a book. Even if I don't really read, even if I don't comprehend, it keeps me safe from knowing the real truth behind the fear that rattles me. It's only a temporary fix though. It's pretty obvious that this anxiety is all memory related, stirred up by what happened last night. Finally able to admit it, I put the book down and let myself go there. I must face it. I ask my body and my memories to show me what they know.

Suddenly, I am back in my abuser's house again. I am four or five years old, afraid of their dog. I actually cried when a dog jumped on me while I was taking a walk this morning. Generally, I shy away from strange dogs as I often find them threatening. I become a scared child again and naturally shrink away, and that's what happened today when the dog jumped on me. I became a scared five-year-old child, and that's where I've been ever since!

September 15, 2003

I wake in fear, the desire to withdraw strong, anger potent. A memory circles like a predator, not fully revealing itself, but clearly letting me know it's there. Before long I will be its captive and then who knows what will happen.

I barely have enough strength to get out of bed, but I force myself. I have to get on with life and at the same time prepare for this memory that is sure to come with its usual force, enough to knock me off my feet again by all accounts. "Breathe!" I remind myself. "Breathe!"

I forge my energy body, doing the magical pass as Chuck taught me, telling myself that I am different now, that I'm doing life differently. I have a new way of thinking, a new way of seeing, and a new way of acting. I'm creating a new life and a new self. I will not get stuck in the old patterns. They fit an old me and an old way of life that no longer exist. I must remember all of this as I prepare for a new workweek too. I have money to collect this week. I must not be afraid to stand my ground. I must be strong enough to ask for what is owed me. I must gather enough ego to establish my new self more firmly, rather than crashing in the old way, giving my energy and my time away for nothing.

I must remember that I am very talented and capable. I know these things; I accept these things about myself. I am worth every penny I charge. I am worth every dollar I earn. Self-esteem must be the driving force over desperation and fear now, part of my ego development but fully imbued with new spirit as well. I am worth the effort it takes to change, and although the *I Ching* suggests I not let ego make my decisions, I don't think this is what it meant. What I'm working toward is appropriate ego building and support, in alignment *with* spirit.

The truth is that I've shortchanged my ego, far too often ending up without proper compensation for the work I've done because I feel sorry for people. I get drawn into other people's hardships and lower my prices out of empathy, but that just leaves me angry because I'm left at a deficit myself, unable to remain financially viable as a result, and that's wrong. It's okay to be considerate and compassionate, but it's another thing to give away so much that I myself suffer. Unfortunately, it's been a lifelong habit of mine; the minute I hear that someone needs or wants something I give or volunteer in some way. It's about time I recognize the impropriety of that. My goal is to make enough money to live simply but comfortably, including savings for the future. And there are always emergencies to consider too! So yes, appropriate earnings are necessary!

Today is Monday, a new day and a new week. I have plenty of work lined up and I *will* get paid properly for it. I promise myself that! I will create a good life for myself! I promise myself that too!

Nothing is more powerful than my own intent! The truth is, I'm already doing what I've set out to do, living what I've been envisioning for a long time now. I really am moving forward and changing now, though worry continues to interfere. At the same time it reveals its truths, that it gets me nothing, that it's totally nonproductive. In fact, it holds me back, as devastating as being caught in the clutches of my abuser and his old energy. I must keep moving forward! It's the true prerogative of the soul, for once life has begun there is no going back. All energy is focused on moving forward, even if it's only one small step at a time.

"Be confident," Jeanne tells me. *"Push out of the shell, break the shell and get away from the mess in there. Go finish the projects on hand; get paid a fair price. Don't get exhausted. Pace yourself. Love yourself. Be proud of yourself. You are worth every dollar. You are already there; now just keep going."*

The slowly circling memory that approached this morning reveals itself more fully as the day progresses, edging closer and closer. The sun sets, darkness descends, and I feel it creeping nearer. By ten o'clock at night I am its prey, its talons gripping me. Though I've been feeling its energy for days now, suffering incredible anxiety and depression, it is finally coalescing into something more real. The screaming on Saturday night simply sparked what was already smoldering. It's inside me, a huge monster of a growling dog that won't leave me alone, won't stop gnawing away at me. It's been there forever, slowly sucking the life out of me.

September 16, 2003

Though glimpses of enlightenment and boundless energy have come as I've taken this journey they get stolen away as soon as a memory like this surfaces and I forget that I'm on a magical journey. Only the darkness shows itself then. If I want those momentary glimpses of magic to be more permanent I must get "him" out of me, rid myself of everything related to my abuser; memories, energy, thoughts, ideas, and otherwise. That's why this recapitulation process is so important. I believe it is the only way to completely heal. It has so far proven its worth in so many ways. Of course, I want to hurry it up and be free, to close the door on this chapter of my life as soon as possible.

"The door will close on its own, when the time is right," Jeanne says. *"You can't slam it shut. That's not how it works."*

I meet with Chuck and we process what's been brewing. I can do no more than curl down into my lap and hide my face in my hands, full of terror.

"In this memory, I am old enough to know why he's bringing his dog," I say, shaking as I talk. "I've always known, but I've kept it hidden from myself."

And then I stop talking. I can't go on. I can't tell him what's being recapitulated, but I let it go through me. I let it happen. I shake and shiver and moan. It's all I can do, but it's enough.

"I can't talk about what happened yet," I say, sitting up, thoroughly drained, "it's not a complete memory, but enough is coming through and I don't like it!"

"You'll get through it," Chuck says. "Remember, you got through all the other memories."

"I've forgotten how hard it is, how demolishing."

"I know," he says kindly. "At least you're starting."

As usual, when the session ends, Chuck asks how I'm feeling. I notice how queasy and shaky I am, but also that I'm not feeling so hunted, not so anxious, just empty. If he hadn't asked and brought attention to my body I don't think I would have felt anything, just the usual numbness. When I get home I crawl into bed and pull the covers over my head and stay there for an hour. My throat hurts, a huge lump forming. I am crushed, totally spent.

"You have to deal with this," I hear Jeanne saying.

I know. I have to go through this entire memory. I can't have this traumatic past in my life anymore, but I don't feel as strong as I used to be. I'm not as strong as I was as a little girl.

September 17, 2003

I am a little girl flying through the air in a horse drawn cart. My hands clutch the reins. I fly low, skimming over roads, going fast through villages, terrified by the incredible speed of it and yet I can't stop. It's as if the horse and cart are in control. Then I feel someone behind me, putting his hands over mine, whispering in my ear.

"You can do it, trust yourself. Look, you *are* doing it! You're fine. You're the one. You are making it happen," he says.

I start to turn around and realize that I don't need to see who is behind me because I *am* doing it. The truth is, I'm handling it just fine. As I fly along, more consciously in control now, it dawns on me that things are better than I'd realized. Suddenly, I know that I am in full control of everything, of this process and of the outcome. I am stronger and more capable than I've ever felt before. And then I realize I'm not scared anymore.

Just as I tell myself to relax and enjoy the magical ride, I wake up, not in my physical body, which is still asleep, but in my awareness, in my energy body, which sits straight up, fully alert. I see my hands on the reins, clear as day. I realize that I must totally trust myself if I am to manage this magical ride. I feel how skillful I am, how in control, and I sense a new confidence blossoming. I'm enjoying the ride, the sensation of flying along with total abandon, when I feel myself letting go, dissolving. It's too much!

With a terrifying jolt I wake up to find myself clutching my gut, moaning in pain and terror. I am a child again, in the throes of stomach cramps. I woke up every morning with these same cramps and had to drag myself out of bed to go to school, knew I had to keep moving or I would die. I feel like I'm dying now! Letting go still means death! I remind myself that I'm not dying at all but fully living now.

"Be positive! Be positive!" I chant. "Be positive!"

After a half hour of chanting, forging my energy body, and drinking a cup of coffee I succeed in shifting into a more positive mood. This pain, I remind myself, is just offering me another opportunity to know yet another truth about my past. Perhaps this is what the candle on my bellybutton was suggesting in my recent dream, that this is the next place to shine a light, to resolve what my gut knows and feels, for when I pay attention to it, it tells me the truth. The anxiety and fear lingering deep in my bones and lying nestled in my gut are ancient, long dormant, being exposed now for what they truly are, the results of long ago abuse and torture, the real truths of my childhood. The mind may conjure, attach, and distract, but the body does not lie!

I sense that I truly am on the brink of new life. I can't let these memories cripple me, can't let them drag me back. I need to push through, not get overpowered by what comes up—that's not a healthy approach. I'm going to have to face all this more fully at some point and fully let go, but that's enough for now! Get up. Shower. Wake the kids. Go to work. Focus on today. Today is all that matters, just today!

Intense pain bombards my midsection, my gut on fire. I try to work through it, ignore it, yell at it, but no imperatives ease it. I finally focus my breathing on it, cooling it. I forge my energy body and it releases. I keep telling myself that the body doesn't lie, the body knows all, and that this phantom pain is trying to tell me something. Is it pain from being held too tightly? I'm not sure yet, though I have two dog memories, one with a small dog and another with a larger dog. I am devastated every time I think about them and then the pain creeps back in and I feel a great weight and my body is falling, collapsing. In the memory, I am in so much pain and unable to breathe that I pass out. The memory is totally encased in fear! Unfortunately, I no longer have numbness to hide behind. I feel *everything* now!

I've noticed how the recapitulation has evolved as I've gotten used to handling the memories, and as I've evolved too. Much as in my dream of the flying cart, I've gained a modicum of control. I'm able to handle all the feelings at once now. Physical, emotional, and mental anguish flood me simultaneously and I experience them fully, as opposed to the slower dawning of each facet of a memory in the earlier part of this recapitulation process, when each emotion and feeling came in its own sweet time, separated from each other by hours, days, or weeks. They may still take a while to fully coalesce, to gather momentum, but then it's like a great wave crashing over me, and yet I refuse to drown or get dragged under. I'm staying above the water as best I can, trying to remember how to fly that magical cart!

Forging my energy body throughout the day, breathing into my gut, the seat of self-esteem, will power, and assertiveness, preparing for more flying lessons, I gain insight into what lies before me now.

These are my rights: *to do, to act.*

This is my challenge: *to face the shame.*

My innocence was destroyed, crushed by my abuser, by his ugly pedophilia, but I have the power to take it back. And I have the power to rid myself of the shame I have been carrying ever since, the shame of being abused, the things I could never speak of, and all that that has entailed. I have the power, the intent, and the will to fly this magical journey to the end.

And then it begins to dawn on me: *if I can really learn to trust myself then nothing can stop me.*

September 18, 2003

I dream that I have a set of double doors in my body, at my midsection. I am lying flat on my back when they swing open, quite forcefully, first one door and then the other. I feel them burst apart with a great explosion of energy, a powerful burst that I have no control over, as if giving birth. Nothing can stop it. And then wave after wave of energy crashes out of me through the doors. I identify them as waves of pain and sadness, waves of fear and resentment, waves of guilt and shame, waves of jealously and regret, etc. As wild and uncontrollable as a tsunami they come, one after another. This is Stage One, I learn, keeping the doors open to release, to let things out. Stage Two is keeping the doors open to let things in.

As the dream continues, I am made aware that I must go through this first stage so I can achieve total emptiness. As I lie there and release wave after wave, I keep thinking that it's almost over, but soon discover that there's more. Many more doors, doors at ever-deepening levels open up and release more waves of pain and more waves of fear. I am also fully aware that the end result will be attainment of complete beingness and complete goodness, and that in the end I will discover my ultimate purpose. For I am made fully aware that there is a purpose to this life and to all this work, for all my lives and for everything I have ever experienced.

I learn that the purpose of life is really about *giving*, about letting everything inside be used for the good of the world. It's about having no fear, and about total submission to forgiveness, toward self and other. I am made aware of how important it is that I learn to fully trust myself as I finish this recapitulation journey, and to never stop growing and evolving—to keep going no matter what. These are the things that matter in any stage of life, I learn.

I am further shown that although the process may be quite painful and though it may seem endless right now, it will come to a natural slowing down time and, eventually, a natural ending will occur, that each stage has its natural closure, just as all of life has its ending time. I am shown that there is still anger inside me too, and I am made aware that I must keep the doors open so that it can naturally and easily flow out. I am aware that in Stage Two, after the emptying of Stage One, I must still keep the doors wide open and let what needs to happen come as it will, and to trust that process too, for that is the ultimate journey, to journey through life with an open and trusting heart. I understand that my heart must remain empty and receptive to all that is to come. I understand that this is a true path with heart, for an open heart that has known pain and yet needs and fears nothing is truly ready to give.

I wake up in pain, my midsection raw and sore, as if I have indeed just given birth, the entrails of my past drawn out of me like so many babies. I sense not to ignore the pain but to very slowly and gently breathe into it, the instructions in my dream to remain open foremost in my thoughts. As I breathe, I feel my abuser's arm slowly wrapping around me, squeezing ever tighter, my two worlds intersecting. Or maybe they're the same world? It feels as if I'm being laid over something, pushed against something. I breathe, breathe, breathe through the pain and terror. Breathing allows for release of pain and tears. Breathing keeps the doors open—Stage One of my dream.

I recall feeling this exact pain in my midsection as a teenager. I remember telling myself it was my punishment and I just had to live with it, to hold it in and bear it because it was God punishing me for being bad.

"Jeanne! Please help me find my way to clarity," I beg, "to fully recalling, fully resolving this memory, to reliving it and then storing it in the cupboard of recapitulation with all the others, neatly stacked, and then maybe *that* door will swing shut at last."

September 19, 2003

By the time I arrive at Chuck's office my sides and ribs are aching, my neck stiff with pain, my body gearing up for the grand telling of the memory of the "dog issues" as we have been calling it. I can do no more than tell Chuck that my neck is hurting and then I plunge right into the past.

"I am seventeen," I say, "the year I always thought of as 'the year my neck broke' because it was so painful. I couldn't straighten it out. I wore a scarf wrapped around it. Not only was it painful, but it was also bruised. I see the bruises now, when I look in the mirror. Back then I would try to straighten my neck out as I showered, hoping the hot water would have some effect on the painful muscles. The pain, I understand now, was from his hands, from my abuser pushing and holding me down."

I feel those hands on me as I tell Chuck what I am seeing and remembering. Even after I talk about it, I still feel it. I try breathing into it, breathing the pain away, releasing it as I have been instructed to do, staying in Stage One, staying open.

Later. I remember that I had a dream last night that I thought was too boring to even write down. I woke up thinking, why am I dreaming about this, about an ordinary calm day at home and work? Now I realize that my dream was letting me know that life will become calm, ordinary, and routine again at some point. In the meantime, I want to get this stuff out of me. I want the pain and anguish gone. I want to be empty. I want to enter the promised land that I've seen on the horizon, this recapitulation's natural end.

September 20, 2003

I'm flying over snow-covered pathways, gliding swiftly along, just a few inches above the ground. I fly through woods and across fields with such ease, standing straight up. It's as if I'm wearing cross-country skis, though I'm not. There are no obstacles and nothing is insurmountable or impassable. I pass some artist friends who are painting the winter landscape. They ask me if I'm painting too.

"No," I say, "I'm just going, just going."

At one point, just as I'm about to cross over a road to enter the woods on the other side, I stop. I have a choice to make. Do I take the road or do I go back into the woods? I don't get a good feeling about the road; it's boringly familiar and my energy dies as soon as I see it. That's my answer.

"No, I won't take the road," I say. "I will stay in the woods!"

And off I go. I'm not interested in trudging along boring old roads, no matter how flat and straight. The thrill of the dark woods is much more enticing!

Gliding over that beautiful landscape in my dream was so exhilarating. As I skimmed across those open fields and sailed through those dense woods, I instinctively knew how to fly and where to go. I was in control in a powerful way, so sure of myself, so decisive, and yet I wake up in a daze after my night of flying, my mood somber.

As if retracing the trails in my dream, pains travel the roadmap of my body, from my neck and shoulders, to my ribs and sides, down into my vagina and anus, connecting all the dots. I refused the old familiar road, choosing instead to reenter the woods, and it seems as if the woods still has things to teach me. Only by going into them, again and again, will I continue to experience the pain and exhilaration of this life-changing process. The woods, though they hold the secrets of my trauma also hold the secrets of my salvation.

Suddenly, the pain in my neck throws me back down the recapitulation tunnel, back into my freshman year in college. As soon as I'm there, I realize what I couldn't have known at the time, that a pain in my neck then was a flashback to the pain I'd experienced the year before in high school! I remember living in a foggy depression for several months during that first year in college, my neck achy and sore. I couldn't eat and I had no energy. I could barely get out of bed every morning. I thought I might have mono but a blood test revealed nothing. This happened during a six-week intersession and I was taking a creative writing course. The class met one day a week and then we all went off to work on our own. I wandered around the college buildings and onto the streets of Philadelphia, my neck achy, lost in some altered state that I only now understand was an actual flashback, though no clarity or resolution was gained at the time. I was probably not yet ready to know the truth, but I realize now that something in my psyche was pinching my neck, trying to get me to remember what had happened the year before.

I was leveled by the "dog issue," both when it happened and during those weeks in college when something triggered my memory of it. So little life did I feel coursing through my veins then. And even now, as I lie in my bed and recapitulate, it feels like I'm dying. The fear of impending annihilation is overwhelming, the fear of dissolution, of truly letting go overpowering, for it does not feel like letting go in a healing sense but in a death sense. And yet, another part of me is fully aware that it's exactly where I have to go, so far down into my own darkness that I come face to face with my own annihilation—the last door in Stage One. Only then will I truly be free.

For now, I take calming herbal remedies and cut back on coffee to control the agitated state I find myself in most of the time. I walk a lot, do yoga and meditate to stem the rising panic, forge my energy body to keep death at arm's length. I want to stay open to this process, but it's so frightening right now. I can only breathe and hope that when death comes I will be ready to receive it. In the meantime, I ask my dreamworld for help and guidance.

September 21, 2003

I dream that I'm with a policewoman. She drives me around in her patrol car. We stop outside a tall city building. The policewoman gets out of the car, pulls out her gun and shows it to another officer and then puts it back in her holster. She tells me she shows her gun a lot. We go inside the building and into a small cell-like room. The walls are painted bright yellow and orange, and the floor is tiled in pink. I have a bottle of organic pear juice with me. I open it up and discover little black flecks floating in it. When I tip the bottle over and pour the juice out, small, writhing black snakes fall onto the pink floor. I stare at them. When I look away for a moment and then back again there are fewer of them. I do this a few times, looking away and then back again, and each time there are fewer and fewer snakes until there are none at all. I don't actually see where they go, but I know they have crawled inside my body, through my anus. I know they are worms of death, wriggling inside me. I lie down on the pink tiled floor and tell the woman cop to shoot me.

"I know you have a gun," I say, "so shoot me."

"I can't shoot you," the policewoman says.

I lie on the floor as memories flood through me. Black dog penises, thin and pointy, jab me in the rear end, like sharp pencils. I am being stabbed to death. I wake up shaking in pain.

Death came in my dream and I didn't like it at all! Death is in the "dog issue" memory, in all the memories. Death is after me! I even asked for it, but I'm not ready yet!

I want to call Chuck and tell him that I want this over with, that I can't do this recapitulation anymore, that I hate him for getting me started on this painful journey! I know he didn't really "get me started." Something inside myself did, but my enthusiasm for the process has stagnated. I am overwhelmed with the horror of the meaning of this dream, with what it suggests I must face in recapitulating this memory. At the same time, I'm aware I should keep the inner doors open and let things out. I know I have to fully face it, but the truth is, I don't want to face it! It freaks me out!

I am thankful for my children. They get me up and moving. It's a beautiful day. We go on a hike and, though I am pained and exhausted by the recapitulation, I am able to shift into having a positive experience with them. Afterwards, I push myself to keep moving, to do little things, to not stop moving in spite of the fact that I have no energy. If I stop I fear I will fall into the darkness of the dream, that death will come today. For most of the day I feel empty and gone, near death anyway. Why do I resist? Why not just face it?

I'm angry at myself for choosing to go back into the woods in that recent flying dream. Though it was a dream decision it reverberates through reality, for just as I was starting to accept myself, getting to a good place, I find that I have gotten dragged back into the deepest darkest woods, to a place where I do not exist, where I am inert and invisible, mere dissociated energy. And when I am there one image leads to another, one painful memory evokes another. I hate it. I hate going back there!

A part of me does want to die—last night's dream got that right! But it's the part that fears the worst, that's scared to face the truth, even though it knows the truth too. When I asked the policewoman to shoot me I wanted that part dead so I could go on pretending everything was all right. But I know I'm going to have to face everything, afraid or not, that I can't kill off a part of myself to save myself from fully facing the truth. The truth is I've already done that, for most of my life, and it didn't work! As long as I refuse to face the memories and the fear of death that they present, I will continue to suffer. Damn!

I lie down on my bed and go back into the part of the dream where the snakes fell out of the juice bottle and onto the floor. They disappeared as I turned my head from side to side, just as when I do the sweeping breath, the recapitulation magical pass that both clarifies and dissipates the memories. The dream is telling me that I will have to gain clarity on this memory as well, that I will have to breathe and look, again and again, at what happened until there is nothing left inside me to cause discomfort or harm, until I face the death I was presented with and live through it a second time, in full recapitulation. For now, however, the dream tells me, everything is still inside me, a nest of black vipers writhing, truth and death entwined!

In the afternoon, I regain enough energy to go outside and do a little work in the yard, not much, but some. Otherwise, I spend the better part of the day fighting the fear, staunchly refusing to go there. As I weed the garden, the pain in my neck returns full force, pressuring me to turn and face the truth. I was hoping it had gone away, but now it's back, worse than ever. If I don't go through this memory my neck will never heal, that I am sure of. It's an injury that's been waiting for this moment since I was seventeen years old. If I don't relive it and release it, I will be crippled for life. Cripes!

September 22, 2003

I'm in an old building. Renovations are taking a really long time to complete. There are three closed doors in front of me, boldly numbered in black: 1, 2, and 3. Upon opening each door I see that the rooms behind them are unfinished, the floors unsafe to walk on. One of the rooms will be mine when the renovations are done. I field questions about the progress of the renovations, confidently speak to people about the work being done, the construction and painting, explaining that the projects have to be done one step at a time, that such work, to be done properly, takes time and patience.

Progress is slow and methodical, yet I am so confident in my dream, sure that all is going according to plan. But am I stalling, holding back, just making excuses for the slowness of the work? My neck is still extremely sore, my throat dry, my stomach ill with fear.

"Things will be okay, everything will work out, it will be fine," Jeanne says.

My neck cries. My neck cries a stream of tears. I've wanted to call Chuck all weekend, but I have no words. I have only pain and my crying neck. I take a shower and try to wash it all away. I step out of the hot water and tell it that I have to leave it, that I have to go to work.

"We will talk about it tomorrow," I tell it.

It's eleven at night and my neck is killing me. In addition, a painful spot on my arm has appeared. This is all part of the memory building up, seeking release. I also realize that all the negative feelings and the dark depression that make me want to go lie down in the woods and die are part of the memory too, the after-trauma memory, what I had to deal with when all was said and done. Oh, God!

September 23, 2003

I dream that my hairdresser is putting me back together again, rebuilding me, one part at a time, putting my physical body parts back together again. I am being restored to wholeness, made to look and feel good.

When I wake up my neck still hurts. I was aware of trying not to clench it as I slept. I'm careful as I get out of bed too, though I feel hands on me, holding me down, my neck and ears scraping

121

on the ground, burning with pain. I move slowly as I get ready to meet with Chuck, careful not to disturb too much. I just want to get up to his office and let what comes come. I'm ready now. I want to begin the rebuilding process now, like in my dream, attend to the beautifying of a newly restored me, but I have to go through the final breakdown first. I have to die first.

After my session with Chuck I go home and get back into bed. I don't go near the memory. I just lie there listening to the rain on the roof, my neck hurting. I cancel my dental cleaning for tomorrow because I won't be able to tilt my head, open my mouth, or sit in the chair for any length of time. I need to do something nice for myself, even if it's only saying a prayer. Is there a God? Is She/He listening? Do you hear me? DO YOU HEAR ME? I'm in so much pain!

I didn't fully recapitulate the "dog issue" memory in my session with Chuck after all. I just couldn't. I couldn't talk. I could only peer into the woods and try and make out what was happening. Parts of it are still fuzzy, incomplete, and other parts I can't go near yet, though I know they are there, waiting in the shadows. I guess it'll all become clear soon enough, and then the pain should subside, the fear and depression too. I wait for clarity. In the meantime, I have a fever. I'm dragging, want only sleep, though one morning soon I hope to jump out of bed, excited to start the day, for I am tired of this heavy struggle, this exhausted body, this pain-filled soul.

I sleep for a few hours and then get up to eat, knowing I must nourish this body, keep it healthy, so it will have the energy to carry me through this darkness and into the light, for I see the light waiting for me.

I'm coming. I promise. I'll be there soon!

September 24, 2003

I dream that I am nothing more than dry pulp and brittle paper. Then I am crumbling into bits and pieces.

"Oh, I am really nothing, nothing," I say.

And then I feel myself turning into dry dust, to nothing more than ashes blowing in the wind.

Ashes to ashes, dust to dust. My dream highlights the daily unfolding of this strange and wondrous process. One night I dream of how slowly the renovations are going, the next I dream of rebuilding, and now I must face destruction again. My dreaming self reminds me of the complexities of the process, letting me know that yes, it's slow, tedious, often discouraging work, but it's taking place nonetheless, a little here, a little there, one step forward, two steps back. It's like working on an old house. You never know what you'll find behind the walls, beneath the floors, or under the roof. I must deal with what is uncovered each day, address each issue that arises. Full recapitulation and total renovation require it!

I notice that my neck pain has eased. Somewhere in my dream it released, crumbled into ashes and dust perhaps, the first sign of real release that I've had in a long time!

I have to remember that I really am doing okay, that I'm almost single-handedly rebuilding myself in so many ways, my business included. I'm getting more work as I do more work on myself, two evolutionary projects progressing simultaneously, my inner work and my outer work. In both instances, so much has already changed; so many new doors of opportunity are opening, within and without. I must trust myself and the process.

Though I am not really made of paper and dust, my dream does illustrate some major aspects of this healing work, as I face the death of the old self and the old defenses, of that which is no longer necessary or productive. I will only more fully move on when my fears are finally faced and when I let go of everything without attachment or need, when I finally release it all, like so much dust in the wind.

The new me, however, is not flimsy, destructible paper but real flesh and blood, human, coursing with emotions and feelings. And I am strong—really strong.

Please let me have a good day. Please let me have a good day. Please let me have a good day.

Feeling fragile yet determined, I gather up the pieces of myself that crumbled during my dream. Sweeping up the ashes and dust, I mix a mortar and paste myself back together again. Building my energy body, I give my limbs energy and make them move. I breathe. Pulling air into my solar plexus and exhaling out my throat, I join these two painful areas, these two badly damaged chakras, with a prayer of encouragement: *Please help me stay together. Please help me to be strong. Please help me to believe in myself. Please help me to trust myself. Please help me to learn to love myself. Please help me to be prosperous so I can care for my children. Please help me to learn what love is.*

In the evening, I am overcome with pain and rising panic during parent's night at the middle school. I say goodbye to my children, telling them I don't feel well. Leaving them in the care of their father, I run to my car, drive home, and hop right into a hot bath. Lying in the steamy water, seeking relief from the explosive energy coursing inside me, I imagine detonation, blowing into smithereens, like in my dream disintegrating into nothing more than powdery dust. The dark side of me wants death, annihilation, the frightened side wants comfort. I cradle them both in my arms, holding them under the water, giving one its death and the other its comfort. And me? I'm in the middle wanting to run like hell and never come back!

September 25, 2003

I wake too early, annoyed by the kitten pushing things around on my dresser. She's getting bigger, but still acts like a baby, always wants something, a kitten that lost its mother at birth. Lying in the darkness, I cradle her in my arms and notice how different I feel today. Even before I get out of bed I sense that something has shifted. Last night I wrestled with death, got caught in its depression, but today my mind is already lighter and clearer, my body more solidly present.

I take another bath before I have to get the kids up for school. Soaking in the warmth, I realize that I did really well this month financially, that I have more than enough money to pay the bills, even something to put toward the tax bill. Once again I feel the shift, the lightness inside me wanting to anchor even deeper, asking me to finally get it, to get that I will be just fine.

September 26, 2003

My first thought is to go back to being hard on myself, to invoke an old regime, but I know that won't work. I need a change in tactics if I am to stay on the healing path. I must learn to be kind and caring to myself, to be soft and gentle, to be the light-minded, clear-headed being who arrived yesterday. But I am equally aware that it's okay to be angry and to express anger appropriately. Sometimes it's time to fight in a new way, with awareness and a strong sense of purpose. I sense that I will need my strong aware self today.

"I never feel safe," I tell Chuck when we meet, "except maybe under my covers, but I don't think that's a great place to be anymore. I'm always hunched, sure that an attack is imminent."

"Breathe, you can breathe," he says, sweeping his head from side to side, invoking the recapitulation breath.

"It hurts to breathe, it hurts to turn my neck."

"I know," he says. "Breathe gently, be very gentle."

Following his instructions, I take a slow breath and turn my head and almost immediately I know what happened. The "dog issue" spins its ugly tale. And just as my dream of the snakes pouring out of the bottle of pear juice predicted, the recapitulation breath is the key to clarity and resolution. As I breathe and sweep my head back and forth, I realize that by the time I'm in the barn and tied to a post I'm already partially out-of-body, already dissociating. It's what I've been re-experiencing for the past week or longer, that dissociated self, my depressed body weakened and feverish by its lack of wholeness. As I sweep my head back and forth, inhaling and exhaling, the fogs of time dissipate, the picture clears, and the memory plays like a movie. I clearly see my abuser going out of the barn, leaving me tied to a post, and something clicks. Flashing further back, I am there at another time, in a similar situation, tied up, when he walks out and leaves me alone.

"Men are coming!" I shout. "He's bringing those men!"

"Stay with it," Chuck says, "just let it happen."

I am in full panic mode, frantically trying to untie my hands when my abuser comes back, not with men, but with a dog. He yells at me, "Shut up!"

"Remember the doggy game? Remember the doggy game you stupid dog bitch?" One large hand around my neck, squeezing tightly, he screams into my ear. "Bitch! Just a dog bitch!"

"He's more physically violent than ever," I say to Chuck. "He's fuming because I'm not compliant. I fight him and the dog doesn't like it!"

This is all I can say as waves of pain envelop me. I hunch over in my chair. I spend a long time in those waves, in deep and bitter drooling pain, trying to look at the whole memory, trying to fully know it and release it. This is a big moment and yet I cannot fully release it. It stays inside me, swirling and churning like the black flecks in the pear juice of my dream. I try talking about it, but I can't. I don't know where to begin. I can't figure out how to release it either. I just want it to go away; I just want it to be over. I'm so tired of it all, so bored with my abuser, with what he did to me, and how I feel.

"Perhaps I had memories of the abuse, perhaps not everything was repressed," I tell Chuck. "The flashback that I just experienced, that memory within a memory, brought back a spark of having been there in that compromised position before, because as that flashback went through me I thought he was bringing back the group of men who had raped me before, but in this memory he only brought his dog. It's clear though that I had remembered being there before, as that previous memory of the men was so clear. Maybe I always knew. Maybe a part of me always knew, though I don't recall having any real memories, only a vague sense that something happened to me. I've always had that."

"After that issue with the dog, I went into a decline," I tell Chuck. "I was physically unwell for months on end, emotionally withdrawn and deeply depressed. I isolated myself, going to bed very early every night, moving through my days as Zombie Girl, feverish and half sick. During my freshman year in college the same decline came over me and I wandered around sick and depressed then too. Something must have triggered it."

"I think this is a turning point," Chuck says, and we leave it at that.

This memory feels particularly violent, perhaps a turning point in my recapitulation, but definitely more like a breaking point in my abuse because of the vicious way in which my abuser treated me. I was crying, terrified of the dog, and I have a feeling my abuser was angry with me because I upset the dog. The barking of the dog would give him away, perhaps spark an investigation, but I was in such pain that I couldn't cooperate. I fought back and it made him so angry that he got rough, rougher than usual. I reacted differently and he retaliated with violence beyond the norm, even for him.

What I couldn't articulate to Chuck was that my abuser let the dog have me. It's almost too disgusting to put into words. Have me? He raped me. The dog raped me. I was so relieved when it finished and finally ran off, but then my abuser raped me too. In the orchard, at his daughter's graduation party, months later, I knew I could get really hurt if I didn't cooperate. I didn't want to go through that again. Instinctively, something told me that if I just followed his instructions I'd keep myself safe. I went numb. Compliance meant protection and, ultimately, survival.

September 27, 2003

I dream that I'm lying naked on a wooden barn floor, partially covered by straw. I see my artwork hanging on the walls. I am exhausted and, indeed, people are telling me to rest. I am too weak to move. When I look down at my body I see that I am brown skinned. Then I am standing outside. Some men drive up in a truck. They have come to look at some junk that is for sale. They get out of their truck to have a look around. I go over to a pile of old chairs and clothing and find a pair of pants to put on. They're too big, but I don't care. I don't care about the men in the truck either. Then I ask someone why there's a field of flowers in the middle of nowhere because I see a tall stand of flowers off in the distance, growing in the middle of a dry empty field. They tell me that the large gladioli protect much smaller plants, which are beneath them. I walk closer and see that an herb garden has been planted, the tall gladioli like sentinels keeping the herbs safe. I notice then that I'm on a derelict old farm and I sense that it is being returned to its former glory.

I am struck by the significance of the men in the trucks, the clothing lying around. Have I returned to the empty storage shed where I sequestered my sixteen little girls in a dream a few weeks ago? In spite of the men, it seems I have finally reclaimed my energy in this dream, though I am still weak. It's as if I am newly born onto the straw-covered barn floor, like a fawn or calf. I am brown skinned in this dream, just coming to life, emerged from and merged with earthy darkness. The dream also seems to be about resting after the hard work of recapitulation and birthing of a new self. There is no pain of memory here, only the exhaustion of birthing into new life. Time to recuperate and not be bothered by the past anymore.

My artwork on the walls of the barn is indicative of the work that I have done to get to this point, for indeed my artwork has been a crucial part of the process, an expression of the deep inner work I've done. The dream is also about rejuvenation, about conserving energy for nurturing new life to come, for I am in the garden now.

I have no attachment to the men in the trucks; they are simply there. They can come and go, they can look at me, but I'm not really interested in them. They don't scare me and there is no emotional charge when I see them. I can choose to ignore them or to acknowledge that they are there, but the truth is that my energy is not drawn to them. I will not let them get in my way or interfere with me. They can't touch me or hurt me anymore.

My brown skinned body suggests the reconciliation of my darkness and my light, for I am mocha colored, a true mix of all parts of myself. I am whole and beautiful. The barn and farm are under renovation, as have been all the buildings in my dreams lately. I am newly planted, for I am both the protective gladioli and that which is growing beneath, guardian and nurturer both. In fact, the farm suggests a totality of healing; new growth, nurturance, nutrition, sustenance for body and soul, rest and rejuvenation; all very important changes taking place, both in dream reality and true reality.

I work at the studio in the afternoon. In the evening I try to relax. I have a glass of wine. Cry. Breathe, breathe, breathe. Don't let him kill me; don't, don't. He can't have me anymore. I remember my dream and go back into it. I am safe there. I am safe among the gladioli and the herbs. For now I am safe, though there is still more to come, that I am certain of.

Heavy rain, matching my somber mood, comes with the night, washing my sorrows away, the debris of my memories. Even as they wash out of me, I know that I still have to go back to that barn and to those memories again, to retrieve whatever is still there, to retrieve what has value. What could there possibly be of value? Well, me, of course!

September 28, 2003

The other day, I abruptly shut the door on a memory that flashed before me while I was talking to Chuck about the dog memory and I have yet to figure out really why I did that, though I was certain, at the time, that it was a good idea. Was it because I instinctively knew I couldn't handle it while I still have the dog memory to finish? Maybe it will come through more clearly now. The closing of the door, however, was abrupt and definite, a loud SLAM! A part of me is not ready!

My recent dream of the renovated farm—being born, taking time for rest and new growth—showed me a way to handle my trauma. Men in their trucks will come, but it's how I react to them that matters. Will they always be triggers? I don't think so, and the dream seems to concur, for in reliving and resolving the traumas the triggers lose their charges. It is the point of this recapitulation work, to dismantle the bombs within by facing what triggers them in the world. Thus, where men in trucks once sparked fear, in the farm dream I am complacent in their presence. "There they are again," I say to myself, almost bored, "but they can't hurt me now." I know all about them. I know who they are and what they did. I can live alongside them without feeling threatened or in harm's way. I can turn my attention to other things now. I can rest and care for myself. I have the power within myself to feel safe, all bombs successfully defused.

I understand what it means to nurture and protect and how to do that too, the way the gladioli in my dream protect the herbs growing beneath them. It's about interconnection, bridging within and without. This is only possible once all traumas and triggers are fully understood and integrated. One day there will be nothing left to hook me anymore, inside or outside of me, and that will signal my full healing. I also sense that there must be some greater purpose to my life, for there is a whiff of something to come, something I don't even know about yet. I only sense that it is something very rewarding.

The kids return from their weekend with their dad and anxiety, my old nemesis, creeps back in when they walk through the door, reminding me not to get too excited yet, there is still more recapitulating to do!

September 29, 2003

I'm dreaming a pleasant dream. I have lots of work, a nice house, and I drive a new car. It's raining, but I'm very happy as I drive the car into a large clean garage, feeling contented. Then the scene shifts. Now I'm in gloomy darkness, wading through knee deep water, through endless connecting pools, on a long journey. I walk into a canal of murky water, concrete walls rising high on both sides, tall marble figures along the tops of the walls staring down at me. I spy a small town far ahead in the distance, like a light at the end of a tunnel, but where I am all is in darkness, surrounded by water.

Things changed rapidly in my dream, from happiness to gloom, reminiscent of how quickly my life fluctuates in reality now, from the good mental status that I've achieved and begun to enjoy on occasion, to the murky past, with more to recapitulate still. In the dream, I am fully aware that my journey is not done, that I am still living in two worlds, and that each world is equally real. There are signs that I will go deeper still, perhaps not only in my recapitulation but in my real life as well. Life is a journey that never ends after all!

I realize I've been in a kind of avoidant daze since Friday. It all started when I abruptly cut off talking with Chuck, slammed the door on the first sighting of that new memory. I just couldn't talk about it, so I turned my back and went trudging away, away from the glimpse of utter emptiness and devastation that I saw. I walked FAST, trying not to look back, and I've been walking away ever since! It's like being in the dream on the farm, ignoring the men in trucks when they pull up, going about my business, determined not to look at them. I was not as accepting of them as I first thought. I was trying to pretend that they weren't there, that I didn't care, but the truth was that I was trying to keep from having to confront them. *I was avoiding them.* What I really need to do is confront them and get this damn thing over with!

In spite of my insistence that I need to gain a measure of detachment, I realize I will never have detachment if "they" still have power, and "they" always will unless I confront them.

September 30, 2003

I am jittery when I awaken, the memory pushing. I will meet with Chuck this morning. I'm already preparing for the worst, holding in and clenching down as usual. I need to get on with this recapitulation, let the memory come, but my body is closing in, perhaps not agreeing with my decision to go there. Or perhaps it's just doing what I've always asked it to do, keep its secrets from me.

I drive to Chuck's office. I don't want to do this. I don't want to do this. I don't want to do this. I sit down, take the EMDR pods that Chuck hands me and as soon as I feel their familiar pulsation I am gone. I can't utter a single word. I sink into pain and horror. Nothing is clear but I am lost nonetheless, lost in the past, lost in feelings, emotions, the brutal weight of what my body knows. Chuck sits opposite me, quiet, patiently waiting. We sit like that until the session ends, me hiding my face, him calmly waiting. I go home, eat something, and go to work. The memory presses, begging to be fully revealed, but I only want to get away from it, get out of it. I am sad, pursued all day by whatever it is.

I have already recalled that my last year of high school was bad. Now I understand how terribly depressed I was, withdrawn and lonely, and why. I understand the hysterical outbursts I'd have, involuntary explosions of raucous laughter that abruptly ended in choked back tears. My co-workers at the weekend job I had then witnessed it often enough. I can see them staring at me uncomprehendingly, seriously concerned after one of those sudden outbursts. They could see that something was not quite right, such bizarre behavior, but I always said I was okay, though the shock of such moments did not quickly wear off. I too knew that something was not quite right. I could retreat into myself for days, weeks, and months. It was my only salvation. How fearful I became of anything to do with boys or men, or anyone getting physically close! Closeness meant suffocation.

Here is what I know for sure: my abuser prepped me for the dog, in order to gain control and do what he wanted to do. I feel shame, the horrific degradation of it, how disgusting I am, how disgusting the act was. This too I know: he fucked me like a dog, talking, snarling in my ear, wearing me down. I didn't have all the words back then, but now I understand what it was that he did to me for all those years; he constantly groomed me to participate in whatever sick fantasy he came up with.

When I revisit the rapes in the barn, those with the dog and those with men, I hate myself. I loathed myself then and I loathe myself now as I recapitulate. I was in such pain and agony, but helpless, unable to save myself. I contemplated suicide. A girl at school tried to kill herself by taking pills and something else, but it didn't work. I stood at the end of the hallway looking out a large picture window and saw her being taken away by ambulance, her small thin frame covered by a white sheet. I wondered how many pills she'd taken and why it didn't work. As I dragged through my depressing, unhappy life I tried to think of other ways of committing suicide, quick and certain ways, but I didn't really want to die. I just wanted the pain to go away.

There was a mail strike during the spring of my senior year in high school. I was waiting to hear if I had gotten accepted into the two art colleges I'd applied to. Waiting for the strike to end was excruciating. Finally, phone calls came instead of the usual acceptance letters. Yes, I had gotten into both schools. Suddenly, I saw a way out. I just had to hang on, get through the time remaining, and then I would be free. At last, I could get the heck out of there!

Chapter 4

Cracking

October 1, 2003

I wake up shaking, collapse imminent, fear eating away at me, everything finally breaking through. I wrap my arms tightly around myself, my strength coming from inside, but I can't stop the shaking. Is this the truth, finally hitting? The truth that it happened? My whole body holds that truth. My whole body shakes with that truth. Believe it, it tells me. Believe it! Believe it!

I can't go back into that barn memory for very long, thoughts of it horrible, demeaning, disgusting, reminding me how much I hate myself, how much I absolutely loathe myself. It's nearly impossible to push such feelings aside and recall the positive aspects of my adult self that are carrying me forward toward new goals and new life now. As I continue to do this recapitulation I see those new goals and that new life off in the hazy distance, still out of reach, yet certain nonetheless. It's the ultimate reward for this difficult work and I have no doubt of its reality... some day.

Thoughts of the barn trigger recapitulation. Suddenly, I am back there again. My abuser walks in with his dog and his toolbox containing Vaseline, rope, and tools. I am a seventeen-year-old girl again, puffing up and away from her body with every frightened breath, blowing up until my teenage self escapes, just a balloon sailing away and only my body remaining, becoming what he wants, nothing more than a vagina and an anus, without feeling, not human. From my position on high I watch as he methodically goes about his strange business, poking and prodding. When he's done, I sink back into my body where it lies on the ground, writhing in pain and full of self-loathing.

I struggle through the day in a bad mood, the memory still weighing heavily. In the afternoon I drive down to see my parents and the damage done by a storm that blew through their area a few nights ago. I am shocked to see my parent's yard. No longer lush and shady, it is utterly destroyed, changed forever, close to a hundred trees knocked down, lying like fallen toothpicks. I stand and stare at the desolation, reminiscent of so many of the dreams I've had during my recapitulation, so like the destructive storms and tidal waves that my unconscious brought me, both signaling and supporting my changing self. I see how nature's intent to force change when necessary, both within and without, is without precedent. Clearly, change will come when it is time, and nothing can stop it or hold it back.

My parent's express no emotion, no wonder, no sadness; they just shrug their shoulders while I grasp it all at a deeper level, that it's my own process displayed before me; it's where I am, just as devastated. I won't drive over and see the damage on my abuser's property, despite their insistence. "It's much worse than here," they tell me, but I can't, I won't. Instead, I drive home and crawl into bed, cowering for an hour under the covers, emotionally exhausted. The fact that only the trees behind my parent's cottage and only my abuser's property were damaged does not escape my attention. Nothing else in the area was effected, barely a leaf ruffled. At the same time that I face the destruction of all the old beliefs about myself, as I go through my own ravaging process of change, the old world is literally being destroyed.

October 2, 2003

I am seventeen again and all I want to do is curl up and hide, pull the covers over my head and hide in the safety of my bed until the pain and anxiety lessen. I don't know why I feel this way. I know something is wrong, but I don't know what. I yearn only for a sleep of forgetfulness to take the pain from me so I can get on with my life.

As I recapitulate my seventeen-year-old self, I discover how truly miserable I was, deeply depressed, barely present, a hollow ghost of a person. I was serious, somber, extremely quiet, barely able to communicate, but also ever-watchful and alert, like an animal aware of its vulnerabilities, aware as well of its natural predators. My final year in high school was the worst year of my life. Although the abuse was inaccessible, the memories already repressed, the pain inside me was real. Although I could not really explain the moods, the withdrawal, or the self-loathing, the residue of that abuse tortured me daily. Every day I wished for death in order to be freed of the pain that had no name. Death seemed a logical solution. I thought about it a lot. I yearned for it, for eternal sleep, more as a romantic notion than in reality, but when it was not to be granted I went for real sleep as much as possible.

I was aware that people thought I was too quiet, sensed them looking for signs that I was okay, though they never spoke directly to me, nor would I have been able to share something that was such a mystery. Once my gym teacher heard me laugh and said: "Oh, she laughs!" I think she was relieved. How could I have spoken of something that even I could not pinpoint? It took me until I was in my forties to realize that there really was something legitimately wrong with me. When I first began seeing Chuck that was all I knew, that there was a disturbance inside me, something gnawing for escape. Though I had no idea what it was even then, I was finally ready to take it seriously. I knew by then that I did need to talk, that words would be my salvation, that talking would eventually lead me out of the darkness that I had lived in for so many years, that whatever it was inside me that wanted to reveal itself would eventually find its way to the light, that my time of pain was nearing an end.

Even now I would rather not revisit the pain, but I also know that I must make sense of it, try to find the meaning in all of it. I must fly back into those bad years and pick up that poor seventeen-year-old self and bring her forward into now. I am the only one who can rescue her. No one else can do that for me. I must comfort and protect her like one of my own children. I must bring her to a place of safety, confidence, and healing.

I never realized how painful healing would be.

October 3, 2003

I dream that I'm at a place of healing and cleansing, a center run by Chuck and Jeanne. Every action is observed; they are constantly taking notes. I take part in activities at the center. I go sledding, enjoy the thrill of speeding down a long snow-covered slope. There are two small dogs running loose outside, one black and one white. I pick them up and take them inside, making sure they're okay. I'm aware that things are coming to a good end, that

I'm learning how to participate in and enjoy life again, that I really am healing.

"It doesn't matter what the feelings are, just let them go through you," Chuck says when we meet in real time. "You don't have to search for details; you just need to release whatever is blocking your energy. The objective is to let go."

After seeing Chuck I go home and lie down for almost two hours. It's almost eleven in the morning when I peek out from under my covers. I feel like staying in bed all day but sense I'd better get up and move, go to work, though I have no energy. I am absolutely washed out. It must be all that letting go!

I go to the studio but am in too much pain to do much. I make a cup of coffee and drink only half of it before going back home where I crawl right back into bed. Abdominal pain courses through me and I get my first period in four months. I'm so woozy I can't get up. I argue with myself for a little while, but in the end decide to just give up for the day and stay in bed. This too is letting go, I tell myself.

By four in the afternoon I am still exhausted, still sad and empty, one minute angry because I have to go through this and the next trying to calm myself into accepting it. How I hate it though! I feel robbed of all desire for life. Is that what I'm trying to win back here, my desire for life? I remember my dream of being at Chuck and Jeanne's healing center and the implication that life will one day be enjoyable, but first I must take care of what needs to be taken care of. Those two little dogs, the black one and the white one, need to be taken care of, the light and the dark sides of myself assimilated. The reconciliation of those two opposites will be my ultimate salvation. But could they also indicate memories of being raped by dogs, more memories still needing recapitulation?

How I yearn to be a happy and loving being, able to find pleasure in my life and my work, but I know that won't happen if I don't let the memories go. I keep thinking that I'll be better soon, that in one more week I'll be better. Maybe that's all I need to do, take small steps, one day at a time, work on the release for this day, get through this day's recapitulation. In the end I will be free. Someday I will be free.

October 4, 2003

I dream that I am in an art studio. Gentle breezes blow through the open windows and fill the studio with good energy. The air is filled with feathers, floating and twirling about, catching the sunlight. I am lighthearted and happy, full of good energy too as I dance across a table piled high with art supplies and half-completed art projects. Stepping lightly and surefootedly, I leap off the end of the table and float through the air, as light as a feather, and like a trained dancer I land lightly on the tips of my toes.

In spite of my happy dream, I was up and down all night with severe bleeding, running to the bathroom, blood seeping down my legs. I am hopeful that it will lessen during the day, though I have no energy and even less inclination to go to work. Try as I might to psych myself for the day ahead, my intentions prove futile. I am no happy being of light today, no floating feather, but heavy, bloody depression. I decide to stay in bed again.

Healing energy seeps in under the covers while I doze. Tiny fingertips, with a cooling touch, soothe my pain, massaging lightly, drawing forth the certainty that lots of calmness and lots of persistence will be necessary, lots of faith in myself and my abilities if I am to totally heal, regain my physical and mental strength and stamina, and move on into new and happy life. As this gentle massage is happening it also dawns on me, so abundantly clearly and with a deep sense of knowing, that I will complete this journey and somehow make this healing recapitulation work my future work in this life. I am certain that it can and will do its transformative work on me now and for a long time to come. I am aware that I still have a few more struggles to contend with, but I am certain that I will live a good, successful, and fulfilling life. It's my time now.

Please help me keep these positive thoughts. Please help me regain my strength and my energy. Please help me have faith in myself and my abilities. Please help me to forgive myself and others. Please help me learn how to trust and to love. Please help me teach my children to be good citizens of the world.

I've discovered something important today; that change will not happen, not even consciously-willed change, such as adopting new habits, if I don't rid myself of the root cause of my problems. I have to release the all-pervasive fear, completely eradicate it, or any idea of change is just another cover up, another false idea that I'm taking care of the issue. The intent to change by itself, no matter how strong, isn't going to have any effect without doing the actual hard work of change, in this case, the complete and conscious eradication of what controls me.

Eradication of the fear will provide the room for change, and only then will my body be capable of handling change. Until the fear completely leaves, I am just pushing it around inside me, restocking it, re-encapsulating it in some other body part, not getting rid of it as I should. And now that I'm aware of the reason for the fear I can deal with it better; I can tackle it now. How can you tackle something you don't know about? When I say I can tackle it now, I don't mean I will fight it in the old way. I mean I will let it flow out of my body. I will let it go! Maybe that's what all this bleeding is about.

Help me, please, all of you, Jeanne and all my spiritual guides, to get rid of the fear, to be free to get on with the life of fulfillment that I envision and am working toward. And thank you for all you have done so far. I need you.

I am beginning to think that I do indeed need to write about this process of recapitulation, to get it out into the world, releasing it not only from my body but into a life of its own in some creative fashion. I am certainly capable, but it requires that I let go of the fear, ALL of it, in order to be able to write my story and let it be released into the world to be read by others. That would be the ultimate letting go of fear!

The fear, as if sensing my decision to let it go, grips me all day, but its persistence only leads me to understand it better and I am thankful for that. I notice how it creeps out of the dark storage tanks I've kept it in all these years and settles upon my body, how I tense against it, automatically resistant. Well, Mister Fear, from here on out, I will be taking a different tactic!

October 5, 2003

I feel beaten, pummeled, left in shards. I have no energy. I just lie in bed, weak and depressed. Am I just feeling sorry for myself? Don't I need to acknowledge the sadness in some way? Extend a little empathy to myself?

Inertia has been a big problem these past few days, my depression intensified by this mysterious heavy bleeding I've been experiencing. I thought I was done with all that! Perhaps this bleeding is part of the recapitulation, my body finally purging itself of all the old stuff it has held onto all these years. And I have to say, though involuntary, this bleeding seems appropriate, like the ancient practice of bloodletting to restore a sick body to health. Bleed on, if that's what this is all about, and get rid of the fear while you're at it!

Without my consent, sexual abuse was imposed on me and determined the kind of life I would lead. I have been a sexually abused person my entire life; I see that now. I understand that it has defined and controlled me on so many levels, but that it has also gotten me where I am now. Sexual abuse has provided the strong backbone of my existence too, so I must respect it rather than hate it. I must extricate from it the inherent good strengths and advantages that such a life afforded me and integrate them into who I am becoming, for though I suffered greatly I invariably gained a great deal as well.

I must constantly remind myself that nothing is more important than this process of disassembling and reassembling myself, nothing more important than taking control of my life now. This is my time to live and I am taking it. It's what this inner work is all about; changing my perceptions of myself, transforming myself from depressed victim of sexual abuse to fully alive individual. I must give myself permission to become the me that I could not be in the past, the me that has been waiting and wanting to live. And although I may occasionally get lost in the dust and debris of this process, having to contend with inertia and guilt, depressed and not able to see where to go and what to do next, I intend to stay on this path, for it is truly a path of healing.

October 6, 2003

I am a male knight in shining armor, in a castle high on a cliff, a sword at my side. As opposed to previous dreams that took place in ancient castles, this castle is stylishly modern. The view is serene and beautiful. As I stand at a large window and gaze upon the distant landscape, a voice speaks, telling me that I am still tightly entrenched in my recapitulation, and rightly so, as I still have deep work to do. It tells me that I must go through each step of recapitulation and release if I am ever to be fully present in my life, if I am ever to fully enjoy this beautiful castle, the view, and the surrounding lands. As I turn from the peaceful scene outside the window, I am immediately drawn into the vast darkness of the castle. The voice tells me that everything I must still encounter is in this darkness.

As I draw my sword and proceed into the darkness, a shadowy female figure appears. Dressed in a floor length gown, she follows close behind. I am told that I must complete every task that appears before me if I am to free myself of this shadowy presence, and yet I am also told that this shadowy presence is crucial to this journey, a part of it, a part of myself. I am informed by the voice that I am both the male knight and the female shadowy presence and that I must enable and draw equally upon both feminine and masculine energies as I undergo this recapitulation process. I am told that I must bring the yin and yang of who I am into full consciousness and action. Rather than relying solely on the feminine aspects of my being, the maternal, nurturing side that I have focused on as regards my child self, I must also incorporate aggressive male energy when necessary. Sometimes it is right for even a pacifist to fight, I am told.

I am directed to take up my sword of determination and force my way forward when appropriate, not defensively as in the past but confrontationally, with the intention of ridding myself of all that does not belong to me or serve me. Nothing must stop me, I am told, for it is only through such forceful action that I will penetrate the mysteries of the self, complete my tasks, and finish this recapitulation. Taking these words to heart, I charge forward, fully embodying the strong and determined knight that I am. Bravely confronting what lies ahead, I sweep the darkness with my sword, and though I cannot see a darn thing, I am aware that I am accomplishing my task, slicing through all that blocks my path.

As I work my way forward, going from dark room to dark room, I am told that everything has the potential to be good and that one day I will live peacefully in this modern castle, with all that is in the darkness, and the light too, fully revealed and fully known, with my masculine and feminine sides fully expressed and enjoying equal partnership.

In the end, I am told, all *will* be recapitulated and resolved, and life *will* be good. That is certain. I am also told that I am the creator, the director, and the chief actor in my own reality play, that I am responsible for all parts and all scenarios, that everything was designed a long time ago by a higher aspect of myself. And then I learn that my higher self is the voice that is speaking to me throughout the dream!

There was nothing frightening in this dream. In fact it was laden with a peaceful determination. The voice of the higher self spoke to me so calmly and encouragingly throughout the dream, assuring me that all is going according to plan, that my life is unfolding as it should, that *everything*, including my life as a victim of sexual abuse, was planned. Not only that, but it was planned and agreed upon by me! So much for my supposition yesterday that sexual abuse came unbidden into my life! The voice implied that everything was created and set in motion a long time ago, that all I had to do was enter life and live it, and then, when the time was right, *remember*. I was told that all I have to do now is complete the final challenges I have laid out for myself, this recapitulation tops among them!

October 7, 2003

I meet with Chuck and without hesitation go back into the barn, into the nagging remainders of memory that have been haunting me for weeks. Like the aggressive knight of my dream, I know I must cut through all the blockages in my path if I am to access the full truth of what really happened to me when my abuser brought his dog into the barn along with his Vaseline, his tools, and his rope.

I sit huddled before Chuck and tell him as much as I can. Haltingly, through clenched teeth, I choke out one word and then another. One sentence meets another until the bare essentials of the tale are pretty much sketched out. I am still in the midst of the recapitulation when the session ends, aware that I haven't told him everything. I drive home very carefully, barely able to see in this world, crawl into bed, and tumble right back into the memory, every ugly part of it. In fear and trembling, I call Chuck and leave him a message. Then I wait, and wait, and wait, and wait for him to call back. It takes a long time.

"I have to tell you the bad stuff because I'll never get beyond it if I don't," I say, my voice that of a frightened child. "I kept thinking it wouldn't matter if I didn't tell you all the details."

"Oh no," he says, "you have to tell them. That's how you let them go. Okay?"

There is silence on my part as I struggle with what I must tell him. I hear him breathing, patiently waiting for me to speak.

"Tell me," he finally says, very gently. "It's okay."

And then I do. Like ugly black tar, thick and sticky, I pull the story out, gagging on every word, about my abuser pounding the stick tail into my anus and the finger penetrating my vagina and the sneering talk in my ear; the words he used, "doggie way" and "bitch," and how he told me I liked it because I orgasmed, and then he pulled the stick out and fucked me in the ass, "the way dogs do it," and then he got his dog on me and I felt Sharp! Sharp! Sharp! PAIN! And I saw the dog run away and I thought, "Oh good, it's over now," but it wasn't, because my abuser fucked me again because now I was "a real bitch," now I was "a hot bitch," and then he stuck the stick back in and walked away, leaving me like that.

"I had to pull the tail out. I had to pull the stick out," I croak. "Why did he hate me so much?"

"He didn't hate you," Chuck says. "He was just so caught up in his own perverted sexual fantasies, his own very strong and sick drive."

"During the rape at the graduation party, which happened after this, I did whatever he wanted. I was obedient."

"You knew by then that you had to be, in order to survive; it was a matter of survival. You had gained knowledge," Chuck says. "All that had happened came crashing down on you and it became the catalyst for getting you out of there. It's crashing down again now as you recapitulate and you have to talk about it because you can't let it dominate the second half of your life the way it dominated the first half."

"Deep down inside, I think I always knew what had happened to me, but I didn't know what to do with it, and if it ever came up I squelched it as best I could. I pushed it down as deeply as possible and covered it over and left it there, like a dog covering its shit. But now, with time and memory, it has come surging up and I can't squelch it down again. I have to let it out."

"You can't let it take over your life," Chuck says.

"I won't," I promise. "Just for a day, to recover from the whole shock of it, the whole-body shock."

I hang up and make a cup of tea, my hands shaking, my body shaking too, and read this message on the tag of my teabag: *You are not a human being having a spiritual experience, but a spiritual being having a human experience.*

It jolts me right back into the mystery of this life, of life in general and my dream in the castle. It reminds me of who I really am, hints at the bigger picture as was revealed as I cut into the darkness of that castle, that I am a multi-faceted being, that I created this life, and that there is so much more to come. It's all about facing and fully knowing the truth of the self, all parts, so that I may ultimately discover for myself that, yes, I am indeed a spiritual being. Though at this point I still do not know the deeper meaning or greater purpose of this life, perhaps one day soon I will find out.

"Go where your heart takes you," Jeanne says, *"on paths that lead where the heart says GO! Follow the echo of that command! Follow it forever, where the heart leads. You will know. You will know. Spiritual path! Follow your own heart. Spiritual awakening! Go there!"*

I am wobbly all day. I keep thinking about just getting through the week, that I just need to get through this week and I will be okay. Maybe that was it, maybe that was the last of the memories. Maybe it will be better now. When I talked to Chuck I kept saying, "I'm alright, I'm alright," but I was hurt and angry, my voice brittle, ready to crack.

I try to come back, to shift, to get back into my body, back into this reality, but I am drained and weak, still in as much pain as ever. I try to relax into this body I have selected to be in, this human form that my spirit resides in, this body I have never felt comfortable in, that I have dragged around all these years and now don't know what to do with. If I truly am a spiritual being having a human experience then I must find a way to like who I am, and to perhaps someday love myself too.

I do hope that I will achieve some joy in the end, some satisfactory ending, like in my castle dream, and that I will one day know the reason behind all of this, why I came here to go through all of this. And I can only hope that one day peace *will* come.

October 8, 2003

Please help me. It's only six in the morning and already I'm shaking. Please help me get through the day. I have to get the kids up and off to school and I have to go to work. I have to live in the present, in spite of what happened in the past. I am strong. Chuck said so. I can do this. I can do life. If I keep working I will be okay. If I stay focused my mind is clear. And I must remember to eat and breathe. Chuck told me that yesterday too, eat and breathe.

I send the kids to school, go for a walk, and then drive to the studio. Though emotionally shattered and distracted by the recent rash of memories I actually get a good amount of work done. Money worries pop up immediately as I ponder what to do about my car, which has been having issues. I remind myself that everything will be fine.

Night. I'm home, in the safety of my own room with the door shut, lying on my bed, scrunched up in a little ball. It's not that comfortable, but it's comforting. I'm in pain, but I feel safe and alone, which is also safe; being alone is very safe. I need this aloneness. It's a form of self-preservation, especially when the overwhelming terror and the strong desire to disappear come, when the urge to wipe myself off the face of the earth comes, the urge to do something drastic for the pain because it's killing me. I refuse, however. As exhausted and in pain as I am, I refuse to be overpowered by my abuser ever again. I will not let him have control. Although his sick exploits became my experiences, they don't have to be mine forever. Like an archeologist, I will continue my dig, excavating my long lost body and soul, scraping clean the artifacts of self, eradicating him like the remnants of some ancient disease. I will not leave one stone unturned, one particle of myself unexamined, nor one iota of sickness inside me.

As today ends, I am one more day beyond his sickness, another day closer to my own salvation, another day closer to the peaceful castle on the cliff.

October 9, 2003

I wake in the middle of the night, hot with anger. Tossing in bed, reality blurs. I have no idea where I am. I can barely make out the wall opposite me. It's not familiar and then it looks very familiar. I seem to be in my old childhood bedroom. I see the outline of the closet doors, dark against the lighter painted walls. I am a child again, writhing in fear, but I am also an adult writhing in anger as the room shifts from the present to the past and back again. I am caught in an undulating time warp, unable to get my bearings. I finally break away and sit up. I must ground myself!

I fall back to sleep and dream that I'm getting my hair done. The hairdresser shows me a special vacuum cleaner that sucks up everything in its path. The anger begins to churn again and I watch as it spews out of me in projectile vomiting all over the hair salon, black as tar.

"Don't worry," I tell the hairdresser, "it's not what you think. I'm not sick. It's just anger."

I hope her vacuum cleaner can do what she says it does!

In the morning, anger still boils inside me. I try not to take it out on my son. He stayed up late again. I'm worried that he isn't getting enough sleep and doesn't use his time properly. I realize it's his challenge in this lifetime, but it doesn't help that he won't get up when I call him. In the end, I have to yell at him, something I hate doing. I'm not really angry at him. It's just this old and bitter anger, leftovers from my experiences with my abuser that have me fuming. I AM ANGRY! ANGRY! ANGRY! There, I admit it. I'M FUCKING ANGRY!!!

After the kids head off to school, I take a fast and furious run, breathing out waves of anger, running and releasing, my feet pounding, pummeling out the anger in my body. Afterwards, I beat on my bed with a big stick. BEAT! BEAT! BEAT! And something shifts. Now I have energy! Anger gives me energy!

The anger stirs inside me all day. Snakelike it climbs higher and higher like fiery Kundalini energy. I keep busy at the studio, working, moving, anything to keep it under control, for I find that keeping one step ahead of it seems to be the best tactic, though its flickering flames lick at me all day. Flashbacks come too. I see my abuser's leer, his drooling fixation on my genitals. I turn my eyes away, focus on something else, try to forget, though I cannot deny that I had similar flashbacks while running today. I'll have to recall them more fully, relive them, wear out the pain and intensity of them just as I've had to do with all the other memories, until they no longer carry a charge.

The most recent memory with the dog in the barn is still fresh and painful, woundingly sore. I haven't achieved distance from it yet. It still makes me shake, still makes me hide in my bed like a frightened child.

October 10, 2003

"I just want to get under the covers and stay there," I tell Chuck when we meet.

"Is that how you feel right now?"

"Yes, but life intrudes and I can't stay there for too long, just long enough to get my fix. The pull to stay there is lessening though. Life tugs at me a little bit more each day."

"Yes," Chuck says, "now it's time to turn to life."

"Please, please help me," I pray. "I feel like I'm falling apart, splintering. Maybe a new memory is coming, or more of the last one trying to show me something, but I can't handle it now. I don't want to hold onto fear anymore, but it's painful to let it go too. I don't know how to let go without breaking apart. All day I've felt pursued. All day I've wanted to hide, but I haven't let myself. I pushed myself to get through to the end of the day and then I took a long walk, trying to shake it off, but whatever it is has followed me home and here I am, stuck with it, and so uncomfortable in my own body! Please help me find a way to not be afraid all the time. I don't want to be afraid anymore."

And then it becomes clear what I can't escape, that a new memory is trying to make itself known. All the signs are present. I crawl into bed, seeking some of the old comforts, seeking freedom from the pain, but before I know it I am falling, falling, heading right toward a pit of darkness where the snakes of fear lie waiting.

"Just breathe," says Chuck when I call him in a panic.

"I can't, I can't catch my breath!"

"Breathe slowly. As you breathe, your body relaxes. You need to relax into it, relax into your body by breathing."

"Why am I doing this to myself?"

"I don't think you are doing it to yourself," he says. "It's just happening *to* you. Breathe, breathe, breathe! Not too much, just enough to quell it, but not enough to start anything."

"I just want to get through tonight! I just want a night without fear!"

"You can do it," he says.

Okay, I can do it. I am exhausted enough to sleep and finally drift off, though I toss and turn quite a bit. The phone rings a few times in the dead of night. I don't answer it, but the ringing leaves me slightly disoriented, wondering what kinds of tricks the universe is playing on me.

October 11, 2003

Last night, I dreamed about the man who likes me, who continues to pursue me, who still shows interest though I give him absolutely no encouragement. I can't remember the details of the dream, but they centered around the fact that I never feel that good when I'm around him, which is so true!

It often feels as if his real intent is to capture me, as if I were some strange and exotic butterfly he's been in pursuit of for a long time. He has a habit of just showing up at the studio and then he stays for a long time, soaking up my energy, hungry for whatever he thinks I have. "The Amazing You!" he says, and when he says that it feels as if he's actually taking something from me, siphoning some of my "amazing" energy, adding it to his collection, the same way he collects bits and pieces of stuff. I've noticed his van filled to the brim with who knows what. I don't want to be collected and stashed away, taken out of my box only to be admired and then packed away again. My instincts tell me to stay away from him and indeed I offer no incentives, yet he pursues me still!

Oddly enough, he stops by the studio in the afternoon. Come to collect my "amazing" energy perhaps? He invites me out again, says he wants to be friends. He pries, asks probing questions, and when I give him nothing starts in talking too much about himself. He's an interesting guy, in some ways, though I remain staunchly uninterested. When he finally grasps that there is nothing to be gained he gives a sad sigh and leaves.

I take a walk after work, hiking at my favorite spot. Jeanne tells me not to go down into the far meadow where in the gathering dusk I see a shadowy figure sitting on the bench at the trail's end. And my inner little girls all chime in too, saying, *"Turn back, don't go, don't go, turn back!"* The bridge spanning the river is beautifully lit by the golden setting sun, so ethereal, and the voices, with their high-pitched warnings, are so golden and ethereal too.

"Turn back now! Save yourself. Turn back now!"

I heed the voices, grateful for their insistence, for I am not interested in being energetically compromised.

It gets suddenly darker as I hurry through the woods that will take me back to the parking lot, a little freaked out at having to feel my way in the dark. I keep wondering if the shadowy figure is behind me. I tell myself that the experience is good for me, part of facing my fears, an opportunity to test my ability to relax in my body and let go. I finally get to my car and ride out of there like a bat out of hell! Safe at last!

For the most part, I keep to myself, a private, introverted person. I don't have friends. I prefer it that way. The result is that nobody really knows that much about me, only what I've been willing to reveal. I'm a mystery even to myself. Here I am, 51 years old, and I don't even know who I am. I was married for sixteen years and at the end of that time I said to my ex-husband: "You don't know who I am. You don't know what I think," but really I was saying it to myself. "I don't know who I am, and I don't know what I think or feel," and it was the truth.

At this point, I know a lot of things I didn't know about myself a few years ago, but I still don't know who I really am. I keep thinking I should be dead, but I'm not. So why am I not dead? For what purpose am I still alive? My abuser didn't kill me and I didn't kill myself, so there must be a reason for my continued existence. What is my purpose in this life? I can't believe I'll be selling painted children's furniture for the rest of my life. I wait for the answer to be revealed—hopefully sooner rather than later!

Though I do wish for a person to share my life with, I have to do this inner work on my own and it actually helps to be alone, to have the full focus and the full brunt of experiences all to myself. Such a fantastic journey with such a tremendous amount still to learn! I regret nothing, and yet I hope for everything. At the same time, it's not the right time for a partner. I am all I have right now, and I will just have to be enough!

October 12, 2003

I dream that I'm back in the house I grew up in. The place is falling apart. Leaky pipes in the cracked ceilings bulge and drip, puddles forming on the floors, everything about to collapse under the weight of decay. I find an abandoned baby in the basement. I'm a little miffed that it was left there for me to rescue, that it's assumed I'll take care of it. A little girl appears too, another being to care for. The whole scenario reminds me of how my parents never dealt with anything that needed to be taken care of, structural and emotional problems alike. Just ignore things and eventually they go away, seemed to be their motto, but I know that's not really true, that everything eventually must be reckoned with. As I am thinking this, I look out the window and see my brothers coming toward the house, talking and laughing together, and I know there is hope. They are carpenters and builders, and I know they will take care of things here, so I can leave and move on. I don't have to worry anymore about my parents or the choices they made. I am being freed to go live my own life, as I wish.

Then I dream that I'm in a small apartment in an old high rise building in New York City. Here, cats and kittens need to be taken care of. Things are crumbling, needing repairs, and the toilet leaks. I don't want to be in yet another deteriorating structure, with things going wrong, with responsibilities foisted upon me. But then I realize that this is not my house or my mess!

"Don't take on other people's issues!" I tell myself.

I wake up, feeling a great need to keep my world small and manageable, to live in my house and work in my studio, stay limited to the road between them, stopping only at places I need to stop at along the way; the gas station, the grocery store, the library; to not interact too much, to not expose myself to too much, to limit my contact with the outside world, to be here because this is where I find myself, but also to be as withdrawn as possible. But I also realize how limiting that attitude is, and besides, it's the way I lived my childhood, as withdrawn as possible. Is that really what I want? At the same time, it's what I must do as I continue to focus on this healing process. I must pull inward and save my energy for this recapitulation. And so, yes, I must stay within the narrow and known, at least for the time being.

A part of me says that it doesn't want to be in this world at all, that it wants as little involvement as possible. But I realize that's the frightened child speaking, the petrified, abused child inside me who still wants to remain hidden and safe. She doesn't really want to be here in this body because all she knows is that life in this body is painful and frightening. "If I just stay hidden, then I am safe," she tells me. That sentiment offered the only solution to a childhood of neglect and abuse. The baby and the little girl in my dream remind me that my parents didn't have a clue as to what their kids really needed. We were left up to our own devices, to survive or not. Somehow we all flourished.

Now, as I change and begin to ponder new life, as I begin to allow myself to feel happy and secure, and as I venture out into the world in a new and different way, I begin to gain some confidence. I begin to wake up to the possibility that life can offer more. In the old days, when I did that, I wouldn't get very far because—WHAM!—something would come along to remind me that the world is not safe and that to be too happy is foolish, and I'd crawl right back into my burrow, happy to hunker down and become safely invisible again. I know that my world now is not the same world as when I was a child, nor even the same world as a few years ago for that matter, but the old fears are still deeply embedded in my body and psyche. They still weigh heavily as I recapitulate, revealing that they were legitimate fears once, showing me how they protected me and kept me safe. But the old voices are countered with new voices now, calling me to be alert, awake and aware, rather than shy, fearful, and withdrawn. They encourage me to be daring and unafraid, to face my fears and declare them largely unnecessary now, guiding me in how to be fearless as I walk my new path of heart, teaching me that there is more to this world than meets the eye.

My dreams instruct me that it's not advisable to live in the old world anymore, nor to take on other people's issues, but to free myself once and for all. And that's why this recapitulation is so important and this moment in it so critical, for I am called more loudly to detach from the old and prepare for the new. And that I must do on my own, for no human protector will arrive to save me or travel this part of the journey with me. Everything is in my own hands.

"Oh Jeanne, and my guides, please help me," I pray. "I need help. I feel so alone and in such need of help, even though I know I must do this on my own."

I have rarely asked for anything in my life and only recently begun to realize that it's okay to ask for help, that everyone needs help at certain times in their lives and there is no shame in that. I don't ask for too much, only what I need, and sometimes not even that, but it has been shown to me that if I ask I will receive.

I meditate before heading out for the day. Immediately my inner girls come pestering, telling me to just stay in bed, to let the world go on without us.

"Don't go," they say, "don't leave us! Stay here; it's not safe, it's not safe."

"It's okay, I'm an adult now," I say, "I can take care of us. I can do this. I am strong."

As if to prove that they are stronger they pull me right out of my body. Like a cluster of balloons, we rise. I break free by breathing into my heart center, by doing quick, shallow heart centered breaths. In a matter of seconds the tug of war is over.

"*Open your heart, open your heart,*" Jeanne says, as I plunk back down into my body. "*It has been so closed up. Open your heart! Everything you need to know and learn will come through your open heart.*"

And with that I jump out of bed!

It's my son's fifteenth birthday. I call over to his dad's and wish him a happy birthday, letting him know that we'll have cake and presents together on Tuesday night when they return home from a long holiday weekend. Then I venture out into the world, drive over to the studio and put in a few hours of work.

Later in the day, I go home and crawl into bed, my inner girls getting the better of me after all. The truth is, I've been recapitulating all day, reliving how I felt in those weeks after the rape with the dog in the barn, when I was sick and withdrawn for weeks on end, most of which I spent in bed. I'd drag myself through the school day, getting into bed at an early hour every evening, feeling sad, sad, sad. I'd pull the covers over my head and just lie there in a numb state, blocking out the world as best I could. I could hear everyone else in the house, but I'd just stay in my room, safely isolated, slightly feverish and far, far away from everything. Nothing touched me or intruded. I think maybe my little girls were trying to get me to remember this when they insisted I stay home and in bed this morning, letting me know that we haven't finished the memory yet, that we haven't investigated what happened in the aftermath.

I stay in bed now, consciously giving in to the girls, letting them show me what I need to learn. Perhaps this will be the last recapitulation and so I will not fight it. I will not fight the fatigue, the depression, the sad feelings, such old stale feelings. I recall what Jeanne said this morning about opening my heart, and I breathe slowly into my tight little heart, into where it hurts so badly, into where there is just lonely sadness and old bruising, the soreness of my childhood pain. I must go through it again, let myself feel and weep and heal. I must finish this recapitulation and find out the real reason why I'm here.

After a while I get out of bed. It feels good to be up and moving, pumping energy through my body. I vacuum the living room and rearrange the furniture, letting the feelings of my seventeen-year-old self flow through me as I work, even though they are not smooth and flowing feelings at all but wrenchingly painful. I let her sadness tell me the truth, that I barely made it through the last months of the twelfth grade, so overwhelmed was I by the pain, confusion, and sadness of what I was hiding from.

"Do you think that guy should be behind bars?" Chuck asked the other day, speaking of my abuser. It threw me when he asked that question, and I reacted as if he'd punched me in the stomach, but I couldn't stay there.

"Yes, of course I think that, that he should be punished," I said, "but you can't ask that of me! Oh God, I can barely take it all in myself, and I don't really care about him. I only care about keeping myself alive through all of this. Okay?"

I promise myself that I will write about this someday, warn the world to be careful, to be aware, to look, really look at the children, because they do not tell you everything. Children are as complicated as adults, perhaps even more so because they don't pretend to have all the answers. They are more open to new ideas as they constantly seek to figure things out, as they look for explanations for things they don't understand, things that children shouldn't have to worry about, like fear and pain and sexual abuse, things that even some adults have never had to deal with.

At night, I kick all thoughts and memories of my abuser out of my bed. I leave them lying on the cold floor beside the socks I took off and then I snuggle into my warm bed, alone at last, intending to sleep soundly through the night.

October 13, 2003

I dream that I'm standing inside a cavernous warehouse situated high on a hill, looking down upon the nighttime lights and shadows of a town in the valley below. The buildings in the town are no longer decaying or under construction, as in previous dreams, but whole now. I see that they are all empty, cleared out. Hollow feelings of sadness, of deep loss, sweep through me as I realize that I'm leaving this place that once was so important to me. The old world is done now. It's high time to move on.

It really is time to leave it all behind and move on now, to take the next step on this journey to wholeness and find the means to release what I have held in abeyance for so long, my feeling and emotional self. It is constantly clear to me that I must suffer again if I am to gain access to that self, that I must learn everything about my past and myself, who I was and who I might be in the future. It is only through taking this painful journey into my private hell that I will fully recover all that I have kept from myself, and heal in the process, as strange as that may seem. It is only by suffering that I will be truly free.

I take a long walk on this nice sunny fall day, the air so crisp, the leaves colorful against the clear blue sky. I notice that even a beautiful day doesn't seem to matter when I feel like this though. I could kill myself on a day like this and it wouldn't matter. Is that what I feel like doing, killing myself? Not now, but I sure did back then, when I was a kid and in such pain. "I don't feel good," I would tell myself. "I'm sick. It's okay to go to bed because I'm sick." In declaring myself sick I'd give myself permission to withdraw, and I would pamper and comfort myself by getting under the covers and going numb, falling as easily into numbing nothingness as into a dream. It was a kind of death in itself.

Shaking myself free of the overlapping of worlds, the old gloom a little too close, I walk quickly, breathing, breathing myself back to the reality of this beautiful day and the progress I'm making. Afterwards, I drive to the studio and quietly set about getting things done. I let my mind go on its merry way while I work, planning how I might someday write about all of this, perhaps a memoir penned by *Slave Girl*. I doubt I could do it under my own name at this point, for I am still too hurt, too afraid, and too humiliated to expose myself. I am full of self-disgust and self-loathing, in agonizing pain, knowing that I did all those things, that I was a participant in such deviant activity, that I am no better than he. I don't know if I will ever come to terms with that.

If I dare to write about this it will mean that I am ready to publicly speak about it too. Even if I never fully expose who he was, my writing this personal story could be a device to help others open up and talk about their own sexual abuse, to find someone trustworthy to confide in, and to validate their own experiences. I know that if you keep it in you will slowly destroy yourself and then the abuser, even if dead, will still be in control; he will have won. Only words can stop him, even if only spoken aloud in the privacy of a therapist's office. That much I have learned is true.

"How did you do it? How did you survive?" Chuck once asked me.

"Sheer luck and will power," I said, "and knowing that my abuser was never going to get to the real me, that he couldn't get to my thoughts, and no matter how far he reached into me, or poked a stick into me, or hurt me, he could never reach far enough to destroy that tight little fist of spirit that I kept safely protected deep inside me."

I still feel it bundled up there, a hard nut to crack, but little by little I chip away at it, the lumpy weight of it more real than my own fist holding the pen that is writing these words.

I know now that I was merely a pawn in his game, but I refuse to think of myself as a victim, as of no importance. I *was* something. I *am* something. My story is not a story of abuse alone but a story of transformation, not of death and destruction but of transcendence.

October 14, 2003

I dream that I walk into an art gallery. As soon as I step inside my body explodes. I see my hands go flying off, one landing on the back of a chair, the other on top of a large framed painting on the wall. My feet shoot off in opposite directions too.

"Stay calm, you can handle this," I say, as the rest of me bursts into a million pieces, as I watch myself fly through the air, like so much confetti shot from a canon.

I'm vibrating, not quite in my body when I wake up, still in pieces. It's all I can do to stay present. I try pulling myself together by breathing, try calming the vibrations, but the thought of seeing Chuck in a little while sends shockwaves right through me and pretty soon I'm in full panic mode. Am I still afraid of him? He only wants to help me. Oh God, I feel so ill! Is this the longed for emotional release? Am I finally letting go? It feels like I really am bursting apart, and I'm scared. I'm fucking scared.

"I'm in a dark hole and I can't get out," I tell Chuck when we meet. "It feels safe in here, but I know it's not. I know I need to climb out, but just thinking about leaving and I start to shake. It's like my dream, the feeling that I'm just going to explode."

"I know," he says.

"I'll be okay. I know it's part and parcel of the struggle on the long road to redemption. Don't worry, I can do this."

"You have been doing it."

"I know, and once I've finally fallen apart I look forward to reconstructing, to putting the pieces back together in a new way and becoming the person I truly am. I look forward to that phase of the journey. In the meantime, I understand that this phase is important too."

I go home and crawl into bed. I don't stay long, just long enough to shake off some of the fear. Then I get up, do errands, and go to the studio. I get through the morning okay, but around noon deep sadness and loneliness hit me hard. I go home for a half hour and lie down under the covers again. My cats come around to check on me. Looking seriously concerned they tap me on the shoulders, purring, as if to say, "*It's alright, it's alright. Hang in there. You will get through this.*"

I eat some lunch and take a walk before going back to work. A couple of people stop in at the studio in the afternoon, so I'm not alone. I have a long list of things to accomplish and I'm able to stay focused, directing my energy in positive ways rather than letting it seep out in sadness and regret.

In spite of my pain, I am so lucky to be doing this work with Chuck. I have to let myself be vulnerable, go to him trusting that I will be safe. Jeanne was so right when she appeared before me and told me that he was safe and that I could trust him. He has accompanied me on this entire awakening journey and now some kind of spiritual flow happens when I'm with him. I can read his mind. I know what he's thinking. I know what he's going to say before he says it. We're riding the same energetic wave.

October 15, 2003

Sadness wells up from the caverns deep inside me. Only sheer power of will suppresses it. Only two days until I meet with

Chuck again, until I can fully acknowledge what lies coiled inside me. His presence is so necessary; not only is he my witness but his insight is invaluable as I encounter what is so overwhelming and frightening. I pray that I get through these days, focusing on work and children and life, staying balanced in the outer world while keeping my inner emotions, ready to bubble up and spill out at last, under control. Such a false sense of power though, for I am steeped in pain, all that I hold back only letting me know how crucial that I let it go, a precariously painful game.

I am pulled to withdraw into my inner world, to crack the hard nut of resistance that lies deep at my core, to push through and finish this recapitulation once and for all. I remind myself that I can't do that right now, that I need to work, that I need to concentrate on life, and that the recapitulation will more fully come when it and I am ready, though I do give myself permission to sit for a while and do this writing. I will always write. The words seem to write themselves. Without thought they flow, and they will continue to flow until I have said all that needs to be said.

October 16, 2003

I dream that I am in the woods where I was abused. I'm trying to save someone before it's too late.

I wake up with the clear realization that I *was* abused. It's all true. I was abused. I was abused. I was abused. I feel the truth making its way to the bottom of my clenched self, sinking in and loosening the hard casing that has protected me. Like a caustic chemical, those words—I was abused—eat away at the layers of toughness and shame, and the deep, deep pain that has become so difficult to bear.

Sometimes I still wonder why I survived. Sometimes I still think death would have been easier than living this hell for fifty years. But I didn't die. Out of this misery and pain there will eventually emerge some joy, though for now I still struggle with the pain and the deep need to let go, the need to weep big gulping child's tears. I am in such pain!

"Let it out, Jan, let it out," Jeanne says. *"It's okay, it's okay. Let it out. Let it come. Let it flow. Open the door to your*

pain and let it out. Open the door. It's an emergency situation now. Do it now, before it's too late. Chuck is there for you. He will help you. You will be safe. You are safe with him. He knows. He cares. He wants you to heal."

"Yes, I want to heal too. I want to let it go too. I know how important it is. I want to feel safe. I want to know I will be okay. It's so hard to accept another's help, to rely and trust and feel safe without shame and guilt and humiliation. How do I let go and not feel all that?"

"It will all wash over you. It will all flow out and away and it will be gone. Don't you want that?"

"Yes, I do, more than anything I want that. I want all the pain and the shame and the blame to just wash away."

"So, let it go. Tomorrow is the time. It is your chance, when you see Chuck. You can tell him you are ready, that you can't hold it in anymore, that you need him, and that you are afraid. He knows. He knows how afraid you are. He knows the evil that has followed you. He is ready to help you escape now. It's time to escape; it's finally time. Let the agony go, let the pain go. Let it all go. It will be hard, but you can do it; let it go."

"Thank you. Please help me. Tell everyone to please help me. And then maybe I'll be able to forgive myself. Maybe then I'll begin to feel clean and whole, clean and whole at last."

I go to the studio and concentrate on work. Some days, staying focused is such a battle while on other days it's my saving grace. Today it shields me from the pain, but every now and then the sadness rises up and reminds me. And so, I am able to admit that I have suffered and that I hurt. It hasn't really consciously dawned on me, until lately, that I got hurt or even that my abuser hurt me, but I do hurt and he did hurt me. He hurt me in a lot of ways, and it's only by going back into the memories and staying in my body that I begin to discover the source of the pain that my dissociated self has protected me from for so long. Even with that dissociative protection in place I have suffered greatly my entire life, the mysterious pain a shadowy enigma I could never solve.

In the weeks that followed the dog incident, when my teenage self was just trying to deal with the sadness and the bad feelings about herself, she buried all the pain. And I have just buried it again; it's what I've been attempting to do for days now, but I'm not allowed to do that anymore. I must keep it present in my awareness, the knowledge that at the core of me are rivers and rivers of pain. I can't hold those rivers back anymore. It really is time to let go, as Jeanne said. And there is nothing I would like more! Just how to go about it is the question. I wish I could push an "eject pain" button and have it fling out of me, but instead I am having to dig deeply and shovel it out, load by heavy load.

Tomorrow I see Chuck again. I have to keep reminding myself that he's safe, as Jeanne says. No need to feel ashamed or embarrassed or loathsomely disgusting in front of him. I have to continue telling him everything too. If I don't, it will just stay inside me festering, making me feel worse and worse, and I want to feel better now. I want to feel better.

"So tomorrow, please, please," I ask my little girls, "let's make a pact that we won't be afraid. Okay? For one day, we won't be afraid. What is it that we're so afraid of? Is it really the pain?"

It doesn't take me long to realize that yes, indeed, I am afraid of the pain. There's a reason for it; it has served as my punishment. I deserved it; I needed it. It's a major factor keeping me from more fully experiencing the deeper truths of who I am, from what lurks beneath the pain. In bearing the pain I am doing my penance, but I am also assuring that I won't have to feel the self-disgust that lies beneath the pain. I have protected myself with the pain, used it to keep me from worse feelings. I am sure that if I release it, all hell will break loose and all the ugly truths behind the pain will be revealed as well. That's why I'm afraid of the pain. It has protected me from all that I believe about myself.

Oh God! I just realized how one misconception has been feeding another, one false block building upon another. The real truth is that I don't deserve the pain! I don't deserve to be punished! But that was all part of the plan: blame the victim! Blame the victim and she'll keep quiet. Hurt her and frighten her to death and make her feel disgusting. Blame her for your disgusting behavior and she will be your slave forever.

Well, it's time to stop. Please. It's just time.

October 17, 2003

I dream that a big dumpster is dropped at the end of my driveway. I wonder if it's being delivered at the wrong address, that it's supposed to go to the neighbors, but then realize, "Oh, how appropriate, a dumpster. What a great idea!"

I wake up tired and grumpy and yell at the kids to get up and ready for school, louder than I've yelled at them in a long time. I feel angry and sad and disgusted, knowing that yes, this is indeed dumping day. All the old stuff lies piled high inside me, waiting to be dumped into the dumpster of my dream.

Oh Jeanne, please help me. I need to vent and expel. I need to get angry and sad. Please help me to get through this.

"If I release into the pain then it all becomes real and then it all really happened," I say, sitting down across from Chuck.

"Jan, he hurt you," Chuck says, straightforwardly. "He hurt you. That should be your mantra: he hurt me and it's not my fault."

"He hurt me, he hurt me, he hurt me, he hurt me. FUCK! FUCK! FUCK! FUCK!"

"Jan, put your shoulders down, put them down," Chuck says. "Release to the pain, and let it go. Acknowledge it, let the experience in, that you are not to blame and that he hurt you, and then let it go."

"I'm so afraid to admit it, to make it real. If it's real, is it my fault?"

"No, no, no, nooooo!" Chuck says, and then once again, "Jan, put your shoulders down, put them down."

"He hurt me and then he made me feel guilty by making me keep it to myself, that damned code of silence."

"The veneer is so thin now," says Chuck. "You're getting there."

I'm busy at the studio all day, though a familiar little voice inside me teases: "Do what you've always done, ignore it and it will go away! Ignore it!" The temptation to ignore is indeed great, but I am wiser now and I know it will just prolong the agony. I am dealing with full acceptance now, with the actual truth of my childhood, with the final collapse and annihilation of the person I always was. I am facing the unknown emptiness that surely lies inside me as I accept the truth of my abuser's presence as a lifelong entity dwelling inside me, usurping my energy.

After a day of intense work at the studio I go out running in the evening, powered by anxiety and fear. The college students in the house next door are playing loud music, too loud, and it's feeding the crazy in me. Instead of letting it get to me, however, I use it to face where I am. If I dissociate in the usual manner, I can ignore the memories and the way they make me feel, but that's the old way. I'm not doing that anymore. The counter solution is to stay fully present as I let go and experience the disintegration that I am certain will come, though it terrifies me to my very bones. The obvious truth is that my abuser can't get me now; he can't do anything to me. So what am I so afraid of? He's old; he probably doesn't even think of me. He doesn't care about me at all and never did. He's just an old geezer now. I have absolutely no connection to him in this world, none whatsoever. So why am I so afraid? Do I just fear the old fears?

Physically spent after my run, I am calmer in one sense and yet still tense, and I keep hearing Chuck say, *Jan, put your shoulders down, put them down.* The pain in my arms and neck underscores the incessant hunching, but if I relax I feel pain in other places—waist and ribs, vagina and anus—and then it's too much. So I hunch my shoulders instead, controlling the pain, keeping it bearable and tolerable, keeping it contained and away from more vulnerable areas. He hurt me! He hurt me! It was not my fault. I am not to blame. He hurt me. He hurt me a lot. It hurts! Oh God, it HURTS!

"You should have a vacation," my son says to me. "You need one, but I realize that if you have a vacation you can't work and you need to work. But *if* you had a vacation you would probably work better."

He's right, so sensible. My daughter on the other hand confronts me with another truth.

"In the mornings you're fine and happy, but at night you're a cranky mess. Your voice is like bullets hitting me," she says.

This makes me feel utterly terrible. I apologize and explain that I'm a morning person and by night I'm exhausted.

"I'm beginning to see that," she says.

Oh please, help me get through the night. Thank you for my children and the happiness and distraction they bring, for the truths they speak and for their deep concerns. Please help me to be a good mother. Thank you for Chuck who offers refuge. Thank you for my work, which I love, and please help me get through this great task still before me. Please, please, please help me. I need your help. I am so lost.

October 18, 2003

I dream that I am in a small airplane that someone else is flying. I can see everything from my perch in the open cockpit. The pilot takes the plane through many rolls and dips and then heads straight down, nose pointing toward the ground. I hang on for dear life, afraid of crashing, increasingly concerned with the moment of impact. At the same time, there is a calm peacefulness to the whole experience. I'm actually enjoying the ride. It's only the moment of impact, the expectation of explosion upon hitting the ground that concerns me. At the last second the pilot pulls up and we land safely, gliding gently down to the ground. I get out of the plane slightly bewildered, unsteady, and I hear someone say, "She can't handle it anymore; she's cracking."

That's how I feel right now, like I'm cracking. The harsh and brittle tone of my voice is affecting the kids. Their once so stable mother, so reliable and dependable, is just not present, but I can't stop what's happening.

"Get a grip, woman!" my daughter yells. "You beat me with your voice!"

I don't mean to. It's not fair to them, but I can't help it, I'm cracking. The veneer is finally cracking. I tell her that I'm dealing with some personal issues that have nothing to do with her or her brother, that they are not in any way at fault or involved, and that she needs to forgive me for not explaining further. I ask her to just help out, just help.

I woke in the middle of the night with such bad feelings, despising myself, but when I woke this morning I was clearer, able to see them as old feelings and not necessarily how I feel about myself now, but the tension of them is still in me, for the truth is, they are strongly held beliefs, hard to deal with in the middle of the night when I'm coming out of sleep and dreams, feelings of worthlessness, self-disgust, self-blame, thoughts that I'm bad, despicable, and ugly. When they take over I do go spinning out of control, and it's all I can do to hold on. The pilot in the dream, however, is showing me how to gain control, how to come out of a tailspin and land safely. I am being shown that I must get control over what is happening in my body and, like my daughter says, get a grip! If I can do that, all will be calm and fine, and there will be nothing to fear!

As the day goes on, I face the slow unraveling of my old self. She pops up repeatedly, wanting to be heard, but her approach to dealing with things is the old way. I tell her it doesn't work anymore. When I say this, she goes away and things are calm again. At the same time, I am aware that a sort of crashing has to happen, that I will only fully heal in the total cracking of the old self and the old façade that has housed her. It feels like I'm almost there. I am slowly, slowly giving in. The end is in sight.

October 19, 2003

I dream that I'm going to be married. I am sequestered inside a tunnel made of wooden slats, like ribs, covered in white fabric. I am dressed in a voluminous white wedding gown and told to wait for the ceremony to begin. I don't want to be married. I'm extremely uncomfortable about the idea, a reluctant participant. All of a sudden, men rush in and grab me. They push a stick into my vagina and prop me up on a throne that sits at the far end of the tunnel. They exit, leaving me alone in the empty tunnel. Sunlight streams in through the white covering and gentle winds billow the sail-like fabric. Suddenly, I feel safe and happy. A sense of purity that I have rarely experienced flows through me. I want to stay here forever. I am at peace at last.

I hear people outside, calling to me, telling me to come out of the tunnel, urging me to join them. I know they are waiting for me, expecting me to come out.

"No, I don't want to join you," I say, realizing I have the power to refuse.

I discover that I control everything and that being in the tunnel is the best place I could possibly be. Why should I leave? I sense that to go anywhere else would be disastrous, that I would lose all the peace I've gained. Can't I just stay here? Then I become angry and it's the anger that makes me refuse to budge from the throne. The anger makes the tunnel grow longer and longer, pushing me backward at great speed, until I am sitting on my throne at the end of a tunnel that now appears miles long. The more I say "no," the more I speed backwards, the longer the tunnel grows and the more at peace I become, until everything that was bothering me has receded, until I am far, faraway. The sounds of the people outside the tunnel, talking and laughing, grow more distant and indistinct until they are only faint murmurs in the distance. I feel so incredibly safe in the sunny whiteness of the vast tunnel, pure and chaste, untouchable at last. I know it's necessary that I stay here.

Eventually, the people outside the tunnel go away and the only sound I hear is the hypnotic sighing of the white fabric billowing in the wind. Shhh... Shhh... Shhh... I stay seated on the throne, completely at peace in the vast and sunny whiteness. After a while I don't even feel the stick in my vagina, for I am far, faraway, safe and protected, and there is no pain anymore.

Then a new dream begins. A man takes me to a house that is not my own. I feel like I'm trespassing, but I know it's necessary to be here too. The man leaves me alone with piles of paperwork to do. I sit at a kitchen table going over numbers, long serial numbers with nine to twelve digits in them. There are stacks of papers to organize as well. At the same time that I settle into working I am also slightly uncomfortable, as if the stick were still in my vagina from the previous dream.

After a while I get up and walk outside. A high fence made of chicken wire, about eight feet tall, surrounds the property. On the other side of the fence I see a beautiful garden, well tended, very ornate, with pathways and ponds, trees and benches. I yearn to be there, quietly strolling and at peace, but I can't get to it. It's not mine. It belongs to someone else; as does the house I am working in. Again, I have the sense that I'm trespassing, that I don't really belong here, or anywhere for that matter. I'm bothered by that, but in the back of my mind I also know that if I can just sort through all the paperwork then things will be okay, and then I can achieve anything, even that beautiful garden. The fence is tall, but I can see everything right through it. I take that as a sign. The garden is within reach and when I've finished the task before me I'll be able to access it.

It's a rainy Sunday today. I'd like to go back to sleep, stay in bed all day, hidden from the world under my quilt, safe and protected like in the white tunnel dream, for the atmosphere inside it was so exceedingly beautiful and calm, so desirable. I crave it, am drawn there, as if to a field of poppies. I could stay there forever, overcome by its heady, soporific properties, living a dissociated life. The other dream proposes the real work of this recapitulation, being in an uncomfortable place as I face the real tasks at hand. In the second dream I am not "home" yet, not yet in the garden either. I am still caged in, still in the discomforts of recapitulation and transition. These dreams present the current dilemmas as I wrestle with the old self who values her dissociation, loves it in fact, and is still drawn back to it, and the new self who really does desire to enter the garden of new life, so near and yet still out of reach. The tunnel or the garden? The choice is mine.

If I remain in the tunnel and refuse the life that is calling to me, I will not progress. All the work I have done will be for naught. I will stagnate, the veils keeping me from fuller life, an incomplete recapitulation and the stagnancy of dissociation my only legacy. Yes, there is a sort of peace and purity to it, to having uncovered the abuse and taken it as far as I have, but in this tunnel dream I am electing to remain a victim. In the dream of working in the caged property I anticipate the beautiful garden that will one day be mine. Dissociation or recapitulation? The choice is mine.

I have no intention of remaining a victim, but I see how my dream world is showing me where I easily get caught. The tunnel is addictive, filled with the white noise of the wind billowing through, blocking out true life on the other side of the veils. By the end of the dream I am far away from bustling life. In fact, I feel quite wonderfully at peace, so far removed from the cares of the world or the need to be involved. I have to admit, I am drawn to the serenity of it, but the truth is it's dissociated serenity. It's just an illusion. Such a life offers nothing really, except maybe the fulfillment of an infantile desire to withdraw and be protected from reality. If I stay in the tunnel, reminiscent of the inner tunnel of my dissociated child self, I will remain in the uncomfortable position of the victim queen, a stick stuck up my crotch for the rest of my life. I would remain always a bride-to-be, on the verge of new life, never taking the fuller journey to all the experiences that being in the real world offers. No, thank you! I am far more interested in what comes after this journey of recapitulation. I am much more interested in that beautiful garden!

I must stay on course and remember that I am here, at this point in my life, in order to do this recapitulation, and that there is a bigger plan, as the garden on the other side of the fence reveals. Somehow, I will get into that beautiful garden. It is my future. That I am certain of.

It's evening. I am in agony. I am suffering and I am dying. I am dying a little bit more each day, the old me is dying. I wake up in the middle of the night and I want to walk out into the garage and turn on the car and asphyxiate myself, but I can't tell Chuck that. I keep that to myself because I know it's the old me talking, the teenager, the abused one; she's the one who wants to die. Going into the garage is the only solution that comes when I wake in the night, *her* solution to feeling deeply ashamed and full of self-loathing, looking for a way out, desperate to annihilate the pain. When I wake in the morning I can't believe how strong the intention and desire for death had been in the darkness of the night, and also how unrealistic, but it makes all the sense in the world when I wake in the night in such old pain.

On the other hand, I really am experiencing a dying, the dying of the old self, and it's not by my own hand but by the slow breaking down process that is this recapitulation. Little by little, as I let go of my old defenses, I face the annihilation of all that once kept me safe. Along with that comes this sense of not knowing who I am or where I am. The tunnel of my dream pops up as a perfectly viable solution then. I could just stay there forever. Even though I am impaled on a stick, queen of my own painful delusion, there is a kind of serenity that is undeniable behind the veils of illusion.

In a sense, my dream is showing me what a dissociated death is like. Yes, there is the absence of pain, but there is no real healing as the abuse remains unresolved. It still has control. There is the slow receding of life as the spirit moves further into the white tunnel of death, such a sterile and lonely place. Though life went on outside the tunnel, no one came in to get me, for they could not penetrate the veils that divided the worlds and I stubbornly refused to get up off my ass and get the heck out of there. I just sat there, as if drugged. And after a while I could no longer hear the people outside the tunnel calling to me, distance and the sound of the wind blocking all communication. Though there was a kind of peacefulness in the tunnel, it was a veiled illusion, related to old states, just as the thoughts of death that come in the night are from old states.

My worlds are overlapping more and more now and how I choose to respond at this point is critical. I am fully aware of that! I have the opportunity to chose differently now, to not die an old death but to live a new life, for I am really in the transformative process, not of dying but of being born. Who I will become is on the line, now more than ever. The last vestiges of my old self are making a final plea, asking me to stay behind in the old world, teasing me with such grand illusions.

"Look how wonderful it is here," the old me says. "You don't even notice there's a stick up your vagina. Isn't it beautiful here? So peaceful! And you are queen of all you behold!"

October 20, 2003

I am in a dark hole. Nothing like the white tunnel of my dream, this place is pure hell. A part of me still feels like slamming the door on all of this and returning to that peaceful tunnel, but I know that's a total copout and that my memories would bug me forever, forcing me to remember again and again, torturing me forever in my private hell. I'd end up a madwoman, and then I'd never get out of this dark hole.

I need help. With a sad and humble heart I reach out of my dark hole and call Chuck. I tell him that I'm just trying to find something to hold onto, something to keep me anchored. I keep reaching out and there's nothing there, only the old me and my child self hating herself, feeling so bad about everything.

"Have some empathy for that young girl," Chuck says.

"I do, I'm trying," I say.

"Instead of fighting her, you need to mother her. You are an adult now and even though this is hard for you it was worse back then."

"You are so right! We are not stopping," I say, suddenly re-enthused, "we are going to finish this!"

"We're almost there," he says.

October 21, 2003

Last night, I dreamed that I was gathering children to go to an event, making sure everyone was with me, no one left behind. Such an appropriate dream, as I will be meeting with Chuck this morning. And so, I set the intent that all parts will be fully present no matter what happens. It's time to allow the "letting go" process to proceed now with all parts fully engaged!

Thank you, Chuck! EMDR proves its worth. I am able to release, both physically and emotionally during the session. Afterwards, quite exhausted, feeling washed out and wrung dry, I go home and lie under the covers for a while. I make a promise to not be so hard on myself, to take the pressure off, to soften and allow for things to naturally happen. After a while, in a much better mood, I get up, eat some food, and head over to the studio.

I stay present in my body, working calmly, but late in the afternoon the anxiety creeps back in and all of a sudden I'm afraid. The nice buzz of calmness I've been feeling completely wears off and I'm back to my old reality again, poised like an animal, sensing danger lurking nearby.

"There isn't anything to be afraid of," Jeanne says. *"It's all over now; it's over."*

"Just because you say so doesn't make it true," replies my body.

Has the EMDR unearthed something deep inside myself that I'm not aware of? Do I need to remember more, release more? Did I become too open, too relaxed, too vulnerable too quickly? When I feel like this, my instinct is to protect, to dive right back into that white tunnel, safely protected and hidden from the world, and myself. I sense my body going into overdrive, on heightened alert, ready to fight or flee.

I make it home from the studio in one piece, but by the time I arrive I am near hysterical. It freaks everyone out! The cats scatter and the kids scramble into their rooms. I go into mine, still wondering if maybe I got too open too quickly, not just the release but the emptiness too much to handle. I realize that just because I intend something doesn't mean it will happen as I want. I have to be patient with the process. A sense of impending disaster stirs in me, my body anticipating a sudden and brutal impact, the same fear of crashing as in my recent flying dream. Instinctively, my body clamps down and holds in.

I notice the chakra points along my spine are tender and raw, as if each one has been bruised. Once again, I wonder if I've opened too much. I caress them one at a time with slow and gentle breaths, but beneath the surface I still feel the hot heat of hysteria waiting for its opportunity to release. Instead, I drink a big glass of wine, effectively putting the fire out! Then I go to bed. I'm just not ready to surrender yet.

October 22, 2003

I roll over in bed, half asleep, and suddenly I am crashing, crashing, crashing, in full release, cracking and exploding! I want to scream! I want to cry, and yet I hold back still! But I have feelings! I have real feelings! Like waves they crash over me, tidal waves of needs that I've ignored, needs asking to be recognized and dealt with. I am child and adult, child, adult, child, adult, tossing and churning in the onslaught of feelings crashing over me. I am not going crazy. Don't panic. Don't panic. I'm only opening. I'm just opening all those closed doors, unlocking, letting things flow. I am surrendering, surrendering, surrendering.

Today I worked quietly alone, painting at a private home. I will be there for a few days, making some good money too. I dealt with flare ups of anger all day while I worked. I studied them, addressed them, and maturely tended to them. Unlike the waves of feelings that washed over me this morning, they came in short furious spurts throughout the day. I calmly noted their presence and let them slowly seep out. I've noticed that the anger sits on the outside, flaring up like flames on a log, while inside, at the hard core of the log, lies sadness and pain, more deeply encased and harder to access.

I don't want to close up again. I don't want to harden up or seal off my feelings again but intend to keep the fires burning, just enough to keep the alchemical process, the fiery cauldron of self, in a constantly transforming state. For this is the moment I have been expecting. This is what I have finally surrendered to, the fires of transformation and change. And so, I vow to consciously remain more open than usual, while simultaneously keeping the fire under control, for I still have to be careful; I don't want to hurt anyone or anything. I vent with measured control but refuse to do more than that. I breathe to calm down and to keep open the passages that might otherwise close over.

It's a cold night and the inner flame warms me in a strangely comforting way as I tend to it, but how I wish I had someone to hold me and tell me that everything will be okay. It's lonely inside my cauldron of fire.

October 23, 2003

I wake up early, at five, feeling energetically strong and yet the fires burn still, anger flaring up in little spurts. To control the burn I lie very still and mentally walk around the rooms of the house I'm painting, focusing on how to tackle the problem areas. In spite of the mental focus I start to feel myself floating away from this sad, sad body. I become a poor little girl floating up on the smoke, rising from the body of flames, like a spirit rising from a funeral pyre. I know she just wants to escape and that I can help her by acknowledging and letting go of the anger, by releasing it. I have to, so that I can do more than just survive because, frankly, I fully intend to be transformed by this process.

I realize that if I release the anger the sadness will also release. If I hold onto the anger, I will only continue living a life of dissociation and I'll never fully access the truth and the means of salvation. If I let the anger go then the truth of it releases as well, the reality of it and why it resides inside me to begin with. Release of the anger will lead to release of the truth of it all, because there can no longer be denial if I acknowledge the anger.

Eight at night and I am exhausted after eight hours of work, painting a large room, an enormous job with lots of nooks and crannies, more doors than imaginable, plus the ceiling with all the lines between the acoustic tiles needing to be meticulously painted with a small brush. My neck is only slightly sore, but the rest of me is tired and edgy, with such a need to combust! There is still a part of me that no longer wants to carefully tend the flames but instead to say, "FUCK IT!" and burn in one giant bonfire, set all the feelings, all the anger, and all the frustration alight. But I can't do that, it just doesn't feel appropriate, and so I leave the licking flames of discontent and jump into a hot bath instead, from one cauldron to another. Immersing myself in the soothing waters, I hope that maybe things will finally simmer down.

"Everything will be all right," I say, calming myself with the kinds of soothing words that Jeanne might use. "I don't have to run anymore. I don't have to hide. I don't have to be afraid. Let the fear go. Let the anger go. Let the feelings go. Let the sadness go."

October 24, 2003

I dream that I'm in a play. I'm not sure I want to be here, but I know exactly what to say and how to say it. I deliver my lines perfectly, reading directly from a script I hold in my hands. With no self-doubt or inhibition I move about the stage, a natural actor. Another woman is also in the play, though she doesn't quite understand how to act out her lines. Her delivery is stilted and unnatural. I get a pleading look from her at one point that says: "Please take over, you know what to do. Please?" So I do. In the beginning I can barely speak because my voice is hoarse and dry, but the more I speak the smoother my voice becomes until everything is flowing out of me effortlessly, comfortably, with great confidence. Some children sit on the floor before the stage watching the play. When the play ends they are each offered a small gift bag of toys. I watch one little boy lay out the toys from his gift bag in a geometric shape, creating an intricate mandala, with him sitting right smack in the center of it.

I had the sense while I dreamed that I was both women, one uncomfortably out of place and the other very confident and exactly where she was supposed to be. One receded while the other stepped up to the challenge and did a beautiful job. The dream perfectly reflects where I am right now. The old me is being challenged to back down. It is not her time to act anymore, and the new me is asserting herself in her new role as lead actor in the new life I am creating. During the dream everything felt so right!

"I meant nothing to my abuser," I say to Chuck as we sit down for a session.

"It might actually be freeing to fully realize that," Chuck suggests.

"Yes, maybe, because from a certain perspective there was nothing personal in the abuse. The fact that I dissociated from my body points out that he didn't really need or want *me* at all. He just wanted a body, even a lifeless, empty, girl-gone body. As much as I wanted to matter, I never did."

"Is that freeing?" Chuck asks.

"I can accept that I meant nothing in the context of what he wanted, a human body for his games. Yes, it's freeing to know that it wasn't personal. But everyone wants to matter, and I am no exception. I had so little emotional support or comfort in my life and I sense I looked for an inkling of affection and caring from him. But I acknowledge that 'I' never really existed for him, except my body and what he wanted it for. If I hadn't dissociated but instead reacted, he may have killed me."

"The fact that he needed a willing body for his games made it more important that he keep you alive," Chuck says.

"But the truth is, the real me meant absolutely nothing to him. That thought sends me right to the pits of emptiness. I understand that it's up to me to fill the emptiness with something else beside the old ways of seeking comfort, to not look to others or wallow in self-pity and rejection, but to give myself the gift of unafraid life, to fill the emptiness with my own energy now, my own agenda, not someone else's but solely my own. It's time to live life on my own terms. That's how to take back my power."

"And I don't have to be afraid anymore, which is probably the greatest gift I can give myself, the gift of no fear," and then I remember the little boy in my dream who sat so quietly, creating a mandala around himself, essentially showing me that I must do the same now, not protect or isolate myself in an old way but live my new life fully from my core, from my own spirit.

My talk with Chuck brings up so much stuff, old issues still unresolved, and by the end of the day my head is swirling with them. I try to walk them off after work, breathing slowly, trying to clear my head but that just makes them worse. What's emerging is the fact that I carry a deeply penetrating sense of guilt that keeps me in denial. But why do I still feel so guilty? Even after everything I've discovered, why do I still feel like it was my fault?

I don't consider myself a victim of sexual abuse but more a *participant*, and there is tremendous guilt attached to that! I was there! I did all those heinous things! I also still resist accepting the deeper truth, that it really did happen, nor do I want anyone else to know! The people who have been coming forth recently, speaking out about Catholic priests having molested them, how can they do that? I feel absolutely terrible for them, but I suffer such shame and guilt around my own abuse that it would be impossible for me to ever speak out. But why, after all the work I've done?

I must reiterate that technically I know it wasn't my fault, but I was always taught to take responsibility for myself, for my decisions and actions. I also know I am not *really* guilty, that I *was* sexually abused, and that I participated *against* my will. Why then have I contemplated suicide all evening, for the last several hours been steeped in thoughts of death? The truth is, I'm still stuck in the memory with the dog in the barn. It's been chasing me all day, so to speak. Did the conversation with Chuck bring it up again? It brings me right to the questions of why the guilt, why the shame, and why the incessant need for denying that it even happened? Is death better than facing the reality of the dog memory, and of the entire thing, the prolonged sexual abuse of my child self? Would I ever really kill myself?

"I wish you were dead!" my son yells, after getting off the phone with his father. "My life was so much better before you two started hating each other!"

This is in reference to our divorce, of course, but I have to wonder why this message comes at this moment. I assure him that we don't hate each other, that we just have our differences, but this does not appease his anger. He goes into his room and slams the door, leaving me to deal with my own frustrations, for I have been stuck in the past all day, in the frustrating time after the dog incident when I stayed in bed as much as possible. It was then that I wanted the solitude of death. For months on end I was utterly retched. Just the thought of that time and the heavy blanket of memory falls over me with a thud and before I know what's happening I am muffled under it.

I leave the living room where I have been sitting, writing in this journal, and escape to my bed. I am seventeen again, under the covers, effectively muting out the world. As I recapitulate, I am in both places at once, here in the present under the covers in my adult bedroom and also back in the past under the covers in my childhood bedroom, experiencing emotions that are so real, though the memory is decades old. Finally, I have enough. I sit up and ask my present day adult self to use her intellect to figure this out once and for all. My mature adult self fully realizes that the abuse wasn't my fault, but a frightened part of me still refuses to accept that possibility.

"Why do I feel like this? Why am I doing this to myself? What is happening to me?"

As soon as I pose those questions guilt comes flooding back, as strong as a tidal wave. On its back rides shame, cutting through the water like a shark. I dive back under the covers. I am not going to kill myself, but I am back in the memory, all the old emotions swirling in my head and me trying to figure them out. At the same time, I don't believe there is any figuring out to be done because it's all so intense and there's no way out. The only thing that makes sense is staying under the covers until it feels better, but that was the old escape. Is that the only thing that will work now too, staying under the covers where everything is muted, faraway, and nothing can get me? It reminds me of the tunnel dream with the billowing tent fabric, dissociation a safe yet deadly option. I know that's not the way anymore.

"We don't need to torture ourselves anymore," I say to my seventeen-year-old self.

"You don't believe me," she says.

"I believe you," I say. "Is that what this is all about? Do you think I don't believe you? Do you think I don't believe what you have been telling me and showing me? Well, I do, I believe you. I was there too."

"No, you weren't."

"Yes, I was there with you at the time, but I also grew up and left. I am so sorry I had to do that, that I had to leave you back there bearing the burden of that memory, but we don't have to stay there anymore. We have the whole story now and I have no doubt of its realness. I believe it. I believe you. Please come with me now into a different world where we can be free, where we can start a new life. Leave the memory now, leave all that bad stuff behind."

"Even the guilt?"

"Yes. It's not our guilt. We are not guilty. I am not guilty. You are not guilty. Come on, say it: I am not guilty."

"I am not guilty," she mumbles. "I am not guilty. I am not guilty," her voice getting stronger and stronger until she is yelling. "I am not guilty! I am not guilty! I am not guilty!"

"Do you really think I don't care about you?" I ask her. "Do you think I just want you to go away, stay back there?"

"I want to stay back here."

"No, you don't. Not really. You have to come with me now. You have to because there is no wholeness without you. We have to integrate and begin a new life together. We can do it. And maybe we do need to speak about it again, all the details, but in our own way and in our own time, when we are ready."

Ah! I sense that this idea frightens her, as it still does me, but I will not stop talking. There is too much at stake here. And the possibilities are endless as to how things might unfold, so no more hiding or refusing life when it comes!

"We'll figure this all out," I tell her, "but first we need to understand our feelings, whose are whose and what they mean, and then we need to figure out how to deal with them."

"Okay," she says.

"I've said, so many times, that I need to re-experience the memories and the feelings, but this time without the old numbness that helped us back then. This time I want to experience them full force, to make them all fully believable. Are you helping to make them believable?"

"Yes."

"Okay, I get it. Now let's try to sleep," I say, "and in the meantime I ask for clarification in my dreams."

October 25, 2003

I dream that I'm having an open house at my studio. I go to use the bathroom. I am sitting on the toilet when the door opens and in walks a little girl with her mother. There are no doors on the stalls so I am fully exposed. I try to pull my underpants up, which have gotten rolled in a bundle, but I can't pull them up without doing all sorts of gyrations. The little girl, watching me go through my antics, bursts out laughing. "They stick like glue!" I say, and this makes her laugh even more.

The mother and daughter follow me back to my studio. In walks another mother with another little girl, this one dressed in a 1950s matching hat and coat, sky blue and trimmed in white fur. This little girl comes over to where I'm sitting on the floor, trying to hide. She plunks right down in my lap. All of a sudden, I feel sick to my stomach and puke right onto her shoulder. It looks like half-eaten chunks of dog food. She asks me where it came from.

"Oh, my bad little doggie did that," I say.

"Where is he?" she asks, excitedly.

"He's hiding because he's so ashamed," I say, but she just laughs at that.

"Here, bad little doggie!" she calls, but I have made him up, so of course he doesn't appear.

I clean the little girl up and send her off to look around the studio, wondering what her mother will think of a strange woman having held her daughter close enough to puke on her shoulder. I feel bad, like I will be accused of something. I want to go home and lie under the covers, but then I feel guilty about that too because I promised myself to stay at the studio all day.

The girls are innocent! They are sweet little children. I AM ALSO INNOCENT! They are not guilty. I AM NOT GUILTY! My dream shows me just how pure innocence really is. Those little girls are so small and trusting. The first little girl just naturally laughed at how funny I looked as I tried to pull up my pants, not in the least bit afraid or embarrassed, and the second one believed me when I said the dog puked on her. And why did I puke on her? Do I feel like the bad little doggie my abuser accused me of being? Am I still feeling guilty about that? Don't I want to accept the truth of her/my innocence?

That tiny, pretty little girl dressed in her matching outfit with little ankle socks and Mary Jane shoes is straight out of the 1950s, and she reeks of innocence. It's obvious that she could not have defended herself against a grown man even if she tried, and neither could I. This is so clear to me now. I realize that I've been trying to figure this all out from an adult perspective, with all the knowledge, logic, and judgments of an adult, but I was not an adult back then. I was that tiny innocent child, two, three, four years old, who couldn't defend herself at all. What child could? Who would blame a two-year-old?

I have been blaming myself all these years, blaming my two-year-old self for what I now clearly see was not her fault, nor was she to blame for getting caught in a madman's fantasies. I've placed such unreasonable expectations upon her my whole life. My dream, on the other hand, is reminding me to take a step back and look at the situation from a different angle, from the perspective of innocence! I have to understand just how innocent and pure my little girl self was if I am to resolve this, and then I have to get her to understand that as well. Both of us have to step back and reconstruct this with these new insights in hand. She could never have thought up any of the things that happened to her; innocence is untainted, doesn't have knowledge of such sexual brutality, nor could she have prevented what happened. She didn't have any means at her disposal. That's where we are right now, facing the truth of all that!

So, no more guilt. The burden of guilt is not my burden. It falls directly on the shoulders of my abuser, thus the absurdity of the puke on the shoulder of the little girl! The little doggie girl that I was when I played all those terrible games with my abuser was not bad either. She was innocent!

I have a busy day ahead of me, which will keep me stable and focused, though my head swirls, all the confusions of my sixteen little girl selves begging to be reexamined from this new guilt-free perspective. To begin with, the seventeen-year-old self thinks death is her only recourse and that it will bring her peace. She is the one who went out into the garage one night and turned the car on. Do I feel guilty that I grew up and she is still haunted by the memories? She was unable to kill herself then and I won't let her do it now, but I'm not sure yet how to help her.

I take an hour off for lunch and then go back to work and right back into analyzing the dream. Methodically painting, I seek meaning in the details of what came to me in the night. I remember that the adult me had bad feelings in the dream. I tried to hide, first in the bathroom when I got caught with my pants down and later in the studio where I hunkered down on the floor. I was ashamed of being caught with my pants down and of puking, but the truth is that I don't have to feel ashamed about anything. The girl who saw me trying to get my pants up didn't care and the girl I puked on didn't care either. They had no judgments, as they were innocent children. They were simply curious and reacted innocently. It's so obvious that judgments are learned. Somewhere along the way, innocence gets lost and judgments begin taking over. It's time to take my innocence back and free myself of the judgments that were imposed upon me. My dream instructs me to return to the truth of my early innocence and remember that innocence does not judge, it simply is.

In my dream, the adult me clearly perceives the two girls in this light, that they do not judge, they simply are. In contrast, my waking self has been confused by all the judgments and ideas I've imposed on myself my whole life, about all the rapes that occurred over the years, as well as all the many "doggie" games I played with my abuser. These judgments have only added to the confusion and created even more judgments. To keep looking at everything from a nonjudgmental standpoint, as Chuck has always suggested I do, and to fully understand and embrace the innocence of the child, is the means to moving past and erasing those harsh judgments. The truth is, I never thought of myself as *innocent*. I only ever thought of myself as a sinner. Everything was my fault, after all. Even if I never did anything wrong I lived in a world where sin, guilt, and shame were common themes, far more acceptable in the Catholic world I grew up in than innocence ever was.

"Your child self is giving you the gift of innocence," Chuck says when I talk to him. "Even though the four-year-old that you were didn't ever feel innocent, that little girl in the dream is bringing it back to you. It's a gift."

Something seeped through from my dream world into this reality and shifted things because I don't feel like killing myself today. I'm not fighting or hiding or in a scrambled mess either.

The end of the day. I lie in a hot bath and automatically cover myself with a washcloth, but then I pull it away. I forgive myself, even though it was not my fault. It was never my fault. I acknowledge that I have always felt so ashamed of my body, always wanted to hide it, even from myself. I intend to change that. I don't have anything to be ashamed of. I am that innocent little girl in the coat of virgin blue, full of hope and trust, so openly innocent. When she looked at me, her eyes invited me to know the truth that I am innocent too. She sat in my lap and gave me the gift of innocence, as Chuck said, while I sat there feeling bad and dirty, trying to hide my shame and guilt. It was shame and guilt that I didn't deserve, that I don't have to carry anymore. I am not a bad little doggie. It's time to wash myself of that idea.

Oh God, please help me. I need another dream. How do I let it all go? How do I empty myself of the shame and guilt and take in the innocence?

October 26, 2003

I dream that I get several phone calls from a strange man with a pleasant accent who insists I visit him. I discover that he's a Buddhist monk. My daughter and I visit him at the Buddhist center where he lives. I ask him what he wants from me and try to write down what he says, but the pages in my pad are already covered with writing. I attempt to write over them but what I write is totally illegible.

"At least tell me your name," I say, getting frustrated.

"Nicoleen," he says, and then he leaves.

My daughter and I walk around the stately grounds of the Buddhist center and go into a small cabin. As soon as we step inside, my daughter begins yelling. She yells at the top of her lungs for a long time. When she stops I give her a big hug and the two of us just laugh and laugh. From there we drive to my parent's house. My mother is in her room trying to remove ticks from her arms with lit matches.

"Why do you have so many ticks?" I ask. "No one has that many. Didn't you notice them crawling on you?"

"Well Jan, that's just the way it is," she says bluntly.

I watch as she burns holes in her skin. It must be very painful, but she doesn't even flinch. There is something about her and the process that disgusts me, that she has let things get to such a point. Then I dream that I am with a man who keeps asking me if he can do anything to help me. He constantly shows up, bringing me coffee and food. He desperately wants to be available to me, and he insists on being generous. He just wants to give to me, he tells me, that's all that matters now.

My lovely daughter, accompanying me on my dreaming adventure, shows me the means to releasing the tension and how to accept my innocence—to just let it all out! It's the answer to my question. Thank you, dream world! I'm already experiencing the joy and liberation of all that yelling and laughing because, frankly, the desperation that has clung to me for the past few days has completely lifted. I feel much lighter! A part of me really did experience the satisfaction of release in the dream.

I have to say, the Buddhist monk and the man who kept asking me if he could help feel so familiar, as if I know them already, for they were so real! There was such insistence on their parts that they be included in my life.

The swirling madness of the past few days has definitely receded and I am experiencing quieter brain activity. This is mixed with physical tiredness and the exhaustion of balancing work with the needs of the kids. It strikes me that I don't have to do it all on my own, that I can ask their dad to help more. I don't think I can sustain this running around after a full day of physical labor, getting them to and from activities every afternoon and most evenings without some help. Since they live with me full time, except for every other weekend, I am doing most of the daily parenting too and, frankly, it's exhausting.

This transformational process has definitely gotten to a new stage, a slow breaking down taking place, the long promised dismantling well underway. I am fully employed in this process, like a vulture at work, pecking and picking at the carcass of my old self, old bones snapping, splintering shards stabbing me as I try to swallow their jagged chunks of truth. Why not spit them out? I sense I have to ingest them all as I try to figure out where they fit in this sad puzzle of my old life. Perhaps I should hammer each bone into dust, mix with paint and pigment and paint my pain, begin the drama of the rest of my life with the past securely locked into a still life painting, archived and varnished so that nothing from that depiction will spill out as I continue this dismantling of my old self and my old world.

That's where I am right now, in the process of acute deterioration, not growth and rebirth yet, but still in the very slow and painful dissecting of the old self, the only self I have ever known. She must be broken down if I am to transform, ashes to ashes, dust to dust, like in a dream I had not long ago, until the old me is nothing more than powdery dust blowing in the wind. This decomposing is as much a part of this recapitulation as gaining access to the memories is.

My teenage self has deteriorated to a lump under the covers. She is in such pain right now as I pick away at her, but I have little energy to give her. I can't even bother to throw aside the covers and tell her to get out of bed. Her life has no meaning, she says, her body only a vessel of pain, her mind swollen with the nightmarish scenes of horror and torture from long ago, playing repeatedly. She wants to give in.

"Why didn't he just kill me?" she wonders. "Why didn't he just kill me?"

Suddenly, I am with her, back in my childhood bedroom where it's quiet under the covers. No one misses her, her absence barely noticed. Though she can hear the voices of her parents and siblings no one asks where she is, no one calls her name, no one needs her. She feels as if she has died because it seems that she doesn't really exist at all, she's just a ghost.

"You see, no one really cares," she says, "I might as well be dead, then it would be over, it would all be over."

I have to admit that she's right, that was pretty much the essence of my life at that time, a deep pervasive sadness with little or no human contact. I realize now that I was deeply depressed, but at the time all I knew was that I was alone with my pain, believing I could never speak to anyone of what I was feeling or experiencing on a deeper level. Burying it was the best recourse, even though I didn't really know what was wrong with me or the real reason I felt the way I did. I rarely spoke to my parents and they rarely asked me about myself, nor were they demonstrative or encouraging. There was no sense of being loved or valued. My mother, burning ticks off her arm in my dream, speaking coldly and without emotion, is true to life. I cannot refute what both my memories and my dreams tell me.

In my dream last night, when my daughter yelled and yelled, I was so happy for her ability to express herself that I just stood back and watched her in awe. Now I need to drag my teenage self out of that bed and get her yelling too!

I know I'm not complete yet. There is still a part of me that is unfinished, a part of me I haven't tapped into yet. Perhaps it's the writer in me, as I continue to uncover the desire to write, still carry the inking of an idea that I need to tell my story, that it's important, that it may help someone else, that there are plenty of others out there who are as lost as I was, as I still sometimes feel. I don't need to ask myself why anymore. I can pretty much say that the whys have been answered. Why am I like this? Why do I feel this way? Why am I always so afraid? Why am I always so sad? Why am I always so lonely? Why do I sometimes freak out? Why do I have such strange pains? Those mysteries have finally been answered. And although I may always be a loner and always a little sad, I hope that I will learn to not be afraid.

As a child I believed in fate, that my path was laid out and I had no choice but to accept it; a fatalistic attitude to be sure! It was how I saw my parents live, as they just rolled with the punches. Once again, it reminds me that my mother's remark in last night's dream that "it's just the way it is," was what I heard often enough as a child. No attempt to protest or change anything was ever made. It's a model I adopted and followed for quite some time. Eventually, I woke up to the certainty that there were other ways of living and that it's perfectly appropriate to react to what life brings. It's okay to say no. After a while I began to develop my own personal strategies and set of values, moving further and further away from my early parental influences. I've changed even more now. As my inner strength and spiritual energy have emerged, as I attempt to follow the signs that lead me, as I continue to integrate all parts of myself, I experience life differently. I'm taking back my own power, developing the ability to make decisions on behalf of myself that are good and productive, from the heart, rather than just living blindly, beaten down by life. At the same time, I believe that everything that happened to me was and is meaningful, even the bad stuff. And I am here to discover it!

I'm learning what it means to live more consciously aware of myself in this world too, broadening my overall worldview in the process. As I've dismantled what the shaman's call the *foreign installation*, all that we are taught to believe from the moment of birth, I've learned to see life in so many different and previously unimaginable ways. I have not just embarked on a shamanic recapitulation into my past but have gained the fuller insight that *all of life* is a shamanic journey. I now know that I am much more than just my present self. This life is only one meaningful part of a much bigger and grander journey. Of that I am sure!

October 27, 2003

I dream that I'm painting the ceilings in a cavernous room. "The art deco phase has ended," I say, "so what's next?" There is no light in the room. It's gloomy and sad, and it makes me angry. I am intent upon changing it.

The cats kept waking me up and I got angry during the night. What am I going to do with these emotions! Helpful as it was, even the yelling that my little daughter did for me in my dream the other night did not last long. I am like a magic pot. As soon as I express and release my bubbling emotions, I fill right back up to the brim of the pot with more bubbling emotions! How do I rid myself of those negative emotions tied to the memories? I guess I have to change, but I think of changing and immediately fill with fear. If I stay the same I am in control.

Last night's dream tells me that I do need to change, especially that which is still hanging over me, the ceiling that I am painting in the dream. I must determine what is most important to me now and slowly make changes in that direction. The art deco period is indeed over, no more highly stylized attitudes, no more staunchly guarded emotions. It's high time to move into the more modern phase of *realism* where everything is real and accepted for what it truly is.

In another dream of last night my daughter yelled again. I think that little girl inside me needs to express herself and I need to find a way to let her do so in real life too. But right now I need to focus on getting up and going to work. Ah, life!

I work for six hours and come home exhausted. I noted all day, however, that work keeps me sane. Physical and creative work calm the voices and the emotions, giving me ample quiet time in which to figure out what to do about them. When I am inside my creative bubble everything else disappears, everything dissolves, even the fear, and then I rule. It's my kingdom. I can be totally alone, totally contented and absorbed, and nothing bothers me there. If I can keep turning the fear energy into creative energy then I should be able to handle everything else too, even the things I believe will never go away: the sadness, loneliness, and pain. I think I will always have them. They are a major part of my inner network, but certainly they too will lessen with time and recede into the background, though it is my opinion that they will never completely disappear. I do notice, however, that when I'm in my creative bubble they do disappear! So perhaps there is hope that one day I will be completely symptom free.

As I experience this steady deterioration of my old self, this slow falling apart of the old, I notice that the poor girl hiding under the covers has no contact with anyone at all. No one is asking her if she's all right. No parents are looking out for her. She is alone and lost. There is only me. There has only ever been me.

October 28, 2003

I meet with Chuck. I bring up my parent's neglectfulness, their lack of affection, how unaware they appeared to be during my childhood. I think they chose to be that way. We often presented as the perfect family, but it was far from the truth.

"A child needs affection," Chuck says. "Your abuser zeroed in on the parental neglect and knew you were available, ready to be groomed. He took over where your parents left off. In a very basic way, you were ripe for affection and he offered it."

I nod when Chuck says this. I feel the truth of it. The little girls inside me agree and I feel them nodding in agreement too as I talk about my current need for affection.

"I'm afraid my loneliness might lead me to make a wrong decision," I say.

"How so?" Chuck asks.

"Just because I'm so desperately lonely doesn't feel like enough of a reason to be in a relationship, as strange as that may sound. I know a lot of people seek relationships for that very reason, but it just doesn't feel right to me, it never did. I'm not so much bothered by the loneliness itself as much as I'm afraid of potentially choosing the wrong partner. When I enter into a new relationship I want it to be right this time. I want to be ready for it, and I don't think I am yet. I'm still working on finding out who I am and trying to have a better relationship with myself. I don't even want friends right now. I just want to be left alone, to do this recapitulation undisturbed. I am determined to know myself at the deepest level before anyone else does!"

"You'll have to have a relationship at some point," Chuck says, rather bluntly.

"Maybe not! Maybe a relationship just isn't right."

October 29, 2003

I dream of being in a room where everything is boxed up, furniture piled high, ready to be moved out, but I am reluctant to leave. I sense that someone is looking at me. I catch a glimpse of a face in a window and my first reaction is fear. I hide myself behind a pile of furniture in the middle of the room. I stay like that a long time, hiding my face in my hands. After a while I walk over to the window where I had seen the face and see a smiling woman looking back at me. She wants me to look for an eraser, shaped like a frog. It's in a small box, tied with a ribbon, she says. It strikes me as a ridiculous request and my first inclination is to brush her off, but then I realize that I had seen the box earlier and so I tell her to come in.

"I know it's here somewhere," I say, looking around.

I wake up in moody reluctance. Just as in the dream, I don't want to move, I want to stay where I am. The woman in my dream creatively urges me, suggesting perhaps that it's time to erase the past and move on. Everything is packed up and ready to go. What am I waiting for? I've done the work. Enough stalling, hiding, and making excuses. My dream tells me that it's time to take the leap!

There is a part of me that is like that smiling woman in the dream, but I can't find her today. What follows me out of bed is the energy of the first part of the dream, the reluctance to be part of life, even though yesterday I was beginning to feel that maybe the worst was over, that maybe now I could begin to live that new life that I sense is waiting for me. Yet here I am caught between worlds again, simultaneously ready to leap and yet so scared, so eager and yet so reluctant. I just can't do it today! The little leap frog of my dream is just going to have to stay boxed up a little longer.

I push myself out of the house early and am busy all day. I come home exhausted at four. The kids and I have an early dinner and while they do homework I read, do laundry, and take a bath. I finally realize how drained I am, but also how much lighter I feel as the evening wears on, as if something is being worked through me on a very deep inner level, slowly resolving itself.

As I turn in for the night, I realize that throughout the day I've been allowing the truth of what happened to me as a child to sink in. It's really hitting me, but I'm letting it. It's time. There's no point in staving off the truth.

The phrases, "the truth of it" and "the truth will set you free," came to me last night, spoken repeatedly, sinking into my subconscious and as I worked today I kept hearing them. And I thought about "the truth of it" and what that really means as I bring the truth home, really accept the truth of what happened, and more fully integrate who I once was with who I am right now, even as I simultaneously wonder who I might become. I sense how I really am changing on a very deep and visceral level. And that feels pretty darn good!

I feel no desire to have an interaction with my parents around any of this, though occasionally the thought pops up. Even Chuck brought it up the other day. The truth is that this remains a deeply private journey of discovery and it's only in keeping this process going, in a deeply instinctual unfolding, that I will ever set myself free. It isn't about them. It doesn't concern them, or even him, my abuser. It's about me and my ability to integrate my past, and all my parts, and evolve. I am not a victim and I will not be a "survivor." I intend to figure out why I've survived and discover what comes next. There has to be more to life than mere survival. I've already done that!

I am certain that the tremendous feelings of guilt, which I suffer constantly, will pass as the truth sinks deeper in and as new life comes to greet me. I still believe that art and writing, which have been the mainstays of my existence, will remain significant in my future. Not only are they my escapes, my safe places where I can be me, unbothered and unafraid, but they provide my income, and clearly they are on my path of heart.

I prefer my solitude, though I also admit that I like being in a relationship, and so what Chuck said is probably true, that at some point I will need to have a new relationship. There is still a part of me that protests that idea, the part of me that craves only to be alone. I have to figure out how to have both, to take care of my spirit while at the same time offering my physical self new life too. Both are equally important.

October 30, 2003

My father stands before me in a dream wearing a long white tunic. I sense that he's dead, speaking to me from another realm. "I'm sorry about the men," he says. "I'm sorry I couldn't do anything about them."

My father is physically deteriorating in real life. Death is hovering nearby, waiting patiently, and though I have often lately tried to have real conversations with him, it has proven impossible. I think the dream is telling me that he can't communicate in this reality anymore, but his spirit is willing to speak on his behalf. Or did I just dream that because I *wish* he could talk, even on his deathbed?

November has arrived too soon, bringing too many family commitments, Thanksgiving and an endless string of birthdays, right up until Christmas. I have little interest in family contact and dread having to be involved in yet another year of familial duty, but I push all that aside. I've got a busy day ahead of me and I need my energy for work. I must prepare myself to go out into the world and face my fears, for I admit that I am still afraid of everything, but today calls for me to be a professional and to be fully present.

In spite of the fact that I have been under great mental and emotional stress, my business is doing really well. I even paid my tax bill in full and on time! Thank you to my spiritual helpers, you good and compassionate souls! My pleading and prayers to you work, both my dream pleadings and my waking prayers. I still think reality sucks, but I am in it until I die, so I had better get used to it and learn to enjoy it! And I do feel so lucky to be where I am today, like a sturdy vine that has emerged through cracks in a concrete sidewalk to find the light; always a vine seeking the light.

"Some horror, some horrible thing is about to happen," my teenage self warns me as the workday ends. I take it that she means a memory is on the rise and as soon as I get home I go right into the bathroom and fill up the tub, always a good place to soothe and displace emotional heat. The hot water does the trick, loosening things, and the memory comes easily, rising like a bar of soap to the top of the memory pool.

In the memory, I am a teenager. I decide to clean myself with *Comet*, the super cleanser that is "tough on stains." I read the label on the can, check out what it's good for and decide that it will work on me because I am dirty and disgusting. I make a paste and rub it all over my body, starting with my face, my acne spots, my breasts, belly, genitals, legs, until I am covered with pale green paste slowly drying and cracking, the strong smell of chlorine, the burning sting of it irritatingly perfect, releasing me. The pain of it justifies my own inner pain as I step into the shower and scrub it off, scouring myself with a rough cloth, intent upon ridding myself of my dirt and stains, intent upon making myself clean and pure.

All it did in reality was turn me red and blotchy!

October 31, 2003

I wander the deserted streets of a strange, futuristic city in a dream. Some disaster has happened, but life goes on. The city is constructed of modern terraced buildings. There are no doors or entryways to the buildings on the street level where I'm standing and I can't figure out how to get up to the terraces that stretch high above me into the sky. I see people, restaurants, vegetable and fruit markets, life happening on the higher levels. Try as I might I can't figure out how to get up there, though I am intent on finding a way.

Then I am in my childhood bedroom, which is painted starkly white. My mother is there folding clothes. She doesn't notice that I have big spoons hanging from my labia. I try to get her attention by digging into my vagina with the spoons, but she never looks at me. A woman doctor comes in and tells me she can help.

"I can't get it out!" I tell her, feeling intense shame and guilt. "I can't get it out!"

The doctor brings me to an office building and into a large room where a gigantic telescope is suspended from the ceiling. I lie down on the table beneath it. The doctor digs into my vagina, using whatever she can find. I feel nothing. I only want to be rid of "it." While she is digging around inside me, I look out the window of the room and wonder if anyone can see in. Then I realize it doesn't matter; I am nothing, I am not special, and I don't care if anyone sees me. I just want her to dig it out, the guilt, the tremendous sense of guilt attached to my vagina and what happened there. In frustration, the doctor pulls down the telescopic contraption, now a giant drill. I wake up as she turns it on and drills into me.

I am confronted with the truth of my mother in this dream, ignored by her in spite of the bizarre portrayal of the sexual abuse—the spoons hanging from my labia. As usual, she sees nothing, hears nothing, cares not to know. When my father's spirit came to me in a dream the other night it was telling the truth, that he couldn't protect me, he was incapable, but it also acknowledged that he knew about the abuse. I must accept the truths about my mother that are revealed in this dream. She is not capable of or interested in knowing the truth. The best I can do now is move on into the future, to the city of new life, as revealed in the first part of the dream, with the truth fully revealed and accepted by me, for me. My parents, this dream underscores, are not important.

Once again, my dreams stress where I am in the context of this changing journey: still between worlds, but the worlds are looking clearer, taking shape. The new world of the future looks bright and intriguing, yet I'm not quite able to access it, though I am fully determined to find my way to higher levels and new life. Then I get pulled back into the recapitulation and the old world, having to face what my child self already knows so clearly, that my mother was in her own world, that she was blind and deaf to my experiences as a child. I have to admit that it doesn't really bother me, for the truth is that I am more interested in the unfolding of this journey, the discoveries I'm making as I recapitulate, and the exciting possibilities that lie ahead than I am in the past. As I continue this inner work, I will empty myself of all the bad feelings, and I will do it for myself alone. The dream does suggest, however, that I must dig deeper still, though I hope not in too violent a way!

Every time I confront how neglected I was, I am given the opportunity to tend to my child self in a much deeper way. I don't have to be ashamed. I am not dirty and disgusting. I am beautiful. I must accept the fact that my parents were simply lacking and then let them go. It's time to move on. I don't owe them anything. I don't owe them a damn thing. But I'm still angry. How hard is it to hug your children? How hard is it to tell them you love them? I make sure I hug my kids and tell them I love them every day. I feel terrible if I miss that opportunity.

"Are you running from safety?" Chuck asks.

I see that the book of that name by Richard Bach, *Running From Safety*, is directly in his line of vision and he keeps glancing at it as we talk, and so I am not surprised when he asks me this question.

"Yes, I'm running from the old safety," I say. "It doesn't work anymore, but I have yet to find a new place of safety and that has been a big problem. It's not easy to find a place to settle that feels safe and good, where the old me is at peace and the new me is happy. But hopefully I will arrive at it soon. I know I must look deep inside myself. I'm aware of peacefulness deep inside myself, sitting and waiting for me to just reach in and grasp it, but I may have to journey much further before I reach it, much further than I've imagined."

"Be patient," Chuck says, "just be patient."

"I want the past to recede now," I say. "I want it out of my face. It can be in the background, I don't really care, but I need it to give me some space now, give me some air."

I need to give myself some air too, and utter calmness. It's what I need more than anything at this point, calmness of body and mind. I've been in a state of shock now for a few years, hanging in there as this recapitulation has unfolded, and I've been willing to go the distance, but it's time to move on now. Time for new life.

Chapter 5

Basically Sane

November 1, 2003

I dream that I am in a modern house. It's totally empty. My daughter comes in with some other children. I want to be alone. I tell them they have to leave. She protests, telling me they're having fun and she doesn't want me to spoil it. I fly into a rage and physically tackle her. She fights back, strongly and fiercely. As we tumble around like two cats, hissing and scratching each other, a sudden change takes place. Now we're in a very old house, rusty claw-footed bathtubs stacked about, dusty broken stairs, a derelict house. My daughter jumps up and begins screaming at me, loudly. I feel completely helpless as I experience her verbally letting go. The amount of stuff she seems to have to express is incredible! I make square shapes with my hands, signaling that she should box it in, but she looks at me like I'm crazy. There's no stopping her; it's totally impossible! She shouts on, letting go with gusto.

Then I am driving along ice and snow covered roads. All the other cars are slipping and sliding all over the place, but mine is not. I have perfect control. I drive effortlessly and flawlessly, without any consequences. Then I am feeding orange slices to a kitten. The kitten speaks to me, saying, "No more," and transforms into a human baby. Turning her back to me, curling into a fetal position, she says, "It is enough now."

Once again, I am dealing with two worlds in these dreams, the old and the new, though I prefer to be in the new world now, in the modern house that I want to be alone in. I am pulled out of the new in the beginning of the dream when my daughter enters, my inner child showing up again. I get angry at her for invading my new space, so angry that I fly into a rage, but the truth is clearly shown: we are not done yet. I have to let her express all that has been repressed. I feel completely helpless as I watch her explode, though my psyche allows me to gain a little control in the second dream by letting me drive with ease. In the end, the anger, the emotion, having been released, is transformed back into its animal nature, into a docile kitten and then a sated baby ready to rest, to finally recede into the past, everything recapitulated, everything done. This dream portends the future completion of this transition through these dual worlds, with issues still needing attention given appropriate expression and put to rest, naturally.

I went to bed last night feeling terrible, still full of such guilt and shame, and then I cried and cried, trying to hold it in so the kids wouldn't hear me. I didn't feel free enough to really vent, but the child in me was not going to be held back. Good for her!

November 2, 2003

Everything is a dream. The memories have the essence of dreams or nightmares, affecting me the way dreams do, but they also fade the way dreams fade. I'm beginning to experience that now, as a lot of the memories no longer carry the impact they once did, as they recede into just being memories, no triggers left in them. This is what I have expected. I'm not so sure the physical memories will fade as easily though, the pain in my muscles persistently hanging on, though I constantly relax and release. Perhaps there is still more for my body to tell me, but I'm so tired of having pain, of needing to cry and scream, of being unable to express myself. I'm tired of the shame and the fear that cling to me like dirt, tired of the loneliness and the black emptiness inside me.

I sense it's time to focus outwardly now, to literally be in the world more. Energy expressed, in some fashion, is healing, while energy held inside is burning pain. I spent yesterday outside with the kids, working around the yard, hanging out. It was so good for all of us, noticeably so. My body relaxed, my mind relaxed, my mood relaxed. I need to keep finding ways to shift my focus outwardly, away from my inner work, try to be more present with the kids, not so self-involved, though that is still necessary too.

I remain intent upon continuing my journey along this spiritual path that has been unfolding before me. The dilemma is how to do that while also staying fully present and available to this reality. I'm sure I'm not the first person to have to figure this out! But I have already proven to myself that if not dealt with the pain will stay inside, swirling around, causing incredible illness, holding me back. Night and day it still grips me, but it is only in its release that salvation and transformation will come.

I made it through the day! No big events, except the need to cry, tears sneaking out when I least expected them. I eased them gently out, acquiesced to letting them have their way. If in no other way, at least in slow and incremental release, I will survive this process and achieve new life, that I am certain of.

The kids are okay. We had fun for a second day in a row, took a hike, picked apples, and they did homework. We talked a lot. It was good, but I still feel distant, separated by a wall that I can't quite scale, though at times I can see right through it!

November 3, 2003

I wake up feeling lost, in an old doubtful place. Sadness and uncertainty fight for domination, the old world once again trying to assert itself. I must be strong and stand firmly in this new reality. I can't give up now!

The truth is, it's often hard to get motivated, even though I have so many good things happening right now, for life really is quite magical, but I have years of shocking discoveries still to process and assimilate. I feel like a transplant from some other planet who has to figure out how life in this new world works. Even so, I am fully aware that the recapitulation is not totally done. I don't, for instance, think that I've released all the anger yet, or expressed the sadness, and I still have blocks of fear and shame to deal with. Though I continue to soften a little bit more every day, getting myself to a place where I feel good about things is a very slow process. I must be patient.

My horoscope for the month underscores exactly what I'm going through: *a time of great change.* It even states that I will find myself projected into a new world and that it will be hard. Yes! The advice is to stay in motion and not get stuck in old patterns of behavior. Yes! This is something I am very conscious of, that the only way to affect change is to keep moving. When in motion other things can happen—think snowball effect—while when stationary nothing happens at all!

I seek to break away from my old behaviors and habits— every single one of them—and head into new life totally free and unburdened. That old world has just about depleted my energy and if I stay in it much longer I don't think I will survive. I've faced this truth of death before, knowing that if I did not do something to help myself then I was making a pact with death. That has always scared me out of a depressive state long enough to catapult myself into something new. Once again I face death. What else is there? We all face it every day. I have a choice to make every morning: do I let the old stuff bury me or do I brazenly go forward? I choose to brazenly go forward, even if I have to drag myself along!

This recapitulation will heal me, and it will cleanse me too, but only if I can find a way to forgive myself. That is the final healing.

Shards, splinters of brittle glass, stabbing and piercing, bleeding and hurting, this is what I feel as the day goes on. Why can't I cry then? My mother, so cold and closed, showed me how to close myself too. No doors ever opened in her; even in the very beginning I knew there was nothing there for me. So I closed my own doors and fled behind them to that small tunnel inside myself where I rolled up tight enough so that all the bad and scary things were far away. Now, I am opening the doors, expelling the old ghosts, airing the dirty laundry, learning to breathe. I am discovering that I am whole. I am being reborn, a perfectly formed being, gulping for air.

Why is birthing so painful? I should know how to do this. I should be able to handle this. I should be happy and carefree now. Why wait any longer? But the old me tells me that to feel happy for more than just a few seconds is dangerous because something bad will surely happen. Bad things always happened in the old world. But I'm not in the old world anymore. I must keep reminding myself of that. Maybe now I will be allowed to be happy, maybe now I can let down my shoulders, unclench my jaw, relax my fists, and breathe. Maybe now I can finally live.

Constant movement in body and mind get me through the day. I hope I can keep this up because a softening is finally happening. I am able to cry more easily now, with real tears, and not just that hoarse croaking sound I'd been making for so long. If I can keep moving and not let either my mind or body settle on the old stuff then I may be all right. I am hopeful that one day I will feel almost normal, not so deeply disturbed or filled with such shame and guilt, my two crippling companions. It's time to send them off. I pump myself with positive reinforcement, intent on becoming the good mother to my inner child, letting the old voices of shame and guilt fade away, letting the new voices of renewal and freedom rise and take over now.

I begin to understand how the mother I got in this lifetime prepared me for the life I lived. Her neglect not only sent me into the arms of my abuser, but taught me how to survive on my own. What was most painful to me also presented me with my greatest strengths. I must grapple with this dichotomy as I continue this recapitulation, finding a way to accept everything, the negative and the positive, everything as necessary, meaningful, and valuable, even that which caused the most pain.

I am beginning to see my parents more objectively and honestly now too, able to accept them as they are, but also able to accept just how terribly neglectful they really were. My siblings and I joke about them, about how distant they were and are, about how little they communicated, how little affection and interest they showed, how little guidance we received. I'm surprised we all grew up into such highly functioning and fulfilled adults, or even that we made it into adulthood at all. Somehow we received enough.

In the end, I know I have to let it all go, shed all the old issues and ideas, until the memories are gone from mind and body, until I am innocent once again.

November 4, 2003

I am sitting in the woods in a dream, quietly waiting, for what I'm not sure, but I feel contented and at peace. I laugh and am immediately ashamed.

"Why won't you let yourself be happy?" I ask.

"I am too afraid, too afraid," I say.

"No," I reply, "you can't do that anymore. You have to let happiness be a part of your life too. It exists, and it belongs to you too. It is part of life."

I gain distance by softening and releasing the memories when they come, rather than letting them dominate. I free myself one memory at a time, letting the feelings attached to them go too.

I do yoga, going deeply and more fully into each pose, holding them as I soften and release, breathing all the while. I am learning to let good things happen by not letting the bad things get control. The memories may still flit in and out of my life, but they can't have me anymore.

I sit in the car waiting for my daughter to return from an audition, trying to relax, but I can't even breathe. I am in extreme discomfort. What am I holding onto now, and why? "It's fear," Chuck said, when we met this morning. He recognized it when he mimicked what I do, clenching up his shoulders and pulling into himself. He shrank in and looked so old and pathetic that it scared me. Is that what I look like?

I know I don't need to be afraid anymore, it's an old ally, but my body hasn't quite understood that, not wholly. I need to keep shifting so I don't fall into the old body habits, the old postures. I need to hold myself differently, walk differently, stand and even sleep differently. Chuck said the old habits will always be with me, they are in memory, physical memory, so I have to catch myself and change with *consciousness*. I'm in the process of doing that now, changing everything.

"Behaviorists and shamans alike agree that it takes four to six weeks of intense, concentrated effort to change behavioral patterns," Chuck said.

I've begun sleeping curled up in a ball again, a habit that I broke for a while, but I've recently gone back to the old comfort of it, solely for that comfort. As a result, I am waking up in great pain again and it stays with me all day. I notice that as I unclench one part of my body, the energy that had been caught there doesn't flow out and become part of my whole body energy but tends to circulate, as if looking for another vulnerable area in the body in which to settle, as if there is no outlet for such energy, that it can only exist in clenched muscles. But I have the discipline and expertise to change it. With concentrated effort, and enough time, I should be able to change the way my energy works. I know how to do yoga and meditation, how to breathe a flowing breath, how to open the crown of my head and allow my energy to release and how to allow healing light to flow in. I know, instinctively and consciously, how to release energy.

Chuck said there is usually a final effort on the part of the habit to remain attached, when it stubbornly refuses to move. Maybe that's where I am now, at the point of final push and refusal, the old stuff hanging on harder as it feels my efforts to pry it loose. I haven't hurt like this in a long time.

"Please, Jeanne, help! Help me let the fear go. I don't want to carry it; I don't need to bear this burden any longer. I want to dump it!"

"*When the moment is right it will happen,*" Jeanne says. "*It's just not ready to release you yet.*"

November 5, 2003

My body expresses everything I'm going through. I am so stiff and in pain that I just hobble around now. Am I fighting, am I holding back, or is this what letting go feels like? I do yoga and breathing to help things along, a little bit every few hours. When the yoga and breathing themselves become uncomfortable I back off. I have to take this very slowly, institute a very gentle practice, without pushing too much.

It's raining heavily. I try to stay calm, but fear creeps in with the pounding of the rain against the windows. I override it. I handle it. I have so many commissions going right now and it will be another good income month if I can just stay focused and get everything accomplished.

What is there to be so afraid of?

Before I even finish asking that question I know that it isn't even the question to ask anymore. The question to ask now is: How to keep ridding my body of the fear that cripples me? And the answer to that question is: by physically relaxing every muscle in my body, over and over again, until I have trained them to be loose and stay loose. If at all possible, that is my intention.

I struggle with my body all day, try to find new postures, new ways to sit, walk, and rest, but I am still in such pain no matter what pose I try. My entire body is clenched from head to toe, as if I am perpetually cold and shivering, the muscles tense and gripping, but I am gritted against fear and pain, not cold. As I relax slightly, I notice that my shoulders stay scrunched up. It's as if I'm trying to become invisible, to shrink and disappear, and I probably am, in body memory. For fifty years I've been trying to hide, that's all my body has ever known.

November 6, 2003

I wake in the night, yelling loudly and hoarsely, my throat wide open, my body clenched. I'm surprised to find myself on my back, stretched out, taut, rather than curled in the usual fetal pose. Sudden, bitter, fiery anger rushes out through my legs and I kick and kick and kick at the invisible man trying to grab my legs, trying to spread them apart and rape me. I am fucking furious!

"Just hold on for one more day," I tell myself, shaking violently. Just one more day to get through. Then I see Chuck.

"*You will be busy,*" Jeanne says. "*You will get paid for your hard work today, and you will have the job done so you can start on the furniture commissions tomorrow. The furniture will be a lot of fun. It's okay to be happy. It's okay to feel good about yourself. Tomorrow you will see Chuck and then you can tell him everything you feel you want to tell him. He understands.*"

"*Relax. Try to unclench throughout the day. It's the first key to getting someplace new because without first unclenching there will be no release. As long as you clench then you hold everything in. Start to let go, just gradually at first. Find a way to send it out and away, not just to another area of your body, but out into the universe, out through the crown of your head if that feels more appropriate. No posture will feel comfortable if the clenching is still going on; there will be no progress if the clenching is still occurring.*"

"*Breathe, meditate, relax, cry, yell, kick, do whatever you need to do to release, in any way that it needs to be expressed. Don't hold it in, don't, there is no need.*"

"*Your mother does not control you. Even though you still hear her scolding voice, she doesn't have control. You are in control. Even though that scared and traumatized little girl is locked inside you, you are now in charge. You are the mother now. Let the little girl go free. Help her to cry and yell. Help her to express all those tears and all that pent up anger. She needs release from your body. Help her, free her. Tell her it's time to do it differently now. Tell her that everything will be okay. He isn't here anymore either. No one is here to scold or yell or threaten or rape. You are safe now."*

"*Speak to your little girl self,*" Jeanne concludes.

"Okay, thank you, Jeanne."

"It's just us now, and Chuck," I say to my inner child. "He knows how much you need and desire to feel safe, and he knows how bad you feel. He knows how scared and alone you are, but I am here too. I am a mature woman now. I gave life to my own two children and I can give it to us too. I can give you life. Let's see if we can climb to the top of the dark tunnel today, right up to the opening, so we can come out now. I am waiting; Chuck is waiting."

I climb into bed after a long day at work, the pain in my body signaling a memory about to emerge. I lie in a ball and wait.

"It won't hurt so much next time," I hear my abuser saying as he opens me up, stretching my vagina with his tools and his penis. Then I hear my mother's voice, louder than his, saying: "No one will ever know about this!" Then I am lying on the ground. My abuser lies next to me. He is talking intimately to me, as if we were lovers, touching me, patting me, telling me it won't hurt so much next time. "Every time it will hurt a little less," he says. I am keeping secrets, forced to keep so many secrets. Secrets are swirling through my body, between my legs, in my head, painful secrets. I need to cry. Anger in my throat. Anger in my legs. Anger in my teeth and jaw. I break away and roll out of bed, wondering if I'll be able to sleep at all tonight.

November 7, 2003

"Black waves of memory and pain keep coming," I say, sitting down in Chuck's office.

"Don't let them take over," Chuck says, very sternly.

"They are unrelenting. I can't stop them."

"Well, you have at least three choices the way I see it," says Chuck. "You can be knocked down by them. You can shoot through them, or you can ride them. Choose your attitude. Don't let them destroy you. You *will* live through this. You won't let them destroy your life. In spite of them, you will have a good life."

"I get it," I say. "It's how I choose to deal with them that's the key, and not so much that I have them. Just deal with them in a positive way."

"So how are you going to tackle the waves as they come in?" Chuck asks. "Are you going to get knocked down?"

"No, I'm going to ride them!"

"Your abuser's energy comes in one form or another, but he doesn't have control over how you react. He will show up, but you pick the method of attack."

"Sometimes I can't do it," I say, "but that's okay too. I'll just have to live with it. I'm strong, I know. And, as you say, I'm in control. I will handle it."

The day is exhausting and I feel teary, but I don't let the black waves control me. All day, I ride them quite well, but even as I ride them I keep thinking they're trying to tell me something. Something is striving to come to consciousness, to bridge the worlds. It has something to do with my mother. It's something I'm not quite ready to go to, at least not willingly, though it keeps resurfacing, something to do with her and my abuser. The tension, however, is too great. As soon as I get home from work I sit on my bed and do the sweeping breath, the magical pass of recapitulation.

A scene begins to emerge. I am in it and I am watching it at the same time. It's foggy and unclear. I see my mother talking and laughing with my abuser. Suddenly, I feel the tight grip of my mother's hand on my arm as she hurries me along the path crossing my abuser's property and heading down toward our house. My mother is furious. *No one will ever, ever hear about this! Do you hear me!* Frantically, she pulls me along, her fingers digging deeply into my arm.

Something happened! Something happened!

I stop the magical pass and pull away from the memory. But my mother hated my abuser! She still talks about him with obvious disdain, but in the memory I saw her looking happy with him. "They are horrid people!" she exclaimed as recently as this past summer. Imagine if she knew, if she knew who and what, and still she didn't protect me?! *If* she knew, she kept it to herself, making it all go away by ignoring it. Did she slip up the time she called me to tell me about a cousin, aged twelve, who had a "benign growth" that the doctors later discovered was a pregnancy?

"But she's only twelve," I said.

"Oh, it happens! Believe me, it happens!" she said, quite emphatically, so much emotion quite unusual for her.

I wondered for a long time about that phone call, just why she called and gave me that information. It was so out of character. We rarely spoke and I had no connection to the much younger cousin in question. Why did she think my cousin's dilemma would interest me? Was she calling to see if I might have remembered my own twelve-year-old self in the same position, a pregnancy explained away as a "benign growth?" At the time I had no such memory, any stirrings of memory still decades away. Her tone was one of agitated, yet slightly sinister excitement: "You'll never believe this... guess what happened to your cousin!" Did she use the news to absolve herself of her own carelessness?

Do I dare ask her? Do I confront her? Is this all true? Is this the way it was? Did she know? Did she have some relationship with my abuser too? Can I believe my visions, my flashes of memory? Why can't I confront my parents? They are so fragile, my mother especially adherent to her rules, her life neatly compacted, orderly and tight, with no place for frills, such as love and joy, so locked away are her feelings. The truth is, I am afraid of her. I am absolutely afraid of her and her screeching denial. I know how devastating it would be for her to hear that I remember my childhood. I have to be careful. It's a delicate situation and I'm sensitive to her moods. She hates when anyone talks about personal issues. She shuts down immediately.

She's a hard and unapproachable old lady now, tightly closed. Who is she hiding from now? Only herself and her own memories perhaps? I also see her vulnerabilities and her mistakes. I see her and my father as two unhappy people. They don't exist anymore in the way I always thought of them, in the way I thought of them when I was a child. They don't really exist for me at all anymore. They are just two empty gray ghosts. Poor little old man and poor little old woman.

The memory keeps returning, wanting to show me more, stressing that my time of recapitulation is far from over. There is still more to learn. I intend to ride the waves, but if they knock me down I will just get up and prepare for the next one. One day soon there will be no more waves.

November 8, 2003

I dream. I am in a blizzard, carrying a change of clothing. I cross an expanse of railroad tracks just as some trains come chugging along, huge and powerful, steam and snow swirling about them. As they come barreling down the tracks one after the other, I realize I just missed getting hit, so silently did they slide along the snow covered tracks. The streets are all blocked because of the snow, cars stuck all over the place. I go into a building and down into the basement where I get stuck too, unable to find an exit. I meet a girl and ask her the way out. She points to a door. I exit and go back outside and into the blizzard. Walking along the narrow snow covered streets I feel quite lost. Eventually, I come upon a car abandoned in a snowbank and decide to take it. As I back the car up, I bump right into my father. I hear a thud as I hit him and watch as he falls to the ground. I drive away, leaving him there in the snow. Afterwards I find him lying on a bed in a dark room under a pile of crumpled blankets. When I call out to him he doesn't answer. I realize I probably killed him.

During the dream I am carrying a bundle of clothing, indicating my firm intention to change. When I met with Chuck yesterday he urged me to change, to find a way to keep going, no matter what comes at me or gets in my way, to beat the black waves of memory as they come barreling along, one after the other, like the trains in this dream.

"You get out of the way, you move on, you don't let them destroy you, you keep going, you find a way out," he said.

Well, I certainly accomplished that as I navigated through this dream! It's a little strange that I killed off my father without batting an eye or feeling any emotion, though my intention has been to kill off my mother, in a metaphorical sense of course! It just proves my lack of emotional attachment to my parents in general, especially as I noted right before bed last night that I see them as dead already. Heartless as it was to drive off and leave him, it was the only reaction I had. I didn't even question it. I guess my dreaming self wanted to underscore my complete detachment!

I feel pretty good today, in better spirits than a long time. Murder has its positive aspects!

Yesterday, I was afforded a new look at my mother in that snippet of memory. The realization that she probably knew what was going on knocks my socks off! I can't feel anything for her right now except anger. I will eventually let it go, but right now I also feel a deep sense of loss at never having had a real mother, of having been a casualty of other people's dysfunctional lives. And when I encountered my abuser it only added to the whole mess. I'm not feeling sorry for myself, just stating the facts as I see them!

If my mother really knew that I was being abused all along, and if she had something going on with my abuser, then she used the same tactics to keep me quiet that he did: threats. If I spoke, I destroyed everything, all of their lives. I understand now why she was so mysterious, so different from other mothers, why she kept to herself, why she was so reserved and angry. My mother's anger could leave you cold, and it did leave me chilled to the bone often enough; it still does. But I also know her intimately. I have been trying to rid myself of her my entire life, to become who I truly am and not just a carbon copy of that angry woman. I had all the markings of becoming just like her, frightened and angry too, but I've always chosen to question who I am in relation to the world as I experience it. Even as I struggle in my darkness, I seek always the light. I refuse to be the carrier of her secrets. I even refuse to continue carrying my own!

It just dawned on me that obviously my parents knew! What have I been thinking? Why has that fact not sunk in until now? My father took me for an abortion in the middle of the night. They had set that up ahead of time, so of course they knew! At least they knew something! I think my father knew a lot less than my mother. When it was discovered that I was pregnant her anger was abusive and self-protective, worried as she was that I would ruin them in the eyes of the world. Maybe her real worry was that I would spill the beans about her liaisons with my abuser. Wouldn't that have created a mess for her!

Still, to this day, I see her holding everything in. I see her anger. When she was sick a few months ago I saw something I didn't like in her, an icy coldness, a disconnect from feeling and emotion that I've seen and experienced often enough but never wanted to accept, her inability to truly relate and truly love. She has distanced herself from her emotions so totally that it's visible on the outside now; there is no warmth, no spark of anything loving about her. But Chuck is right, I can't let this control my life; I have to move on. Okay, I am moving on.

This new knowledge is devastating, yet something will come from it; I will change. I will put on that change of clothing I carried all night long and the snow will melt and I will find my way to another place. It's interesting to note that my mother was nowhere in my dream last night. I think that is significant of my entire life, she was absent as a true mother. I wasn't allowed to kill her off in my dream, as I did my father. It's not her time yet. There is still a lot to learn about her, and myself too, I gather.

I go for a cold and blustery walk. It's like being in the blizzard of my dream, the wind so vicious I almost turn back but challenge myself to charge into it instead, as if it were the painful waves of recapitulation.

"Please cleanse me!" I beg the wind. "Please cleanse me!"

I feel that I must suffer, that I must do something drastic and painful to gain forgiveness. Why can't I simply forgive myself? Why the need for more punishment? I have already been punished enough. As I walk, realizations continue to hit hard, how strange and deceptive my parents were and are, how in denial. I must not judge them but keep in mind that they did the best they could, based on who they were and how they chose to live their lives. I don't feel that I owe them anything, nor do I feel obligated to love them either. The truth is, I feel only sorry for them at this point.

I must remember that I am doing all this deep inner work for myself, for my own evolution, striving always to keep an open and trusting relationship with myself and my own kids. I am not doing this to have a better relationship with my parents. They are already dead to me. I take note of and accept in my mother the same things I struggle with in myself, but I am determined to work through them and resolve them. I find my parents draining to be around, but as things have unfolded I feel a need to ask them something about the past, though I'm not sure how to do it yet. If I could get confirmation from them on just one thing I could get beyond my own denial. Did they know? Or do I already have the answer? Was I given it in that dream when my dad said he was sorry for not protecting me from the men?

I watch the full moon eclipse from the street outside the artist's gallery where I am working in the evening. I join a small group of people on the sidewalk, eating up the moon energy. A pink cloud blocks the intensity of the moon until the sky finally clears and then we watch as a shadowy scrim slowly makes its way across the moon's bright face, as if invisible hands were pulling ethereal drapery, veiling its holy light. Later on, I feel the pull of the moon in a crick in my neck as I turn down the covers on my bed and climb into the dip in the futon mattress made by my body over the past few years. I snuggle in, a little moon being settling in for the night.

"I need to change," I say out loud, and the cats leap over me like cows jumping over the moon, full of energy, too frisky for sleeping on this moony night.

"*Don't sleep in that tight ball tonight or you'll just stay the same,*" Jeanne says. "*Shift, dig a new hole in the futon, lie a different way, change your old habits, try something new, flip the mattress over and start again. Read the moon for new thoughts, read the stars and planets as they shift.*"

I look up at the full moon glowing outside my window, searching for my own star, a place to rest and be safe. The clock turns to twelve-thirty, but I am unable to rest, to find peace. It's cold out tonight, but I am hot and uncomfortable. Restless as the cats, I toss and turn. My fetal body pose has so deeply marred the mattress that it's impossible to find another comfortable spot. The bed is molded to another person—the old me!

Another hour goes by and no sleep. Better to acquiesce. Better to write it out. Better to state the truths. I accept the truth that I lost my mother almost from the beginning. She made a decision to cut herself off. Perhaps I became a reminder of uncomfortable memories and decisions. Perhaps I held too many shameful secrets. Was I a constant reminder? But of what? And why does she speak with such hatred and disgust in her voice when the name of my abuser is mentioned? Was there something between them? It's possible. It is very possible. Did she lead another life too, live in another world too? Was there actually something going on? A flash of memory adds to the mystery. She is yelling at me and my abuser's daughter to get out of the kitchen. She is there with him. What are they doing in the kitchen? Did he get her too, or was his preference for little girls? Or did he not care? Was it just the conquest that mattered?

With these questions thrown out to the universe, I turn out the light. Even the cats are finally settling down, curling up at my feet for the night. Maybe now we can all get some sleep!

November 9, 2003

I want clarity. I want to clearly see through the veils and know everything, if at all possible. The memories are, of course, helping me gain clarity to a certain extent, but they also make me question my own sanity. They are so shocking, how could they possibly be true? Over time, clarity will eventually come. I trust that. In the meantime, I write everything down. This writing has proven to be a critical part of this process of freeing myself from the past. It's a soothing activity too, soothing to my poor tired soul, soothing to that exhausted little girl inside me, and that sad and depressed teenager too. I come back to this writing again and again as a method of release, as valuable as the physical and emotional release, as I finally give the long held-down words an outlet. As I write, my spirit is calmed, even my muscles seem to relax as the words take shape, expressing not only my pain but also my sadness and disappointment about the turn my early life took as a result of decisions made by the adults in my life.

As each new day dawns I set the intent to channel my energies into creativity and to follow my heart as never before, trusting that this recapitulation process will lead me out of the woods, never to return. But I am also aware that I must leave behind the people who have inhabited my life until now if I am to evolve, especially the parents who thought they were good parents, who thought they were doing the right thing. I must leave them to their own devices, leave them behind in the darkness of the woods and step out into the sunlight, for that is where I belong now.

I have finally discovered what the woods held for me, their dark mysteries now unveiled. I have pieced together what I know so far, rewritten the story of my life based on the memories that have been revealed, a new life story greatly revised from what I previously understood about who I was and how I got to be me. And I have accepted this as my truth. I have learned to accept that my life was once largely driven by fear, anger, and depression, though I also accept that it has been a meaningful life, even wonderful in many respects, though I have come to understand now that I have not yet truly lived. That is what I look forward to, to fully living life.

What does "fully living life" mean? In the past I thought I was living just fine, but I have discovered that I lived in fear and illusion. With clarity comes a different sense of life, a sense of the magic beyond illusion, a sense of belonging that I have rarely experienced. To fully live now means to let go of the fear. That is the key; to let go of the fear and to trust that life will unfold in good and positive ways. As long as I keep telling myself that I'm afraid then I remain afraid, but if I allow myself to be open and trusting then everything is possible. As long as I remain caught by fear I will remain crippled in body, mind, and spirit. My challenge is to be mindful of what is going on inside of me at all times, or as much as possible, checking that I am staying true to my new self and my new intended path. If I feel the fear, I must breathe it out and let positive affirmations take its place. It may not be easy, as it means painfully opening up passages—mental, physical, and emotional—that have long been blocked. It means being vulnerable, trusting that I will be safe. It's a constant battle, but well worth the effort!

I believe my mother knew, very early on, that my abuser was doing something to me. I feel also that I witnessed him doing something to her, a sense of something happening between them in that bit of memory. What did I actually witness? I need to let myself go back and look very carefully so that I might retrieve and understand more fully, so that I can move on from here.

I do the sweeping breath, letting my neck and shoulders relax as I breathe in and turn my head one way, then breathe out turning my head in the opposite direction. Back and forth, from shoulder to shoulder I sweep my head, breathing in and out, in and out. Gradually, as I relax, allowing my eyes to soften their gaze, things become clear. I see my mother so full of shame, but I realize now that it wasn't about me. I realize now that it was about her and him. Two scenes flash repeatedly before me, teasing me, inviting me to investigate, to go deeper, to take a closer look. Do I go? I acquiesce. How could I not?

In the first scene, I see the color green. Why do I see green? The floor and the counters of our kitchen were of green linoleum and green Formica. "Go away! Go outside!" They yell at us, me and my abuser's daughter, but I stay at the screened door looking in. He is holding her up against a countertop. I smell the screen, the stale smell of dust clinging to the sun-warmed mesh, and I hear them grunting like animals. "Don't hurt her," I think, for I know on some level that what they are doing hurts.

The second scene is outside, the memory that came earlier. Perhaps he was bringing me home and we stopped to rest because I see us sitting under a tree. I am perhaps three years old. His penis is out of his pants. He is teaching me to put it into my mouth. Then she is there, my mother. He stands up fast. She laughs. He grabs her arm. "Don't hurt my mommy!" I say. "I'm not hurting her," he says. They are laughing. Afterwards, when we are walking home along the path she is so furious with me that I think I have done something wrong. Whatever it is, it must be my fault. She yells at me, screaming into my face, her voice harsh, yet tightly controlled. I look into her smoldering dark eyes, staring coldly into mine, and shrink away. I am afraid of her and her bitter anger.

I pull away from the recapitulation, do a few last breaths to sweep away the memories, exhaling the negative energy of them, leaving it to the universe to hold the memories for me now, while I breathe in the fresh air of release and liberation. As usual, I feel lighter afterwards, but more puzzled too. Did she see what he was doing to me? Did she choose to ignore it because of what she was there for?

If it had gotten out that she was having an affair with that man in particular it would have destroyed the entire life she had constructed with my father. She had every reason to keep it quiet. It was nineteen-fifties America. She was a Catholic living in a very isolated place, surrounded by in-laws, trapped under the thumbs of my well-off grandparents. I heard my mother bitterly and angrily expressing her disappointment to my father often enough: "We should have gotten away from them when we had the chance!"

I carried the secrets I forged with my abuser and now I also understand that I carried the secrets my mother forged with him too. It explains my fear of my mother and the deeper shame I still bear, relating specifically to her and the treatment I received from her as a child. My mother always held herself to a high standard of social propriety, but I now suspect she was hiding a lot behind her restrained, tight-lipped behavior. It's clear to me now that a lot of anger was always brewing just beneath the surface of her reserved demeanor, especially apparent in a condescending attitude that popped up whenever there was something she didn't want to confront or be confronted about. I witnessed and was the recipient of both the anger and the control often enough, not to mention her stinging condescension. I still feel the bite of it to this day. Anything that was troublesome or didn't fit into her idea of what was proper had to be kept out of sight, never to be aired or shared. Well, I guess I'm letting it all out of the bag now!

In not facing the truths of my own life I am just following the example set by my mother. In so doing I keep myself as tightly controlled as she has kept herself, locked in a fantasy world where nothing bad ever happens, simply because it is vehemently denied. Meanwhile my body and psyche have been trying, my entire life, to alert me to the fact that something just isn't right in that make-believe world. I have to accept what I see in the flashbacks and memories or I will never be free. I too am an expert at denial. It's my inheritance! It's so easy to *not see* what's right before my eyes and, at the same time, it's so hard to *see* what's right before my eyes too!

My memories are the truths of my existence, the roadmaps of the life I have lived thus far. I have to accept what they inform me of, painful or not. I realize I ended up carrying a double secret, my relationship with my abuser and my mother's relationship with him, both of which were never to be spoken of. I ended up afraid of both of them, afraid of my abuser and afraid of my own mother. I learned how to survive by being complicit with the adults who mattered in my life, even as they made choices and decisions that had devastating effects on me.

I am not blaming or judging them. I am just trying to discover the truth. I am learning to unburden myself, to let it go, to undo the damage. I will no longer play a part in the family game of denial. My parents have always chosen to remain closed and in denial, and that doesn't seem to have changed, and so I won't interfere. Even attempts to talk about my father's health are rudely and abruptly silenced. They continue to construct walls and lock doors, no prying allowed, you can't come in, so I don't even try. If they are ever ready to accept responsibility for the mistakes they made I will be ready to listen, but until then I understand that they can't go there, and I accept that. They shut down a long time ago. I need to save myself, not them. I am not shutting down at all.

I take a bath, wash my hair, and realize I haven't eaten since yesterday at lunch, so I eat and watch some movies on TV until the kids get home from the weekend with their dad.

It's late now. The kids are asleep and I'm restless, unable to stop the swirling, mind-numbing thoughts that will not leave me alone. I turn on the light, sit up in bed and write, seeking calmness and clarity.

What I've been discovering has been pretty devastating, but I understand so much more now. I don't have that nagging question of why my mother was the way she was anymore. I don't judge or condemn her actions with my abuser, only her neglect of her children, and me in particular as regards my abuser. She seemed to suffer from a persistent lack of understanding of the need to protect a child. Basically, she let us all run wild, unsupervised, knowing that eventually we would return home. At the age of two I was wandering around our rural neighborhood, either alone or with my older brother. There was no traffic to speak of, everyone knew everyone else, and we knew the area really well ourselves, hiking and playing in the woods as much as we did. In many senses it was a perfectly idyllic place during an idyllic time, but there is a shadow side to everything. My mother chose to ignore the evil lurking in that beautiful countryside, or so it would seem.

I see more clearly the lack of connection I had with my parents, with my mother in particular, how cut off we really were and have always been from each other. She was never the soft maternal type, in spite of having so many kids, seven in all. She once said that she didn't really do anything special to help us all grow up and become good, productive people. She just sent us off into the world, hoping for the best, figuring we would find our way. I can attest that we figured it out, but when it was our turn to be parents, we consciously made the decision that we would raise our children quite differently from the methods of our parents. None of us wanted our own kids to suffer as we had. We have tried to do parenting differently, most likely making our own mistakes, but who gets parenting perfectly right? With so many factors involved, it's a tough job!

How do I feel about my mother now? To be honest, I feel nothing for her. I feel her coldness, as I always have, but I also see that she chose a path of self-preservation, thinking, I am sure, that it was the right path, based on the times and her situation, and how important it was to her that one never, ever speak about things that were shameful. To this day I would still describe her as cold, reserved, angry, controlling, holding in a tremendous amount of stuff. As children, if we followed her rules and were perfect then everything was fine, but if we rocked the boat, if we brought shame to her in any way, boy, she let us know it! Her method of attack was most often verbal, but I once witnessed her chasing one of my brothers down the stairs with a frying pan, aiming for his head. He reached his bedroom in the nick of time and slammed the door shut while she beat a hole into it with the frying pan, screaming the whole time, "I'll kill you! I'll kill you! I'll kill you!"

My friends would talk about their mothers, shopping for clothes with them, doing things with them, being invited to go places with them. I had no such relationship with my mother, but I would sometimes make things up, pretending she cared about me. In reality, I grew up in fear of her, confused by her, feeling unloved by her. I didn't understand love as a child. No one ever said they loved me. I thought love only happened between a man and a woman. I didn't know it was a universal concept to be shared by all. When I'd hear my friends expressing love for their parents or siblings, it embarrassed me. I didn't understand it. It was quite frightening to imagine having that kind of relationship with my parents. To utter the word "love" to them! How unthinkable! A foreign concept, for no love was expressed, even the word itself was rarely spoken in our house. Along with everything else, that was just the way it was.

November 10, 2003

I dream that I purchase a horse, a beautiful, large and healthy horse. And then I set him free. I watch him run and run and run. I have bought him solely to set him free, not for any other reason.

The recent revelations help me understand everything better. I now understand my mother's barely contained contempt for the family of my abuser, as well as her own self-hatred and barely contained anger. I often wondered what she was so ashamed of all the time. Who truly knows how another really thinks or feels? Perhaps her relationship with my abuser was mutual? Perhaps it just happened, or perhaps he pushed it, but perhaps it explains how I got involved with him. It is a well known tactic, the pedophile cozying up to a mother, the child being the real target.

I understand my father's lifelong suspicions, always suspecting my mother of having affairs, and perhaps she really did. I especially remember the years surrounding the birth of one of my younger brothers as being especially contentious between them. They did a lot of entertaining, but my abuser and his wife were never included. Outsiders always, they were not among their social group. My parents associated with them only in passing, but obviously they must have felt it was safe for me to play with their daughter.

I go back into the recently recapitulated memories, doing the sweeping breath. The scene on the path plays out and the actions of my mother and my abuser begin to clear. They told me to go away that day, but I didn't. I stayed nearby, just as I had stayed outside the kitchen door, worried about my mother. I see her walking up to my abuser and I where we sit beneath a tree. He jumps up, but she only laughs. I hear their laughter coming down through time and I realize that they knew each other! They were friends, not contemptuous strangers, and it didn't seem to matter that his penis was hanging out. She was wearing loafers and a light blue sleeveless summer dress, just like the one I was wearing, matching mother daughter dresses. They sent me away, but I watched, crouched behind a bush, as he took her hand and drew her to him.

Surprised at the clarity of the recapitulation, I pull away and clear the scene from memory with a few additional sweeps of my head. As uncomfortable as it leaves me, I decide it doesn't matter. It's just another piece of the puzzle, giving me answers to so many unanswerable questions. Could it have happened? After all, anything is possible. However, I still must contend with the feelings I carry within. I received no support or protection from my mother. I am deeply disappointed in her. I always was. I used to dream that a beautiful woman would come along and claim me as her child, save me. I wanted to be rescued, but that was a secret I kept to myself. I never understood why I harbored such a fantasy, nor could I fathom my deep feelings of abandonment. On the other hand, I was extremely independent. And, truthfully, it was enough for me to know the adults in my life were present, but I didn't really need them.

Having now been in therapy for a few years, and aware of projection, I am well aware that I must mother myself with the characteristics of the perfect fantasy mother that I once dreamed of. She has finally appeared. She is me!

November 11, 2003

I dream that I am with my mother. All excited, she leads me down a pathway, intent upon showing me her new house, a modern white structure on the outside, made of carved ice. As soon as we step inside disappointment sweeps through me because I see that it's the same old house on the inside. I realize she needs her fantasies. I feel so sad, but I also understand that this is how it is always going to be with her, no changes will ever take place on the inside. She can pretend all she wants, but there will never be change at a deeper level. I see her clearly now.

"I need to talk about my mother," I say to Chuck, but it takes me a long time to open my mouth and speak of my recent discoveries.

"It explains a lot, especially about your mother," he says, when I tell him the memories that came to me.

"Yes, it explains why I always felt so cut off from her, why I felt she failed me so badly, why she didn't protect me, and why I felt such a burden of shame and guilt at such a very young age."

"To witness your mother having sex with a man, any man, and then being shaken and told to never, ever speak of it, is such a terrible burden for a young child, for anyone, even adults would have felt shame if they had been threatened like that," he says. "Did she see what he was doing to you?"

"I think she saw something but chose to ignore it, and in ignoring what he was doing with me she chose to not be my mother. She brushed me off, no attempt to protect me. In turn, I became afraid of her anger and her threats. I'm still afraid of her, but I try to ignore it."

I talk about finally seeing my parents for who they are, the compromises they made, the fact that they did indeed throw me to the wolf. But my journey is not their journey. They made their decisions and took their own journeys and I am making decisions on how my own journey is going to proceed from here on out. I leave them behind to reckon with their own choices.

"Well, at least you are *basically sane*, aka BS!" That is Chuck's joke as we end the session.

I want to be able to see things more clearly from now on, to stop and look at the why of something and really decide, with all the knowledge I now have, if I am on the right path for me. I intend to stay on my own path now, out of the woods and into something new and different, that path of heart and spirit that Jeanne told me to focus on not long ago. When I go walking now, I rarely go into the woods. I choose not to. I don't feel the need to anymore, and I don't want to. I just don't want to.

To be a small child and to be held down by an adult so he can rape you and sodomize you and hurt your body and your soul is the worst kind of pain, the worst kind of abuse. And to have it happen over and over again will, I think, either destroy you or make you strong. It didn't destroy me so it must have made me strong. In spite of no love, of being abandoned, of being terribly neglected, a strength of will and character grew inside me. I refused to be destroyed and I still have that strength. Now I need to direct it into life-giving, life-affirming energy. I need to grab it and run with it, finally learn to live.

I am no longer hiding from myself. Within myself I am free and aware, open and safe. I am safe now, safe in my own body. I have strength and creativity to channel into new life. Run with it! Run with it! Now is my time to live, not to die, not to think that my life is or was terrible, but to think that my life is just beginning. My life is just beginning!

All day I remain stunned, perhaps in shock. I haven't allowed myself to go back to the memories yet. Chuck pushed a little, asked if I thought my dad knew.

"Yes," I said, but I couldn't go into it, the stress of it too much. "I can't now."

"That's fine," he said. "I didn't mean to push you."

I will have to go back into the memories and face what else is there, for I saw more in the haze of it. Maybe I can get it over with quickly so I can move on, for it is too painful to live in this state, under such stress and pain. I will see Chuck again on Friday, just a few days away, but it seems like weeks, the days so full of torment. As Chuck said, my recapitulation is like the view of the Grand Canyon at dawn, the depth and width of it only revealed as the sun rises, as the morning fog and mist burns off. From the moment of darkness just before dawn, he said, as the day slowly arrives, more and more of what lies there is revealed. I had to agree with him. My story is like that as it unfolds, for there is so much to take in and hold in my sight. Perhaps it really is as vast as the Grand Canyon, though not at all as beautiful!

My feelings of abandonment ran deep as a child, perhaps they still do. Worse than having no mother at all was the cold mother I got. She must think I have forgotten everything; that I would never remember. How could I? Children forget, after all. Hasn't she ever heard of flashbacks? I would sometimes find her staring at me, cold empty stares that showed no feeling and I wondered what she wanted from me, what she was thinking. Now I wonder if she was looking for signs of memory, wanting to see if I remembered what she had done. I do believe she knew what was really happening to me and yet she did nothing to stop it or protect me. I am Slave Girl in more ways than one. I carried not only my own trauma but also the sins and desires of full grown adults, my innocence compromised again and again.

Do I have other memories? Please help me get through this quickly so I can begin my new life!

November 12, 2003

I sleep very deeply, through the whole night, and wake up feeling lighter. Maybe today will be easier.

It might be time to do a more intensive yoga, a different approach with some deeper breathing and more releasing work. Can I handle it? I know it might trigger things, perhaps even be painful, but I think the next step is to purge my body of all that does not belong to me. Part of this purging has to do with my parents, as I must consciously release from my body the memories of their treatment of me, for the memories have remained embedded in my physical structure, in my muscles and bones, just as much as they are stored in the memory bank in my brain. Even as I release them from my memory, I must also fully release them from my body or I will continue to suffer physical pain and ills. That I am certain of.

I do not mean to imply that I alone suffered deprivation at the hands of my parents, my siblings too had to deal with the climate of the household, the lack of emotional warmth and love, and the idiosyncrasies of the parents we got. But I now more fully understand my own child self turning away and concluding that she needed a different kind of mother. I saw my mother as having so little to offer that I did not care to engage her, far better to create a fantasy mother who did not judge or turn a cold shoulder but was always there with a smile and open arms, accepting of everything. Did my mother see me as an enemy? Did I constantly remind her of her sins? Did the sight of me cause her to hate herself, and me?

As soon as I think about being a child in my parent's home I am back there again, feeling abandoned. The problems I had then become real again and my parents become who they were then, cold disciplinarians, my father with a good deal more feeling than my mother, but equally unavailable, cut off by her dominance. I recapitulate them within the context of our old relationship, my child self weighed down by life with them as parents, but when I emerge from my memories I do not carry the old feelings about them forward. Each time I revisit my childhood, I gain a new perspective and understanding of who they were and why. As I dip back and forth into the past, I gain new information, moving further away from the old feelings of my child self, releasing them from my psyche and my body, releasing my parents as well.

I recall my mother being so angry at my father that she would lock herself into their bedroom for hours on end, refusing to come out. My father, pleading at the door like a little child, would disgust me. I suspected something was seriously wrong, that they weren't doing things right, that it wouldn't be that way if they knew what they were doing. When my mother closed herself off and withdrew so childishly, my father's neediness emerged, and I saw him as a child too, though I was but a child myself. Afterwards, when she rejoined the family, my mother was composed once again. However, the locked door communicated the underlying truth of a deeper dysfunctionality. There were other times when piles of dishes would go crashing to the kitchen floor in angry outbursts or the telephone would get slammed down in a screaming fit. But more often than not my mother just sat in her armchair, reading novels, while the lives of her seven children went on before her unseeing eyes.

I don't enjoy going back into the memories, yet I feel that I must if I am to discover who I am. I must remember to breathe as I open those old doors and enter the rooms of the past. I must remember to consciously release the physical holdings and the emotional strangleholds, as I grasp the true content of my strange past and then let it all go. It is only through such sacrifice that new life will come. I am the sacrifice; the old me is suffering a kind of death so that a new me may one day emerge.

Yesterday, while at the studio, I had a sudden feeling of breakdown, as if I were going to suddenly crash and splinter like a plate glass window. I was intensely afraid. I imagined Chuck asking me: "What are you afraid of? The truth?" Perhaps I am afraid of the truth. Perhaps I'm afraid that I really am just like my mother, choosing to hide from life, choosing to live in silent denial rather than fully embrace life and live. Am I still in denial? Have I not accepted it all yet? What I struggle with is an old feeling that what I am doing for myself is forbidden. I am not allowed to value myself. I am not allowed to take this journey to freedom, to give myself so much importance that I or my life matter. I am nothing, of no importance, and in one sense I do think that. I don't matter more than anyone else, but I am on a healing mission now, and that matters.

Life looms ahead, real life is in reach, but as soon as I enter the territory of the inner self, daring myself to take the next step toward that new life, my mother's rules and judgments show up. The ghost of her voice has trailed along beside me during this entire recapitulation, judging and making comments, reminding me what is allowed and what is not. It only belongs here now because she is showing me what I must free myself from, for as I do this recapitulation her voice is one of the biggest echoes of the past, and one of the biggest catalysts egging me on to new life too.

The other echo of the past that haunts me is a look of total disgust on my father's face. I have seen it my whole life, in reality and played out in memory. When I see it I am sick to my core. It is a look of absolute fear. It is a look of complete disbelief, horror, and even fascination. It is a look of total incomprehension too. Yet it is also a look that clearly grasps that the entire world is exploding right this minute, everything is blowing apart, and there is nothing to hold onto. That look on my father's face is immediately followed by his shoulders slumping. He is stunned by what he is seeing, but his reaction says that he is deciding to look away, to keep his own secret, accepting and yet rejecting the truth of what is right before his eyes. It is a look of absolute fear followed by total submission. What he is looking at I don't know yet, but I sense it has to do with my mother.

I wonder what my little girls have to say? They have been very quiet. I think they are quiet now because I have found what they wanted me to find. I have found that I had no mother protector, no father guide. I was alone. They want me to fully take that in and realize what that means. I found the kind of comfort a child would need in creative fantasy and by pulling the covers over my head, by blocking the pain that coursed through me, whatever its origin, seeking an antidote to the constant loneliness, filling the emptiness with something familiar, something safe. That was my addiction, not to drugs or alcohol, but to the familiarity of denial and catatonia.

"Caution! Be careful!" my little girls warn me.

I must be careful who I befriend, they caution, for I feel the inclination to seek out comfort, in a relationship perhaps, but it would be a fatal move at this point. I am not ready. I must remain isolated and alone a bit longer. I must gain more self-esteem and strength of character. I must trust myself and believe in myself. I must allow myself to experience life outside of the old habits and behaviors. I must still work through this recapitulation process and discover who I truly am by turning my old fantasies of the good and loving mother and father into a reality within myself. I must be good and loving parents to myself. And I must learn to trust myself if I am to one day trust someone else.

Was my mother really having an affair with the man who groomed me, who sexually abused and raped me for sixteen long years? Did my mother know what he was doing to me, choosing to ignore it? Why? Did she not want me interfering with her own pleasures? Was I a pest, in the way, abandoned to wait under a bush while they went at it under the guise of walking me home?

"Children don't remember anything. What they don't understand won't bother them. What they don't know can't hurt."

Those are the common excuses adults use to get away with things in front of children. I believe they thought I was not affected by it at all, that I would forget, that I would do as they wished, that they had me under control, and in essence that is what happened, for I blocked out what bothered me, forgot what I saw, obediently did as they wished; I kept quiet. But they forgot about the fear, always present, and even though it worked in their favor it remained deeply embedded in me as a reminder that all was not right. The fear covered the hurt, the feelings of abandonment, the need to self-punish, and at the very bottom lay the truth of the abuse, long buried as they had predicted, but now it has uncoiled itself, a mighty snake, and it is emerging from its black cauldron with each revelation, its forked tongue licking away the mists of time, revealing the truth.

Why did I have to go through all this? Why did I survive? I am certain that when I am at journey's end I will discover the meaning of all of this, though I don't quite understand it all yet.

When I walked out of the studio the other day I heard an angry voice, very loudly saying, "I hate my life!" I was shocked to hear it! Where did that come from? Surely it is not the voice of now, but the old me, desperately struggling, lost and alone. And yes, I did hate my life, especially the times when I was alone for long periods, when I isolated myself for weeks and months, lost in the black cauldron of despair, long before I ever knew of such a thing as recapitulation. Now I realize that I was down there with the snake of recapitulation, that he was holding me captive in an attempt to remind me, to wake me up to the fact that the blackness was familiar. I am in that familiar blackness even now, but I also look out and see that there is more than just this dark cauldron, and that I am not alone. I know that I can reach out and connect with where I am going next, with what I am being shown, and with a new mysterious, unknown self.

A memory comes. My father is walking along the path, coming upon my mother and my abuser where they lie having sex on the ground. He doesn't see me, but I see his face and that look of utter pain and devastation is written all over it, that look of fear. It hits me badly in the pit of my stomach, makes me feel like I put that look there, that it has something to do with me. I bear his look of disgust and fear until I am totally lost in his pain. I am writhing in pain as I see that he can't deal with it, and suddenly I hate my father. I hate him because he is showing that face to me, his weakness on full display, and I hate him for that. There is no rescue here, I realize. He did not come for me.

He watches them. I see in the set of his face that he is resolving to do nothing, to not confront. Transfixed by fear and sadness he stands there motionless. I watch him. I hate him. He is not going to rescue me; he doesn't even know I am here. He is so caught up in his own misery that he is not aware that I am a few feet from him trying to hide and make myself small so they won't hurt me, so my mother won't yell at me, and so that he, my abuser, won't hurt me either. I see my abuser doing it to my mother. I must stay as quiet as possible so he doesn't do it to me too. My father is just standing there, watching, his mouth gaping helplessly open, and as his face crumbles so does he, right before my eyes. I hate him. He disgusts me. Somewhere inside me I know he is supposed to be a father, he is supposed to do something, he is supposed to be a man, but I only see a sad and frightened child, his face a crying child's face. I am even more abandoned now. I have no strong adult in my life to take care of me. I am three years old and I am totally alone in the world. And yet I feel ancient, for I see what they refuse to see.

I pull out of the memory and away from the pain. Enough for now! Enough to contemplate and integrate. I have seen that look on my father's face at other times in my life, and every time I see it on him I hate him. It shows how weak he really is, how needy he is, and when I see it my immediate reaction is hatred. Now I understand why.

What did I do with the knowledge that I gained that day when I was a child of three? I had my abuser's daughter to act out with. I had my bed to hide in. I had a pet rabbit. I used to crawl into her cage and curl up around her, but one day Muffin was dead. I couldn't believe it. I went into her cage and tried to wake her up but couldn't. I loved her and needed her, but she was gone. My brother and I dug a hole and buried her in a cardboard box.

Today, my father is still like a frightened child to me. My mother is the ice queen living in her cold house of ice. I am glad to finally see them so clearly, to understand, to step back and see them for who they really are, and for the truth I have gained that they could never do anything for me. How many examples of the truth do I need? Why hold out even the tiniest bit of hope that they could be real and truthful now? I see that they have always been incapable, interested only in hiding. It's time to let them go. Can I abandon them the way they abandoned me? Can I be that cruel? I don't think so. Part of me wants to be, but I don't think I can. I will have to let them go in my own way, in a loving way.

At the studio I work on a painting that I am calling "Small Darkness." I am painting at my easel when I suddenly feel myself curling into a ball. Though in reality I remain standing, a part of me rolls tight as a fiddlehead fern, curling into a small dark place. From this place I see my father coming along the path; a skinny man, limping, the aftermath of childhood polio, tie undone, white shirtsleeves rolled in the heat, dark swathe of hair over worried brow, thin face and dark, sensitive eyes. I see his hands parting the overgrown vegetation blocking the path and then, with a catch in his breath, he sees them, she groaning beneath *him*. I know what's going on; I have seen it before. I shrink into a little ball and cover my ears because I don't like the doggie game sounds. I don't like the doggie game.

My father's face crumbles into a mask of disgust and something else, I don't know what, but when he turns and walks away, his limp more pronounced than ever, I see that he is really only a scared little boy, his world suddenly, gruntingly collapsing in that pile of squirming flesh on the ground. My mother, pressed between my abuser and the earth, is playing the doggie game. They yip and lick and roll and finally *that*. I know about *that* because he did it to me. He did it to me when we played the doggie game too, when I was the mommy dog and he was the daddy dog, and he did that hard sharp hurtful thing he said doggies do. Now he does it with my mommy. I stayed hidden when they told me to go away. And then I see my daddy stumble away, not even seeing or hearing me. I am so quiet and rolled up so tight in my small darkness, but I see him, and I see them, and I know things they don't know because I am silent, watching.

Later, at night, there is shouting. I hear them in their room next to mine. She is louder than him. She is shouting him down into quiet. "I don't want to lose you, I don't want to lose you," he cries. Bitter laughter. "Don't worry about that, you'll never lose me," and she makes her decision, her haughty, selfish decision to have what she wants and leave that man with the crumpled face to go on with his hard life, and that little girl, me, to hide under the covers in that small darkness where no one goes but me. I keep all the secrets there with me in the pockets of my soul where no one goes, not even *him*, my abuser. Though he tries and tries and tries, he will never get into the small darkness of my soul.

I stop painting and clean my work area at the studio, moving to break the spell of the memory, rearranging the tables and easels, making the workspace more flowing and functional. As I move, the energy of the memory clears too, rearranges into a solid picture of what happened, and I am set free. I feel lucky to be alive, lucky to be BS, basically sane, as Chuck says, and lucky to have a better life ahead of me because of this inner work that I have elected to do. At all costs, as painful as it is, I must continue this recapitulation, unburdening myself of my parents, as well as the memories. There is nothing I need from them at this point; I can easily let them go.

This shedding of layers and layers of old stuff is slowly but surely transforming me. As the old layers fall off and I move on I learn that I am good, I am a good girl. I have nothing to be ashamed of. I have nothing to be afraid of. I breathe it all away, out into the universe where it swirls around and mixes with all the other breaths of release, eventually dissipating, disappearing, gone forever, the pain and the memories all gone forever. Then I breathe in new air and new life. I breathe in my own life.

November 13, 2003

I dream that I am in a warehouse. There is something sinister going on. I am told to be quiet and watch the street below, to keep my eyes open for someone. I look down on men on the street, anticipating that something bad is about to happen. I'm supposed to stay hidden, not let anyone see me, and I don't really want to be discovered, but I'm very uncomfortable because I don't like what's going on. I'm not supposed to blow my cover, but suddenly I don't care. Energy surges through me until I feel tough and hard, until I am standing up straight and tall. I know how to yell too. So I yell and yell and YELL! Boy, does that feel good!

Where is Jeanne? I haven't felt her presence in about a week. She came to me not long after she died, in visible form, energetically real. Then she went away, but she came back and I've felt her nearness ever since, but where is she now? And why doesn't she come to me in physical form anymore? I miss her that way. Has she gone somewhere else? Is our connection done? Is a spirit more in tune to the needs of people on earth right after they leave? It was utterly fantastic, unbelievable, when she came to me and told me to trust Chuck. She stood before me with such compassion and kindness in her eyes, and then suddenly he was standing beside her. "Trust him," she said, pointing to him, "trust him," and I have come to trust him. Many other times I've felt her calming energy pour into me. I want that again.

Please come back in that way again, Jeanne, in that visceral way. I didn't even know you when you were alive, but every time I saw you I got chills. I got a feeling that I *should* know you. You didn't know me either and yet here we are, having this strange and wondrous relationship. Why did you come to me? Why did you choose me? Why have you accompanied me on this journey? And why can't I find you today? Do you think I don't need you anymore? I would like contact with you again. I yearn for the feelings I've experienced before, your calmness and your love, for that is what I feel in your presence, that I am loved.

Wherever you are, I still need you to help me. I have had you for only a short time, but you are so real to me. You are a crucial part of my healing process. Give me a sign that you are still here. Give Chuck a sign too, though I haven't spoken to him about my connection with you, but I will at some point, when the time is right. Is it possible for the three of us to have a numinous experience together? Are we spiritual partners, the three of us?

"Everything will be fine," you always say, your calmness so intense and satisfying, so palpable and real. I feel that you are still here, still present, but also far from here. Please let me know you haven't abandoned me. I long for your touch again!

November 14, 2003

I am sitting in the front seat of the car next to my father while two or three of my friends sit in the back. He has picked us up from an evening event. I am around sixteen. This is a memory, not a dream, though it comes in dreamlike images, a little hazy at first, clearing with each scene as I do the sweeping breath, the breath of recapitulation.

"Mom is having an affair," my father says.

"What?!" I blurt out, turning and staring big-eyed at my friends in the backseat.

"Mom is having an affair," he repeats, in a monotone.

I am mortified by this pronouncement, not sure how to respond. It's embarrassing, to say the least. Suddenly, another memory emerges. I am older, married, living in Sweden. My sister tells me that Dad thinks Mom is having an affair. "He is driving us all crazy," she says. He believed my mother's lover was contacting her by telephone and he wouldn't let anyone except him answer the house phone when it rang. If there was a hang up when he picked up the receiver, or if someone said, "Sorry, wrong number," his suspicions were proven. He was driving himself and everyone else crazy.

These memories of my parents have been difficult to assimilate. Did she actually have affairs?

I begin to feel so much lighter and freer as I sit and talk with Chuck, the heaviness of the memories lifting, like storm clouds dispersing, bringing relief.

"I am not burdened by constantly asking why anymore," I say, "nor am I trying to figure things out all the time. I feel like I'm finally getting what I've needed to know for such a long time. The nagging questions about myself have been answered."

"What comes next is acceptance and acknowledgment of all those painful feelings that are buried inside you," says Chuck.

It's easier for me to talk about what my parents did to us as a family, in general terms, but extremely difficult for me to hone in and express how I feel about what specifically happened to me. That we all suffered is easier to accept, but to tap into my own feelings of rejection and loss, to feel them and understand them on the deepest level is excruciatingly painful.

"How can I heal if I can't even acknowledge that I'm hurt and in pain?" I say.

"You have to revisit where the painful feelings come from, how they got there in the first place, and then you'll be able to accept them," Chuck says.

I am reminded that I will be seeing my parents on Sunday. I have to take my mother and my aunt to a baby shower. I tell Chuck that I will go with no expectations, wanting nothing. I will be totally neutral, challenging as it may be.

I leave the session, so grateful for all that I have been given. Oh God, thank you for saving me and for protecting me. Thank you for giving me the power to survive a fate worse than death. I have survived and I will continue to find a way to go beyond survival. Thank you for Chuck, who listens endlessly to my rambling, searching soul. I would not have survived this last phase without him. Thank you.

Later in the afternoon, with my daughter in the car, we come upon an accident. A van sits at an awkward angle in the middle of the road, debris strewn about. As I prepare to turn into my street I see the second vehicle, a terribly smashed car, wrapped around a telephone pole, the windshield crushed, the roof pushed in, a person sitting upright in the passenger seat, covered with a bright red mask, which a second later I realize is blood. I have the chilling sensation that the person is dead. It is not something I want to dwell on, but the image is imprinted on my mind. The person in the van, an older woman, is struggling to get out of her car, looking stunned, looking like her leg is hurt. Paramedics arrive as we turn the corner. I realize the accident just happened.

"Why did you make me look at that!" my daughter says, angrily, blaming me for driving past the scene, for putting her in the position to have to see that bloody face, which I frankly don't want to think about either.

"I'll never get that out of my mind!" she yells, reflecting my own thoughts perfectly.

She is like my recapitulated child self, having to witness something horrific, unwittingly present at a specific moment in time, subjected to seeing something disturbing. Clearly this incident is a synchronicity, occurring just as I am dealing with what I saw so many years ago. Do I blame my parents for putting me in the position to see what I saw, in the same way my daughter automatically blames me?

I calm her down, telling her that I would never want her to see something terrible, but sometimes things just happen, we look and we see something unexpected and shocking. I tell her that I don't want to think about it either, but accidents are a fact of life and sometimes we can't avoid seeing what's right in front of us. Sometimes it's better to take it in and talk about it rather than try to hide from it. She understands and easily talks about how scared it made her feel.

"We can talk about it again if it bothers you," I say, as we turn into our driveway.

I give her a hug and she's in a much calmer state as we walk into the house together. Shaken by the incident myself, I find that our frank conversation has calmed me as well.

I call my mother to make plans for Sunday's baby shower. My father answers the phone. He sounds happy. They have been out to lunch with friends, he tells me. He puts my mother on the phone, but she's hard to talk to. I ask her some questions regarding the shower, but she doesn't give me any answers. I suggest a time that I will pick her up. She sounds hesitant, but still says nothing. What is with her? I am not very patient.

I am faced with changing how I automatically react to things, just as I advised my daughter to do. It's time to heal, and if healing is to happen I can't run and hide from the things that must be dealt with. I must face the pain head on and release it. It seems impossible to do that while constantly being confronted with the people who caused it all to begin with, but that's where I am right now, having to face what is right before my eyes. The old me wants to run away and be alone with my pain, curl up like an animal and lick my wounds, but I have to face where I am now and stay in the tension of it. Time to stay put and face the truth. It's the only way to really heal.

November 15, 2003

I have my life story pretty much recalled now, a sense of completion coalescing. At the same time, I wonder how I'll ever get to the deeper feelings of abandonment and loss that I'm just beginning to acknowledge. How will I ever access all the feelings I've pushed away forever because they cause so much pain? I must be willing to face them and talk about them, just as I advised my daughter to do.

On the other hand, there is a part of me that begs me to just walk away now, knowing I have a skeleton with some muscle and skin on it, and that the feelings don't matter. But I realize how wrong that is. Of course the feelings are important! It's what my daughter and I talked about last night. It's critical to this healing process, the very thing that Chuck has been trying to teach me. To walk away now would be just another avoidant move, leaving me as empty and unfulfilled as ever. I made a commitment to myself to suffer through this. I must complete the journey. Rather than walk away, I must surrender more fully and deeply, and keep going, one step at a time.

Somehow I will find a way to acknowledge to myself just how hurt I really am, as that seems to be the crux of this stage of the recapitulation. Can I be totally honest with myself about how I really feel and have always felt? I must get over the idea that it's selfish to be doing this inner work, and get in alignment with just how right it is. I must face everything honestly, what happened in my family life, what happened to me physically, and how it all effected me on the inside. The truth is, I lost any real connection with the adults who were closest to me in the first few years of life, those whose job it was to protect me, my mother and my father.

Even now, as I face that truth, the old inclination is to just forget about it, to lock it up, to leave it buried. There is that part of me that still wants to insist that it's not that important, that I'm not that important, but I know that's wrong. If there is anything I am learning as I take this journey, it's that everything that arises is important in some way, and that this whole journey is leading me to discover just how much I do matter, to myself especially. If I am to finish this journey, the procedure remains the same: to release what I carry inside me, otherwise I will never reach the completion I so desire and I will continue to suffer needlessly.

Actually, I am less stunned by the latest discoveries now, my ability to handle the shock of it all strengthened by the years of doing recapitulation, each new memory less intense, each truth easier to assimilate. As my story nears completion, and as the final questions about myself get answered, my need for order is satisfied. Like an architect, I build mental structures in which to house my past, in which to compartmentalize and lay to rest all that I have experienced, all that I have been. There is still work to do, more structures to design and build, but I sense the end is in sight. There are still undeniable truths to face. There are rules, ideas, and conventions that have been imposed upon me that I can no longer believe in or uphold. There are new personal experiences of spiritual import that must be fully assimilated and allowed to guide me toward a life of meaning and purpose. All these things and much more must be fully resolved if I am to take this journey to the end. I must completely break with the old world structure, someone else's mental design that I can no longer live in, if I am to discover that I truly do matter and just what that really means.

As a child, I never thought beyond my own little world, never suspected that there was another way to feel or think or perceive, the world I lived in being all I knew. I followed the rules, did what I was told. I was ashamed to even think of myself as an individual needing love. I was ashamed of wanting a mother to love, comfort, and hold me. I was ashamed to say that I was hungry, cold, sad, or sick. I was ashamed to tell anyone what my abuser's daughter did to me, let alone what he did to me. I was ashamed to cry. I was ashamed of all the secrets and all the feelings I carried. And now I'm trying to find a way to speak about it in a new language, in the language of feelings, so foreign and yet so intriguing.

Time to get up now, do the errands, get the kids up, and go to the studio for the afternoon. It's Saturday and though I really wish I could just stay under the covers I have to go out into the world. I have to learn to trust myself, learn to be safe and unafraid.

"*Be careful, Jan. Take care of yourself. Someone loves you. Someone, somewhere, loves you,*" I hear, as clear as a bell.

Jeanne! Not gone at all but with me still, right next to me, in me. And with that I get up, a new spring in my step, hope in my heart, ready to face the world.

I meet with a new client, a gallery owner. We hit it off immediately and she buys a good amount of my work for her space in a high end area on the New Jersey shore. It looks like I'll have some good commissions coming in too. The prospect of new work gets me in a good mood, and a nice fat check isn't bad either! Thank you, thank you! I ask for help and I am rewarded, the universe helping me focus on what's important now—work—so I can earn a living and some self-respect, building up my confidence at the same time. It's like I'm being told: don't think about relationships or the future, just stay with what's important right now, at this very moment.

When I told Chuck about the voice inside that said, "I hate my life," I immediately said it wasn't true, but he challenged me, asking me if it wasn't a little bit true.

"Maybe," I said, "probably," and finally, "yes, it is true."

Of course it's true! But it will get better, life will get better, it's better already. Everything will get better as I get better. And now, I get to enjoy another day.

I feel like I've gotten to a new level, some of the puzzles completed, some of the mysteries solved, though there are still a few unresolved issues, especially as regards my parents. How do I let them go? Should I feel sorry for them, pity them? My inclination is to try and figure them out, find out why they were like that, why they did that to me, because if I can find excuses for them it eases my own guilt. For I am as guilty as they are, a part of it all. I watched, I saw, I was involved, guilty of their secrets and their intrigues. I cannot deny that I was a major player and that I still harbor bad feelings. I see the look of disgust on my father's face and know that we share that feeling.

Chuck has explained that I don't need to be ashamed of having basic needs that every human being shares: to be loved, but to also *know* that you are loved; to be protected, to be safe, to be allowed to ask for comfort; to not be ashamed of wanting these things. They are basic needs and instincts, he says. So why have I been so ashamed of claiming them for myself? They were never as obvious as he makes them sound, but I know I must allow myself to experience them and not be ashamed of them. I must not be ashamed of my desire to be loved. In the end, I know that I must grant all of these things to myself, but for now it soothes me to think that somewhere and somehow they will also come to me from another being, for isn't that how it's supposed to be too?

I need some good dreams tonight, answers to how to let the feelings of guilt and shame go, so I can move on now.

November 16, 2003

I dream that "letting go" is right, and then the past and my parents tumble away in a snowy avalanche. In an instant they are gone, wiped off the face of the earth.

"I couldn't do anything about it," I say. "It was an act of God, a natural disaster, unavoidable."

I stand at the top of a mountain and peer down into the clouds of snow billowing up from the deep valley into which they so suddenly disappeared.

I'm slightly worried about being around my parents today, having to deal with them face to face. I know I can't change them. I will never be able to do that, nor do I really want to be any closer to them. I am more interested in letting them go, in ridding myself of what is not mine, for it feels as if I am possessed by family pathologies that have been handed down through generations, on both sides of the family. Indeed, I have long felt that we inherit more from our families than just our genes, that many other characteristics and traits are passed on, in my case: depression, denial, shame, guilt, fear, and anger, to name a few.

In my family there is a definite lack of interest in the paranormal, in anything spiritual, in finding meaning and purpose in life beyond what reason dictates. Only the rational matters, all else is ridiculous. I have grown up like a fish out of water in that rational world, for I have always been a spiritual seeker and have had so many experiences that could only be called otherworldly. I must remember who I am, a spiritual being having a human experience. And I must let my parents be who they are and not get upset by how they have chosen to live. I can consciously move on, because it's right for me to do so. I don't really need an avalanche to take them out, but in essence my psyche it letting me know that what I am doing in this recapitulation is pretty radical, for who makes a conscious decision to leave their family?

Now that I have a clearer picture of my parents, especially from what was revealed in the latest memories, I can step back and study them from a new perspective. I do understand that what happened wasn't my fault, that the adults were making all the crucial decisions, determining the foundations of my childhood, absenting me from any control. I guess that's pretty normal, but in my case it went way beyond what was normal. The only control I had was within myself, but the truth is, we were all living a lie.

Today presents a different challenge, as I must face my parents armed with new knowledge and insight. Do I have to put on a fake persona, wear a mask in a sense, present what they expect, cheery old me, to avoid any unpleasantries? If I am too quiet they accuse me of something. If I am too outgoing they scold me. How am I going to do this? I must get centered and calm! Of course, I must just be me, the new me, the me I am becoming, for it does me no good to be otherwise! I remember a voice in my dream telling me that it doesn't matter, that all the frustrating things don't matter, just let it all go! Let the avalanche begin!

The truth is that I really don't want to go to my parent's or the baby shower! Maybe my car won't start. Maybe my mother will cancel. Maybe I'll get sick. No, I will go. I just have to relax. This is a big test, to see if I can let things go, because I do know that my parents are never going to change. I know that. The only way for me to survive any visits with them is to be totally detached from them, from the past, from what I know and remember, and from all future expectations. I must remember that there are still things to learn and so I must be silently aware, present as an attentive observer, for that is how I will navigate the world from now on, as a detached observer. That is my challenge, to fully live in the world while also remaining fully aware that there is so much more than meets the eye, and I must do it all seamlessly, without drawing attention to myself. I must be real, centered in my body, present in the whole mess of it all without personal need or attachment. And that is how I must navigate this day too.

It only perpetuates my own torment if I stay attached to my parents as people who hurt and damaged me. If I blame them I compromise my opportunity to grow, and I can't let that happen. I have gained knowledge now, and I am ready to move on. I know my basic needs will never be met by them, in spite of my desire to still try and find some love and caring in them.

"Well, Honey, they can't. They can't ever do that for you so let them go. Let them go," Jeanne says. *"Let the little girl give up trying too. In her heart she knows. Let her go free. Free her from them. Free yourself from them too. You don't need them or anything from them. There is nothing to be had from them. Please stop looking. Grow within yourself now. You are the key here. You are all that matters. They were simply vehicles, alien beings who brought you to this planet, and you were allowed to survive and get to this point in your life for some other reason than them. They don't deserve you. They are complete strangers, aliens who have taken on human forms and human sins. They can't possibly offer you anything; they don't have anything to give. They can only control and feed off each other as they tried to control and feed off their kids, but the kids survived to be real, to escape, although you all struggle with those barren childhoods."*

If I think of my parents as aliens inhabiting human form then I can detach from them quite easily, seeing them as mere vehicles to life and nothing more. It offers the perfect approach to handling this day, enabling me to interact with them, armed with a fresh new perspective.

"They studied up on how to act, but they never became real humans," Jeanne says. *"Their life force is dying out now."*

I don't need to be afraid of them, aliens among us. My abuser is another evil alien, the three of them interfering with so many lives for so long, but now their energy is low. I need to keep all of this in mind as I get ready to go. Thank you, Jeanne!

On the hour-long drive to my parents, I keep reminding myself of their alien status. When I get to their house I am met by two very old people, my mother not really wanting to go to the shower, not wanting to leave my father, my father not wanting her to leave him. I begin to feel sorry for them.

"I don't like to leave my house," my mother says, several times. "I don't like to leave my house."

What she's really saying is that she doesn't like to leave my father, but she doesn't say this directly. I don't think she can admit it, even to herself. I see that they are totally dependent upon each other now and I have come to take them away from each other. I am the enemy. Luckily, my aunt is traveling with us to the shower, another hour's drive. My mother sits in the back seat and is quiet for most of the trip. I concentrate on driving while my aunt chats. The party is okay. I talk to a few people. I leave my mother to herself.

My aunt rides home with a friend and I drive back alone with my mother. She has nothing to say, but I keep up a good chatter so there are no silences. I even dare to tell her she needs to make an effort to be nice to her new daughter-in-law, the one who is expecting the baby.

My dad hasn't eaten, but he's in a good mood when we return. I notice how quickly my mother's mood shifts when they are together again. My dad's medications are helping him, he's not so depressed, so she isn't either. I see their deep dependency after so many years together. They are so wrapped up in their lives, their being old together. For the first time they actually seem to be a unit, needing each other so intimately that they can't help but let down some of the old walls between them.

For me the past is much clearer now, but for them there is no past, there is only now. They are wrapped in their own very real and very immediate problems and no one else is important. I feel sorry for them, but I also feel they aren't burdening me anymore either. I am free to be me, to be the real me. They have turned away at the very moment when I am ready to turn from them. It's clear that I can let them go. I watch them moving away from me, tumbling down the avalanche of my dream, feeling no connection to them whatsoever. I look upon them and see them for what and who they really are. I don't feel like a daughter, just a being who has traveled through a great deal of life with these two odd people.

I see that they have been at war within themselves and with each other for a long time. My six siblings and I have been the wounded on the battlefield of their lives, but that is over now. They are old, turning toward each other because they really need each other as they traverse a new phase of life together. I see this new bonding between my parents as solidifying an old contract. Their pact is complete, their lives near completion. They just want to be left alone, undisturbed, in a house where nothing will ever change or be revealed. My time with them is done. I accept that I am moving on. I am not sure what final conclusions I will come to as regards them, but as I drive home I feel such distance and a sense of relief. At the same time, I know I was blessed with new insight today and I am satisfied with that. For them the past is forgotten, there is only now. However, I must still continue my journey back into the past, recapitulating and attempting to figure myself out. Nothing is more important to me in this moment in my life than that. I too am in a new phase.

The feelings I overcame this morning, not wanting to be around my parents or go to the shower, were perfectly reflected in my mother. She did not really want to go either and I doubt she wanted to be around me. Who knows what she really thinks of me, but today I was there to take her away from my father when she did not want to leave him. She had to give up control, but as soon as we walked back into their house I could sense her steely energy taking over, reclaiming her power, on familiar territory once again. She survived the outing and he survived while she was away, but now she was back. It was her domain and I was not wanted or needed.

I realize that a small part of me still holds out some hope that they will come through, that they will recognize me for who I am, be grateful for my presence in their lives. But if I am honest, that will never happen, for they are a tiny isolated island of two, closed off and cut off from reality. Once again, I let them go. I see that dream avalanche and have only good feelings as I let them tumble down the treacherous mountainside again and again. The fact is, they are already gone; they have always been gone, two alienated beings. Unfortunately, they had a lot of kids who needed real parents. It surely is amazing that we've all matured into such BS, basically sane, adults!

Where do I go from here? I must find within myself all that I have yearned for and looked for outside of myself. I must take back my projections. It's time to take this inner journey a little deeper, while simultaneously looking eagerly forward and outward to where I'm going and who I'm going to be.

November 17, 2003

This thing with my parents is just going to have to wear itself down, as I will not let it wear me down. They will fade away just as the memories have faded. It's amazing to me, however, that people are willing to die still carrying all that stuff that has kept them on hold their entire lives. Will they ever give themselves permission to truly let go? Maybe only in my dreams!

My daughter is sick today. I get my son off to school and go back to bed. Suddenly, everything goes deadly quiet inside me. Where am I? I lie still, in eerie silence. I do not feel life or air circulating inside me. I am not breathing. For a few seconds, longer than that, I lie in this stillness that is like death. Then I force myself to breathe again, laboriously inhaling. It's as if I've forgotten how, as if my body has shut down. Is it possible that I could simply stop breathing? Just the thought and I am spontaneously enveloped by the same experience! It's impossible to breathe! I have to force myself to concentrate on the process. Breathe dammit! Sitting up, gasping for breath, I wonder what's going on. Perhaps it was a memory of being suffocated by a heavy weight, for that's what it felt like, too much weight pressing on me and I couldn't breathe!

Am I not done with memories? Or maybe that was just a reminder to not hold things in as I see my parents doing, to breathe myself free of old needs and desires. Even holding onto a tiny hope that my parents might find a way to acknowledge me, to notice the real me in some way must be let go of, tossed down the avalanche. I am not a child and, as I have said so many times before, I must be my own mother and father now. I must also let go of the old belief that having needs is something to be ashamed of. Such a suffocating idea! Everything must become valid and part of this process, and so nothing is to be judged as shameful; everything has something to offer. I must stop looking to my parents for acknowledgement and fulfillment of my needs. Even seeking the tiniest acknowledgement from them will hold me back. It's time for me to take over, in full consciousness, and give myself permission to accept that I am a human with human needs that must be filled if I am to evolve and live more fully, as I hope to. And I must remember that I am all I need to achieve that!

I am finding my way to responding appropriately to my own needs and feelings. It's a challenge to not look to others, as is the usual pattern. As the shamans say, breaking the old patterns involves dismantling everything that holds the world together as we know it, as a known, predictable, and safe place. It involves constructing a new world based on a different concept of reality, one anchored in knowing that everything constantly changes and evolves, that everything is impermanent. The only real security is to be found in the self, as one experiences life in flux and learns to constantly leave behind what is no longer useful or necessary. As I dismantle my old world, I must remove the old voices from my head, turn down the old family protocol, and find my way to my own heart's wisdom, to gentle self-love and self-appreciation for the journey I have taken. And so, I will not be a child looking to my parents for fulfillment of my needs any longer, nor carry even the slimmest hope of reconciliation or acknowledgment. I consciously snip that very thin thread that has held me to them for so long and watch it all go tumbling down the avalanche.

I am moving on, facing the legacy of the neglected child within myself, in my own way now. I will receive the devastated child self into my heart and allow her to release all the emotions she has held encapsulated in her own heart all these years. I fully intend to accomplish this monumental task of individuation, redemption, and transformation by staying totally within myself. Yes, I am my own mother and my own father!

November 18, 2003

I dream of making my way to a newly constructed city. Work is still underway, whole areas fenced off, huge holes in the ground, foundations being dug. I finally arrive at a building, a newly renovated structure that is near completion, with beautiful rooms and ornate staircases. The staircases are roped off. I am part of a tour group, though I'd rather be alone. The group moves down a hallway to stand before a row of glass doors. We look out onto an

Italianate style piazza. It's winter outside, nighttime, and the piazza is covered in snow. As beautiful as it is, with the piazza lit by gas lanterns, I am not interested. Instead, I move down the hallway and open the next set of glass doors. The others in the group follow me as I step out into a sunny park. It's summertime here. The park is vast, with meandering pathways, large trees and ornate gardens overflowing with flowers, everything in bloom. This is more like it!

An old friend of mine, a man whom I once worked with, holds my arm as we stroll calmly along in the sunny garden. He keeps morphing into Chuck and then back into himself again. Suddenly he becomes Chuck and heads straight towards some woods, dragging me with him. I don't want to go! I'm having such a good time in the sun and I'm fearful that he'll abandon me in the woods, that I'll have to find my way alone in the darkness. I realize, however, that I can trust him, that he always has my best interests in mind. As soon as we enter the woods, however, I panic. All I want to do is get away, go back into the sun and just be alone. I free myself from him and run out of the woods, back into the sunshine, into a vast field of flowers.

I am so happy to be out of the woods and alone at last, but the fragrance of the flowers overpowers me, and just like Dorothy in the field of poppies in *The Wizard of Oz*, I fall down in a swoon. A cloudlike cocoon immediately envelops me, gently lifting me up and away. I am floating along, feeling safe and happy in my white island cocoon, when intense black feelings and fiery emotions suddenly fill the cocoon, almost as overpowering as the fragrance of the flowers. I am aware that they must be dealt with, that they are the last challenges on my journey. I breathe and breathe, cooling the fire of them, telling my little girls that we will deal with them later.

Eventually, I meet up with the same group of people I'd entered the garden with, each one of them also encased in a white cocoon now. We float companionably along in our separate island clouds, not engaging but energetically aware of each other. At one point, I feel Chuck's cocoon brush quickly past me. He is with my old work friend. No longer morphing back and forth, they are now two separate beings in two separate cocoons. I watch them float off together and suddenly feel abandoned.

"Oh well," I think, "I'll just have to deal with it alone, as usual," but then I realize that Chuck is leading us somewhere, that the whole group is following, and I am too. We are all comprised of blissful, happy energy that propels us forward, a unit of likeminded energy beings. As soon as I realize this, I am no longer afraid. Everything feels so energetically right! There is great excitement as we begin to float around a corner, our group happily anticipating what is to come, for there is such beautiful golden light streaming towards us, and we can hear the excited voices of those who have gone before. Whatever awaits us around the corner is going to be wonderful indeed. I awaken to happy sounds echoing in my ears as the first energy beings in our party round the corner and send up a shout of delight.

The initial dream setting is a brand new city, work still underway, and yet one building is near completion. The park where most of the dream takes place, is lush and fully grown. Nature, in its most pristine and natural state, both its light and its dark sides, is as important as the new inner structures I am in the process of constructing. The theme of light and dark, revealing the rapidly changing state I am constantly dealing with, is apparent throughout the dream, as I encounter winter and summer, dark woods and sunny fields, white cocoon and heavy black feelings and emotions. Back and forth I go between these two extremes as the dream unfolds.

Chuck, in true form, leads me where I still need to go, into the darkness of the woods, underscoring that if I am to be fully ready for new life, I must deal with what still holds me back. At the same time, in reality, I have been experiencing longer moments in the light and so my desire to get out of the woods and back into the sunlight underscores the progress I've made as well. But as I bask in the floating cocoon in the sky, enjoying my energetic wholeness, I get drawn right back into what I must still face, and the peaceful cocoon also becomes the alchemical cauldron for doing the work within. I cannot escape the intensity of the feelings and emotions of my child self heating up inside me. Clearly, this is where I must go next, into the cauldron of self. Yesterday, I had declared myself to be my own mother and father, determined to take this journey of transformation alone, *within myself*, and here I am challenged to do just that, but so much more as well!

The truth is, I am not alone. I am never really alone. At the end of the dream, what actually made me happy was being in the company of other energetically aligned people. It was as if we were one being, the bliss and happiness of the group so satisfying and unique, a soul group or something like that. At the same time that I was having such an energetic experience with others, however, I was still a separate being in my own cocoon, having my own feelings and experiences. I also noticed, that I did not flinch or hold myself back as I experienced the enthusiasm of the group energy. There was no sense of negativity in what was to come as we headed around the corner at the end of the dream, and nothing else rushed in to undermine the experience as usually happens in real life. Fear did not even enter my mind, and I quite naturally and innocently embraced the anticipated good feelings. Indeed, it all felt so right, and those good feelings stayed with me as I woke up. As I heard those happy voices, and the gasps of delight as the first in our group rounded the bend, there was no interference from the old cautious, fearful self.

My dream shows me what to expect as I take the ever-deepening journey within, as I continue this process in the fiery cauldron of self. A natural reconciliation will take place as the destruction of the old dark world and the construction of the new light one unfolds. It is also implied that a new balance, a steadier unfolding of the recapitulation process, and life too, will take place if I can remain aware of how and where it's attempting to lead me, and if I can more fully acquiesce to this most natural process. It underscores a sense I've had lately that what lies ahead, so mysterious and unknown at this point, will occur naturally and be energetically right. It underscores, as well, the truth that I am a spiritual being having a human experience, as the final scene fully embodied spiritual energy.

I must let my spirit guide me to discover what needs attention both inside of me and outside of me, my dream tells me, so that everything unfolds naturally. My psyche has it all laid out. All I have to do is dream on, awake and asleep.

I meet with Chuck and just sit for several minutes, unable to move or say anything, the good feelings of the dream long gone. Like an amnesiac, when I go into recapitulation mode everything else shuts down, everything is forgotten. But the dream got it right, for I am steeped in the heat of a new phase now, overwhelmed with what is boiling inside me. Eventually, I am able to explain to Chuck how I'm feeling, what I'm struggling with, knowing that I must somehow forge the ability to handle all that is pressuring me. Fear, as usual, has me in its grip.

"You are experiencing very powerful feelings and you have to let them come and let them go through you," Chuck says. "It's okay to have feelings. Every time you let them in, one of those little girls comes home."

"I kept thinking that since they were negative, fearful feelings I shouldn't let them in, but now I understand that they are the feelings that my little girls have been holding for me."

"You will get through this and become a whole person," he says. "Having feelings is key to your growth. Let the feelings go through you. Let the girls speak. Eventually, you will be at peace."

Chuck understands where I am, but I know this is my challenge to face alone. As helpful as he is, he can't solve it for me. No one can solve anything for me. I have to figure this out on my own. How I elect to deal with all of this is my choice. And as I wrestle with what to do next, I have to stop hating myself and blaming myself. I have to stop feeling sorry for myself too. That just gets in the way of progress. I'm not going to get around the next bend if I don't step up to the challenge and keep going.

"I want to get unstuck, but I can't seem to move on. I'm so afraid!" I say.

"You can't stop now," Chuck says. "You're fifty feet from the summit. You've already come twelve thousand feet. A new situation will change it, a new relationship will allow you to see that this isn't it, this isn't all there is to life."

"I'm afraid of having a relationship, of allowing someone in, of being vulnerable, of having to trust someone with my soul."

"When you're ready. You're not quite there yet. Almost, but not quite."

"How do I stop hating myself?"

"Be kind to yourself," he says. "Just be kind to yourself."

It's evening. There's no electricity, supposedly out for the next three hours. Something to do with a transfer station being down, affecting three towns. The house is cold. I sit under blankets, surrounded by candles. The kids took their homework over to their dad's, where there is electricity. I could go to the studio, but I think I'll just stay put.

I was depressed and sad all day, but I kept telling myself to just keep going, almost there, just keep going. Except for a few times when I needed to lie down, I focused on work. I think I'm still in shock over the recent revelations about my parents, need time to let it sink in. It's another new angle to fully grasp, like something out of Greek mythology, the mother giving her daughter to the abuser so she can have a passionate romance herself. Is that what it was all about?

I have a memory of my abuser bringing me home one summer day. I had been at his house, playing with his daughter. I was very young. He molested me along the way and when he brought me home I was dripping wet. He said something about it being "hard to keep them out of the water," meaning the stream that ran alongside his property and which we had to cross to get to my house. If I did what he wanted my reward was that I could play in the cooling waters. They laughed together, my mother acting flirtatiously. There was an easygoing familiarity between them.

November 19, 2003

Such a dreary, rainy day. I'd rather stay in bed and cater to my depressed feelings than get up and be in the world. I've kept up a pretense of being just fine. Whenever anyone asks me how I'm doing, I say, "Fine, I'm fine!" What a fake! But the truth is, I can't do it anymore, it's too exhausting. At the same time, I don't want anyone to know just how tormented I really am.

I am reminded of what Chuck said, to be kind to myself, but that's difficult when I feel like punishing myself. I already know that if I'm hard on myself I can control the feelings, which are driving me crazy. That is my usual first recourse. Instead, I must meditate on calmness, meditate on being kind to myself, meditate on letting go, even at the expense of collapse. It will be all right; everything will be all right. That is my mantra now, *everything will be all right*, but inside I am collapsing, the shock of the latest revelations wearing off, the truth of them sinking in, hitting me right in the gut. All I want to do is react as I always have, by disappearing, by dissociating, leaving this painful body!

I find myself entertaining thoughts of cutting. I would do it to transfer the pain. I could never do such a thing in reality, too shameful to have scars that someone might notice and ask about, but it's what I *feel* like doing, the aim to get control over the internal pain so I can function. The only relief I really get is in my work. It is my outlet and my stability, and the only real bleeding I will allow for is in the flow of paint from my brushes.

The truth is that I am constantly being shown, in dreams and real life, that I am very capable and competent. I am being guided toward something new and I know that all I have to do is stay on the path, keep on track, one step at a time and I will get there, wherever that may be. Anywhere would be better than this! Somehow I will get through this, though sometimes I feel like I must be crazy, that none of this is real and I'm just plain nuts, but when I talk to Chuck about it, I know how real it is. He helps me to stay focused on the process while also investigating the doubt and fear that come to interfere and drag me back. But the truth is, I am really only interested in moving forward now.

For most of the morning I am in a fog, even the busyness of the studio is no match for this recapitulation. I work slowly, trying to concentrate on the tasks at hand, but have to lie down and let stuff go through me every now and then, not even sure of what it is. I don't even know what I'm feeling. I just know that I'm so sad. The idea of cutting myself emerges again. It would transfer the pain to a specific spot on my body. I could locate it and identify it then, rather than suffer this elusive but constant pain and anguish. I have to be careful. I don't really want to hurt myself, for I am already in so much pain. It's more than emotional pain, for I am feeling bodily pain too. My vagina hurts. My legs are cramping. My head hurts. I need to cry and actually do make some jagged little starts, like the feeble mews of a newborn kitten, but can't release more. My skin is tender, as if battered and bruised, but even so I won't let the pain show on the outside. I must appear to be fine!

When I feel lost like this I conjure up Chuck's voice. I talk to him inside my head, asking myself, "What would Chuck say about this?" He always answers, and that keeps me going.

The pain begins to dissipate around lunchtime. By three I can actually feel the fog lifting as my whole psyche releases. The heaviness leaves, pushed out by an effervescent lightness that fills me with tingling energy. Pretty soon I can see and move better and I don't need to curl up any more. It seems the cocoon of self, the alchemical cauldron, did its work. I really did bear the tension of the feelings today. I let them burn through me, the heat finally escaping and with it the pain. By nighttime I am tired but calm. Something seeped out of me today, evaporated into thin air, and I stand transformed.

What comes next? In my dream the other night, the inside of the renovated building showed a lot of progress as compared to the many other dreams of renovations. It's pretty clear that the inner work I'm doing is proceeding along very nicely, almost done, though the staircases are not quite safe yet. They were roped off in the dream, posted with a warning sign to keep off, but everything else was looking pretty spiffy!

I saw things differently by the end of that dream as we all floated along so easily, energy beings wrapped in our separate cocoons, all going in the same direction. It was really quite a marvelous dream, and though I long to be granted access to those staircases and to what is on the higher levels, I have to deal with the basest of feelings and emotions first, the very natural things that keep me so earthbound. I will not elevate to a higher level until I have accepted and released them. My experience today was quite magical, the sensation of effervescence a real boost, offering a hint of new energy to come.

My body showed me today how it finds its own way to release. I don't have to cut. I just have to stay present and be willing to let the process unfold. Eventually, peace will come.

November 20, 2003

I am in a clearing in the middle of a forest, a white square painted on the ground. I get into the center of it and begin wrestling with a man. People crowd around to watch, cheering me on. Like Neo in *The Matrix*, I fight without thought, naturally and instinctively knowing what to do. I never tire. I am in the flow of everything. I am unbeatable.

I awaken, the energy of the dream pulsing and vibrating through my body. I am aware that it is a mandala dream, with myself now firmly and powerfully taking possession of the center of the mandala, as it should be. But who is the man? It could be my abuser, I suppose, or it could be just any foreign energy. It could even be myself, I suppose, wrestling with my feelings.

Still the middle of the night, I hear the sound of heavy rain falling in driving sheets, the wind blowing it violently against the side of the house behind my head. I hear my son cry out in his sleep, and then it's quiet again, just the rain endlessly falling. I sleep no more, and then it's time to get the kids up for school.

It does feel as if this is one big fight to the finish now. In the dream, my energy was really good and the ability to fight came so effortlessly, so naturally, far easier than holding back. I feel weakened by the intensity of the feelings and emotions as they come up and go through me, but I see that I am gaining new strength as I let them go.

Where is Jeanne? I have been looking for her, needing her, but she seems distant lately. Are you off on some mission again? Are you done here on Earth? Have you gone on to a new life? I still need you. I need your steadying hand, your soothing voice, your calming presence. Please don't go yet. Have things not turned out as you wished? Have I disappointed you?

I ask my other guides where she is, the other beings in spirit whom I connect with, my brother, my grandparents and others I don't even know except by their energy. I am aware of them watching over me, though none of them have appeared as she has. Jeanne has spent time with them, they say, but she isn't with them anymore. She had to go back, they tell me.

"Back where?" I ask, but they don't say.

"But she's still with me, right?" I ask.

"Yes," they say. "She's in you. She will help you."

I'm tired of accepting things are they are. I want to be done with always settling for next to nothing. It's an old idea that no longer has any appeal because the truth is I want a good and comfortable life. I want love and happiness. I want to accept good things into my life. I want to stop hating myself so I can allow myself to love another person and let myself be loved in return. Right now, all of that seems impossible. I still feel so distant and sad, like I will never make it out of the woods, that I will always be stuck here in my cauldron of self with my little girls and my parents and my abuser, that I will always be tortured, that I will always be alone because even when I have been with another person I have always been alone. I don't know if I can stand that anymore.

All day I feel like crying. The heavy fog inside me lifts long enough for me to work and the phone rings a lot so I am busy, but all I can think about is that tomorrow is Friday and I will see Chuck. I need him. He's the only one who totally understands what I'm going through, and yet I feel so shy around him, and ashamed, though I know he doesn't judge me. He understands, but I think I need him too much. Perhaps that's why I feel so shy. I need him too much.

November 21, 2003

I dream that I am with a woman who owns a restaurant. She cooks for me. I watch as she slowly and carefully selects only the best and freshest of ingredients. I know she has it right, and that I must allow myself to accept such kindness and nurturing but that I must also learn to do the same for myself. It's very necessary. I must learn to be kind to myself.

I am fully aware of how important it is that I find a safe way to release what I'm holding if I am to gain any lasting relief. I sit and meditate on what lies at the bottom of it all. Below the shame and guilt I meet the endless sadness that has plagued me my entire life and the feeling that there is nowhere on earth to express it. But now there is Chuck, and the kind of support he offers is priceless. I know he can guide me through this. It's my own doubt that gets in the way, for there is still doubt, and that feels right too, for how could I not have doubts? How could I not wish for such evil to be a figment of my imagination only? How could I not wish to alleviate such suffering with a coating of denial? How could I not wish to tell my child self that it was all just a bad dream? I suffer again whenever I think of others suffering as I have suffered. I have had the truths revealed in so many ways and still doubt arises, asking me to face the truth of such evil, even as it asks me to go still deeper into it. Doubt has become a useful tool and so I accept its rightful presence.

Jeanne and my other spirit guides have told me that it's all true, that everything I have recapitulated is true—all of it. It doesn't matter why anymore, it just happened. I have to accept how my life unfolded. I have to fully believe and fully understand what the abuse has done to me, but I also have to realize that it's over now, the time of suffering is over. I have to remember that once I am fully released from the memories life will open up in new ways, the past will recede into the past, no longer negatively impacting my life. This is what I am being taught as I take this journey and it is also what I am beginning to experience. It is the ultimate goal of recapitulation: freedom. This is what Chuck has been teaching me. Now I need to go to my appointment with him and tell him that I am ready to let go a little bit more. He is waiting for me, always ready to begin as soon as I walk in the door.

Shit! I did not have a very satisfying session with Chuck. I am angry at myself. I know I shouldn't be, but what the fuck! As much as I wanted to I just could not let go of anything! I just sat there shaking, in the grip of fear, holding the dam back with all my might.

At noon I meet with the woman I am doing writing and editing work for, the restaurant owner. Just like the woman in my dream, she makes lunch for me. We sit around, sipping wine and chatting. I begin to feel that perhaps one day I will have people in my life who I can really and honestly relate to, for I notice how real I am with her. And I'm a lot more relaxed than when I met with Chuck this morning!

The kids are with their dad for the weekend so I am free to work at the studio later into the evening than normal. I am eager to take advantage of the extra time but find it hard to concentrate, for I am stuck in a well of sadness, in the cauldron of self again. One short burst of tears comes, but the dam still holds. I know I will just have to sit tight and let release happen in its own way, in its own time, naturally. That too is recapitulation.

November 22, 2003

I wander through large cavernous rooms in a dream, a gym, a movie theater, lecture halls. I greet people in my usual pleasant manner and as I enter each room I wonder if I might fit in, if this is the place to be, but in the end no place feels right. In the end, I am alone, happily aloof and detached. Only that feels right.

I am still between worlds, though it feels as if the new world within is beginning to solidify, as my dream suggests. I am becoming more innerly stable. I even experienced a touch of connection to the outside world yesterday, during lunch, but it was tenuous at best, for I still have deep work to do, especially as regards the fear that still pulses through my body day and night. I still make decisions based on fear. Until I have conquered my fears, standing like gargoyles guarding the gates to my new world and my new self, I am not free.

I know that a good amount of healthy fear is necessary for survival, but the kind of fear I suffer from is unhealthily stagnating. Disentangling myself from its grip is proving to be a slow process, but it explains everything that is currently wrong with me. Fear is still the biggest block, sitting squarely in front of me, and yet it still makes so many important decisions. Of course, *I* should be the great decision maker, not fear! To my credit, I have been pushing myself beyond my inherently introverted nature, placing myself in many different situations lately, learning to be extraverted. To be in the world, I must cultivate and give life to an outer self who can more fully live in and enjoy the world. Indeed, as this process of recapitulation has progressed a new model of self-confidence has slowly formed. The fear, however, is tenacious. Clamping down daily, it reminds me who has ruled for so long. It's so easy to fall back into its embrace, which is as reluctant to let me go as I am to let it go. However, if I am to advance, I must fight it constantly, from morning to night, and even in my dreams.

I need to become stronger than the fear, trickier too, more aligned with my desire for change and not so easily fooled by it. I have survived this life by utilizing my inner strength and now I must bring it forth and really use it. The first order of business, however, is to take better care of myself so that I am not so exhausted and anxious, so on the edge of panic all the time. I need to eat, sleep, and exercise; take care of my body so I can take on the difficult fight within my psyche. If my body is in good condition and my mental status strong then I will be ready to wrestle the demon on the white painted square of my dream. The man, the demon, is named Fear. That I have no doubt about!

Everything that I desire will remain out of reach, locked, roped and fenced off until I tackle the fear. I just have to use the cauldron of self in the best and most efficient way possible. In the past, I used anger to fuel myself to action, which is what happened yesterday; I got angry at myself.

"Don't," Chuck said. "Don't be angry, that's not good."

So how do I deal with the fear otherwise? By being kind and compassionate to myself? By continuing to be open to things that scare me? The truth is, in keeping with the new me, I must *feel* my way through all of this. Ignoring my feelings has never been helpful.

Today, however, is my mother's eightieth birthday and if I am to get through this day I must leave my feelings aside and attend the celebration in a detached manner, as a stranger among strangers. It's a challenge to even think of honoring the woman I call Mother, a woman who has never felt like a mother. She gave her daughter to the devil in order to satisfy herself. It was a long time ago, it's true, and she has a knack for putting things bluntly into perspective. "Isn't that a little old? Isn't it time to get over that?" I can hear her say. But she doesn't understand that damage once done and not repaired only gets worse. I only have to think of all the drippy faucets that plague every sink in my parent's house. Unlike them, I intend to repair the damage before it ruins me completely.

The truth is, I've been purposely distancing myself from family lately and I would rather not go to my mother's party. I have no energy to spare, but my dream is offering me the proper method of approach: while acknowledging that I no longer fit in, I must act pleasantly while also remaining aloof! And so, decision made in the right alignment with where I am, and not out of fear or duty, I pick up a gift of flowers and drive down to my parent's house with my daughter. She will stay for the night with her girl cousins and be driven home by my brother in the morning. My son elects to spend the day and night with a friend instead.

We arrive to a full house, twenty or so people. After dinner my sister reads a long poem she has written about my mother, heartfelt and sprinkled with a good deal of humor. As she reads, I realize that my sister has half of our mother down, the half that she presented to the world, but the other half, the secret half, is left unspoken. I know there is another story that is just as true as the one my sister speaks of.

As my sister reads, I reflect that we all see what we want to see, we remember what we want to remember, we know what we want to know. We may have all grown up in the same house but we each had our own unique experiences, and though we all got the same parents we also all had very different relationships with them. As I sit among my family, I am aware that the past was a long time ago, an ancient time full of ancient feelings. I am aware that I have *chosen* to go back and relive it, to find meaning in it. The rest of my family is not part of that choice or of my journey. I feel my separateness from them as I realize that I am taking an inner journey that only I can take, a journey that doesn't really have anything to do with any of them or the world of family. Indeed, it is a uniquely private journey, mine alone to take.

As these thoughts go through me, I feel myself move slightly, not my body, for my physical body remains stationary, but something inside me shifts and suddenly everything is different. One instant I am thinking my thoughts and in the next instant everything goes quiet. I go quiet too, utterly calm and still, inside and out, and I see that everything and everyone is highlighted in bright white light. Brilliant luminous energy flows from everyone and everything. I am almost afraid to blink; I don't want to disturb the beautiful vision. Then just as suddenly I am flooded with a rush of emotions. Feelings of sadness and loneliness envelop me as I become aware that my solo journey is one I *have* to take, that I *have* to go where it takes me, and that I *have* to leave everyone behind, all these beautiful beings.

As this is happening, I am sitting on a step leading into the sunken living room. Everyone else is sitting in the living room, crowded around on all the available seating, spread out before me.

Suddenly I shift again, into greater heightened awareness, and then I know that it's all true, that everything is true, that this experience in this moment is true and all I have recapitulated is true too. I know it unconditionally, without a doubt, that all of my experiences are real. Then I hear Chuck's voice whispering in my ear, saying, "Yes, it's true, Jan. Yes, it's true."

This personal revelation is replaced by a new sense of knowing, as I feel another very subtle shift happen and I perceive what is really going on in the room. I hear everyone's thoughts. I feel their feelings. If I turn my awareness toward any of the people in the room I perceive all that they normally keep hidden. I notice my mother waiting to defend herself should my sister say anything unsavory about her. She's nervous and I instinctively know that she's afraid of her deepest secrets being revealed, of the truth being spoken. I see and feel how uncomfortable and frightened she is that someone will expose her.

One brother is not agreeing with what he is hearing, he knows more. Like me, he doesn't really want to be here, at yet another meaningless get-together. He feels that no one is really being honest. He suppresses an undercurrent of negativity, the bitter truth that no one dare mention. We are all holding it down, ready like my mother to swipe it away if the merest drop dare spill into the room. No one really wants to face the truth.

Then there is another subtle shift and suddenly the floor is vibrating and shifting, as if an earthquake were rumbling through the room. A jagged crack begins at my feet and crosses the room, slicing the floor wide open. A river of vibrant energy pours out of this crack in the floor, flowing into the room like thick mist until it is about a foot and a half deep. What once was solid is now a vibrant, moving, flowing river of energy. I am aware of a muffled silence, as if my ears were plugged, and I go one level deeper into people's thoughts and feelings, as I clearly read everyone's inner dialogue.

I notice that my mother does, in fact, use her hand to bat down all the little issues that come too close for comfort as my sister continues reading her poem. She rejects the accolades as well as the comedic truths, pushing them away from her. Clearly she is unable to fully acquiesce to being the center of attention. Unaware, my sister continues reading, sweetly honoring our mother, while our mother grows increasingly uncomfortable, faking pleasure at being feted, giggling, but more than a little embarrassed. I see, however, that she has no effect on the energy that flows through the room. It merely absorbs what she flicks away, continues flowing unabated, still vibrant and alive.

As I look around the room at my siblings I see that some of them have moved on and don't carry anything with them from the past, perhaps they have forgotten everything, or perhaps it just hasn't caught up with them yet. Others do. I feel alone in my discoveries, yet I also sense that everyone can perceive in this way, if they allow themselves. As I sit with my feet in the flowing river of energy, I feel everyone's emotions and memories roiling into the mix. Mine are there too, my story mixed in with all the others, interwoven with all the stories of all our lives, an eternity of lives. I experience all of this without attachment and without fear, it simply is. Everything is crystal clear, and I am aware that this is reality, this is what's hidden just below the surface of what we normally perceive. And then I hear Chuck's voice in my ear, whispering again, "Yes, it's all true, it's all true, all of this is true too," and I know it is.

As my sister finishes reading her poem the crystal vision fades. The numinous light, the heightened awareness, the river of energy, all dissipate and the floor becomes solid once again. I feel slightly disoriented, uncertain as to what has just happened, though I am utterly calm and contained. I am also slightly sad, wanting the heightened awareness to return, though now I am eager to leave as soon as possible too, to savor my numinous experience alone.

The brother whom I had earlier perceived as suppressing underlying negativity gets up immediately and leaves. I get up and go into the kitchen to wash dishes. It feels important to distance myself, to hold onto the feelings and images I've just experienced, to bring into focus the knowledge just gained. I realize that I experienced a shift in the *assemblage point*, an expression Chuck has often applied to my unusual experiences of heightened energy and seeing acuity. According to the Shamans of Ancient Mexico we all have an assemblage point, which is normally fixed in one position, that of normal reality, enabling us to perceive the world as we all see it. We can be jolted out of that fixed position by a knock on the head or some other kind of bodily shock where we might find ourselves outside of time and space, observing what is happening from a different vantage point. We can volitionally shift the assemblage point too.

I don't know how mine got shifted. It seemed to be such a subtle thing, but somehow it moved and there I was, having a most interesting experience! And, I didn't freak out at all! Instead, I was able to hold my attention on what was happening during each new shift, as if a cogwheel were turning every few minutes, clicking me into a new cog, a new position from which to view the world. I was simply present in the awe of it all, and I easily maintained a sense of cohesion within myself through the entire experience. It was so amazing that I didn't want it to stop! I guess I was ready for it. In fact, it felt like the most natural thing in the world!

I let it all sink in as I wash the dishes and listen to two other brothers, accomplished musicians, play their guitars and sing, harmonizing quite beautifully, always a nice treat. After a while I take my leave, politely and graciously, maintaining the pleasant aloofness of my dream guidance. The last thing I do is give my sweet daughter a big hug, assuring her that she can call me if she needs to. And then I head out.

As I drive home, I accept the truth of what happened during the shift. In spite of what I learned about everyone else, my personal truth was underscored: I *chose* to take this recapitulation journey and I must forge ahead on this truth-seeking mission alone, going where it takes me, though it means leaving everyone behind.

November 23, 2003

Difficulty falling asleep last night, tossing and turning, the chronic pain intense, letting go impossible. I replayed the numinous experience over and over again, trying to hold onto its vibrant beauty, seeking calmness and a place of no pain in its magic. Then I fell asleep and was swept along through unsettling dreams about my mother, going over the same things, creating a rut, getting stuck. In the light of dawn, I am aware that I will remain like my mother if I do not face all my truths and if I am not totally honest with myself. I too have to deal with dark self-hatred, and I still believe that I do not deserve life or love, but I will not wick away my feelings or tamp down the uncomfortable truths that come up like I saw my mother doing yesterday. I intend to face them all.

Yesterday, when I saw into the depths of the people in the room I was given the gift of insight and now, knowing what I know, I must accept everything and move on without attachment to any of it, taking my journey to the end. At this juncture, I must allow myself to accept the truths as they are revealed, grieve, and heal. A one day at a time affair, to be sure!

The most difficult truth to face is the idea that it wasn't my fault, that I didn't have anything to do with what happened to me as a child, that I am not to blame. Beyond that I must try to accept that I do deserve to have love and life and all that those things entail. Wanting anything for myself still feels totally wrong though; it has always felt wrong. I am not allowed to want something that will make me feel better. I get so angry for wanting the hug that Chuck offers me at session's end. Why can't I accept a hug? "I can't let him do this," is what I think and then I feel such anger because I want a hug more than anything.

This is Sunday, my quiet day of rest, the kids not back until later. I take a walk. I feel a loosening and am able to release a little, crying in short painful bursts. I felt such compassion for all my siblings yesterday and today I try to find a way to feel it for myself. I brush it off, thinking, "Well, I don't matter as much as they do," just as my mother brushed away the kind words in my sister's poem. On the other hand, I am fully aware that I need to break through the old stalemate within myself once and for all and breathe away the anger and hatred that I carry within.

While dreaming last night, it was so clear to me that I must accept my mother's choices and not expect anything from her. I must not interfere with her well laid out plans for how to do life, which are of her own choosing. We all make decisions as to how we will live our lives. She will always keep herself closed off, distant from feelings and truths. I must not look to her anymore, and yet a small part of me still yearns for some recognition.

"Don't look there anymore," Jeanne says, quite out of the blue. *"Don't even think of them, don't want anything from them. Look for what you need in yourself."*

"How? I'm not sure how to do that yet," I say, delighted to hear her voice.

"Just be aware, all the time, that they are not real parents," Jeanne answers. *"They have nothing to give. Feel the loss and move on. It is very painful but necessary to break the connection to that dark past."*

"Why do I continue to desire, to want something from them, even when I am aware I will never get anything?"

"Break the connection. Within yourself sever the ties. Make the decision and finally cut the need for them. Cut the need that existed from the very beginning, the child's need to be loved and protected."

"That is truly the biggest need of all!"

"But it won't ever be fulfilled by them. They never could and they won't now," Jeanne says. *"It's over. Childhood and family are over."*

Thanking Jeanne, I acknowledge this truth. There was no love or warmth in that room yesterday. We were all separate beings, with little or no connectedness. No love emanated from the parents toward the children, nor was there love from the children to the parents either. There was a strange sense of tolerance on all sides, and a grim sense of fate, that it was just the way it was, the way it would always be. It was not depressing to realize this, only striking to finally grasp it. In the state I was in yesterday all of this was very clear, the truth so easy to acknowledge and accept. Today I must face the truth with my assemblage point back in its customary position, back in this reality. And Jeanne is right, I must give my parents up, give up my inner child's need for their love. It should be pretty easy to do that, to say good riddance and be done with them, but I am not vindictive or hardhearted. I will have to adjust to the emptiness that I feel now as I write this, and as I let them go yet again, in yet a deeper way.

I want the softening within me to continue and I want compassion to fill the emptiness. I don't want to go all mean and hard on myself again, nor be angry at my parents for what they could not do or give. I want to allow myself to really feel, even if it's only pain and sadness, for I should not deny myself any feelings that arise but acknowledge them and let them go through me. My recapitulation is not a selfish act, nor a self-indulgent process, but an attempt to get to the bottom of my soul, to excavate the last remnants of a mostly terrible childhood. In the end, I hope to be empty and fully ready to receive new life. It's a funny thought to think of myself as being empty enough to give birth to myself!

It's four in the afternoon, and I'm back in bed in my pajamas after meeting my brother and his wife at the studio. They delivered my daughter and then we all went out for lunch. I could barely eat a thing, sipped some soup, but had no appetite. Afterwards I raked some leaves and did a little work around the house. Now I'm exhausted. Sadness overwhelms me and I try to not get angry about it, just let it go through me, as I have intended. If I get angry I will fall back into the old ways and I don't want to do that!

Yesterday, a shift of the assemblage point happened, not just inside me, but in my outer perception of life and this world. I was granted a totally different view of reality and it was all so clear, everything transparent, everything knowable. Amazing! Things are different now as a result of that experience. I'm a believer now! Everything that happened to me *is* true. Everything that happened yesterday and everything that happened in the past, all true. I can't deny it. The truth is that my abuser was evil. He didn't care about me at all, about what he was doing to a tiny child, he only wanted to satisfy his own desires. I believe that both he and my mother used me for their own purposes. Here I am at last, at yet a new turning point, trying to get through the muck of it all, and finally allowing the child inside me to weep.

It's all true. I just have to look at my mother and know that. Even though she is now eighty years old, an old woman, I am certain she was once capable of what she did with my abuser. She was capable of treating me badly and of controlling the lives of all of us in the family with her emotionlessness, demanding that we remain silent and closed up so as not to disturb her own memories. She hides so much. That was clearly revealed to me yesterday.

When my sister was reading her endearing poem, I witnessed how uncomfortable my mother was, but my sister was only complimentary, no biting sarcasm. She was gentle and fair as she described the person my mother always presented to the world. At one point my mother acted upset. "I don't think I like that!" she said, when something in the poem got a little too funny or started to sway from the expected. I couldn't help but feel anger towards her for hiding so much, for never being real or honest, for pretending that everything was perfect when the truth was quite the opposite. Everything about her was fake. The real person never revealed herself. Can you hate your mother? Is it possible?

I do need to leave her, to leave both my parents in an energetically deeper way now, not in anger, but because it's the right thing to do and the right time to do it. This kind of leaving underscores the deeper truths I've uncovered during this process of individuation and recapitulation, as I fully accept myself as my own person now, as a solitary being on a solitary journey, moving on alone, with compassion. It's a tricky period because I know how easily I can tip into anger and self-hatred, the old standbys, just waiting for me to slip back into their familiar embrace. It will take some time to fully own this leaving and this self-acceptance. I am only now accepting what I've learned during this recapitulation. It takes a while for things to sink in.

I have to look at all of this from a shamanic perspective too, as Chuck always encourages. In one sense, I felt such deep emotion and had great feelings of respect for everyone in the room at my mother's party during my shift in the assemblage point. I felt deeply for and about everyone, including my parents, but I also felt a deep sense of detachment. Where we each are in our journeys, in our karmic work, does not have anything to do with anyone else. It was clear to me that our choices, whether made consciously or unconsciously, are ours alone to make and the consequences of those choices are ours alone to deal with. No one owes us anything. I did not get attached to feeling sorrow or pity for anyone in the room, even myself. I felt a total lack of pity, in fact; what the shamans call a place of no pity. It was a place of total detachment, or lack of attachment, for I clearly saw that we were all responsible for our own lives, down to the minutest particle, even our own energy. It was such a fascinating moment when I was able to observe, without a hint of personal attachment, all the energy in the room and know that this was reality, the reality that underlies everything, and it was totally impersonal!

I get drawn from further exploration of my numinous experiences, and the truth of that energetic reality, right back into the messier reality of my personal life, the realities of work and that I am worried again! I have lots of work, lots of commissions lined up, but bills are due again and I have no cash. People owe me money. I need to start tracking it down, more aggressively collect what is owed, some of it outstanding for quite some time now. That's where my weakness in business lies, in getting paid for the work I do, as it's so terribly hard for me to ask for money! I must not get angry at this struggle, but face it. It's really just my fear of confrontation, but there will be no more sidestepping issues now. It's time to change my tune, time to get back into a place of no pity!

November 24, 2003

A huge block towers over me, a tall stone formation. No matter what I do, I just cannot move it. All night I tell myself to release, to let go, to just keep going in spite of everything that stands in the way. I remind myself, as I sleep and dream, that nothing must stop me, that it's so important to not get stuck.

"I have to get on with my life," I tell myself, "keep going."

Get the kids up for school, breathe, just breathe, make the breakfasts, make the lunches, get everybody off for the day. Breathing into my upper body, into my heart, so painful, so painful, but I have great success in the third chakra and I am able to facilitate some release. Tender there, in my solar plexus, I feel like crying, and that's good, that's good. At the same time, I am frantic and scattered, in pain, afraid of what I still have to face, but it does me no good to worry, so I head straight out to work and work until I am exhausted, until I can't do another thing, until I am tired to the bone. Then I go back home, make dinner and crash. Get ready to do it all again tomorrow.

November 25, 2003

I wake in pain, every inch of me hurting. Stiffly, I get out of bed, wondering if I've been tense like this all night. I am in so much pain I can barely walk. I hobble out to the kitchen, put the coffee on, and the day begins.

I meet with Chuck. We have a good session. I talk about everything I need to talk about. The shift in the assemblage point that I experienced at my mother's birthday party is what the shamans call "tapping into the energy and seeing the world as it truly is," he explains.

"What a good experience!" he says.

"I'm leaving the family fantasy and going off on my own journey where I definitely have helpers," I say, though I still do not mention that Jeanne is one of them. It doesn't feel like the right time yet.

"You have another family. Someone is helping you, Jan. You are definitely being led," says Chuck, as if he already knows.

"Yes, I am! Someday this will all be in the past, but for now I'm going with the flow, going where the current takes me."

He teaches me a shamanic ritual and suggests I do it to keep things flowing smoothly, to help when that big stone block looms in front of me, when I feel stuck or when I'm in pain. Stand in cold running water, he tells me, preferably in a river or stream, but even under a tub faucet, or even standing *next* to a river. Imagine everything flowing out and away, being carried away by the current.

"Go with the flow," he says, as we end the session.

I'm happy I was able to talk, to finally say all the things I needed to say. I notice that I feel fairly optimistic after the session, that my self-confidence is stronger, more deeply owned. The heavy self-hatred has lifted and I'm not sad at all, though I notice how the sadness sneaks back in when I'm tired or stressed, when something painful gets triggered. I feel it creeping in, like a poison ivy rash, slowly spreading, irritating and annoying. "Oh, you again," I say when I feel it there, and then I breathe it out. I imagine myself standing next to a river and the flowing waters taking it away, the sadness, the pain, the triggers of memory, all flowing downstream and into the ocean, mixing into the great seas of the world, one with everything. And then I am calm.

"How am I doing?" I ask my spiritual advisors as the day progresses and as I continue to feel pretty good about myself.

"Okay, but you should focus more on your own work, don't worry about others. Don't worry about the daily stresses. You need to stay focused on your work; that is where your energy needs to go now. Everything else will work out just fine."

So, for the rest of the day I concentrate on letting go of all the painful stuff when it arises, unclenching and letting it flow out of me into the great river of energy. I imagine standing in a churning river, everything flowing swiftly away, the heavy weight of people who zap my energy and drag me down, who are harmful to me, carried away by the current. Faces of injured girls keep popping into view whenever I step out of the imaginary river and sit to meditate for a few minutes, my only intention to lull myself into a deeper inner calmness, but their faces will not go away. They line up in front of me so that I am forced to see each one of them. They are hurt, sad and angry, definitely injured, with swollen eyes, noses, and cheeks. They are covered with cuts. At first I feel shock, I try to push them away, but that makes them more determined and when they tumble at me like a deck of cards hurled into the air I feel their pain most intensely, until I can't take it anymore. Shifting focus away from their sad faces, I go to my breath going in and out of my nostrils, just feel my breath going gently in and out, in and out. Their faces go away then, but I feel them wanting to come back. I feel them needing me, wanting me to take their pain and send it into the river too.

At night, I take a hot bath. I lie in the tub soaking a long time, until the water is cool, and then I sit up and put my toes over the drain and pull the plug. The water rushes past me and I feel the drain sucking at the soles of my feet, feel everything being sucked down and away, my pain and the pain of countless others. I become very calm. The flowing water gives a gentle foot massage and my whole body relaxes. As the last of the water trickles past my feet, I imagine all that I have released today going down into the drain with it. As the tub empties, I begin to feel the weight of my body. So heavy I feel. I am real. I am a heavy body, solid, touching earth. I am here.

November 26, 2003

I wake up to find myself scrunched in the old position, rolled up on my side, shoulders and body tight with fear, anger in my bones. I've been trying to avoid the fetal position, sleeping instead on my back, my legs stretched out. Obviously, it didn't work last night, but as I roll over and stretch out my legs I notice immediately that my mood changes. When I get out of bed I feel pretty good too. I hope the changes last through the day.

I wake the kids and get them off to school. They'll be with their dad and his family for the Thanksgiving holiday. It gives me a nice stretch to work on my recapitulation without having to worry about affecting them.

I work until six-thirty, almost afraid to stop, fearful of what will come in the emptiness of no work, but then decide it's better to not exhaust myself further. If I get too tired the old bad feelings drape over me like a net and before I know it I'm caught. Instead, I've been trying to monitor and manage them. I notice that when I regulate my energy I am better able to manage the old feelings, but if I'm exhausted I might as well just forget it. I've been trying to figure out why some days are better than others, why some days I wake up in a good mood and some days it just seems to be the luck of the draw. Perhaps my sleeping position really does matter, the old pose apt to trigger old feelings. I make a mental note to sleep only on my back.

Home alone, with no pressure to do or be anything and yet I'm totally clenched. I expect to be attacked! This is what it has always felt like, a sense that I am never safe, that I am about to be ambushed. This is PTSD. But why now, when I've been making such good progress, so far along on the road to healing? How do I convince myself that I'm safe?

"In the breath," says Jeanne, *"just breathe, and breathe, and breathe, slowly letting out the tension."*

I do as instructed and realize that instituting distractions only postpones the inevitable. Relief only comes in confronting everything and letting it go through me, in breathing it out or releasing it in whatever way it needs. In other words, I have to experience everything in order to be done with everything. That is at the crux of recapitulation as a healing process. What comes to me in my pain and sadness is asking me to acknowledge it and release it, to transform its energy into new and useful energy; for what other outlet is there except through me? Am I really still afraid of everything? No, I don't think so, and I'm discovering that all this fear and clenching is just a waste of energy. The sooner I'm done with it the better.

I call Chuck. We had agreed that we would talk today and determine if I need to see him on Friday, at our usual time, even though it's the Thanksgiving holidays. It's hard for me to know how I'll feel on Friday, but I tell him that for now I'm okay. He leaves the decision up to me, telling me to call him tomorrow.

November 27, 2003

In a dream, I am sitting in the lap of a female friend who is an energy healer. I am in her arms weeping, laughing, and weeping some more.

"I feel your pain," she says. "I feel so sad for you."

We are in a large auditorium with people milling about waiting for a show to start. My daughter is with me. I get off the lap of the healer and see Chuck in the crowd. I signal to him that I'm okay. He comes over and we speak briefly, then my daughter and I walk around the auditorium waiting for the performance to begin. We stop at a concession stand. A large woman in a green pantsuit jumps from the stand and falls to the floor with a thud. She can't get up. I ask another woman, standing nearby, if she'll help me get the large woman up off the floor. She ignores me.

"I am talking to you!" I shout. "Can you get on her other side and help me?"

The woman puts her nose in the air and walks away, so I put my arms around the big woman and hoist her to her feet.

"You are so strong for such a little person!" she says, beaming at me.

"Thank you!" I say, happy to have been of assistance.

I select a few pieces of candy from the concession stand, some for my daughter and a few for myself. We go to our seats and wait and wait, but the show never starts.

Then I dream that I am in the same auditorium, this time with a large portfolio of artwork. I lay the portfolio on a large table and leaf through it. There is a painting of a river scene, a proposal for a restaurant. The artist has painted a large gray, ominous looking battleship in the middle of a river. There are three different views of the battleship and the artist has even written an essay explaining why he thinks the restaurant should be an old gray battleship.

After I talked with Chuck last night I cried, more than I thought I could or would, feeling the depths of my own pain and sadness. I acknowledged it, allowed myself to feel it, and then dreamed a similar scenario, with the healer in my dream also feeling the depths of my sadness and pain. Later in the dream, I was able to help another person. I felt such compassion for the woman who fell to the floor and automatically rushed to assist her, someone whom I felt was in far greater need than myself. The show, whatever it was supposed to be, never started, but perhaps the "show" was just about being present in the moment, the impromptu moments of release and compassion, and being available to experience the gentle being I really am at my core. And I got the message that I am strong enough to handle things on my own. Whatever arises, I am enough.

The river painting was beautifully executed, but I couldn't imagine such a thing as a dingy gray battleship being turned into a restaurant. In contrast to previous dreams of battleships gathering on rivers, portending the need to prepare for battle, this battleship hints at a time of nurturing, a time of turning my attention to something healthy, food to nurture my body and soul. I sincerely doubt that it signifies more battles on the horizon but rather the retirement of the old warship into something good. The war is over, destruction has occurred; it's time to rebuild and heal, swords into pitchforks and the like.

I have a sense that when this inner journey is done my energy in the world will be useful to others, that what I protect so staunchly now will be available in a new and nurturing way. I felt such compassion for the woman who fell down and yet in reality I don't feel that compassionate toward others right now, though I feel I *should*. At the moment, I just don't have the energy. I'm so exhausted right now that it's all I can do to muster energy and compassion for myself. So yes, I get that nurturing and caring for myself is the first priority! Perhaps the other woman in the dream, the one who wouldn't help me pick up the large woman on the floor, was telling me that I could use my energy in that way if I wished, but she was going to be careful to conserve her energy, two aspects of myself in conflict over how I'm handling things!

Every now and then I just stop and listen. I close my eyes and just sit and listen. If I listen hard enough and quietly enough, and am open and receptive, I receive messages from Jeanne and my other spiritual advisors. I know they are there, working on my behalf, and I realize there are many more than I had at first imagined. I don't even know who they all are but sense that many of them have been in my life for a long time. They hold me in their intentions. I am well cared for. I have a new family guiding me now, as Chuck said, and I am well aware of that; I feel them. I'm learning how to access them by simply remaining open. None of them are ever far away, all I have to do is reach out. They advise, protect, and offer compassion and pure, unconditional love too. I can always count on them; they are always there, ready and waiting. I don't even have to dream to connect with them anymore, though I realize they work through dreams as well.

I am home from the family Thanksgiving gathering. It was at my brother's, a different crowd. If it had been the same group as usual I would have removed myself a lot sooner, but as it was it went fine. When I got home I found that Chuck had left me a message on my answering machine. I called him back and told him that I'm okay, that I'll be fine and don't need to meet in the morning. I told him I cried last night and he said it was good that I could open up like that. He is a major part of this journey. Even when we are not sitting together face to face I hear his voice advising me, saying, quite matter of factly, "You will get through this." And then there is Jeanne's voice of course, and in the quiet there are those other guides, speaking to me just as clearly, ready to communicate whenever I'm ready.

The rest of the long weekend looms ahead but, as I told Chuck, I will be fine. It's amazing to me how much I need those two visits with him each week, how the days between are only countdowns until the next visit, how for years now I have wanted only to be there in his office talking with him. I am also amazed that I have continued to have a life aside from the inner work. I am amazed at how far I've come, that I haven't frozen in time but have actually been able to carry on quite successfully, moving forward one slow step at a time.

November 28, 2003

I dream that I'm staying in a hotel, an old rambling place in the Catskill Mountains. The resort is closed for the season, but I'm renting it with my siblings and their children. I'm trying to decide if I should stay or discretely pack up and leave. I'm aware that a bus comes through at certain times during the week. Our rooms are full of stuff, clothing, games, projects my children and their cousins are working on. Long, dark, narrow staircases and corridors lead in and out of the building. I am so reluctant to walk along them. And once I am outside and walking on the beautiful grounds I don't want to go back in and face the depressing stairs and corridors again. I am having a tremendous inner battle over whether I should stay or not.

Next I dream that I am at a party. I am busily working with my hands, conscious that if I keep busy, that if I keep moving my hands, I will be okay, my creativity will get me through everything. Then I stand around talking. I am unusually loud and extraverted. Suddenly, I am overcome with a tremendous desire to be alone. I leave everyone and run down the street to a house that is mine. I go inside to be alone, to do yoga and meditate. Looking out the window at people passing by, I want no interaction. When I am done, I walk back to where I had been earlier and rejoin the party.

Was I shouting or talking in my sleep? My throat is so raw and dry, as if I really have been talking very loudly and for a long time. It's clear that the dilemma around family is not quite resolved, as the first dream suggests, though a part of me knows that I must leave them behind as I move into new life. I am also reminded that once the recapitulation is complete, indicated by the dark, narrow stairwells and corridors, a beautiful world awaits. The second dream, in which I run away to be alone, at first reminds me of the old reluctant and avoidant self who just wants to be alone, but I sense that it's the new and changing me, wanting to be alone for the right reasons, because if I am to keep my energy up to par I must feed my spirit as well as my body. Sometimes it's appropriate and healthy to be with others and sometimes it's better to be alone, as these dreams indicate. The struggle at this juncture of the journey, as I attempt to leave the old and adjust to the new, is to do so in a healthy and nurturing way.

That last line I wrote this morning is so true of the struggle I now face! It's nine forty-five at night and I just got home from work. I worked until I thought I would drop. I became obsessed with working, for I knew it would help keep the pain at bay, which is of course the old way, but it also reveals the real thing that I have been trying to avoid for so long: the moment of disintegration, a necessary part of this process. It's what I've been holding back for years, the specter of death that was and is always present. I sense that the moment of annihilation is soon upon me and I can't stop it. Even working like crazy can't stop it!

As soon as I write those words pain breaks through and I am splintering, falling apart, like painful shards of glass I shatter into bits and pieces. I am falling apart. I am breaking down. I am crying. I am crying. I am crying. I want to call Chuck. I want to call Chuck. I want to call Chuck. Why don't you? Why don't you? Why don't you? No one cares. No one cares. No one cares. He does. He does. He does. Why is this so hard? Why so raw? Death would be easier. Death would be easier. I must be crazy. Oh God! I'm crazy.

November 29, 2003

I am at a formal party being held on a large estate, looking for my car. Walking across a large open lawn, passing among all the guests in their party finery, I enter a large garage. Even though I see my car right away I walk right past it. I come to a door, open it, and peer down into the darkness of a cellar. Then I begin to yell and cry and laugh. I yell and cry and laugh so hysterically and so long and loud and hard that I create a giant black vortex of sound that goes swirling down the stairwell into the cellar. I stand at the top of the stairs and watch the sounds I am making swirl into a black tornado of smoke and fire.

Next, I am in a house that I am sharing with my mother. I have recently moved in and my stuff is all over the place. My mother comes in, very annoyed, commenting on the clutter. I tell her it's okay; it doesn't matter.

"No one cares!" I say.

Frustrated, she throws her hands up in the air and walks out of the room. I hate her. She comes back, bringing people with her, friends from the old neighborhood, people who just want to see what I look like now, so many years later, but her real intent is to shame me. I shift back and forth from my teenage self and body to what I look like now as she parades me in front of them, complaining about what a terrible mess I have made of everything.

Then my daughter comes in and says she's hungry. We go into the kitchen where the counters are covered with bowls, boxes, and piles of fresh food. My mother quickly pulls vegetables out of a fridge, saying that I should cook because she couldn't possibly cook in the mess I've made. I open a second fridge and find that it's filled with rotting food and crawling with bugs. I am angry for letting it get this way.

I am breaking down, breaking through, falling apart. In dreams and in reality I have yelled and cried. I know that all the feelings and emotions need to come out somehow. Some of it will come out in dreams, some in real life, but as long as it comes out I will be thankful. A few weeks ago it was my daughter who was doing the yelling in my dreams, now I am doing it. Some very deep feelings are finally breaking through, and that shows progress!

These dreams clearly point to the work at hand, releasing all that I hold inside myself, the final work of this recapitulation as I let go of my mother's influences, and take on the nurturing of my inner child. I must be okay with all of these tasks, with what must come out, with what must be faced, and with what is asked of me as I continue this journey.

When I opened the door and looked into the dark cellar in the first dream, I knew I was facing pain and fear, not a place I can hang out very long. I prefer to slam the door shut, though I am also fully aware that I must come back again and again to face it and stare it down, even as I let the pain and fear pour out of me in torrents of yelling and crying, and as I laugh hysterically too. The truth is, I am transforming the pain and fear and hysteria into the truth, into what really happened, accepting it and owning it as my own deepest truth. Sometimes I'm not ready, but it comes anyway, like last night when it broke through my barricades. But then this cellar dream came, bringing me an appropriate place to put all that was so overwhelming.

In the second dream I was faced with the "mess" that has been created during this unraveling of life as I have known it, for I am changing and, yes, it is a bit messy at the moment, but that will all change. This was a very frustrating dream, dealing with old assumptions, judgments, and expectations of my mother and the world I grew up in, things I don't really care about or want to entertain anymore, things I never did care about, rules I followed blindly. Even the anger I felt at the end of the dream was based on my mother's assumptions that I was a complete failure, and not my own true feelings about myself at all. I am learning to separate myself more and more from the old world, deciding what is important and healthy to take forward into this new life I am creating from scratch.

My hungry daughter came along to remind me of the real work at hand, that it's a time of nurturing now, of letting go of old fears and expectations, and taking care of myself in a new and different way. I do have to address my feelings around my mother though. I can't just say I hate her and walk away. I have to resolve things with her, at least within myself, and accept this "mess" I've created, or what she perceives as a mess, because out of this mess will come new life. It's all part of the process!

I go to the studio. It's early in the morning, but the kids are still away until tonight and I have a lot to do. If I stay at home I'll just get depressed. Work, work, work. I must keep busy. I stay until around two, going with the flow, getting a lot done. Back home again, the old feelings rise up. I put up a good fight. A lot of the things brought up in the dream about my mother surface again, but overall I enjoy a fairly good day.

November 30, 2003

I wake from dreams I can't recall, but feelings linger, bad feelings of failure versus the new growing feelings of confidence. I have the old taste of fear in my mouth again, as well as the new taste of strength coursing through me. The split nature of my psyche pushes me forward while at the same time it forces me to deal with my deeper issues. I am trying not to panic. It all has me feeling exhausted and a little depressed, a dream hangover!

"Remember," I tell myself. "You have plenty of work. You are making a good living. You are very capable," but the old voices with the old bad messages pull me down, trying to regain control, putting up a good fight, unwilling to let me go.

I remind myself that I am doing work that I love. I have children I love. I have people who care about me in my life. I have my spiritual guides. I have Chuck on this recapitulation journey with me. I am basically sane! Don't get overwhelmed, I tell myself. I must open the door to that cellar of darkness and keep it open long enough to let the feelings emerge from the dark cellar of my own soul. I must continue yelling and laughing and crying down into the vortex, adding to the tornado of churning spit and fire until I have emptied myself. This tool has come to me from my dream world and I must go to it and use it, for my own good. I will get through this phase too. I will be okay. I keep telling Chuck that I'm okay and I have to believe it too.

I'm at the studio by nine where it's warm and cozy on a cold grey day. I realize how much I need this place, how happy I am here. I'm working on some beautiful projects and I'm also satisfied with the work I'm doing on myself. Along with the cellar of darkness there is new light all around me now, from within and without, for I am not only protected and guided but I am indeed happier. I am still struggling, but I am definitely happier.

I'm not sure what's happening. It's late at night and I feel an incredible underlying sadness. I've had a few days of happy and positive feelings, with lots of energy for work, but when I crash at the end of the day the old feelings come back at me full force and I hear those old voices arguing in my head again.

"I hate myself. No, you don't. I can't do anything. Yes, you can. I hate my life. No, you don't. I suck at everything. No, you don't."

I've noticed that when I forget about the pain and fear behind that strange cellar door I feel almost real, alive in a real way for the first time, but when that door opens again, I get swept up in that vortex of fear and annihilation.

I'm amazed at all the things I do in spite of the battles I am constantly waging. While I'm at war inside myself there is another me working in the world, carrying on my daily life, and at the end of each day I look around at what I have accomplished and am quite amazed. I know I am very lucky. I am lucky to be BS, basically sane, with no debilitating addictions, lucky to wake up every day and know that I am doing exactly what I should be doing. I am certain of that. In spite of the inner battles that I must still wage, I am also aware of how lucky I am to have them, for they keep me opening, growing, and searching. In spite of feeling extraordinarily lonely, I also feel incredibly lucky to have the people in my life that I have. In spite of my desire to sometimes not live, my greatest desire is to live as long as possible and to be as creative as possible. I am also aware that without such inner strength and determination of spirit I could not survive.

If I were not to be granted love in my life would I be contented to just have my art, my creative life? It would lack the most essential of elements, real human love and connection. My ultimate desire would be to discover love, to experience it, to find the love of my life out there, somewhere in the world, looking for me too. In truth, I am ashamed to hope for such a thing for myself, almost embarrassed to admit that this is a real desire of mine. I guess that is my other big hurtle, climbing that huge mountain of shame that looms over me, a huge finger above it, shaking in my face, saying, "You ought to be ashamed of yourself..."

A lifetime of blaming myself lies entwined with the fear and pain and hysterical laughter in the darkness of that cellar. The truth is though, the cellar and all that it contains came from inside me, a lot of it of my own doing, created by me in my ignorance and confusion. To prove that, I just have to think how ashamed I am to even consider having happiness and stability, let alone love, as possibilities in my life. I imagine that I don't deserve love, though a tiny part of me hopes and imagines that I might actually find love someday, but keeps that a secret. Far easier to close up, to not even think about it, than to let myself hope and then be disappointed. Far easier to shut it down, toss it into that vortex and let the blackness consume it.

Those are the things I tell myself.

Chapter 6

Darkest Just Before Dawn

December 1, 2003

I'm not staying in bed as long anymore, not hiding as often nor feeling the need to retreat so much. I'm feeling more secure, coming to terms with my feelings, more confident and strong, definitely stronger.

I've kept my body fairly calm and quiet over the past few days, not doing anything to get too upset, not forcing anything with breathing or yoga. I didn't want to stir up something I couldn't handle. After a few difficult crying sessions I've gone quiet inside, cycling down the vortex to a manageable spin, but now even breathing is painful. I'm in pain from my root chakra all the way up to my heart chakra. When I breathe into my heart I feel like crying. It's clear that I do need to keep crying, to let the little girls inside me cry, but instead I'm going to go to the studio where I will be happy and contented, and very busy!

I get the kids up and off to school and head out myself. It suddenly dawns on me that the great sadness welling up in me is related to the recent realization that there were other people involved in the traumatic events of my childhood, not just my abuser, and that I really had no voice in any of it, thus I truly am not to blame. My anger should not be directed inward toward myself, for as a two or three-year-old child I was incapable of defending myself against a grown man.

I keep envisioning a muddy stream, the murky water settling, gradually becoming crystal clear, too bright to peer into for very long, an apt metaphor for where I am right now at this stage of the recapitulation, trying to deal with the painful clarity of all that has been revealed. For indeed, an endless flow of material has come forth from deep inside me, transforming me as viscerally as if I've been boiled alive, sacrificed in the alchemical cauldron of recapitulation. I hope to be done with that cauldron soon, and then I hope to find out what else is out there for me, what else the world holds, what else the universe has in mind. But first, the anger has to be dealt with, for I will not be able to move forward into new life if I am still an angry woman.

December 2, 2003

I wake up hating myself and immediately order myself back to sleep, seeking a better mood. It doesn't work, for I end up in a worse state, dreaming of wandering along endless corridors, lost and crying. Cripes! What a crappy way to start the day!

The day never got any better. It started out crappy and it stayed crappy. I saw Chuck this morning, but I was in such extreme physical discomfort that I couldn't sit still. Edgy, brittle, and angry, I talked about my parents though I didn't really want to, trying to sort out how I'm really angry at them and shouldn't be angry at myself. That was followed by a difficult morning at work because I still could not settle down. I finally went out to deliver some furniture to a local bank, a commission I'd done, some painted children's furniture for their lobby. Everyone who saw me bringing it in remarked over how beautiful it was, except the woman who had commissioned it. She didn't say a thing! I was so disappointed that I cried when I left!

"Why am I doing this?" I wondered. "What's the use!"

I decided to drive home and crawl into bed, but once there I couldn't lie down except for about thirty seconds and then I was up and moving again. I went back to the studio and forced myself to work. I finally got into working on the next commission, which is now almost done.

Chuck said that I am once again in that damned place the shamans call the "in-between" place. He's right. I feel like I've been stuck here forever though. There's no comfort in turning back and I haven't fully moved forward yet. I have no place to turn for safety. The shamans suggest that you just throw yourself out into the void, Chuck said. You have no other choice, they say, so why not just go, take the leap! And the truth is, the old way no longer exists. I've cut so many old ties and old beliefs that a new reality, the painfully crystal clear truth that is almost impossible to look at has been revealed. For that, I am lucky and thankful, still in awe, but I also suffer tremendous grief at having left the old, and tremendous fear at having to face the new and unknown. The studio is my only real sanctuary at this point. It's where I feel safe and anchored, probably tied to the fact that my creativity gets to fully vent, offering a great escape for all that I cannot mentally, emotionally, and even physically bear. There is nothing like getting lost in the activity of painting. Otherwise, I float untethered, but the truth is I'm already in the fucking void! I've already fallen down the cellar stairs and into the swirling black vortex of my own damn dream!

"No regrets, go forward, life awaits," says my horoscope. True reality has been revealed and it is nothing more than a miracle, with more to come. "Miracles are just reality becoming clear," it states. I can certainly agree with that! Reality, the truth of my life as I never knew it, is sharply in focus now. What miracle comes next? I will just have to wait and see!

December 3, 2003

I am at the studio early today, not sure what to do with myself, so I sit and meditate. Suddenly, I am floating. Luckily, I have years of experience of this untethered state, dissociation a familiar reality. I land on my tongue and lie there for a few seconds at a time, quietly and calmly meditating before flicking myself out into the void again where I ride up and down its spinning vortex, like a gyroscope on a string, then back again to rest on my quiet tongue. When I open my eyes and stand up I'm still in the void, still hurtling through space. I'm not really going anywhere though, I'm just spinning in the vortex. I have yet to be spit out into the next phase of my life, though it feels like something must be about to happen, for there is such pressure. If anything, I am surely entering the birth canal.

I try many ways to gain and remain calm as the morning progresses. I'd like to go for a walk, but it's only ten degrees outside, bitterly cold and windy. Just trying to sit quietly becomes increasingly difficult, something I am usually expert at, my tongue meditation no longer possible. Energy courses through my body, pacing like a caged wild animal. At the same time, I am light and airy, totally ungrounded, in a kind of euphoria. Is this what mania feels like? Should I just try to enjoy it? I am also anxious about the prospect of coming crashing down with so much spin that I lose control totally. I am fearful that I won't survive a crash.

I have to trust that I will land safely, that I will end up in a new good place, a better, safer place, without the old life sitting heavily on my soul, a weighty burden on my shoulders. I have to trust that I will be able to handle all the realities of that new world too, not because of someone else but because of myself, because I have worked so hard to get there. After all this work I expect to feel safe, but being safe means something different to me now. It means feeling like I belong in my own body, grounded on this earth, with complete knowledge of who I am. It means being able to be myself to the fullest, without fear, to understand myself at the deepest levels, to remain open and eager, always ready to keep growing, always honing the ability to listen to what my body and my psyche are telling me. Always.

I do know that I have been given the gift of knowledge, the gift of truth, the gift of clarity. I know what I need to know about myself and my journey thus far. There are no more murky waters. Everything has been revealed, very clearly. I'm not sure that I'm comfortable with it all yet, acceptance has been difficult, but after I get used to the harsh glare of it, when my eyes adjust to the crystal clarity, I will be able to handle it. I just need time.

I am grieving, crying. It hits me at odd times this sadness and grief, when I'm driving or making dinner, much the same way the memories emerged, coming upon me when I least expected them, when I was preoccupied with something else. This feels like real grief, similar to the loss of someone close. When my youngest brother died in a car accident at the age of 20, grief at his loss snuck up in the same fashion, strung out over the course of a year or longer. I'd weep in the middle of some mundane task, doing up the dishes or dusting the furniture, a physical activity triggering a deep sense of sadness over his loss.

It feels as if my emotions, caught far down in my gut, are just now beginning to move higher up, catching in my heart, teasing their way up, asking to be let out. It's been so hard to lift them out of the darkness, to feel and taste them, but they're slowly coming now of their own accord. I feel lost and sad as they surface though, devastated too, if I let myself admit it, vulnerable and afraid as I face what comes to me in the void. But the shamans are right, what else is there to do except take the ride?

December 4, 2003

I got pulled into old feelings and depression yesterday. I'm still there, wanting to stay in bed and sulk and feel sorry for myself. I am both sad and angry. What a pathetic combination! I want a big boost, something to project me far into the future, for I long for what lies ahead, yet I am aware that I must stay here and deal with today, with this moment, and where I am right now. Speaking of which, this void really sucks!

My father is dying and he has not one word to say to anyone. I find it kind of pathetic. I know that silence is all he's capable of, though I find it disappointing. I have to accept it. As much as I wish I'd had a wise and emotionally expressive father it's not what I got. I have to accept that too. I feel empathy for him as he faces death, but I have too many of my own stresses right now to worry about him. The funny thing is that even though he has nothing to offer at this most significant time in his life, I feel him wanting something from us, from his children, and that has added to my stresses for I have nothing to offer him either. I can't tell him I love him. I can't even tell him he's a great dad, which he always wants to hear. He has this idea that he's a good and loving father, yet the truth is he's a terrible father and I don't love him, not the way he wants. It would be dishonest to express love for him at this point. I won't do it simply to placate a dying man.

He once said to me, "Even though we don't have much money, at least we have a lot of love in our family." Surprised by his naïveté, I thought, "What planet did you just arrive from? What family are you living with?" I guess he figured he did a lot better than his own parents had done, and perhaps his style of parenting was an improvement in his own eyes, but even if he feels love, he rarely expresses it. I can truly say that he probably feels it in his heart for all of us, for he is at his core a tender and good man, but he doesn't know the first thing about how to communicate or express his feelings. To be perfectly honest, my father is more than a stranger to me and, the truth is, old angers and old abandonment issues arise whenever I think about him.

Family issues are complicated by so many things, so many dynamics, so many secrets and rules, so much that is and was forbidden. But, as my recent experiences have taught me, I must move on without attachment now, and I am being challenged to do just that, in so many new ways. The first challenge is to contend with the residuals of old attachments that still smolder and spark inside me. At the moment, however, I don't care to. At the moment, I am too preoccupied with other business.

Clearly, I have deep work to do as regards my father, and perhaps some of it will be accomplished before he dies. At some point in the future I will undoubtedly have to contend with my feelings about him, just as I am having to deal with my feelings about my mother. Perhaps I will get to a place of compassion and even love for them, but for the moment I have no energy for either of them. I am on a different mission now.

At various points in life we all end up stagnating, we hit dead ends, feel stuck, can't see our way out of a situation, but such points of stress and tension are necessary if new life is to happen. We must bear the tension as we die to the old and birth to the new. I am not going to wait until I die though; I will not be like my father. I am going through my own dead zone right now, as I consciously take care of what still needs attention in my old life, as I prepare to meet my new life in full consciousness as well, with open arms, freed of the past and, hopefully, as a much wiser, kinder, and more feeling and loving being. That is my mission now.

Early afternoon. At the studio. Extremely restless all day, in such pain, tormented by anxiety, but I will not stagnate and die in this state. My intention is to move on into new life, though perhaps I really am in that dead zone I had earlier proposed, charged with bearing the tension as I fully embrace this process of death and rebirth. Already so broken down, must I go even further? And why this pain and anxiety?

I walk around. The pain eases, though I remain agitated and restless, like a captive wild animal pacing and pawing the bars of its cage, instinctual nature wanting only its freedom. Is this my spirit, my true self urging me to get on with this process, or is it something else? I must acknowledge the pain as memory pain from the time when I was captured, abused, treated inhumanely and, yes, wanted only freedom. The only freedom then was in getting out of my body, though now I'm trying with all my might to get back into it. But I must recognize this pain for what it really is, memory pain still caught in my physical body. When my abuser was done with me, when I returned to my body, this is what it felt like, my body shaking and in pain. It's true, it's true, it's all true. I have all the evidence, all the facts, all the memories, and all the pain. How do I get beyond this point? Chuck would tell me to just release the pain, release the fucking pain!

Ten at night, and I'm still asking myself that question. How do I get beyond this point? I already have *knowing*. I *know* everything now. Why can't I accept what I've learned and move on? It feels like I've had my head in a fog all week. Instead of looking down at all that has been revealed, instead of gazing into the crystal clear water at my feet, I've had my head in the foggy void. I don't want to stay here. It's just plain unhelpful. I look to my father and his dying process and find nothing there but stagnation, and yet I see that he is teaching me what I must do if I am to catapult out of my own stagnation—become the conscious being I wish him to be! And yet, I can't seem to find a way out of this endless void.

I am so sick of spinning in this crazy vortex. It's depressing and even possibly dangerous. I have to be careful.

December 5, 2003

I am swirling like a tornado, filled to the brim with anxiety, ready to explode. Then I let go and I am totally and frighteningly spinning out of control. This is my dream and I am still spinning as I struggle to wake up. Caught in the swirling energy of the dream I am unable to fully wake up in reality. The truth is, all I really want to do is stay asleep and in the dream, keep letting go, though it pains me like an invisible knife stabbing viciously. Each time I fall back into the swirling energy I rear back in pain, needing it and hating it, fearing it and loving it, until I finally wake up.

In my session with Chuck I pace wildly, talking all the while about how jittery I am, unable to calm down, still caught in the dream tornado. It feels as if I'm going to burst apart at any second.

"Sit down!" he commands, loudly.

We do the recapitulation sweeping breath. It calms me down, allows for momentary distance from the driving anxiety, but it doesn't last long and I jump up again, the tension in my body driving me to pace. He jumps up too, has me do other magical passes; forging my energy body to strengthen my resolve; doing the sword form, cutting my way through the energy and the tension. Lastly, I swing my arms in a circle, creating a wall of protection to keep the predatory energy of my abuser away. Once again, I try to sit, but I can't for more than a few seconds.

"Now I'm angry at myself! Damn it!" I say, hitting myself.

"No, don't!" he says. "You're doing really, really well."

"But I'm so angry and frustrated, as if I'm about to split apart at the seams and everything inside is going to spill out."

"It has such a strong hold, a powerful hold. It doesn't want to let you go," Chuck says.

"Even if I want it to?"

I sit down on the floor, but I can't find a comfortable position for my legs where the knife-stabbing pain is centered. I hunch down in child pose, protecting and cradling my legs, trying to ease the pain, then get up and sit in my chair again. Then I'm freezing and Chuck hands me my coat and turns up the heat. I do the recapitulation breath until it works again, until I calm down again, finally exhausted. Then I hear a howling, like a wolf off in the distance.

"Do you hear that howling?" I ask Chuck.

"Yes," he says.

"It's the howling of my soul," I say.

I do the sweeping breath throughout the day to combat the restlessness. I swing my arms, creating a circle of protection. I don't want to stop the coming of this death, but I have to be able to function. I finally calm down enough to get some work done, though the battle rages on. One minute I am exhausted and the next revved full of anxiety, the tornado inside me touching down, then spinning off again, before returning and touching down again, oh, so painfully! I pace around the studio and moan a lot until I pick up the kids after school and then drop them at their dad's for the weekend.

It's late now, the cats and I curled up in bed, the inner tornado quieted down for the moment. But wouldn't you know, a big snowstorm is on the way! What will this weekend be like? Me alone, snowed in? Stuck in tornado energy? Oh, God!

I told Chuck that it feels like I'm about to be struck by a car. I see it coming, a huge speeding machine, and I can't get out of the way. It's headed straight toward me and I know it's going to hit me. All I can do is helplessly wait for the impact; pain, fear, and sadness enveloping me while I wait.

"Where is the sadness?" Chuck asked today.

"I hate that question!" I said.

"Where is the pain?"

"In my legs, it's always in my legs."

I was like a tightly coiled wire all day, bouncing around, unable to settle down, tornado energy. Tonight I just feel very sad and I'm trying to let it out, trying to cry, trying to howl like the wolf I heard today at the end of my session, the howling of my own soul.

It's eleven o'clock, snowing quite heavily now, the ground already covered. I'm not looking forward to winter! My legs cramp and my shoulders automatically hunch at the thought of the cold weather ahead and all the shoveling I will have to do, but I will try to forget about it, try to get some sleep.

December 6, 2003

I wake early to several inches of snow on the ground and still it's snowing heavily. I will be doing some shoveling today.

I've been experiencing the same overwhelming fear of a few years ago, when I made the decision to divorce and had no idea how I'd establish myself outside the protective environment of marriage. I'd forged ahead anyway, staying connected to my intent to change and in the end everything did work out. I know that this period of tension and fear will pass too and in a month or two I will be in another place, another frame of mind. I will have died to this phase and been reborn in another. I know that's how things go. Right now, however, I can't seem to see beyond this current phase. I have no idea how I'll survive this tornadic destruction of all that I have held onto, all the strengths and barriers that have protected me for so long, as they come tumbling down, breaking apart my staunch physical hold on reality as I have known it. Nor do I know how I will ever survive my fears of failure as I move ahead into yet another phase of new life, for I always fear that I will fail.

Am I really afraid of failure, as my body tells me? Even though I have plenty of work I feel that I will never have enough, won't earn enough, even when I'm earning plenty! It's probably related to when I was a child and overheard my parents talking about money, my father confiding in me that he didn't have money for this or that and my mother angry all the time because we couldn't afford things. It worried the heck out of me as a kid. We were once so poor I had holes in the bottoms of my shoes, the winter slush soaking my socks, my feet wet all day in school. My father's confidences tormented me and I worried all the time about how I was ever going to earn a living myself when the time came. If my own father couldn't do it, how could I?

Aside from my financial fears, I must also contend with my usual fears of being in the world, of having to be fully present and engaged in life, fully participatory in the greater reality out there, which scares the heck out of me. My old place of safety is being blown apart and there is, as of yet, nothing to replace it. In spite of all of this, full of fear or not, I will not retreat now. I am pushing ahead.

Before I can write another word, the tornado inside me strikes, the once solid structures of a lifetime crumble, and I am crying and crying. I am howling. I am howling while the snow piles up higher and higher and the wind howls back like a pack of wolves at the door. I am stuck in my snow-covered house, my sorrows and my pain, my everything, releasing. There is no stopping it and so I do not hold back. I let everything that is inside me pour out. What feels like the sadnesses of a thousand lifetimes wells up and out of me, spilling out in wave after wave. My heart weeps. My body weeps. After all these years of keeping quiet, I weep a river of tears. I am letting go! I am letting go! I am letting go! I look out the window at the snow swirling down and I weep and weep.

As I weep, I touch the depths of all I never had, the grief of the unprotected, neglected, abandoned child, of the child not cared for the way a child needs to be cared about and loved. I feel the deep loneliness and despair that my child self used to feel. It's as if I'm lying in a snowdrift and no one knows I'm here, the others gone on, not noticing that I've fallen behind, lost in the blizzard. It goes way beyond words. I just release and release all that is inside, empty myself of all that I have ever held back.

At six o'clock in the evening I go outside and shovel the driveway. Eighteen inches! The wind whistles, whipping me with driving gusts, howling around me as I struggle to stay on my feet. I shovel and swear, shovel and cry, fall back into the snowdrifts, stare up into the dark night sky, snow swirling in my face, into my mouth and eyes, until I am part of it all, and I weep again, and then I get up and shovel some more. By the time I'm done, two hours later, two more inches have fallen, the driveway fast disappearing beneath a new thick covering, changing the world no matter how hard I shovel, just like my inner world, still more to release no matter how much I empty.

I go inside and take a hot bath. Chuck had suggested that the hot water might help the cramping in my legs. Little does he know that the cramps have been there forever; I have clenched my legs my entire life. Then I try to eat, but I have little appetite, my stomach twisted with tornado energy, with blizzard cold, like the rest of me. I am shaking with it, and I don't feel so strong anymore either. I was strong and determined when I went out to shovel the driveway, determined to just get it done. I pushed the softening, releasing self out of the way, put on my strong suit of armor and set to completing the task.

A huge lump begins to form in my throat now as I begin to soften again, the last of the old armor looking for a place to settle. I do the sweeping breath, release it, and then ask for sleep, blessed sleep.

December 7, 2003

I dream that I'm driving an enormous Greyhound bus down city streets snarled with traffic. Eventually, I drive out of the city and into the country, to a smaller, older town with narrow streets and sharp turns. I am not really sure how to drive a bus, but

I figure it out as I go along. There are many obstacles in the way; gates that won't open, barriers blocking the road, doors seemingly too narrow to drive a big bus through, passageways and corridors that I must drive down, but no matter the obstacle I manage to get through it or beyond it. In one narrow corridor, hundreds of tiny dogs run alongside the bus carrying colorful scarves in their mouths. I know they want me to stop, but I also know that if I do they will tie me up, and I will be unable to proceed. So I keep going, even though I'm afraid I may be crushing them beneath the wheels of the bus.

At the end of the dream, I drive the bus into a parking garage inside an old barn, part of a history museum. I circle around looking for a place to park and eventually find a spot where people are standing around looking at the ground, staring at a large pool of blood. I pull into the spot anyway, coming to an abrupt halt right over the pool of blood.

"It doesn't matter," I say to them, as I open the doors of the bus. "It's over."

At that point I notice that my own kids are with me on the bus. I had not noticed them earlier as I was so focused on figuring out how to drive the bus, with all its levers and clutches. I am so grateful for having arrived safely and now am delighted to discover that they are safe and sound too. I feel such deep and tender love for them, for having taken the wild journey with me, so happy that we all made it in one piece.

I wake up thinking that when I had talked to Chuck about my parents a few days ago I was really trying to fathom my own dead feelings, not my feelings about my parents per se, but the fact that I survived my childhood by shutting down my feelings in order to survive. They were forced into a silent dead zone and have been there ever since. Now, however, they are coming back to life. Yesterday's torrent unblocked them and I am feeling them at last. This is the reward for spending all this time in the dead zone. My feelings are coming back to life! And the little dogs in my dream were trying to give them back to me, the colorful array of scarves that I perceived as binding were just my own feelings. The dogs ran alongside the bus with such energy and glee, a festive moment, very welcoming, but I was still in the flurry of the energy of escape.

Indeed the Greyhound bus was an accurate symbol for the speed and focus of my intent in the dream, for nothing was going to keep me from reaching my destination. I sped along at top speed, like a well-trained greyhound dog, heading straight toward the barn at the old history museum, an appropriate end to the journey, a final resting place for the recapitulated memories.

It's time for me to accept my feelings, to treasure them and use them, to become a real feeling being. This is what I have been seeking as I have taken this journey. They have waited decades for me to incorporate them into my life. My children in the back of the bus, and my tender feelings for them at the end of the dream just underscore this point. My inner children and I have taken this lifelong journey together, and now we've arrived safely, this phase of our journey complete, our feelings intact. Where we go from here is another adventure.

As aptly presented in the dream, my own two children are taking this recapitulation journey with me too. They didn't choose to do this, at least not consciously, though they did get me as their mother, so who knows! But I am so happy to know that we will all survive this time of transition, as the dream portends a happy ending for all of us, with good feelings all around.

The pool of blood, over which I parked the bus, seems to represent the past and the present, for I sensed it as the spilled contents of my body and soul. It seemed to be all that I have released on this journey of recapitulation and transformation, the memories of abuse, the tears and pain, the sadness that poured out of me last night, remnants of this time of tornadic activity, this breaking down and breaking through to what really matters. It is the blood of my childhood innocence, spilled at the hands of my abuser, as well as the blood of my own birthing into fuller life.

In revisiting the earliest part of my recapitulation, in going full circle back to the very beginning, to the first ushering in of the first memories of being with my abuser's daughter and the games we played together, I see how far I've come, how much I've really changed in the past few years. I am no longer triggered or shocked by any of it. As I go back now, I am able to fully accept the truth of my childhood. It's exactly as Chuck had predicted. He told me, long ago, that one day the memories would not grab me so forcefully, would not pain me so viscerally, that everything would neutralize. That time has come. Now I look at and fully accept the life I lived, without negative feelings or emotions, without self-pity or sadness, without resentment or regret for anything that happened. I have no attachment to pain or sorrow around it. I am in a place of no pity. I see everything mixing into that river of energy that emerged from the crack in the floor during the vision at my mother's birthday party and I have no attachment to any of it. It's only memories now. As I said in my dream as I parked the bus in the barn of the history museum: "It doesn't matter, it's over."

Deep within myself I arrive at a neutral peacefulness. A calm certainty about the whole thing sinks in, but there's another part of me not quite ready to let it all go so easily. Part of me is still angry at my parents, considers them abusers too, for their neglect and denial effected me greatly. I have compassion for them, but it's the same compassion I feel for total strangers, pretty detached, for I have no real feeling connection to them. And something about their lack of love and protection doesn't sit well. Something stirs in me when I think of them. Though the rest of my story feels pretty done, I know I am not done with them yet. Do I want something from them still?

Even though I have been emotionally dead for so much of my life, and in spite of everything I have been through, I do know how to deeply love and protect my own children. Even though my feelings for myself have been buried, I have always cared deeply about others. I must contemplate my parents and their seeming lack of feeling and caring, for if I am to truly get to a place of compassion as regards them, I must face everything that exists between us. And, I must discover if I still want or need something from them.

Though my parents probably think I don't remember anything, the truth is that I remember everything, and what is so very painful to me now as I recapitulate is the total lack of compassion they exhibited toward me as a child. They did not instinctually gather round and protect their child, but left me to deal with things on my own. They took no part, no responsibility, except to consciously decide to never talk about what was so obvious. By refusing to acknowledge and deal with the truth, they chose to ignore the greater repercussions their decisions would have on me, their own child. Perhaps they were just ignorant, but they set me up for a lifetime of pain and suffering. In pretending that nothing was happening, they totally abandoned me.

I have not allowed myself to have these thoughts and feelings before in quite this way, to state this so bluntly or to lay blame at their feet, but it feels like another part of this letting go phase as I face the deeper truths of what affected me so viscerally. The idea of them being neglectful parents would have been a ridiculous notion when I was a child. To have negative feelings about my parents would have been a sin. They were only to be held in the highest regard, infallibly perfect, but now I see them more objectively, from a whole new perspective, as unenlightened beings. I realize how self-centered they were, narcissists really, and in my confusion and self-disgust I did not feel I deserved to be loved anyway. It was a pretty hopeless situation when I think about it now. But it was the dynamic we lived, each steeped in our own issues, and without communication or access to an emotional bond there was never going to be an opportunity for explanation or reconciliation. I understand that now. I understand more each day as it sinks in, as the tornado dies down and as I sift through the wreckage of its aftermath.

I go outside in the middle of the afternoon and shovel the driveway again, the snow having fallen all through the night and into a second day. I breathe, breathe, breathe! Shovel, shovel, shovel, digging through the mess of feelings about my parents, seeking greater understanding of them on the deepest levels. I feel the pain of that sad little girl who had no one to turn to or trust, except another little girl, also caught in the throes of sexual abuse. Such a hateful place to be. I hated myself and my life. I accept the bitter truth of that, let the taste of it go through me, spit it out into the cold snow. And I shovel and shovel and shovel.

It only takes me an hour and a half to clear the snow this time, my back aching by the time I'm done, all that bending and lifting, all that pain and emotion in my body seeking escape. But the physical exercise does me good! By the time I'm done I don't feel so bad anymore, a little sad, but thankful for the shoveling and the opportunity it afforded me to breathe the cold air of release and, in ever-deepening ways, to let my parents go, my sense of attachment and entitlement to something from them released with each shovelful tossed to the wind.

"Your parents were incapable of loving and protecting you," Chuck said the other day. "Your mother was involved with your abuser and your father knew it. That was where they stayed."

"I know," I said. "I didn't even come into it. I was left to deal with it as best I could, swept up by a rising tide of pain that I sought only to dissociate from."

I'm trying to find a way to deal with that rising tide of pain as it resurfaces now, as it brings all that emotional and physical turmoil, all that suffering once swept out to sea back to me for recapitulation and reconciliation. The past has washed up on the shore of the present, as consciousness of all that once was.

As night comes and darkness falls, I space out again, the tornadic activity returning full force. Losing my grip on reality, I am caught in its churning energy once again, angry and hyper one minute, sad and depressed the next, lost in some other world. I feel like screaming, fucking screaming into a metal bucket just to hear the harsh echo pounding into my skull. I grow mean, hard on myself, angrily despising and hating myself. I am no good. I never have been good, so how could I think that I could be good now? I am only bad, stuck in self-hatred, hatred of the bad person that lives inside me. This bad person doesn't deserve anything. I might as well be cold and dead, cold and dead as the two feet of snow on the ground, cold and dead as the hood of the frozen car, cold and dead as the hard chilly steering wheel. I could pound my head against it until it bleeds. I am fucked up, hateful toward myself, yearning for this to be over, for sleep, for peace, for quiet, for my demons to go to sleep and leave me alone. I am my own worst enemy, the pain of my self-hatred piercing me like a knife, stabbing the hated enemy that is me. I hear a howling inside me, the long, loud howl of a wild animal that does not cease.

My own pain exhausts me. Eventually I am worn down, but also mysteriously at a place of real peace. Having gone up to the heights of clarity and then down into the darkest inner pit has left me strangely cleansed. My emotions, so raw now, are as tender as spring shoots peeking out of snow. Even though it's just the beginning of winter the scent of spring is already on the horizon. I have finally cracked through something. I can finally cry because everything is real. The pain is real. The torment is real. The neglect is real. I am real.

December 8, 2003

I dream that I am with a man, walking hand-in-hand down narrow cobblestoned streets. It's the wee hours of the morning and pitch black. I am twelve years old and I have just had intercourse with this man. Since we have had sex I know he owns me now. While I think this thought I am also aware that it's a wrong conclusion, that what he's doing to me is wrong. He leans down and speaks into my ear as we walk, talking nonstop about how much I'm going to like it when we get where we are going. As we walk, I notice the large numbers on the doors of the tall, narrow, attached row houses that we pass, 20, 21, 22... I recognize number 23 as Chuck's house. I know he's home, sleeping upstairs, but I also know he gets up early and I don't want him to see me. I'm so ashamed to be seen with this man and I'm sure that Chuck will not approve. I walk quickly past his house, tiptoeing on the noisy cobblestones, imagining him opening his door, seeing me there, and being disappointed in me because I am with an abuser.

The man and I go into building number 25, right next door to Chuck's house. My abuser's daughter is waiting in the lobby. The man says he will wait outside for us. We are going upstairs to the fifth floor to audition for something. My abuser's daughter is very excited; I am not. She's going to sing, though I know she doesn't sing well.

"I don't audition," I say. "It's not my thing. I don't audition for anything, it's not me," but I go anyway.

We jump into an elevator to go to the fifth floor. We stop at every floor and kids pile in, as if it were a school building, and I begin to relax, thinking that maybe it will be okay, just as I used to think when I was a child in the company of my abuser. We exit the elevator at the fifth floor and walk down a hallway to sign in for our auditions. At the audition table is a pad of paper with a few names written on it, letters instead of numbers next to each name. I sign my name on line c. People mill about, waiting to be called to audition, an assortment of transsexuals and cross-dressers mostly. The school children are all gone now and I begin to get anxious; I don't have a good feeling. I focus on the fact that Chuck is in the next building, sharing a wall, and I begin to silently call to him, hoping that he will telepathically hear me, that he will burst through the wall and save me. I imagine him sleeping, then waking up as he hears my plea and then pounding his way through the wall to rescue me.

"It's your turn," a man says, grabbing me from behind.

"No, it's not! I'm letter c," I say.

"No, you're first now," he says, showing me the sign-in sheet where all the names ahead of mine have been crossed off. My abuser's daughter is behind me, pushing, telling me it's my turn today, that I'm first, just as she did when we were children and her father was on the prowl. I focus on the wall, willing Chuck to burst through it and put an end to this, but I am pushed onto a dark stage where a man dressed in leather garb is sitting on a chair with a huge erection popping out of his lap and a big evil grin on his face. I wake up, my heart beating wildly.

I lie awake, wondering why my heart is pounding so loudly that I can actually hear it. I remember only the man at the beginning of the dream and my name written on a pad of paper. I lie perfectly still, breathing calmly, as the rest of the dream slowly reappears. The ending bothers me, so I go back to sleep, intending to fix it. This time I immediately run away from the man on the dark stage, past the elevator and down into a stairwell. I am aware that the man who brought me there is waiting for me outside the building. I won't be able to avoid him. I am trapped, caught in the stairwell between the man on the stage and the man waiting downstairs. I don't know where to go or what to do. The only answer my dreaming self comes up with is to go into my head, into my imagination, and call Chuck. I tell myself that I just have to pick up the phone and then I can talk to him and ask for his advice. It seems like a feasible plan, and there the dream ends.

The kids came home last night exhausted after spending the weekend with their dad. They told me he never tells them to go to bed so they just stay up all night, that they aren't aware of time passing. I know it's hard for them to tell me this. They love their dad and want to remain loyal to him, but they're really struggling with their feelings. They ask me to intervene. I commiserate with them, but tell them they will have to work this out with him, find a way to communicate their needs and expectations of him when they stay at his house. They agree to give it a try. In the meantime,

I have to find a way to get my own shit together. Crying and swearing while shoveling snow are only temporary outlets, though I did experience a good release of anger and frustration during the snowstorm. I feel somewhat lighter after this difficult weekend. In fact, there was a blizzard outside and one going on inside as well, the cold harshness of inner and outer worlds colliding head on.

I feel the urge to plunge ahead now, more intently than ever. After all, I really do have nothing to lose and everything to gain. My immediate desire is to change how I react to things I have no control over. Rather than panicking, I wish to remain calm and steady, going with the flow.

"Be strong," I tell myself, "no regrets! Have some faith!"

Early afternoon. At the studio. Emotions erratic. One minute I'm with my abuser's daughter and the next I'm plunging into the deepest pool of feelings, yanked back and forth between memories of being with her, then back to now, feeling everything and trying to figure out what to make of it all, trying to breathe, trying to remain calm. I thought I was done with all that! But the truth is, something inside me doesn't feel right. It's as if I've had too much caffeine, but that's not the case at all, though I feel wired in that way. It's more that I'm distracted by this constant shifting between realities. As I try to focus on work it's as if I'm looking into a time machine, the only thing I clearly see is my abuser's daughter and the things we did together. If I shift my head slightly, hold it at a different angle, the image disappears. Is this another shift in the assemblage point, here for my benefit? Or am I creating it, going where I don't really need to go? Or is there really something I still need to resolve back there?

The ringing of the phone breaks the fixation. By the time I hang up I've shifted into a different mood. A big commission came through! It helps to dispel some of my old nagging financial fears, but it doesn't take away the real issues that plague me. No matter how much money I have or make, it won't cure what's really eating away at me. I am now fully in the in-between place, in the void, and there is no going back, but most of the time I can't figure out where I am or how to get grounded. Even in the void there must be some means of orientation!

My new good mood doesn't last too long. Even though I was perfectly calm one minute ago, now I am tensing up again, getting sucked back into the spinning vortex. Somehow I'll just have to steady myself. Focus on reality, dammit!

"Calm down, relax, feel your feet on the ground," I tell myself, jumping up and down. "You are here now, in this reality!"

I go out to get some food. On the way I do the shamanic breathing pass, breathing out the old stuff, breathing in the new me. Staying alert and focused I make it to the store and back safely, breathing, breathing, breathing. The breathing helps me make sense of last night's dream too. It clarifies this in-between stage I find myself in, trapped between accepting the truth of the abuse, that it did actually happen, and finishing up the recapitulation of the sexually explicit horrors I had to deal with. That's what I sensed as I stood in the stairwell at the end of my dream, that it was this bearing of the tension that would lead me to acceptance of the truth.

Chuck is not far away in my dream, nor in reality either, but he can't rescue me. Nobody can. I have to do it myself. But I can reach out and ask for help, as I often do. Chuck doesn't know anything unless I tell him, however, as he's not a mind reader nor is he going to intuit anything, as I imagined in my dream. If I can't speak out loud, he can't hear me or know what I'm feeling or thinking or dealing with. If I don't talk, nothing can save me. I have to keep talking.

December 9, 2003

I am on a sandy beach by a lake, sitting next to a little girl, teaching her to press flower petals into the wet sand to make impressions. We are creating a circular pattern. A woman jogs by and turns toward the lake. She runs right out on top of the water. I know what she's doing and how to do it. I know you can walk on water if you know how to energetically hold yourself up. The little girl stares at the jogger walking on the water. I know she wants to try it.

"It's okay," I say, "go ahead. I'll finish the design."

She goes running off and into the lake, but is unable to stay on top of the water, no matter how hard she tries. I will her the ability to do it, to succeed, telepathically sending guidance.

"Lightness of being," I say. "Lift your soul above your head! Get out of your body!"

"Once you begin, you'll never stop trying," I tell her, realizing that part of her just isn't ready yet.

"Don't worry, it will happen one day," I say, seeing her disappointment. "You'll be able to do anything you want, simply by intending, including walking on water!"

I wake up in a calm state, the magic of the dream pulsing through me, my tender affection for the little girl so palpable and real, the opposite of yesterday's waking with pounding heart and panic coursing through me. The little girl and I worked so calmly on the beautiful mandala, our energy so compatible, the dream no doubt portending a final good outcome to this recapitulation, with the two of us, my inner child and myself, in calm alliance. I knew intimately how the jogger accomplished her feat, for I too have experienced the seemingly impossible with a mere shift of the assemblage point. Sometimes I shift into a magical state and sometimes I shift into the past, it depends on the day. Perhaps it's time to bring my little girl self into this new magical life, to let her experience some of the magic too. I think that's what this whole in-between phase is really all about, bringing all parts into alignment, especially now, as I go back and forth, recapitulating again the very earliest memories with my abuser's daughter. It seems as if I'm searching for some forgotten remnants of my young child self, left back there in the past. Why else would I still get pulled back there?

In spite of the wonderful feelings of the dream, surely hinting at a future reconciliation, the specter of my abuser hangs over me as I get up and prepare to meet with Chuck.

I sit down and immediately bring up the dream from the other night, when I was walking with the man who had raped me, an obvious reference to my abuser. I haven't been able to get over how non-reactionary I was, how I did nothing to save myself, but simply went along with him. I'm not twelve years old anymore, for cripes' sake!

"You need to find a way to react so he doesn't have any power over you," Chuck instructs.

"I could run," I say. "I could run away from him."

"You could, but that doesn't tackle the issue. You need to do something about him directly, deal with him."

"Yes, I know. I have to confront him. If I can do it in my dreams I will be doing it for real because my dreams are my life," I say. "The dream just rehashes all the old predatory stuff; it's where I've been stuck. It's boring now, the same old stuff."

I understand that I need to get creative, find ways to shift and react so I can transcend this stagnancy, in dreaming and in reality. I am tense and clenched as we talk, though less agitated than in the past few days. It's time to get out of the fucking vortex! Time to face my abuser once and for all and have a different outcome. My body reacts to the suggestion and I get up and move around the room, trying to shift away from the anxiety, away from the feeling of being pursued, the energy of my dream still with me.

"I can't let him get me again," I say, "because if he gets me I'm a goner."

"What could possibly happen to you that hasn't already happened?" Chuck asks. "What could he possibly do to you that he hasn't already done?"

I have to laugh. He's right, but when I leave Chuck's office I am still in the grip of my abuser's energy, still walking down the street of my dream, hand-in-hand with him. And I am in a daze for the rest of the day too, kind of feeling like I'm not really here. Even after driving I don't feel like I've been at the wheel. I bump into things all day. I even fall down, stumbling on the stairs at the studio, but it's like a dream, so slow motion that I almost don't even feel it, and in one smooth movement I bounce right back up again, as if I'm a rubber ball. For the life of me, I just can't snap out of it!

December 10, 2003

I wake up with bad feelings coursing through me, cursed self-loathing in my heart, anger on my brain, in high anxiety. I can't remember what I was dreaming, but I know I failed at some great challenge and that I am still caught, for I could not dream myself free of my abuser's energy. But I will not be defeated! I will stay alert and aware today. I will keep busy, keep breathing, keep prying my abuser's fingers from my arm, keep turning and walking in a new direction, calm the anxiety within myself with meditation.

"*Just let it happen, just let it happen,*" Jeanne says. "*It has to go through you. Don't fight it, just let it come.*"

The kids go off to school and I head over to the studio, talking myself into a state of calmness as I drive, preparing for what the day will bring. I will not fight it, but I will not give in to the anxiety either. I will let it go through me, as Jeanne suggests, but I will not be destroyed by it. Sadness goes through me as I drive, sadness from the deepest darkest pit inside me. I whine a little, feel sorry for myself, but then shift immediately, aware of just how tenacious this anxious energy is. I don't want to give it any more ammunition than it already has, so no whining! The fight may exhaust me, but I won't let it win.

"Project ahead, toss a line out and no matter what, keep going," Chuck said to me yesterday. "You'll get through it."

All morning I work with the anxiety, acknowledge it and let it go through me, shaking off the waves as they come, like water off a duck's back.

"I'm okay," I tell myself. "I'm just letting it go through me, and though I may feel crazy, I am not insane, I am not possessed. I am just on a journey, a journey of change, and it will get better. This is just a rough patch of road. It will get better."

By late morning I'm ready for a break. I get out of the studio, go to the recycling center and then pick up some lunch. By the time I get back to the studio I notice a change, the grip of tension released, no sign of it at all. My body actually feels loose and relaxed. It's a remarkable shift! Once again I am reminded of how physical movement is often the key to instigating change, though I also have no doubt the anxiety will reappear when I least expect it. Luckily I have a lot of work and will be very busy for the rest of the afternoon.

As expected the anxiety did come and go throughout the day, but I kept in step with it, letting it go through me, shaking it off. It returned more intensely as I prepared dinner, as we sat down to eat, and as I washed up the dishes afterwards. Like a desperately hungry animal it attacked, but I stayed aligned with my intent to unseat it. I will no longer fall for its old demoralizing patter, its boring old scenarios, the same old stuff over and over again. It can't have me anymore.

"Resist it," I told myself every time I felt it sneaking up on me, tension as sharp as the teeth of a hungry beast pricking my skin. "Ignore it. Resistance is *not* futile. Don't give in. It's not now, it's just a memory of tension. Let it go through you."

In the evening I watch a half hour of news and then take a hot bath, gaining a slim victory over the tension, preparing for the inevitable nightly attack, expecting it to come biting back.

"Why are you still here?" I ask it. "Is this such good sport? Am I so desirable that you refuse to give in, to admit that you can't win? Well, you can't. You never did win and you won't win now. I may be exhausted, I may be overwhelmed, I may stumble every now and then, even fall, but I will never let you win. You've had your time with me, it's my turn now. The truth is, I am *your* most formidable opponent. I will not give in. You can try all you want, but you will not win."

"I have an army behind me now. I have love behind me. I have a battalion that is stronger and smarter than even the most cunning of predators. You too will love me for my strength and my tenacity, far greater than your own. I may cry and I may rage against you, and I may fall, but I will get up again and fight you because you are in my way. Get out of my way!"

I really have progressed! I feel different from a week ago. I am no longer defenseless when awake, and even when asleep I'm aware of my abuser's energy coming in the night, aware of its presence and that I must do something about it. So, instead of waking up full of despair and self-loathing, I now intend to wake up ready to fight! Because, yes, I finally remember last night's dream challenge that so eluded me when I woke up this morning. I was being taught to be aware of how anxiety attacks, how it sneaks in, and what to do in retaliation, how to react and how to fight. And that's what I did today. All day I fought like hell!

December 11, 2003

I dream that I am inside a small two-story brick house that sits in the middle of a wide green field. The outside of the house is covered in ice and the inside is dripping wet, wallpaper peeling off the walls in thick soggy chunks, waterlogged plaster bulging and dripping, ceilings caving in. People are packing up to leave, but I will be staying. I'm worried about the structural stability of the house, but no one else seems to see it as a problem. When I point out the soaked and crumbling walls the others just say, "Oh, that's normal." But I know it's a disaster waiting to happen.

I wake up early, my legs completely clenched, as usual, but I notice that the energy battle within has greatly subsided. My dreamworld took me somewhere else last night and perhaps my abuser's energy is finally getting the message: I won't give in. Even if it's waiting for just the right moment, I'm ready for it now. The bath last night and the fact that I was extremely tired helped me sleep so deeply that perhaps it couldn't get me in quite the same way. I notice that I'm not on heightened alert like I normally am, though I still feel my abuser's energy hovering nearby, a constant rumbling in the background looking for a way in. At least I didn't wake up in a passive state again, not caring at all. Today feels better already. Maybe I will defeat his energy today.

I feel strong now. I understand what's happening to me in a deeper, more concrete way now too. Being able to visualize the anxiety as a real opponent in the shape of my abuser actually adds to my strategy, giving me a visual to make it more real. When lost in a non-visual morass of feelings I can't seem to take action, but as soon as I see my opponent waiting for me in the middle of that white painted square in the woods (dreamed on November 20th) it's clear what I have to do. I go there in my mind, jump into the square, and fight like a master.

I have great strength and inner power. I am strong and smart. I'm going to be fine. I'm going to be better than fine. I'm going to be successful and happy. Happy means being free of my demons, and for now that will be enough, even though I may still be lonely. I can find ways to ease the loneliness once the fear is under control. If I wasn't so afraid all the time then perhaps reaching out to others might be easier. Once again fear reveals itself as my biggest block. It has gotten in the way of everything in my life, holding me back, although I've done pretty well in spite of it, but imagine what I'll accomplish once it's out of my way. Even as I fight this demon, fear, I must also get it to love me for who I am, for my powers and strengths, for defeating it, for being stronger, and for my ability to love and live in spite of its negative presence in my life. I won't let fear win.

All day I've been thinking about last night's dream. It didn't feel like just another house dream. It was different. The house stood alone, in the middle of a field with a large tree growing next to it. It was not a farmhouse, even though it was in the country, but a brick or brownstone building from the city, eerily out of place in that landscape, slightly haunted looking with its façade of thick ice. As I faced the front door I was aware of a row of trees and a much lighter, happier modern house, built of wood, off to the left. Inside my icy dream house the walls were weeping and things were peeling away. The other people in the house pointed out how normal all that was, but for me it seemed strange. Perhaps it reflects how I'm beginning to change, to soften on the inside now, old defenses peeling, old ideas that are no longer supportive giving way. The exterior too was changing, an icy coating that was beginning to melt. This may be the change I've been waiting for, as I'm finally becoming a normal, feeling being.

The house had a certain draw, an appeal, the remnants of something comforting about it, as if it were related to my early childhood, but it had a desolate, empty, sinister feel as well. It reminds me of a dream I had about my mother a few months ago, when she took me to see her new house and it was covered in ice on the outside but unchanged on the inside. Perhaps this house reflects the decision I've made to leave the old structures and containment of family as I move on to something much more nurturing, for it's pretty clear that there really isn't anything to salvage in this crumbling building. As everyone else was leaving they told me that the house was okay as it was, that it was supposed to be like that, but it still didn't feel right to me.

It's clear that a crumbling deterioration of the old has to happen if new life is to spring forth. It's time to leave the old behind and move on to the new happy modern house I could see in the dream. I experienced a similar understanding during the vision at my mother's birthday party, a sense of how necessary it was to move on and leave everyone and everything behind, all that I've always known and depended upon. The realization that none of it was really nurturing or helpful anymore struck me with sadness. I was being shown then what would happen as an inevitable result of my recapitulation and it's what's happening right now. The old house, the old self, is no longer safe, secure, comforting, or even attractive. The new house, the new self, is light and inviting. Why then, in the dream, was I intending to stay in the old one?

I am reminded of Jeanne telling me to let things go, to let the old stuff go through me and be done with it once and for all. It's time to move out of the old house and walk through the trees to where the new house is ready and waiting. I see it right there, as plain as day, and yet something holds me back.

I've had a nice calm morning at the studio after a restful night, but anxious energy is slowly seeping in again, building in intensity. Such an old pattern, I see that now, how it crouches, waiting for its opportunity to sneak up and grab me. I feel it in my body. I can't pretend I don't know what's going on, for I am familiar with the play of opposites, how calmness leads to frenetic energy, a high to a low, for what goes up must come down, and vice versa. What stirs now is hidden deep within my tissues, something awakened out of some deep pocket of memory. For the past fifteen minutes it's been emerging, the old feeling of being possessed by something foreign, but I recognize it as my old demon pal, Fear, conjured by my abuser's energy, that other tricky demon, though no pal of mine!

"Hello, Fear, back again, I see. You must really like me. You fight so hard to keep me yours. Well, you can forget it. I am not yours. I don't belong to you, and I don't want you around me anymore either. It's time for you to leave. Get out! My life belongs to me, and I am not willing to share it with you or any other predators anymore."

I admit, fear actually lives inside me. It's nice to have finally figured this out. I know I've been telling myself this for ages, but it takes a while for things to sink in and be fully realized. Fear doesn't come from outside but is manufactured in a thought, a feeling, a mood, stirred by whatever else is going on inside me. Originally it was manufactured because of my abuser's outside predatory energy, because of what he did to me, but now it's just stuck inside me, for what is there really to fear now? After all these years it has more or less taken up permanent residence. I've fought with it and given in to it many, many times over my entire life, but I'm not going to do that any more. This will be the final battle.

"I'm hanging in there," I tell Chuck when he calls, needing to reschedule for a half hour earlier tomorrow morning, but what I really want to say is that I'm having a fucking hard time! Instead, I give him a rather bland report about my usual state of tension and depression.

"Don't get sad, don't get depressed," he says. "Don't let it get to you. It's actually a good place to be. It means something is shifting."

SHIT! Sometimes when he says stuff like that I just want to scream at him, punch him in the face, say, "You don't know a damn thing! You have no idea what I'm feeling or thinking or needing, so fuck you!" That's how I feel right now, like an angry bitch! Later on I usually realize he's right and then I feel bad for wanting to yell at him. Right now, however, angry bitch rules!

Ten at night. This is killing me. Fear tenaciously hangs on, a monster with its claws in me. I remind myself that it really isn't something foreign, that it's something that has been inside me forever. It once acted as a secret potion, meant to keep me under my abuser's spell, powerless, so he could own me. Even though he doesn't own me in reality, the potion lingers in my blood, emerging on occasion to rule again, as is its habit. Right now it doesn't want to abdicate, it still wants to rule.

I take a bath, try to relax and release some of the tension, the grip very tight now. Well, I'm not about to give in. I intend to defeat it once and for all. Now I'm getting angry and anger is a good friend.

December 12, 2003

I meet with Chuck at seven-thirty and we analyze what's been happening since we last met. Pacing back and forth, I explain that I woke up at four-thirty, rigid, with fear coursing through me and it's been there ever since.

"Like a bead in a can of spray paint, I am being rattled back and forth. I can't get out of the can!"

"The death rattle," Chuck says. "Get out! You don't want it! You are dealing with an alien occupation! You need to shift!"

"Walk in circles," Chuck says, "look at circles, draw circles, breathe in circles, create circular energy to counter the alien back and forth energy. Leave the old house, the cold house of the dream. You are like a heroin addict and the only relief is another needle of the stuff, but it's so bad for you. You can't have it. This is withdrawal; this is serious and tough stuff to handle. The universe is on your side. The universe is helping you. You have help and support. The entire universe is helping you get through this. Let go. You're safe."

"Be kind and compassionate to yourself," he says as the session ends. "Everything will be fine. Everything will be okay. You don't need his energy. You don't need his poison. You don't need any of it. You will find your own energy, but you have to get rid of his in order for there to be room for your own. Let it go."

I am at the studio when I suddenly remember that he, my abuser, paced back and forth, and I realize that this energy is not simply a figment of my imagination but an energetic manifestation of the real man. I see him pacing maniacally back and forth, back and forth, almost frothing at the mouth as he speaks of what he is going to do to me and I am helpless, filled with fear. It's what I've been feeling lately, the fear pacing back and forth inside me, the energy of it setting me pacing in reality too, as if my abuser truly were inside me, forcing me to pace like a madwoman.

I have been drawing circles all day, every chance I get. Chuck was right about circular energy, how it counters the back and forth energy, for when I feel who I truly am, when I feel my real self, I feel circles. When I've had glimpses of the real me I've visualized circles, soft, rolled up, compassionate circles. Circles of softness, kindness, and love. Yanking back and forth energy, pacing back and forth energy, those abrupt and jerky movements belong to him, to my abuser.

I realize that I tend to think circularly too. I tend to write and think within a circular framework, always looking for the final point that will bring me back around to my original idea, connecting me back to the beginning of my thoughts, offering conclusions that make sense to me, based on where I started from. I have been on a circular journey. I've been painting circles of light for a few years now too, glowing circles of color in the background of my paintings. Yes, yes! I am coming full circle.

"Journey on now," Jeanne says. *"Leave the cold, falling down house and go toward the new house that has yet to be discovered. He won't follow you; once you start that journey you will leave him behind. His alien energy will have to go someplace else. Don't worry about him and his energy. He is not your problem. What he does is his problem."*

Maybe in leaving me his energy will go back to him, a reminder of how evil he really is. Maybe the energy will reattach to him and perhaps kill him. Maybe he'll beg for forgiveness. Perhaps he's struggling to die right now, only he can't because I still hold onto some of his energy. If I don't release his energy then he can't die, but if I do he will die his evil death and I will be free. Being free is the most important thing in the world.

An hour goes by and his energy leaves me. I enter a calm, floating, body-relaxed state. I am wholly myself; peaceful for a time in my circular wholeness. I stay present in myself, in my body, just being, empty of the alien energy at last, empty of the fear, empty of the loathing. I feel not the emptiness I had imagined, but the beginnings of something new, something filling, like warm bread dough rising in its bowl, softly, slowly rising until it fills the vessel. With his energy gone I am not empty and alone at all. I am full of my own being. I am alive.

I will have to reprogram myself to be different, receptive and open without fear, so I can learn all the things I never had a chance to learn, all the things that are inside me just waiting to awaken. I know there is nothing to be afraid of now. If I sit very quietly and meditate on what is happening inside myself, I feel a wholeness beginning to manifest and anchor, a knowing that I own this body and this soul. *I own it.* It does not belong to anyone but me. I receive glimpses of my own potential. With the alien energy gone I am not empty but full, full of the self I was never able to be, full of the true me. I am a full body of truth. This I must own. All this belongs to me.

I feel the pull of my abuser's energy, trying to take me back as the day goes on, but I also feel very strong. This is not a losing battle, it's a winning battle, and I am winning. I don't want to go back inside that desolate place, that frozen brownstone in the middle of the empty field, and even though I can't quite get off the front stoop yet, I am working on it. I need to close the door so the energy does not find me again. There is new, fresh life ahead of me now and the certainty that I will be fine. That is very clear. I just need to get off that damned stoop!

The back and forth energy returns every time I challenge it, rattling bad thoughts around in my head, pulling and jerking me around, but I won't let it win.

"You won't win! I'm good! I'm fine! I love myself. Well, I'm *learning* to love myself anyway. I see that I have a person inside me who I've barely met, a person who has been waiting forever, for as long as I've been alive, to emerge and grow, to show me who she is. The bead in the can of spray paint, creating the death rattle, as Chuck called it, is not me, it's the alien energy that has haunted me. Time to leave! Die!"

I wish for my abuser's evil to go flinging back to him. I would like it to kill him. I would like it to have the power to do tremendous, painful damage to him, and I would also like him to know where it came from. Perhaps that is black magic, but it's what comes to me now, and perhaps it's the only kind of magic that will work on such evil. I would like his last thoughts to be of me, the little girl whose life he destroyed, whose energy he stole. As he dies and leaves this earth he can give me back my life. But even if it doesn't happen that way, I won't let him energetically destroy me. I am closing the door on the bleak house in the field. I am going to walk down that stoop, get off the fucking stoop, and walk away without looking back. I am going to leap over the row of trees and make a beeline for my new house!

As I sit on the stoop of the old house in my imagination, I notice that it's deteriorating, the cement between the flagstones is chipped and breaking down. The whole house is near collapse, crumbling behind me. I won't turn around and look, but I can hear it cracking and groaning, falling apart as I go down the steps. How many steps are there? Sixteen, of course! There are sixteen steps, one for each child self, one for each year of abuse and torture. I run down those sixteen steps and as soon as my foot touches the green grass I run and run and run!

The clock in the studio ticks loudly. I have never heard it before. Why is it so loud? Tick-tock! Tick-tock! Tick-tock!

"Run, run, run! The grass is so very green," Jeanne says, *"soft and beautiful. Run, run! No, don't look back! Go, go, go! Hear the house crumbling, falling! You don't even have to look, just visualize it, old crumbled debris. There is nothing left, just a pile of stone and dust and ice. It has collapsed. Keep going forward; look ahead! Run, run! Run from it! It's gone now. The house is gone. You won't go back or even look. You don't have to. You know every inch of stone and ice, all too long a part of you. Now it's gone! But don't look back. Forward, forward now. Gone, gone. Let it go. If you have to you can walk down those sixteen steps over and over again, step onto the grass and run, as often as you need to. Just keep the door closed and don't go back inside or look back. There is nothing there for you, nothing!"*

At three in the afternoon I am still battling the energy, the pull and the draw of it, perhaps even the danger of it. I don't know what to do except allow myself to run down off the stoop as often as necessary, as Jeanne suggested.

"Get off the stoop!" I yell. "He can't get you if you just get off the stoop!"

Whenever I feel pulled back I imagine myself running off the stoop. As soon as I step onto the cool green grass I hear the house crumbling and tumbling and falling and then I run and run. I run like the wind.

A little sadness seeps in as I go through this process, but I tell myself it's just the sadness of change, of leaving more than just him behind, for I feel that I am leaving my whole life behind as well, my family and all of my past; but it's necessary. And it doesn't mean I'm giving in if I have to go lie down or if I need a minute to curl up and hug myself. He isn't getting me if I just take a minute to myself. I have to be careful though, especially if I'm feeling exhausted. I must be careful to not think bad thoughts about myself, to not get angry at myself or consider myself weak. I can be tired and exhausted and still not let his energy get me. I must remind myself that I don't need it anymore, I don't want it. I have to remember how destructive it is, how it wants to keep me in an old place and make me do old stuff. I have to remember that I'm going in a new direction now.

I breathe circular breaths. I run off the stoop as often as necessary, promising myself that soon I will run through the trees and enter the warm light of the new place. Again and again, I leave the old house and all the bleak memories, close the door on all the weeping, crumbling walls, acknowledge the state of the exterior too. I turn my back on it all. I let it fall apart. I walk away from it, detached, knowing there is nothing that needs saving there. I am what needs saving now. Every time I slam that door I imagine the whole thing falling in on him, burying him alive. May he scream and cry and beg for his life. May no one hear him. May his last hours be full of pain and anguish, and may he know why. As he suffers may he think of me, and realize that this is his punishment for the heinous crimes against a defenseless child.

"May your death be slow and painful. May you be alone, cold, and full of fear. May you be lost and no one bother to look for you. May you be screaming and no one hear you. And before you are dead, may the animals tear at your flesh. May the birds of prey peck at you, so that you may feel what it means to be eaten alive by predatory energy, to be slowly devoured. May you feel the pain of it and the deep loneliness of it too. May you find yourself in a dark black pit that is impossible to crawl out of, and may you never be rescued from it. I hate you. I hate you. I hope this is how you die."

After I run off the stoop and collapse that icy dream house a few times, and then kill him off, I feel much better and I am able to spend a few hours of relaxation, though I still feel his energy circling around, for he is like a strange mythological creature that will not die. I avert my gaze and warn him to stay away, just stay away from me! I will not look back. I will not attach in any way. At the same time I mustn't get complacent; I can't let my guard down. But I must be careful to not provoke his energy or give it any reason to be interested in me at all. Even by asking it to go away I may draw attention to the fact that I am asking it to do something for me. It's too risky and too serious a situation to make any kind of pact with his energy, for I know it is as cunning as can be. Even asking it to disappear acknowledges its existence.

Instead, I completely remove him from my thoughts. Instead, I think circles. Instead, I draw circles. I say the words, "circular energy, circular energy, circular energy," as I draw, filling entire pages with circles of all sizes, mesmerizing myself, releasing the old pain, drawing upon my new intent to heal. I breathe circles. I surround myself with circular energy. I bring home a circular pizza for dinner.

Midnight. I am ready for sleep. I have had peacefulness for most of the evening, only minor flickers of fear reminding me to not let it get to me, to not let myself go there. One last time I went back and ran down off the stoop at full speed and across the cool green grass. I heard the brownstone tumbling and crashing behind me as I ran like the wind. And then all was silent. Now I hope for peaceful sleep. Chuck suggested that I should call out to him when dreaming and if he is at all alert to my needs he will come to help me. I intend to take him up on it. We will see if he responds with some backup energy.

As my body begins to relax, as I drift into sleep, my hips and legs take on their usual clenching. The pain intensifies as I tense against the fear that automatically creeps in. An old sense of helplessness comes over me in this state and I feel my abuser's energy trying to get me again. But no, he's not allowed! I will fight. I will fight him in my sleep. And I will call on all the help available, the whole universe, and Chuck too!

December 13, 2003

I called on Chuck last night the way a child calls out to her parents in the middle of the night, trusting that they will show up. I called to him in my dreams and in my dreams he came and calmed my dreaming self.

"It will be all right. You're fine. You're okay, Jan. Let it go. Let it go," he said, sounding so much like Jeanne.

I wake up less rigid than usual, though my hips scream with the pain of the usual all-night clenching. I know it's not just pain that's the problem but more memories, painful memories; the hip pain a direct link to something horrific, something I'm not ready to face. Panic shoots through me at the thought and along with it comes a storm of doubt that I can't do this, that I can't handle this, but underneath is a firm knowing that I can handle anything and that I will be just fine, as Chuck said in my dreams.

I know this pain will end one day soon and I *will* be just fine, but for now the ache in my hips is a clear indication of something as of yet unknown. I think about falling back into the old numbness simply to alleviate the pain, to dissociate from it, to return to the walking dead, my old zombie state, because I know that it lessens and numbs the pain. But it isn't the way to go anymore. I know how to ease the pain in a different way now. I just have to accept it, let it go through me, release it, breathe, breathe, breathe. Circular breath, circular energy. Numbness is *not* the answer, it's just an illusion. It won't last, it's not real. And it won't make me real either. It's just a temporary anesthetic.

"No numbness," Jeanne says. *"Feel instead; feel, feel, feel! Go with what comes, allow it to happen! You'll be fine! You'll be fine! Numbness is bad and bad for you. He wins then, and you can't let him win!"*

"Go back to the brownstone and touch those icy walls and realize that that is what numbness is. Then turn and run away. Run down those sixteen steps, off that high stoop, down all those dangerous and crumbling sixteen steps, and keep running. The grass is cool, green, and soft under your bare feet and you are naked, running from that cold dangerous place, taking nothing with you. The sunlight is waiting for you. Run to it and listen as that old haunted bleak house tumbles down. Hear it crumbling. You can look back if you really have to, to make sure it actually fell down. Fine, look back. See? That heap on the ground? Now run, and keep running naked into the light and into new life. You can do it. Release as you run! Release! Release! Let it all go!"

"You can call on Chuck if you want to. He's there for you. He knows everything. Run, run, run! Look forward to that new house. You can see it through the trees. Even if you can't quite get to it yet, you can see it there waiting for you. See? It's waiting all right, comforting in the right way, so full of light and life. Don't go back. The old place is unstable and dangerous. KEEP OUT!"

"Even as you imagine it, even as you feel a draw to go back and fix it, to feel compassion for it, you must accept that it's falling apart. Its time is done. It's not an option anymore. It isn't available to you. There's nothing there for you. It only contains pain and fear and sadness. It will only hurt and it will continue to hurt you for the rest of your life. Now is the time to get away. Warning: STAY OUT! DANGER! DANGER!"

"Go to your new place. You already see it beyond the trees. You are almost there. Keep going. Keep going. Get up now, Jan. Get out of bed and get started on your day. Move and you will be on your journey forward. Don't go back there. Even though the pull is like a magnet, even though your body thinks it needs it, it doesn't, it really doesn't. It is poison and it can kill you. Don't go there. Look ahead! See beyond the trees? A rooftop!"

I was around other people for most of the day, which was good, but I find so much interaction tiring, though it held in check the urge to go creeping back to the old places of comfort. Whenever I felt drawn I let myself go back to the old brownstone, as Jeanne had suggested. I saw it for what it really was, and each time I ran from it and watched it crumble to the ground my attachment to it deadened a little bit more. Each time it fell I got to see, all over again, that what holds me in check, that what causes such fear and sadness, that what I think offers such comfort, is just a figment of my imagination, a symbol I've been attached to for far too long.

Dinner over, I'm tired now, but my day is not over yet. The kids are seeing a play and I have a few hours until I have to pick them up. After such a busy day the quiet alone time is nice. I find that I constantly look for small gifts of comfort that I can easily give myself, a cup of tea, a quiet moment to breathe or meditate, a hot bath, seeking things to shift me, new and better alternatives to the old tried and true numbness.

"Be kind to yourself, just be kind to yourself," I tell myself, though I often find that hard to do.

I do have other ways to shift now, new ways to settle into calmness. Drawing circles works like meditation, a very soothing act, so satisfying, like writing or painting. Tensegrity, the magical passes that Chuck teaches me, feel awkward at first, not my thing perhaps, but eventually they become part of me, though it takes a while. Maybe it's just the act of moving my body in different and unfamiliar ways that feels strange, going beyond my comfortable and habitual range of motions. Maybe just being physical and in my body is what's so awkward; I'm shy about it, unused to it. Visualization on the other hand, the creative, comes to me quickly and easily. Without awkwardness or shyness I make it work immediately. Going back to the crumbling old brownstone of my dream over and over again in my imagination, dealing with it by visualizing its destruction, has worked phenomenally.

A sudden sound outside my window. I hear the dry brush of large wings swishing by, and then: HOOT! Owl letting me know that everything will be okay and that it's time to pick up the kids!

December 14, 2003

Sneaking up on my vulnerabilities while I sleep, it slips down my loneliness, rides my doubt. Entering at my hips, it knifes me, pinning me down in a rigid hold.

"I need you!" I call to Chuck in my sleep, unable to bear the pain and anguish. "Soothe me! I need soothing."

I want someone to hold me, to understand, to massage away the fear sitting heavily on top of me, crushing me with its depressing old messages of self-doubt and self-destruction.

"Be careful," I hear Chuck saying. "Be careful."

"I can't stop it, but I can fight it," I say, and I attempt to counter it with positive feelings, with all that is good inside me, but as I wake up I feel the weight of it. My old demon, Fear, has gotten inside me again.

I remember what Jeanne told me yesterday and I go back to that brownstone again and SLAM the door shut. SLAM it so hard that the windows rattle and big chunks of ice fall. SLAM it on all that stuff in there, on that pain and loneliness, on that bleak sadness and that cold numbness. And then I turn and head down those crumbling steps. I run and run, get away from the danger and the pain, run from the fear, leave it all there and run like hell across the cool green grass.

"Come on," Jeanne says. *"Make those stiff legs run! Drag them if you have to, but move! Move across the grass toward the new house beyond the trees!"*

"Now listen! Behind you! Do you hear that crumbling, that crashing stone by crashing stone? Do you hear that? It's falling apart. That unsafe structure with the weeping walls and the melting façade is crumbling into a soggy wet heap. Chunk by chunk it is tumbling down."

"You hate that place. You hate it. There is no reason to be there anymore. There is no need, there never was. It was an illusion, an illusion of comfort, but now you see it for what it really was and is, a derelict, bleak, uninhabitable monstrosity, not of your own construction, not of your own design. Someone else put that house there and left you in it. For years they left you there, where you had to go numb and tight with the cold dampness, where you had to creep around looking for comfort. Where you had to fend for yourself as best you could."

"There is nothing good there. The rooms are familiar, the walls, the floors, the details. Heck, the doorknobs are so familiar because you spent so much time there, but that doesn't mean that it belongs to you or you to it. It was your dungeon, your prison. It was where you were held captive and, yes, you may come out of it and long for the solitude and the meager comforts you invented while there, because that was all you had, but you have to learn that there are other comforts available now, that those old comforts are no longer relative. They belong to a very painful past. They belong buried under that heap of stone and ice. So, get away! Leave all that bad stuff behind to fall into a desolate heap. Escape! Run! Run! Get Away! Danger! Run for your life!"

"Look forward, not back. Look toward the future and your new home. It's already waiting, nestled comfortably into the landscape, fitting perfectly into its surroundings, and you belong there too, you do belong there!"

"Go find it. You still have to get through the trees. You still have to go through the last stretch of woods, but it's in sight now. It's clearly there; you can see it. Don't go back anymore. Okay? If you do get tugged back, see only the pile of your past life, see only the cold and icy truth, but don't linger. Move on. Go into new life."

It's Sunday today, another big snowstorm on the way. I go out to pick up a few things at the grocery store and hear on the car radio that Saddam Hussein has been captured, one less evildoer out there. It reminds me of my abuser and my visualizations of his painful death. I still think it appropriate punishment for him, and I do believe that with his demise I will regain my energy and have my life fully restored to me. Of course, I can't count on it, but I would like to think that all the positive forces in the universe, and those already here helping me get through this, will understand my thoughts and deal with him as they see fit. I know that I need to take back my own life, that only as I undertake more of this difficult recapitulation work will I regain my true self and my true life and be ready to live this earthly existence as I wish. But I want to be completely selfish for once and ask that he be punished appropriately, and that he think of me, not of his daughter or any other girl, but only of me, and beg my forgiveness at the moment of death. Once he releases me, he is free to go.

I am also aware that if I set him free, I will set myself free too. But I'm still angry, so I don't want him to simply die. I want him to suffer. I want him crushed, chewed alive by wild beasts, suffocated by his ugly misdeeds. Die you horrible bastard! Die a horrible death! This is my wish. His daughter and anyone else he was involved with will have to work it out on their own terms, but this is what I have to do for myself.

The pictures of Saddam Hussein on TV show a tired old man, unkempt, resigned, looking scruffy and exhausted, like a homeless person. He has lost his power, he is nothing but a shriveled up old man. Is that what my abuser is like now too? Yes, in actuality he is an old man now, his power over me long gone. He's probably sick and old and can't even get "it" up anymore. I am strong, still young enough and powerful enough that I could fight him and probably do some damage. "You could kill a man!" Chuck said once, quite shocked at my show of strength when I whacked the heck out of a pillow with a large stick. Yes, small as I am, I am strong and I could probably kill him, but better to not go there. Better to *imagine* him dead. Better to kill him visually because then I have control, and then I can do it over and over again, as many times as I please.

I realize I still have a big battle ahead of me. Old feelings still linger, more than linger, they reside firmly embedded and to unseat them is going to take more than a few hours work. I must remain alert because just the thought that I might let my guard down allows for an opening, and then I am caught again, the bad feelings return, the old needs resurface, fear enters and I become overwhelmed, feeling that I will be consumed again.

"Fight it! Fight it!" Jeanne says. *"Breathe it out! Change the energy! Change the thought patterns! Change the body! Change the mind!"*

And that's exactly what I do! The kids and I go out and shovel the foot of snow that has fallen, the three of us making quick work of it. Then I take a cold walk around the block with my daughter. The wind is beginning to pick up, the cold biting, and her cheeks are bright red, her beautiful face rosy and happy.

I realize more each day how deeply affected I am by my past. In spite of good things happening, progress in my life, my kids doing so well, work going well, there is still so much deep down inside me that still frustrates and holds me back. I still feel lost, still seek something unknown. In fact, I'm always seeking something, still feel restless in spite of all the good things. To get to the bottom of this restlessness is all that matters now. The living of everyday life seems to take care of itself, while deep inside I still struggle to make sense of this life and what it is that I have not found yet, for something is still missing. I know that finding and maintaining a sense of balance within myself is the only way to really feel stable and secure. And I want to keep growing, to find my center, my perfect inner circle, and spin my life around it, create a circular life.

Back in the warmth of our little home I sit and draw circles. Large and small, circles inside circles, circles overlapping, twirling, swirling, swirls within swirls, spiraling in and spiraling out. I am busy drawing, my arm and hand busy, drawing circles onto paper when the back and forth energy rears its ugly head and demands equal time, when fear rides in like a devil on horseback.

Then I draw circles very slowly and very deliberately. Instead of attaching to the old stuff with worry, I relax as I draw.

"Full circle, I am coming full circle, back to myself," I say, my pen running out, not my thoughts or my words or my circles, just my ink...

The back and forth energy and the fear back off as I keep busy, but I know they are waiting for me to reach exhaustion, certain that then I will have no energy left to deflect their plunging knives. I bake cookies, chat with the kids, cuddle the cats, write, read, do laundry, make dinner, and shovel snow again to keep everything at bay. And indeed, I am tired by the end of it, but I remind myself over and over again that I don't have to go back. I don't have any reason. It isn't necessary to go backward anymore in order to move forward, because everything I need is in front of me now.

"Don't look back!" I tell myself.

The brownstone is crumbling; I feel the ground shaking as it falls. I don't look back. I just have to get through that last stand of trees before I reach the new house and then I will be free. I am almost free.

December 15, 2003

I dream that someone has arranged for me to have my own apartment in New York City. I overhear them talking about it, saying that the apartment faces Central Park. When I hear this I visualize the park at night, during the day, during a snowstorm, in the summer, in the fall, etc. I'm very excited that I'll be living in the city by myself, and that the apartment faces the park, for there's nothing I enjoy more than sitting at a window watching life go on outside. I also like the solitude of living alone. The people who are talking never say any of this directly to me. They're talking as if they don't notice me standing right there, but then I realize this is their intention. They want me to hear everything so I'll know exactly what's going on, so I'll know there are no mysteries, no secrets, no tricks. Everything is very plainly and clearly explained. They want me to feel safe.

There's no school today. Another snowstorm is brewing, bringing more snow and more shoveling, so helpful at keeping the tension and fear at bay. So nice to not have to do the morning routine, and I can let the kids sleep in. I make coffee and bring it back to bed, snuggle in, let my thoughts come.

By the end of last night's dream I was feeling pretty good, sort of resolved to the fact that as far as practical everyday living is concerned I will be fine, that things will work out well, and even that others are working on my behalf. And I have to acknowledge that I *am* being helped, that my spirit guides are a big part of how my life is unfolding. In the dream I was excited about the prospect of being able to look down on the busy park, having a full view of life going on below. But the truth is, if I don't face everything and finish this recapitulation I will only be an observer of life and never fully participating in it. That's really what the dream is telling me.

True things happen.

A voice whispered those words to me as I was falling asleep last night. I wrote them down in what felt like a Cinderella moment; a shift happened and I was struck by a sudden spark of insight just as the clock turned to midnight. I think it means that every step, once taken, becomes true reality, right or wrong, good or bad, not to be denied or repressed but accepted as a meaningful part of life. In other words, life is full of only true things. I used to feel my life was controlled by fate, that my life was planned and I just had to live it, just walk the tiresome path laid out before me. It was a rather negative and depressed idea of life and I rejected it after a while, but I have lately come to understand that while I don't control what happens in my life, life itself creates *me* in its everyday unfolding. I remain autonomous, capable of making decisions that effect the outcome of my life, but even so life is directing me, constantly offering me new possibilities and new opportunities, which I can choose or not. Life itself is not stagnant; it's alive, guiding me every day. This is something I have certainly learned during this recapitulation!

I've been learning to accept the myriad of "true things" that happened in my past because things do happen to us without our say-so, and they are meaningful if we choose to see them as such. I've had so many important things to learn as I've taken my journey through life, tough lessons though they may be.

As I look back over my life I note in its unfolding how one thing has led to another, how one decision has impacted the next, how each step has led to the next step. Surely such hindsight, and staying as present as possible in each moment, will help me remain present and alert in the years to come, especially as I am engaging in life like never before, as I make decisions based on a new set of parameters. I am learning to trust that every moment in my life does have meaning and purpose, and that every moment is confronting me with encounters and decisions that will determine where I go next, taking me where I am meant to be, a curious mixture of fate and choice indeed! Determining how best to engage life, how best to approach it, and with what attitude, is how I intend to remain consciously aware of its unfolding, for I do believe that if I get myself aligned with nature inside of myself and nature outside of myself that I will be in the right alignment to always maximize my experiences of life as a true thing!

I'm eager to learn what other opportunities are here for me, for I am certain that I am here to learn more, that every step and every day of my life teach me more of what I need to know. I trust that, just as I've come to trust the magical unfolding of this unique process of recapitulation over the past few years. I am blown away by how guided and led along my path I have been by all sorts of beings, situations, memories, and innumerable other helpers and guides, not to mention some pretty unique challenges from within myself! I intend to continue accepting what happens—good or bad—as true things. Every experience has something to offer. I see that very clearly now, and just what that might be will only be discovered by going through the experience.

After all, isn't life really all about embracing the changes that are constantly offered, and changing along with them? Life becomes interesting and alive then, fascinating, each day an unfolding of true things. If life is viewed in this manner, how could it not be so? Of course, I have to accept that life may not bring me all I could wish for. Even though I am open and ready for a grand future, I really have no idea how things will unfold, but I can still hope and wish for certain things, like love and understanding, kindness and compassion. I can always set my intent and make wise decisions and choices, but I also have to be prepared to face that some things I want may never come about, that certain things may just not present as opportunities for me. So be it, only true things happen.

A part of me wants to be selfish and beg and plead for things and then not be ashamed of my childish behavior, wishing for positive experiences in my life. But that childish part is also pointing out the truth that I must still deal with my shame around having needs and desires. Perhaps the best way to conquer that shame is to be in a position to have to receive, to be in a position of acceptance, to be given to in ways that I have never been given to before. But if I am to go down that road I must first turn off the old voices that weigh so heavily, that speak so loudly still, that push my face down into the mud and whisper harsh words in my ear: "You dirty nasty girl! Who could ever love you?"

It's amazing how quickly my inspiring insights can fly off, dropping me straight back down into the pits, for now I am covered in the mud of shame! It streaks my vision and clouds my sense of self. Why is it so hard to love myself? Why is it so hard to want good things for myself, to allow myself to accept this new life I already feel and see emerging from out of that mud? New life really does loom brightly on the horizon where once only dark and gloomy thoughts and memories stood. I must stay attached to that new vision, even as I feel negative energies revving their engines for a final fight. The new me is more determined than ever to fight back with all I have. The new me knows that since I've survived this far I can survive anything. I have great inner strength and that is where I go now to sweep away the negatives, the doubt, the fear, and the old memories of pain that come like ghostly invaders. I must keep in mind that true things happen indeed!

Meditating, breathing circular energy, asking for strength and protection, I let the old negative voices go. And once again I slam the door on the old brownstone. And then I move my heavy leaden feet off the stoop and make them run!

"Don't become paralyzed," Jeanne says. *"Don't stay just because that's what you've always done. Do it differently now, move, move! Save yourself, save your life. Run! Once you start, it will be easier. Get off the crumbling steps. Run into the cool green grass, away from that bleak monstrosity of a life. Run toward new life!"*

"You don't need to look back. You already know what's there. You already know everything. He will try to pull you back; he will try to drag you back into the house, but don't go. It's no longer your house. It has been condemned. See the sign on the door? DANGER! DO NOT ENTER! Building subject to demolition and collapse!"

"See, it's crumbling. The inside is weeping, the outside is melting, the structure is weak. Get away! You will not go down with it; you will not be destroyed. You have the power to get out now and run like hell to that new house, the sooner the better. Leave now; leave it all behind. The building itself will take care of everything for you; it will self-destruct and bury it all. You don't have to worry about it. The knowledge you have gained is enough. That's all you need, what you've learned about yourself and the people who have been a part of your life. You don't want to continue living there. You will never be comfortable there again. Look at it. It's totally uninhabitable. You don't want that anymore."

"Look beyond the trees now. See that new rooftop? See the sunlight upon it? See how the new house nestles so naturally and comfortably into the landscape? Go there. It was built for you; master builders built it especially for you. Last night, in your dream, they gave you the key. It's yours now, they said. 'Go see how you like it. You should go see it.' But you never actually went and looked at it in your dream. Why don't you go there now? Why don't you go to that new place? A country place is your perfect home. It's where you belong. It's not just a dream; it's your life."

"He will try to pull you back, but you won't go with him anymore. He will trick you, so be aware. He will come at you with his tools and his rope and his truck. He will try to lock you in the barn because he needs you. He is a predator, but he doesn't exist if you don't show up."

I've learned that I must stay busy if I am to keep both the negative voices and the negative feelings away. I get through the days better now, but then everything collapses at night when I crawl under the covers, seeking solace and soothing. I end up clenched and rigid instead, in physical, emotional, and mental pain. I know this will lessen with time and distance and that this frustrating period will eventually be over. I look forward to that time, even as I work on what still needs to be done in this time.

Every time I go back to the brownstone and run off that stoop I run a little further away from the house and closer to the woods. Although I feel apprehension as I approach the trees, I feel that I am making headway. The woods loom dark and scary before me, but I know how to approach them now, how to face what needs to be faced. There are still obstacles to overcome, probably only within myself now, the last interior battles over issues of self-esteem as I make room for my own positive voice to speak up and be heard, as I leave the old feelings of shame and disgust behind.

I will have to turn off my abuser's voice too, the one that makes me think he still owns me, but the truth is no one owns me. As Jeanne says, if I stay attached to the memory of him then he still exists in my energy field, for he is a predator and that's what predators do, even if only in memory. But I do not belong to anyone except myself. I seek to more fully be myself now, to find a way to feel safe and secure within myself, to not feel drawn to look elsewhere for security, but also to not be afraid to accept it from another should it be offered. I would like to wake up one morning and not be full of fear or self-hatred. I would like to wake up and hear a kinder inner voice, full of love and compassion for myself, instead of the harsh and negative voices I hear now. Some days I wake up out of a positive dream and those days start off well, but by night I am back in the clutches of the old demons again. I hear Chuck saying: "Don't let them get you, just don't let them get you."

"Slam the door on the brownstone," Jeanne says. *"You saw clearly what it looked like in there. You saw the bleak sadness of it, the weeping walls, empty darkness, and intense loneliness. You aren't leaving behind anything you need. You are only leaving behind the negative aspects that have been your life up until now. When you slam that door and run away you are leaving it all behind, you are getting rid of the fear and the negative attitudes and voices. You can do it! Just slam the door and run."*

"Whatever is waiting in those trees isn't any worse than what you already know. It won't hurt you anymore than you have already been hurt. It won't kill you. It will free you. You have to go through it in order to be free and in order to get to that new house. Keep looking toward that new house. Keep focused on that.

Keep focused on sunlight and warmth and love in that new house. Talk yourself toward it with gentle kindness and compassion. Talk to that little girl inside who is still afraid. Bring her forward with you. Mother her tenderly. Hold her and soothe her. Let her know she is safe. Soften into love. Let it happen and it will, first for that little girl and then for you. Let her speak out, let her weep, let her express her fears, and then soothe her. In so doing, you will find a way to be compassionate to your adult self too."

As Jeanne finishes speaking a strong urge to go back to the brownstone overwhelms me. It feels as if I left a part of myself back there. Did I leave my sixteen little girls back there? Is that why I keep going back? The night I had the dream I was preparing to stay, crumbling and soggy though the house was, but it wasn't clear why. Perhaps a part of me stayed behind to protect the girls? Why otherwise would I keep going back? I can't leave any part of myself behind. I must bring everyone forward to safety and new life if this journey is to progress. Jeanne suggests that nothing has been left there, but why else am I still drawn? Why have I felt such a pull? Each time I left it felt like it was the last time, but then I'd find myself back there again, standing on that crumbling stoop, staring at that icy façade.

My daughter and I run errands. We buy a Christmas tree and she decorates it while I make dinner. We eat a little late and then go outside and shovel the driveway in the dark, all three of us, which makes it go fast. Another storm, another foot of snow. I take a bath afterwards, but it isn't as relaxing as I'd like it to be, the old feelings strong, not the back and forth energy, which seems to have left, but the heaviness of self-destructive feelings.

I numbed up today and cut off access to my feelings when they became too intrusive. I did exactly what I've been striving to avoid, but I have to admit that the numbness provides a respite. I know I should be fighting to return to full body consciousness instead, but I'm tired of fighting. Maybe I've lost a little ground today, though perhaps that too is a "true thing" happening. I can only trust that it will teach me something important.

319

December 16, 2003

I meet with Chuck, take the EMDR pods in hand, and go right back into my dream of the brownstone. I run off the stoop and across the grass, as I've been doing so many times lately, but this time I run right into the woods. I walk through the trees and come to a flowing river. I can't go any further. I turn back, for although I have been so focused on moving forward I know I will not be able to cross the river until I've first gone back and made sure that I haven't left any part of myself behind in the old house. I describe to Chuck the layout of the dreamscape with this new addition, the river in the woods.

"The river is raging high," I say, "a wildly flooding river, and I know I'm not going to be able to cross it until it runs down."

"It's the River of Letting Go," Chuck says. "It's everything you've been holding back, all of your emotions. Once you release them and let them flow, you'll easily be able to cross."

"Well, until then I can't even get close. I'm fearful when I think about crossing."

"Why? What is this fear?" he asks.

"I don't know. The whole idea of letting go just makes me hold tighter and I'm so afraid I haven't completed everything on this side of the river yet. I don't want to leave anything behind. I'm thorough that way."

We laugh at that, but it's no joke.

I drive over to the studio after the session. I told Chuck about hearing the words "true things happen" and that I like the idea of *letting things happen* so much better than *letting go*. "Let it happen" sounds so doable, a lot less stressful than "letting go." To me letting go implies that I am holding back and can't let go, which is true, but it also implies that I am at fault, that I am to blame for not letting go. *Let it happen*, on the other hand, allows me to let myself be open, to acquiesce. *Let go* inhibits by its very command and my reaction is: "Oh my God, I can't! There must be something wrong with me! Why can't I?" And I start thinking that I'm incapable and then I just tighten up. The phrases *let it happen* and *true things happen* are more soothing, allowing me to open, to be flowing, to go with the flow; all of which are much more positive, without a hint of blame and without some other voice making demands. Instead, I simply release and open to the possibilities. Or at least that is my intention!

I have been so fiercely intent on moving forward that I've failed to use self-nurturing and compassion over the past few days, those maternal feelings Jeanne suggested I use on myself for a change. Anger used to propel me forward, but I realize that the only way I will be able to move forward now is with new, softer energy from the heart. I must soften and release myself to the River of Letting Go. And I must remember that true things will happen, whether I am afraid or not, in pain or not.

December 17, 2003

An old friend appears in a dream. She wears a one-strap, leopard skin gown that falls off her shoulder and exposes her breasts. She lays evocatively stretched out on a large office table where I am attending a meeting. People talk about her most recent relationship and how it has allowed her to open up to her femininity. Later, I follow my old friend to a large modern house. We knock at the door. When the owner answers, my old friend walks right in, shutting the door in my face, as if I weren't even there. I'm a little miffed by her rudeness, but knock again.

"I'm with her," I say when the owner reappears.

I follow the owner into an inner room where I see a lot of my artwork, including a jewelry box I had once painted.

"Oh, I hated painting that," I say. "It's so full of pain."

And then, as I look around the room at my artwork, I realize that all of it has some painful memory attached to it. My old friend in the leopard skin dress ignores me. Rudely turning her back she goes into another room and begins playing a piano, hammering out a mockingly sad song as I tell the owner of the house about my artwork and the meaning behind it. She's very interested, but we can hardly talk over the pounding piano. I become increasingly uncomfortable and more than a little angry at my old friend's callousness. I know I don't really belong here, that I'm just a visitor. I'm aware that no matter where I go I will be slightly uncomfortable until I have completely changed.

I wake up with intense hip and shoulder pain, not at all as loosely relaxed as my old friend in her leopard skin dress. In the dream her character seemed to be mocking my intention to get in touch with my feminine self, to relate to and relax my body, to learn to love myself. She didn't want to hear me talk about myself either and I am reminded that in reality she always mocked self-analysis, any expression of interest in what makes one tick. In the dream I was keenly aware that her opinion didn't matter. I saw that she was acting only as a provocateur. I didn't feel any connection to her either, though we were once very good friends. She didn't take me seriously in the dream and in fact was quite rude. I realize she was often this way in real life too, my dream pointing out a truth that I have failed to acknowledge. The owner of the modern house was much more understanding, even interested in what I had to say, perhaps a future me? It seemed to be the new modern house on the other side of the river.

I know that until I am done with this recapitulation, I will not live in that new modern house on the other side of the river, though it's clear I found a way to get there in my dream world, just as Jeanne had suggested I do the other day, go take a look at it, whet my appetite for it, get used to the idea of it. But until I do it consciously, by releasing all that still holds me bound to an old world, I will be unsettled and uncomfortable there. The inner room in the house, with all my artwork in it, seems to imply that I will soon be there though, that I will soon cross the River of Letting Go for good, the pain dealt with, the emotions released, a new softer me finally available, able to feel and talk about my own painful past. It's all I hope for.

I get out of bed, reminding myself to flow with life, to let true things happen because they will happen anyway. Go with the flow. What will happen will happen. Perhaps the difficulties of this time in my life are nearing an end, as my dream implies. Perhaps good things will come as I shed people and things of the past that no longer serve the new me. I long to cross the river, to wash my body and soul in its flowing waters, to watch everything that is no longer good or necessary wash away. Perhaps my pain will be reduced and I will emerge from the healing waters a newly cleansed and uplifted soul.

Yes, true things do happen, true things will happen. This current stage entails learning to trust that, knowing that one day I will be safe and at peace. It entails having faith, faith in my spiritual advisors to make their moves when the times are right, trusting that they love me and have my best interests in mind, that they are guiding me always.

It's raining as I drive back to the studio after getting an oil change, a new fan belt, and four new tires. I'm on the bridge spanning the river, a steady rain pouring down, when I drive into a thick cloud. Suddenly I am enveloped in whiteness. Everything falls away and it feels as if I'm floating. I can no longer see the cars ahead of me or behind me. I don't dare brake. I keep moving though there is no road, no bridge, no horizon, no perspective. There is only whiteness. It's as if I've driven into a dream. I have the sensation of falling, as if I have driven off the end of the world and am freefalling into white nothingness.

"Nothing is familiar," I say aloud, and then I realize that this is exactly where I am in my life, that I have crossed a threshold into a new land that has no name, where nothing is familiar, where I don't recognize a thing, where I cannot get my bearings. I am fogged in, floating down the River of Letting Go. Suddenly the world as I know it is gone! I start to cry.

"I'm afraid. Where am I going? Nothing is familiar."

"True things happen," I hear. *"True things happen."*

"Okay, let it happen," I say, but I acknowledge the fear I am really feeling, fear of having no control, of being lost in a void.

I peer into the whiteness ahead of me. Calm myself. Okay, I am still driving, my car is still moving, but everything else has changed. I am insulated and isolated in my vehicle as the rain pours down, the world gone. There is no other reality except what I am experiencing. I feel totally alone, totally vulnerable. I can't stop any of it, nor can I change it. There's an eerie lack of sound, no engine, no tires on pavement. It's how I imagine death, the sensation of letting go of the body, of losing anchoring in the world and body I've always known, weightless and floating, no ground below, no sky above, no boundaries on any side of me, nothing holding me together. I am in endless nothingness, in a great spinning weightless cocoon, though in reality I am driving a heavy SAAB. I fully understand that I am not in control, that I never was, that I am just going wherever I go, so let it happen.

"See, Jan," I hear, *"the universe is with you!"*

One minute I am floating down a foggy white chute, drawn down into the depths of that great cocoon of nothingness and in the next I am driving out of it. Land appears, the horizon returns, the road suddenly and magically reappears. I am on the other side of the bridge, safely across, back in reality, trying to get my bearings, trying to figure out what just happened.

"I have been through something profound," I tell myself.

The experience lasted only a few minutes, but it felt utterly timeless. A part of me accepted it, just as a part of me accepted the deeply profound realization that I have no control, that I have never had any control, and that I will just have to go spinning into whatever comes at me, including death one day.

When I am in calm balance, with my heart open, I receive signs. I receive insights too, and I understand what they mean. I am opening up more and more, feeling intuitively stronger all the time, psychically more in tune with a larger and greater universe than I ever imagined or was able to perceive before. Where this will take me I don't know, but I will go with it, follow it down into that great white cocoon if that is where it takes me, letting go into the unfamiliarity of it all, letting life unfold one day at a time. Today I crossed the great River of Letting Go.

As soon as I lie down in bed at night crying grips me and I am engulfed in pain. I release to it, let it happen, let go in the river of it all. I am not in control. I let true things happen. As I pull the covers up over my head and roll into a ball, I know that my old comforts are completely gone now, replaced by nothing, for I am free falling now, hurtling into space. All is white nothingness now.

December 18, 2003

The world is icy today and there's a school delay. I wake in my own iciness, feeling sad and depressed. Last night I cried a river of pain. It just poured out of me, but I didn't want the kids to hear me, so I cried silently, and today I am like the icy world outside, my tears clinging to me like frozen icicles. I long to let the warmth of them flow freely down my cheeks. I long to freely immerse myself in the River of Letting Go once and for all, and although I am not quite there yet, I am, little by little, getting to fuller release. It bubbles inside me, begs to spill out, all the tensions, all the emotions I've held in check. I must let it happen, without trying or thinking, just let it happen as it will. I must let true things happen, knowing that it will be alright, and that I will be alright too.

I'm enjoying the slow morning, some quiet time alone before I have to wake the kids. I understand that I had to live the life I was in, as it was, until the right moment for change arrived. I've led a fairly productive life, though now I know it was only a shadow life, life's real potential overshadowed by the imperative to keep the memories at bay. Now the memories are paying me back for my safekeeping of them, enabling me to grow and journey on into new life as I retrieve them and shed myself of them. By going back into the memories I have been able to truly go forward. I am in the final phases of acceptance and release now, truly letting true things happen.

The word "submission" comes to mind as I feel myself beginning to submit to the universe more every day, acquiescing to whatever the plan is for the unfolding of my life. Even as I submit to life's unfolding, I am aware that a certain amount of conscious action must take place, as I make decisions to handle what comes at me in a productive and mature way. I really am handling things differently now, and will even more so later on, as I continue to progress and open to more experiences. I understand and accept the unfolding of my life's journey, every part of it a part of me, my early beginnings, my youth, and then adulthood, and now this journey of self-discovery and transformation. In finally releasing all the old ideas and untruths about myself, I free myself to travel on into the future, fully accepting of where I've been and fully open to where I'm going. To all of that, I submit.

I am challenged to handle this new state of nothingness as easily as I accepted and handled the shift of my assemblage point at my mother's party last month, allowing it to become as natural a state as that one felt like, another lesson in detachment. I never imagined that releasing would mean that I'd be free falling without a parachute, but that's what it feels like!

In meditation and focused breathing, I seek calmness. Drawing inward, I envision myself as an alchemical vessel, a retort, a round basin at the belly, a narrow torso that flares out at the neck. The negative back and forth energy is up above in the narrow torso now, still reverberating back and forth, hollow and noisy, but definitely not as disruptive as it has been. I sit patiently beneath it, in the belly of the bowl, keeping a steady fire going, inducing the heat of my soul's intent. The smoke from my fire rises, spiraling upward, pushing the negative energy up, soon to be released. It has been sitting there for a while now, like a dark cloud in my throat. With the fire going constantly I should be able to expel it quite easily, and then I will be free. For now I stay beneath it, calmly tending my fire.

There's a new voice inside me now, telling me to just relax, see where things take me, whispering encouragements, speaking soothing truths. It's not Jeanne's voice but my own true voice, though I have only learned how to listen to it because of my work with her, and with Chuck. As I've become more body centered, I've also learned how to keep fear at bay so that I can clearly hear the voices of guidance within and without. Although fear is still often the first sign that something isn't right, always ready to jump up and warn me, I am learning how to work with it differently too. It's always been a key protective measure, so getting rid of it entails more than just expelling it or asking it to go away. It has involved re-training my body and my senses to react entirely differently to fear, to patiently wait to ascertain a situation before jumping to conclusions.

During the shift in the assemblage point at my mother's birthday party I experienced this, as I sat squarely in the energy of what was happening, totally without fear, totally detached, without a thought of personal danger. It was an extraordinary experience in the midst of ordinary life, and that's what I'm learning life is really all about, a series of extraordinary events unfolding in ordinary human life.

December 19, 2003

I meet with Chuck. I have no energy. We talk at a slow pace, the conversation meandering and unfocused, my thoughts not flowing, my words not flowing. I feel lost in the nothingness of it all, neither here nor there, adrift without an anchor. Where I'll land is a mystery!

I get home from work at seven after a long day at the studio and get right into a hot bath. Later, I make soup, the slow cutting of the vegetables, the slow rise of temperature under the pot, the slow stirring of its contents are grounding, offering a meditative period after a hectic day, anchoring me in patient calmness just as my alchemical retort of meditation anchored me yesterday. Work kept me anchored and focused too throughout the busy day, but at day's end I couldn't wait to get home and into my own quiet space again. As I stir the pot of soup, drawing circles with the spoon, I realize that the old curled up fetal position has been helping me through this final act of release. It was a position of holding and clenching, silence and dissociation once upon a time, but now, as I roll into a ball every night, it offers something else, the means of release.

December 20, 2003

The night was full of dreams. In one of them I was on a long journey. Mirroring my real life journey of recapitulation, I hiked in the mountains with my two children, along mountaintop trails. We entered some woods and walked along a path that was almost hidden by a profusion of beautiful flowering vines. When we looked back at where we had been we could see other people up on the mountaintop following the same paths. Then I was upstairs in a large, new modern house, not quite finished, where I found a gift box, a bright red ribbon tied around it. I opened the box to find that it contained a very small, delicate boy, around four years of age, fast asleep. I woke him up and held him tenderly, feeling such deep affection for him. He was a very sweet and thoughtful boy. I asked him if he'd had a good time and he said, yes, that he really liked my children. The house seemed to be the new house on the other side of the river, large and sprawling, light-filled, not quite finished, a smell of sawdust, carpenter's tools and wood lying around, but it was definitely "the new house," and there were good people there, including the sweet little boy.

I sailed smoothly along through all the dreams without conflict, as everything happened, everything unfolded and flowed so naturally. I moved along the paths so easily too, whether in the flowering jungle or along the steep mountain paths, following the route that unfolded before me, never doubting that it was the right path. The only slightly disturbing part was when I first entered the new house, for I felt out of place there, in unfamiliar territory. The fact that it wasn't finished yet bothered me too at first, but the longer I stayed the more I realized it was *my* house, and that I could live there, incomplete though it was. I was satisfied that enough had been done, and then I relaxed and began to look around and really liked what I saw.

My dreams are telling me to follow my path of heart, to rest assured that I will be led to what is right, as I already have been throughout my life. True things happen indeed! I've worked hard to arrive at this place of peace and calm assuredness. As I walk this leg of my journey I have a new place to anchor in. Rather than the old structures of fear and pain, the darkness of woods and memories, this place is within myself, a modern structure, filled with life and light. Here the boy child appears like a gift, something I have to wake up inside myself perhaps, something that could only be discovered inside this new structure, my own heart, the real place of calmness I have been seeking so long. Perhaps my only purpose in finding him is to gift myself the love I have poured into others. In the dream, I got the boy ready to go home to his father. I must let him go already, release him into the River of Letting Go along with everything else that has been revealed, keeping only what is important for the continuation of my journey.

Perhaps the little boy is the inner masculine child self, finally revealed, the mirror of my feminine child self, usually depicted in my dreams as my daughter. It's nice to know that he's equally as beautiful and thoughtful, as sweet and intelligent a child as my other inner child. He's the first male child I've dreamed of, so he must be significant.

The kids are with their dad until Christmas Eve. I'm a little afraid to be alone for so long, but perhaps it will give me time to discover my new place in the world, as I travel my solo journey, walk on new paths, and take up residence in my new home within, even as I finish this old business of recapitulation.

I think about the sadness that comes over me every time I roll up into a tight ball, the posture catapulting me back to memory but at the same time pulling me forward as I release into all that it holds. The pain doesn't wait now, but is upon me without warning. It doesn't wait for a trigger, but comes when it pleases. Nothing and everything sets it off, and then I am freefalling, releasing and releasing, nothing to grab onto, nothing familiar. Everything is changed now.

I stay focused by following the paths that lie before me, trusting that they are right, eager to see where they lead. I am constantly being given gifts. Even this path of fear-inducing nothingness, leading me through this phase of the recapitulation, is a gift. Being able to finally feel the pain is also a gift, this chronic pain I suffer for that little girl inside me, who blocked it and repressed it, who quietly kept it to herself, so I could go on and grow into adulthood. She dared not speak or cry, dared not ask for comfort or love, always afraid, afraid of rejection, afraid of guilt, shame, and blame. In spite of her youth, and with no knowledge of personal psychology, she instinctively found a way to cope with what was happening to her, within her own body. She separated from her feelings, boxed them up, and sent them deep inside herself. Now I have come along and unpacked them for her, taken on the full brunt of feeling them for her. And they too are gifts, for they are returning to me all that I need, just as the little boy in the dream was returning to me the deepest need, to love myself. Someday I hope to be able to do that.

At the same time that I feel and release on behalf of my child self, I am also constantly given gifts of knowledge, shown how best to deal with the pain of knowing the truth, and the acute physical pain as well.

"Just let it happen, Jan," says Jeanne, *"just let the road disappear before you and hurl yourself forward down that tunnel of fog, into the vortex of nothingness. Scream if you have to, it's okay. Just go with it. You will be safe; you will be safe on your journey. If you can let go of the pain and trust that you will be safe, then the pain will leave your body and you will be reborn."*

"How do I do that? The pain doesn't just leave my body. I have to work so hard at it."

"Sleep now. Dream. Release," says Jeanne. *"Go with the flow; let it happen; you can't stop it anyway."*

December 21, 2003

I dream that I am inside a modern house, looking out a large picture window onto a beautiful wintry landscape. A river flows directly toward me, turning as it nears the house. I notice people walking beside the river. I see that they are crying.

"Something is terribly wrong," I say. "Something bad has happened."

As the people stream past my window I see their grief-stricken faces. Their sadness permeates me and seeps into the house. I see blinking, flashing lights. Ambulances! My contention that something terrible has happened is confirmed.

"A river of tears," I say to myself. "It's a river of tears."

My nephew, a carpenter, is staying with me, having come to work on the house, as it is still under construction. I call to him.

"There's something wrong, terrible things happening," I say. "The sorrow is coming to me; I have to deal with it."

When he hears about the sorrow coming he gets into bed and hides under the covers and becomes a little boy.

"Tell me when it's over," he says, and then I know I must deal with it on my own.

I wake up heavy with sadness, stiff, unable to move, my pain bright and sharp, more pain than I've felt in a long time. I am headachy too, the gloomy mood of the dream weighing upon me. And then I remember Jeanne's instructions as I prepared for sleep last night.

"Just let it happen, go with the flow," I tell myself, and then I am able to relax my body enough so I can move.

I sit up, sadness and loneliness swirling through me. I used to keep the loneliness buried, but now it's up in my chest and throat, the sadness seeping out my eyes. The fire I've kept going in the alchemical retort has pushed more than just the foreign energy up, now all else that has lain stagnant within me is rising with the smoke as well. Things really are shifting and changing. The dream signifies the release of all that I have held inside me, as it is finally acknowledged for all that it was, a tragic life now done, given a proper funeral, the sad, grief-stricken crowd of mourners so appropriate. I too must acknowledge the death of the old, the old sense of loneliness and the old sadness along with everything else. I too must accept the appropriateness of this death.

"I need to kill myself!"

The old voice speaks so suddenly, so harshly. At first, I worry that it's come to drag me back, but then I realize it's letting me know the truth, that yes, this is the death of the old self, and mourning *is* appropriate. How strangely the truth comes! The path is never as clear as I might wish, the next step unknown until I actually take it, and then there I am, in a new reality, underscoring how true things do happen! Sometimes the path is blissfully happy, filled with delight, at other times extremely sad and lonely, but it is my path to take and to experience nonetheless. I seek to gain some balance now between the highs and lows of my journey, between the high mountaintops and the deep valleys of my own psyche!

Once again, I am fully aware of being helped as I travel this journey. I have opened to and been granted all kinds of supports, some of it quite unimaginable, though real nonetheless. I sense that I am always being guided toward *something*, and that I will eventually get where I am going, unseen though it is. As I travel I leave my old supports behind, drop them like crutches along the path, like the crutches of the healed left behind at Lourdes. Not knowing where I'm going, not able to visualize what comes next, not able to imagine the next turn in the road without that old crutch to help me is frightening though. Yet, I am in this great nothingness for all that it brings me and I will stick with it for the long haul, though this nothingness often feels like hell.

My dreams come as visual guides, so I pay attention to them. When I feel lost now, I go back into my dream of hiking on the steep mountain paths. I feel my feet solidly on the ground, walking along that dream path, and then I see what's right before me, the path that lies at my feet in this moment, and it's all I need to keep me focused.

My dreams constantly point out new directions and offer new anchors, but even so, I know I must tumble down that foggy chute on the bridge over and over again, into the vast white cocoon of nothingness until the sensation of freefalling is second nature, until this frightening nothingness is as familiar as the old world once was, until I am no longer afraid of anything. I must accept the journey as it unfolds and trust the process.

"You know you can handle it; you know you can do it," Jeanne says. *"Trust yourself and go with it. Go with the magical moments when all familiarity is suddenly erased and you are thrown into free fall. Just let it happen. Like Alice falling down the rabbit hole, you can't stop it. You'll just have to see where you land."*

The morning before I drove into the tunnel of fog on the bridge, I had written in my journal that I knew my spiritual advisors would give me a sign when the time was right, for I was sure they would guide me to feel safe again and learn to trust myself. And they sure did, though not quite what I had in mind! If I am to learn to feel safe and trust myself, they point out, I must let go of everything, even my sense of stability in this reality! Yikes! As the saying goes, be careful what you ask for!

In truth, my spiritual advisors show me every day that I am taking a journey of extraordinary proportions. I say this in all humbleness, as a struggling human being, simply going where the journey takes me, trusting that my best interests are in good hands. I know full well that I am not in control. I probably never have been, but I see from how everything has unfolded that the only right thing to do is trust in the journey itself, that it alone holds everything I will need as I proceed along its unfolding path. I still struggle though, especially when I'm jerked back and forth between worlds, between realities, when nothing seems real. And the truth is, I don't feel safe yet, though there is nothing I wish for more. How do I get to safety?

"Look forward. Look into the jungle of flowers," comes the answer. *"Keep looking for the path. Get off everyone else's path and get back on your own. Stop helping everyone else and help yourself. Stop worrying about everyone else and worry about yourself."*

"Will I eventually feel safe?"

"Stay on the path. It will lead you where you need to go, just stay on the path. You will know it when you are on it. You will

know it is the right path. Your heart will tell you it is right. Your heart knows. Your heart knows everything. Believe in it."

It's two in the afternoon and I'm at the studio, taking a moment to jot down some thoughts. I just remembered that in last night's River of Tears dream, the mourners came into the house, bringing their heavy sorrow with them, and I thought, "Oh, My God, how am I going to deal with this?" And a voice said: "Let it happen, just let it happen."

My dreams really do offer guidance from another world. I get lost in the nothingness, but then receive dreams of a funeral and mourning in order to let me know that I must deal with my own sorrow now, face my own sadness, appropriately mourn the death of the old world and the old self. The dream lets me know what that means and how to do it, that it's okay to let the sorrow flow like a river. Crying is good, as Chuck always says, it's a release. I am also given dreams of hope and beauty, a new path leading me onward to a new destiny. For now, however, the main thing is to deal with the sadness. It's been inside, pushing at me for a long time, bubbling up out of my alchemical pot along with everything else. I know that if I tap into it and let it flow then everything will be acknowledged. Why do I still hold it back?

My experience of release is that it carries with it such pain, but I have to remember how my dream the other night led me to my new home where I found the little boy. I have to remember that I was guided there, and that I knew it was my place, that I belonged there. This new place of mourning, in last night's dream, is that same house, and this River of Tears is the same river as the River of Letting Go, all the same, and it is the only place to be now, painful though it may be, for it is the place of my salvation and my healing too.

So, no more running away, just steady steps forward now, unburdening and releasing as I go. I can decide what to leave behind and what to take as I pack for my new life, getting rid of what I don't need. It's all right to do that. I give myself permission to release and mourn now too. It's okay to flow with the River of Tears and the River of Letting Go too. I vow to sit beside these rivers of my dreams until I am done with what they are teaching me, and then I will move on from this place too.

It's nighttime, almost midnight. I've been crying a lot, dealing with sadness. I watched movies that I cried all the way through, whether they were sad or not. I took two baths, being kind to myself, loosening and softening my strongholds, trying not to be so hard on myself, trying to love myself. I am letting go, letting it happen, letting the rivers flow, flowing with them.

December 22, 2003

I have dreams of pathways again, but this time they are narrow, closed in paths, so claustrophobic I can barely breathe. I wake at three with intense anal pain, wondering if my dreaming brought on a memory. I get up and walk around in the dark until the pain goes away and then lie back down, still sad and lonely, depressed, my body aching in all its usual places. I fall back into bed, into the wakefulness of no sleep, tossing and turning for an hour. After a while I get up. Fuck it! Let the day begin!

I head out early to do the last of the Christmas shopping, then get some lunch and head over to the studio. I realize I've been in a daze, fogged in for days now, constricted by some unknown thing in both dreams and reality. In the afternoon I suddenly pop out of it, feel an actual POP! in my head followed by a clearing sensation, as if my brain released something, as if something really did "let go." In the evening, however, I am back to hurting, returned to constriction again, the narrow pathways of my dream reasserting themselves.

I take a bath, eat dinner, and worry about money. I'm aware that it's an old stand in, something I do when I don't want to face a real issue. The real truth is that I've been angry for the greater part of the day because I need Chuck so much and have refused to allow myself to call him. Am I punishing myself? On top of that, I feel like a crazy person. I just want to be left alone. It feels wrong to be so withdrawn, but the truth is I don't want to be around people. I can't stand noise or sound or interacting with others. I'm okay if I *have* to interact, when I can't help it, but I retreat as soon as possible, go right back into my shell. The shell is a mixed place right now though, sometimes a place of safety, sometimes a fighting ring. I can't imagine this is a good way to be, but it's where I need to be right now, that I am absolutely sure of. Everything points this out, as I am still in the alchemical retort, still heating things up, still waiting for release. I'm not happy though, and the more I think about it the gloomier I get.

"Hang in there," I tell myself, "it can only get better."

December 23, 2003

I am so steeped in sadness I can hardly talk when I meet with Chuck first thing in the morning. He, on the other hand, has other ideas.

"It's been a wonderful year!" he says.

"It has?" I say, dumbfounded by this exclamation.

"It has!" he says. "Look how far you've come!"

And he's right, I have come far, but when I'm steeped in sadness it's so easy to forget. In saying this, he gives me a new glimmer of hope, a new way to see it all too. I've been thinking and saying that I've had a tremendously difficult year, which is also true, but his version of a wonderful year is much more positive. I think that's what I need to do now too, try to apply a positive twist to everything, help myself along, not just depend on my helpers to guide me. I can be my own guide.

It's sunny and warm today, the sun melting the snow, and I feel myself beginning to melt too. I get my hair done and feel a little better. Even being out and around other people is tolerable, more so than in a long time, but a cloak of sadness still hangs over everything, and the truth is, I just want to go home and watch movies, be alone with my sadness, my new comfort.

This morning while I lay in the tub I thought about being a fulltime writer. How and in what form that would transpire I have no idea, but something beyond the kind of writing I'm doing now, for I feel that I must find a way to turn these terrible memories into something helpful, this recapitulation process so rich in insight and guidance. I must share it in some form that would be helpful and meaningful to others. A memoir might be too overwhelming, for I fear that my memories are too repulsive. As true as they are, do I really want to inflict them on others?

End of the day. Panic sets in. Why? Because I dared to imagine putting my diaries out into the world? Is it really such a frightening proposal? You bet it is!

"*Don't panic!*" Jeanne says. "*Don't! Everything will be fine! You're doing so well. You've had a great year. Look how far you've come! Life will get better yet. It has been getting better and better. Wow, look where you are!*"

"You sound like Chuck! But yes, life is getting better," I remind myself. "Yes, this life will get better."

December 24, 2003

I dream of flooding, streams and rivers overflowing. I ride standing up in an open jeep, driving down flooded roads, great waves of water splashing up like wings on either side of me, as if I were a giant bird soaring in for a landing. Every stream and river has gone over its banks. I am searching for something.

I arrive at my new house, filled with boxes, things still being unpacked. A plumber has come because something needs a repair. When the plumber needs to wipe his hands and can't find a towel, I say that someday I will get things sorted out. He nods, but doesn't say anything, just looks around at all the boxes. I turn and trip over one, thinking, "I'm going to fall." I imagine falling smack on my rear, but he catches me and shakes his head, as if to say, "I don't know how you'll ever manage." I assure him I will be fine.

Then I ride a bike to a new construction site. I pass lots of houses under construction and go down a long driveway that ends at a large house on top of a hill. The worksite is muddy. I look around at everything, take in the details, the unpainted wood, the unfinished structures, all the tools and equipment lying around. I turn away, puzzled as to why I came here, thinking about the house I had just moved into, a finished house. What am I doing? I already have a new house!

At some point during the night I wrote: *I need a greater outpouring of emotion.* And the first dream seems to indicate that all is going according to that plan, as the rivers of release are overflowing, the outpouring process well underway. In the second dream I had moved into a new house. It still needed a few things repaired but was largely intact, though a plumber was needed for something. I was unpacking too, so I wondered what I was doing at yet another new construction site in the final dream. It made absolutely no sense to me. Indeed, the question arises: What am I still searching for?

My dreams and my unconscious are trying to tell me that I can stop searching. I need to stay focused on where I am right now, complete what is right before me. Everything I need now is right in front of me. As my dream points out, I haven't even opened all the boxes yet. There's more to discover right here, now, as I sit in my alchemical retort and recapitulate. I'm just driving myself crazy with the incessant need to keep looking; it isn't necessary. And I do sometimes feel as if I'm going crazy, my emotions and all the thoughts in my head driving me nuts.

"Let the thoughts go. Breathe them out. Let the emotions flow, flow like a river."

It's raining today, a heavy, solid downpour. The fuel man tells me I need to build a cover over my oil tank and insulate the line to the house. He's worried that otherwise the fuel will gel up and I'll be stuck with no heat. This happened last winter. When he says this I feel overwhelmed, another thing I have to attend to. Just as I told the plumber in my dream last night, I calmly say to the fuel man that I'll be fine. But the truth is that my lack of energy and focus leave me nowhere near feeling fine. I really do intend to get everything in the house in working order, but the thought of having even one more thing to do is almost too much. Just thinking about it exhausts me!

I do want to be capable of everything, strong and able and independent. I want everything in good repair, functioning well. I want work to continue as well as it has this past year too. None of this seems like too much to ask. I think about all of this as I go out and do my errands. The kids will be home tonight and I have no food in the house. I also have to get over to the studio to finish painting a toy box, scheduled for delivery next week.

Emotions boiling, craziness swirling, and the loneliness so great. Nothing distracts, noise too hard to take. Like real physical pain it grates on my nerves, as if I am bruised on the inside. I've been alone for too long, but I can't stand to be around anyone, too hard to talk. I feel isolated and sad, cut off, incapable of real interaction. I work at the studio for a few hours, hoping no one will stop in, but I'm happy when I make a few sales out of the gallery space we've set up. By the time I head home, I am ready to burst, my feelings ballooning out of proportion. I'm angry at myself. I want the anger to go away. I want the pain to go away. I want the memories to go, the fear to go. I want it all gone from my body, but it doesn't go, none of it goes.

"*Just let the pain out, let the sadness out,*" Jeanne says.

"It's so hard to allow for that. It makes me feel crazy."

I try to keep my eyes open to what is right before me, right here, right now, but I just feel lost. I cry, but it just hurts. I wish I could cut it out of my body, cut the memories out of my head, cut the pain out, and throw it into the garbage. It inhabits me like an illness. I want to be mean to myself, hard on myself. I get angry. I want to punish myself instead of being nice to myself. I want the memories to go away. I don't need them anymore. Why are they still here!

The kids arrive home at ten, happy and lively after having spent Christmas Eve with their dad and his family. I remind myself that Santa Claus is coming to town and the old stuff will just have to take a backseat. It tries to intrude, but I push it away. The pain sticks around, but I know how to deal with that.

"Okay," I tell myself. "I'm alive. I'm breathing. For this night I am okay."

I fill a bath for my daughter and by midnight she turns in. I urge my son to do the same. The three cats roam around for a while, happy to have everyone home again, trying to decide whom they'll curl up with for the night. I just want to lie down and sleep too. It doesn't take long before three little critters hop up onto my bed. The cats have decided, and with two at my feet and one at my head, we all settle down for a long winter's night.

December 25, 2003

Ho, Ho, Ho! Merry Christmas! The kids open their gifts with happy squeals of delight, pleased with everything. They give me such thoughtful gifts, a pair of pretty earrings from my son and a warm scarf from my daughter. I feel so lucky. I make crepes for breakfast, a family favorite, and then we spend a quiet morning together. I'm quiet inside too, calm and centered. I expect the old stuff will stay away until tonight when I'm alone in my bed again. We're seeing the family later in the day. I anticipate that all will go well. I have no agenda, no old feelings to cloud my experience, my own process of recapitulation and transformation all that matters. My daughter will be staying for a sleepover with the girl cousins, my son driving back with me tonight.

After a small, quiet party at my parent's house my son and I are home again. It was a very calm event. Energetically speaking everything was quite normal. I did not have another shift of the assemblage point nor reach any great insight. It was a pretty normal affair.

I end this day by stressing to myself that I must strive to complete this recapitulation in a more centered state, without being pulled down into such deep despair and self-loathing that I can't escape. I must not get caught in old waves of self-pity, but return to a place of no pity, remaining always aware of the ultimate goal of this great journey of recapitulation, which is, to evolve.

December 26, 2003

I dreamed dreams implying progress, working with paint, experiencing contentment in my work, doing yoga and hot baths for peace of mind and body, offering kindness and love to myself. I need these simple things in order to survive, and not to just survive but to care for myself and be available to care for my kids too. If I concentrate on these simple things everything else will evolve as it should. I see so clearly what needs to be done in this world, as my night of dreaming points out, but my inner world is less stable, less clear. Inside I am ready to shatter.

I imagine that if I can keep myself isolated I will succeed in holding myself together. If I gather myself from the inside, piece by piece, and hug the parts close; if I don't move, maybe I can keep it all together. If no one comes near me, if nothing disturbs me, then maybe I will remain whole. I am like a house of cards. I have pulled the cards around me and if I stay as still as possible the house will stay up. By sheer will I will not move. I will sit inside, barely breathing, because if I breathe it hurts, and if I move it hurts, and if the house falls down then the pain will get me and I can't bear that now. I am too brittle and too sad and too lonely right now. Far better to keep everything in so I don't fall down like a sad little house of cards. Such a flimsy façade, but it's familiar and I know I am safe inside it.

My son is still sleeping when my daughter calls to say she will stay another night with the cousins, so I do not have to make the long drive to get her and she will have a ride back tomorrow.

I read for a little while, finishing a book I bought myself for Christmas. Then I contemplate where I am in this moment, trying to remain apart from the gripping panic that hovers always nearby. I have pushed it aside for a few days, purposefully keeping it at arm's length while I have spent time caring for myself and my kids. It's getting jealous of my time away and I too feel the pull to return to recapitulation mode. I know I will be back in its arms before too long. For now I thwart its needling by contemplating other things, letting thoughts take over, thoughts not quite in alignment with progress, but what the heck, it's nice to fantasize. What if I were to go off to another state and find work, make a big change? I know I'm playing devil's advocate, teasing the old stuff, but then I get serious, knowing what it would do to the kids. The practical inner voices take over then.

"*Just stay put, it will work out*," they say, reminding me of where I'm going and why.

Thoughts unleashed, however, like to weave their stories and before long they're plotting fantastical plans for running away, and like a teenager bored with life I listen for a little while, but I know that running away is the wrong move, that it won't solve any problems, just create more, though I have to admit I do feel a strong pull. It's just the old stuff though, playing its old game, captivating me, urging me to take off, just go, go, go, anywhere, it doesn't matter, suicide of a sort, run from it all. Oh God, I can't, I won't. Things will be good, they will be good. I know they will.

I push the old voices away and sit in the silence they leave behind and suddenly I'm afraid again, fear creeping back in, fear and no trust, such ready mates. I don't even trust my own innate abilities anymore. People ask me how I'm doing and I say, fine, I'm fine. You know me; I'm always fine. But in reality I am full of pain. Deep in my hip sockets I weep with pain. I am female Prometheus, bound and eaten, flesh picked at by eagles, ripped to shreds. I am searing with pain while inside my heart beats drumbeats, sending Morse Code to flesh of my flesh, to my children: I love you both, please know that, just know it. Deep in your own loins know what love is, even as it is torn from your bodies, know it exists inside you, for it beats through all the generations, pulsing through placenta to fetus, to new life. You are my twin hopes.

Memories churn out now. By my searing intent to bring light into my own darkness they are recapitulated and released. Facing forward, turning toward sunrise, I, female Prometheus, unable to block the sun's bright glare from ravaged eyes, know instinctively that this is good work I have set out to do, that you two children of mine are good, that life is good. Though my life bleeds at this moment, still I have moments of bliss. Do not weep for me or feel sorry for me, for I am doing my own soul's bidding, and it is time.

Look forward bright new lives. Leave me behind to pick up the pieces, to sew old wounds and bind shredded organs back into place. I will get through this, but only as I watch you go forward into blinding hope, for you are freed by my fearless work. Wait! Stop a moment and untie me, shoo away the eagles that I may rise and draw your visions as I see them, as I would have also wanted for myself in another life. Go! I set you both free from carrying my burdens as I have carried the burdens of others. I am picked clean by this recapitulation and in so doing you are freed too. This is my life and I will go on from here, I am female Prometheus, female warrior.

There is no answer in running away. The answers will only come in staying put, bound to the process. Like Prometheus I must stay put and bear the final stages of this recapitulation process, looking always inward, bringing light into my own darkness, for that is where my salvation lies. Where it always has.

I pause and listen, listen to what I really need to do for myself as I proceed along my path of change. For the past few days nothing has really changed or progressed, though I have been successful at keeping the old energy at bay. For the most part, I feel calm and relaxed as I sit, but then I notice how bad feelings come so quickly, sneaking in, enticing me to do battle with them again. I go quiet again and listen to what's underneath it all, listen deep down inside myself. I go far down until I reach the energy that used to come only when desperately needed, to the long ago strengths, to the deeply hidden self. It's still there, the deepest inner being, the one who never died. And there I find peace and the answer to my strife. I find myself, the real, authentic me.

"Of course you're afraid," she tells me, *"but so what."*

My son and I spend the day together, watching movies, eating, talking, nice and relaxed. I drink wine. I feel lucky. We play with his small laser light, trying to figure out how it projects images from the tiny stencil heads we screw onto it, while the cats dash madly around trying to catch the light. It seems impossible that something that tiny could create the massive pictures that appear as we aim it around the room, onto the walls, ceiling, and floor. So like my own life, once such a tiny and insignificant thing, now taking me on this massive journey of change, projecting me all over the place.

I sense forces of good pushing me forward, forces of love pushing me towards something new, some unforeseeable goal. I sense an end in sight and that it will be good.

December 27, 2003

In a dream, I discover that the new tires are gone from my car. It takes me a long time to realize that they have been stolen and that I can't run away. I have to stay put and face my demons. I feel like a prisoner. I look around and see bars on the windows, locks on the doors. I'm at the studio. It's dark and I'm trying to work, but there isn't enough light to see by. I realize I never turned the lights on when I'd arrived. Like Prometheus, I must bring light. I go over to the door and flip on the lights. With the advent of light, I find that I am in an old mansion, in a cavernous room where everything is made of chocolate. Even the bars on the windows that are keeping me locked in are made of chocolate. I realize I'm not imprisoned like I thought I was. Not at all! I can eat my way out!

I wake up with the realization that I am no longer a reluctant participant of life, just along for the ride. I haven't been that for a long time really, but it's hitting me now more than ever. Now I *am* my life, fully participatory, in dreaming and waking life. Mentally, physically, emotionally, and spiritually, in dreams and in reality I am everything, and everything is turning out to be energy, for I have the sense of life being the same thing I experienced in my shift of the assemblage point at my mother's party, an illusion in one sense, but absolutely real in another. It's as if when I switched the lights on in my dream I saw true reality, and that true reality is a constant shifting of energy, inside and outside of me, everything in constant play, everything constantly changing. What that entails, at the moment, is how I decide to deal with the shifts between worlds, within and without, between the old and the new, but also between different worlds of perception and experience too. As my dream points out, at each new shift something new greets me, some new awareness is reached, some new experience undergone, some new energetic clarity achieved.

In dreams and in reality, I go deep and then I go high. I go low down into the darkness and then I am shot out into the heights of enlightening vision. And then it's all I can do to hold onto what I've learned as I'm shot off again, trying to remember what one world taught me so that when I am in another I can use it to my advantage. It's a crazy rollercoaster ride between turmoil and awakening, between death and life, between old world and new world, between old me and new me. It's often not quite clear where I am or what to do as I ride this crazy rollercoaster into different realities and energies. Often my first thought is to call Chuck and ask for help, but he's on vacation for the next ten days and I made a pact with myself that I wouldn't call, even though he offers that option. But pacts can be broken, and now I'm back in frantic energy mode, clenching, holding back all that wants release, needing help, refusing to ask for help, wanting to break the pact. I'm in the turmoil, clenching down again because this familiar old way of dealing with things still works! But, it's still a prison, and that too is what my dream was telling me, I am my own prison and my own jailer!

I really don't want to call Chuck. I don't want to be a big baby, a whiny complainer, but I have to admit he's still my only anchor, no matter what world I'm in. I also have to admit that I'm afraid to call him. Whenever I feel the need to reach out, my immediate reaction is that it's better to stay back, stay inside, even though that means feeling like a prisoner and even though I know he may be of help. It's hard to know if it's an old world thought or a new world thought. Does it mean the old way is winning, that I really am stuck in a prison of my own making? Or does it mean the new way is finally having an impact on my strength and fortitude to go it alone because it is only in sitting within the walls of my prison that I will learn what I need to learn in this moment?

If it's a regression, I know it will only be temporary. And sometimes a regression, going into clenching mode for instance, surfaces as a necessity, the only means by which I can survive the next ten days. It's embarrassing to think I can't do this inner journey alone. At the same time, my dreams are telling me that I'm not quite getting something. This shouldn't be so hard. My tires are gone, so there will be no running away. I must sit in the heat of this thing, stay in my prison, turn the lights on and look around. I am not blind like Prometheus, I just have to bring the light in to see that though I may feel like such a prisoner, the prison is really of my own imagining, and upon closer inspection it is revealed as something quite unusual. Chocolate! I just have to look at things in the light to see what's really there. However, the truth is that whatever has me in its clutches continues to gnaw away at me. I'll just have to gnaw back!

"Don't call. Don't call, just hold it in," I tell myself as the day goes on, the anxious energy burning inside me.

I sit in the tension and the discomfort of it, going back and forth, as if pacing in a little prison cell, first in one world and one perception, then in another, wondering what it is that I'm really trying to hold back, the spilling of my guts? The collapse of my world? The loss of my self? I get pulled back down, sucked down into the drain of the old world, into the pits of myself, bad energy reasserting itself, unsettled feelings, clenching and pain taking over, and then I can't stand myself. I know I'm losing ground. The fire I've been feeding in the pit of my alchemical cauldron is out of control, and I know the old way is winning. Am I letting it win, letting it take over? Why do I have to punish myself? Why do I imprison myself? Sabotage myself? Why do I have to hurt myself? It feels like death, the old voices of death. Rather than call Chuck, I close up tighter. And then I am drawing circles and circles and circles, containing, containing, containing, calming myself by drawing hundreds of tiny circles, endlessly spinning circles. And then I can't do it any longer. Death or Chuck. I call Chuck.

"You're with the *flyers*," he says, "entities the shamans say feed off human suffering. They don't want you to change, they want your energy for themselves. If you change, they have nothing to feed off. They get at you through your mind, through the negative thoughts they generate in your head, and through your depressed emotions, tormenting you so they can feed off your anxiety. All of that produces the goods for their sustenance."

"I've been feeling like such a prisoner, as if something has tied me down and been eating away at me, but I imagined it was for good reason, perhaps that I needed to be triggered to remember something or to shift into a new phase."

"It's not a good place to be," he says. "I understand why you're there, but you can't stay there. Distract it, watch a movie."

I tell him my kids are watching *The Matrix*.

"That's your story!" he says. "It's about the flyers!"

"Well, I can't watch it, it freaks me out."

"You don't have to watch it, just live it. You are living it. Just believe, Neo!" he says. "It's a very hard place to get out of, but after a while you will be out. There's nothing there for you."

"I was so afraid to call."

"You can call anytime. Call me on the phone or call me in your dreams, either way works. Right?"

December 28, 2003

In a dream I am a young girl, about eight years old, living in a dreary fenced-in prison surrounded by guard towers. An enormous gate marks the entrance through which trains pass. Once inside the gate, the train yard spreads out in an array of tracks threading off into a vast underground train station beneath tall black factory buildings. There are rows of dingy houses, one of which I live in. The setting is damp and foggy, dimly lit by tall industrial street lamps, everything colored in black, gray, and brown. Industrial buildings and empty factories overshadow the already depressing scene. It's always nighttime.

Every night, I sneak out of the prison under cover of darkness. I make the same trip over and over again, going to a bog out in the countryside where I have been doing the same thing each night for years. I dig up old clothes out of the bog where I've hidden them, pink little girl clothes. My abuser's daughter wants some of them. I know they will fit only me, but even so I put some aside for her. I divide them into two piles and then I rebury them. When I am done I go to her house and tell her where I left them in the bog. I give her directions for how to find them and where to dig. Then I sneak back into the prison through a narrow opening in the fence, quietly and stealthily slipping past the armed guards, a mere shadow of a girl. I stay in the shadows, walking the train rails to get home. My timing is always perfect. I pass everything at exactly the same time each night, every step timed exactly right so that no one notices me. When I get to my drab house I quickly duck into the dark doorway and run up the stairs to my room where I live alone.

I have done this trip so many times, and although I am always on alert I am also confident and calm as I go about it, for my timing is impeccable. Once back in my room, I do the same obsessive ritual every night. I wash my hands, with timed precision. I eat a meager meal. I clean up my dishes. I water a plant on the windowsill. I do these same things each night in the same order and then, when I am done with my chores, I stand silently at the window and look out onto the gray and depressing train yard below. I keep in the shadows of my room, careful not to be seen, never turning on a light.

One night, as I return from the bog, I trip, and suddenly everything changes. The darkness that once shielded me is now pierced by a wandering searchlight. The once quiet train yard is alive with noisy trains rumbling through where normally there are none. It's as if a switch has been flipped and all that was once dead has come alive, all that was dark is now light. My precise timing, which has been so reliable, is off and there is danger at every step now. I am no longer safe. I have to come up with a new way to get home. I sneak through a fence and tiptoe a few steps along a railroad track when the wandering spotlight hits me and a guard shouts. I hear more shouting and the sound of feet running toward me as I cower against a wall in the dark. A gang of noisy teenage boys comes running up to me. One of them spits at me, a huge wad that lands smack on my chest and dribbles down the front of my clothes. He calls me a name too, "Jew-girl," and then runs off. I hear the boys laughing and talking about Jew-girls as they run toward the train tunnels. I am aware that I am a Jew-girl now and I am out at the wrong time. I finally make it home to my room. I stand and watch from my window, fearfully waiting for what is surely going to happen next.

It's still the middle of the night when I wake from this dream and write it down. As I dreamed it was clear to me that I was the little girl in the dream, but I was also aware that I have to be where I am now, in this life, still so full of pain, that I have to go through this phase of the recapitulation until I'm done with it and can move on, just as the little girl had to be where she was, until she too could move on. It's what Chuck said to me last night when I called him, using similar words. It's what I struggled with all day yesterday too.

During the dream, I was aware that in my suffering I was being taught something important, that only through suffering would I advance. I was given explanations during each phase of the dream so I would know where I was and why. I was dreaming about a little girl in a concentration camp setting, but I was really being schooled about my current life and what is happening as I complete this recapitulation, with all of its horrors and pains, as I sit in my prison of self and learn what I must learn. I understood that a shift in the assemblage point, in the dream explained as going from an old "safe" and familiar route to a new "unsafe," unknown one, was a necessary part of my recapitulation and my evolution, that a major shift was necessary if I was going to advance. While I dreamed, I remained highly alert, cognizant of all that was happening in the dream, and at the same time I was fully aware that it was related to what is happening in my present life, as I continue my recapitulation journey.

I am in needle-sharp pain as I lie back down and prepare to fall back to sleep, one long cold silvery needle lying between the sheets of my bed. And then I dream again. This time I am at my old family home with one of my brothers. The house has been put on the market. I have a young child with me. She's afraid.

"Why do we have to move?" she asks, clinging to me.

I tell her we're moving on to better things, that everything will get better now. A repairman is fixing the ductwork. There's a problem with the ventilation system and unbeknownst to us we have been suffocating, he says. He finds where the problem is and says that now we should be able to breathe easier. The repairman looks like Chuck.

As my first dream points out, I'm living in the matrix! It's no joke that Chuck said this last night when we talked. I navigate it daily with routines that keep me safe, in an obsessive-compulsive nightmare! That's how to manage the matrix and survive, but I'm not really in that world anymore. I'm leaving it, facing the final days in it, fighting off the flyers. I'm changing.

This dream signifies a shift into a new phase. First, it mirrors my true life of suffering from Post-traumatic Stress Disorder with its obsessive compulsive defenses, the things I have relied on to keep me safe. There I was, in the bleak routine of the dream, digging up pink clothes in the darkness of night, extracting the innocence of childhood, holding onto a thread of happiness, keeping it hidden and safe, reburying it again and again and then returning to prison life. This reveals how I have coped with PTSD throughout my life, keeping the innocence of my child self buried deep inside myself, living a defended OCD existence, not really living at all but remaining a prisoner of trauma and of routine existence. This is exactly how I've felt lately, like a prisoner within myself. But the real deal is that I am no longer allowed to live this way. Things have to change and they will keep changing, and I will continue to be challenged.

The very dark environment in the dream also mirrors the darkness of my recapitulated memories, as well as the darkness of my present inner environment as I sit in my inner prison. In the dream, I was caught in a place as dark as sitting and tending the fire of my alchemical cauldron, as routinely boring as listening to the old voices and the flyers that try to convince me they have all the answers. The dream was just as dull as my life was before this recapitulation began. It was only when a sudden shift happened that everything changed, much like the moment when I was ushered into my recapitulation, when the first memory burst upon me, its power throwing me to the floor.

And so that little stumble in the dream was the impetus to far bigger change too, an unexpected glitch that threw me into a state of heightened awareness, much like a shift in the assemblage point. From that moment on my defenses were useless. From that moment on everything in the dream changed and I had to be fully present and aware. My surroundings, once so boringly known and predictable, my cursed PTSD/OCD reality, transformed, becoming completely unknowable and totally unpredictable, like being in the void. There could be no safety in hiding anymore. When the boy yelled, "Hey, Jew-girl!" I was suddenly exposed and vulnerable, and suddenly different too. From then on, everything was in the light. Anything could happen.

The first big shift came a few years ago when that first memory was unearthed, the first pink garment that began the slow unraveling of life as I knew it, the first shift that ushered in the rest of the memories. Just as my dream suggests, there is no stopping the energy of something that is bent on change. I know that full well! Once my recapitulation began there was no stopping it, and here I am now, having gone through so many phases, in yet another one. Little do I know what will come next, but I do know there are many more changes on the horizon. How could there not be? The uncomfortability of this phase lets me know that I won't be here very long, that I will be moving on, as my second dream suggests. In the meantime, I'm trying to stay sane and balanced in a world that is no longer reliable, no longer boring or predictable either, a world where anything can happen. I've had enough shifts of the assemblage point lately to know just how true that is!

The dream reminds me that things will never line up in quite the same way ever again, that the universe will never allow for it—I can't go back—and at the same time it reminds me that I can't quite get out of the narrow hell I'm in until something else shifts. And something will shift, for change happens constantly. It could be another simple little misstep or it could be something more drastic that creates the shift; only time will tell. For now, I am living in a danger zone, my dream points out. I have to be here. I have no choice, as I must work through this phase of the recapitulation just as I've worked through all the others. At the same time I hold onto knowing that one day things will shift again. That I am more than certain of.

As I dreamed, I was aware of all these things, that things had changed and they would never be the same again. Upon waking, I see that the dream is all about exposure, that my life is going to keep shifting and changing, becoming even more unfamiliar, perhaps for the rest of my life, because I am choosing to reveal what is in my own shadows, what has ruled me. I may never know where I truly am again, for worlds may keep shifting. I get the sense that this is my training, that for some reason I am being taught to handle sudden shifts, just as I did at my mother's birthday party. The dream implies that these abrupt shifts are tests of readiness for new life, life outside the mundane, life outside the matrix.

When the boy yelled "Jew-Girl," I thought, "yes, I have survived a holocaust and now I will survive this too," and I felt empowered rather than defeated by the assault, for I sensed it meant something important. He spit right on my heart chakra, underscoring that this painful phase too is my path of heart, that I must go through this and face the deeper emotions and the shame if I am to connect to my innocence again, if I am to fully discover who I really am and what I am really made of. I have the strength of the little girl within myself to draw on as I deal with all the emotions she's kept safely buried for me. The act of actually *feeling* all those emotions is perhaps the most frightening aspect of this recapitulation.

The biggest lesson I take away from this dream is really understanding how breaking an obsessive-compulsive routine allows for other things to happen, how one change leads to another, how one small step leads to a million more steps. Things can change in an instant, and then all of life opens up, life becomes a gift rather than predictable drudgery. I must not be so afraid of change, for it occurs naturally, but see it as the catalyst to new life. Change is random and there's nothing you can do about it except go along with it. Even if you fight it, it happens anyway. The way to meet it is with an open attitude. As I am confronted by what life throws at me, I must remain aware that life is a series of constantly unfolding events that are presented for my benefit, for my growth. Life is naturally always shifting, so alive, eager for something new to come along. All I have to do is get in alignment with that idea and be ready to accept what comes, knowing full well that it's all part of the unfolding of my greater journey on my path of heart, wherever that may lead!

At the same time, I do need a certain amount of stability while I undergo the instability of this phase of my journey. I am fully willing to go deeper into my inner world, but I must also remain fully present and functional in the outer world too. I need steady work and a steady income if my life as a mother and provider is to run smoothly. If I can have that, then I can handle everything else. My second dream seems to suggest this, that I must make sure everything is properly connected and in good working order, inside and out. This is the third occasion on which I am confronted with repairmen and their insights. First, there was the plumber in a recent dream letting me know that I needed an overflow valve. Then, in real life, the fuel man warned me that I needed to make sure the fuel could flow properly to the furnace, and now I must repair the ventilation system so I can breathe. Such good advice from all these helpers!

I also know from my work on the chakra systems, within the energy body, that these three repairmen are suggesting that the second, third, and fourth chakras are needing some attention. The second chakra, in the genital region, is represented by water, where I have been facing my childhood sexual abuse; the third, in the solar plexus, is fire, where I am doing my alchemical work; and the fourth, the heart chakra, is air, where the lungs are located. All three of these chakras, when fully worked and realized, in a process such as this recapitulation, and kept in good balance, allow access to the higher chakras and experiences of a transcendental sort. I've accessed the higher chakras often enough under the duress of this recapitulation process, but I can only hope that someday I may access them volitionally, with calm intent! The human part of life is just as important as the spiritual, and I must have both in balance.

The breath of life is the most important link to all the chakras. My recent dream repairman fixed something in the fourth chakra, telling me that now I should be able to breathe easier, hinting perhaps at a lessening of my inner distress and tension. Interesting that he arrived after the boy spit on my heart center. Perhaps my time in the alchemical cauldron has been suffocating me a little more than I realized, a faulty ventilation system is as bad as a stagnant routine!

Please, I ask you, all of my spiritual advisors, to help me, to please send me enough work so I can proceed on my journey without worry for my financial stability as I take this journey that is unfolding, this journey that I am prepared to take, one step at a time, aware that I must go through each phase, and that each phase will take the time it takes. I am grateful every day for this journey and for what I receive. Please help me to live this most amazing life with a fearless and trusting heart.

December 29, 2003

I dream that I'm lying stuck between the rails in the dark train yard of my previous dream. Like a hellish vise, the rails clench tighter and tighter. I am in excruciating pain. I call out to Chuck and he comes and stays beside me all night, whispering in my ear as the rails clamp ever tighter.

"It's all right, it will be all right," he says.

He lies in between the narrow train tracks and feels the rails pressing against him too, so that he can experience my pain, he says. As I push against the ever-tightening rails, trying to hold them back, Chuck tells me that it won't last much longer, that they are not as strong now.

"It's almost over," he says.

Is it any wonder that I'm so exhausted? The days and nights are torture, my body clenching, my legs stiff, my mind lost in darkness. I am pulled up out of it every now and then when someone needs me or talks to me, but then I return to it, falling back down into darkness and dread. It has to go through me, the old energy has to finish out its life within me, until it has lost all its strength, until it is no more. I live in the prison of my alchemical cauldron almost all the time now, aware that I must have all the experiences that come as I take this journey. I have to go through every inch of this transforming process, suffer the pain and the clenching numbness along with the moments of insight. I have to go through it all. So I grit my teeth and bear the tension of the release of this negative energy that is now swirling through me. This is what sitting in the alchemical cauldron is all about, bearing the tension of the transformational process. And if I am to truly transform, it will be by my own intent and by my own doing of what needs to be done.

"Don't be a martyr," Chuck said the other day. "Don't."

Is that what I'm doing? Being a martyr? Holding on as best I can? Bearing the tension? Is that martyrdom? It feels like I'm just doing what I have to do in order to get through this phase. I have to be stronger than the old energy or it will pull me back again, clamp me down tightly between those rails. I will not let it get me today. The sun is shining and I have to turn to practical things, not let fear or pain overwhelm me, not get into a negative slump, but open up and let a little fresh air into the cauldron, into my lungs. I must open up to the prospect of hope and success in the near future. I must listen to what my guides are telling me, just sit quietly and listen to what comes from inside too, for it is from there that I will find the answers I seek.

"Follow your path. It will lead you where you need to go," says Jeanne.

How do I know I'm on the right path?

"Let it take you. Trust it; just go. Believe. Believe in yourself and you will find the light."

Yes, I will find the light.

In the afternoon, at the studio, I am suddenly hit hard. Feeling bad, very bad, but I don't call Chuck. It's too hard. I'm embarrassed, feel pathetic. I'd rather just hunker down and bear it, be depressed and distressed. Familiar old numbing comforts, I know, but my feelings are rampaging all over the place and I can think of nothing better to do. One minute I'm sad, then I'm angry. I'm lost in a nightmare and I can't find my way out. Help! I am lost and going crazy. I am drawing circles and going crazy, lost in circles that never begin and never end. I could stay here forever, going around and around like a spinning record, circling around, never getting anywhere but crazy.

I make the kids take a walk with me after dinner. They protest heartily at first, but enjoy it immensely. So do I, it offers a nice shift. Back at home, I realize how afraid I am of the night and what happens at night, the nightmares that come. Can I get Chuck to come to me again in my dreams? Last night it helped that he told me everything was going to be okay. In reality, nothing feels okay though. In reality, memories of bad things happening creep in and fear creeps in with them.

A memory suddenly emerges. I am five years old. I need help, but I am reluctant to ask, because there is no one I can depend on. Even though my need is very great, I anticipate no one coming and so I hunker down and bear it. I can't explain how great the need is either, I just deal with it. This is why I can't ask for help now either. I am a five-year-old girl who knows that when she calls for help no one comes, ever. So, once again, I elect to sit and bear the tension of this great need out of fear of abandonment. I elect to sit in the cold emptiness of a memory of certain desertion rather than risk asking for a little help. Don't I trust Chuck yet?

All last night I wanted to call him, all day today I have wanted to call too. I cry and still I can't do it. I am torturing myself. He won't mind. He doesn't mind if I call. He wants to help me. Do I want to go through yet another night in this torture, in the danger zone? I want to quit this recapitulation now, to just give up. Saying that doesn't really mean anything except that I'm exhausted and when I get like this I turn on myself, and then I am my own worst enemy. Sometimes, when I'm tired, the old me wins. I know there is no going back, but I can't see anything except this dark and dangerous place that I am in at this moment. It's taking all my energy. I can't see beyond it. I am just a five-year-old girl again, not trusting, alone, embarrassed to say that I need help.

I call.

"Tell yourself to float up, to get out of the rails," Chuck says. "Float above it all, then fly away. It's the way to free yourself from it, from the danger zone."

"I forgot I could command myself to do such things!" I say, suddenly lighter, re-infused with insight and energy. "You are so right, I can do anything I want. I'm in charge!"

"Let me know how you make out," he says. "You can do it, make yourself fly out of the clamped rails. Make it happen!"

It's as if a shift in the assemblage point just happened, for I am in a new and better place after our call. It's suddenly clear to me that if I have the ability to ask for help in my dreams, then I have the ability to help myself at any time. I've been so focused on needing Chuck when I need myself even more. I have everything I need. All the power is within me. It's my dream.

December 30, 2003

I am in a small teacup-shaped pod, hovering above the train yard. I am tethered to the rails by a connection of black hoses that go into the pod and then into me, reminiscent of a scene in *The Matrix*. The pod is filled with water. I hover above the rails in my pod for a few seconds before getting yanked back down. I use all my power to raise my pod back up again. I can't figure out how to detach the hoses, but I'm able to stay aloft for longer and longer periods of time, rising up a little higher each time. I look at myself and see that I am covered in white feathers, that I am a swan sitting in my pod of water. I'm too heavy a bird, I think, I need to be lighter, like a robin or even a much smaller bird like a wren, but alas, I have ended up a heavy swan. A great force repeatedly tries to gain control over me, yanking my pod back down to the tracks, attempting to clamp me down between the rails, but I won't let it. "No! I am in control," I say. Fierce battles ensue as I will myself higher and higher. I get pulled down repeatedly but am always able to regain enough power to float back up again. At the same time, I remain frustratingly attached by the black hoses. I cannot fly out of the pod, sever the hoses, or completely get away.

While prepping for dreaming last night I had decided that one way I could get out of the train rails was by turning into water so I could flow away or by turning into a bird so I could fly away. The two ideas seem to have meshed in this dream. Chuck had suggested that I float above the rails, and float I did, but even though I had wings I just couldn't fly.

With the dream still fresh, I call Chuck, following up as he had asked me to do. All the elements, the intentions are there, he tells me, but the one piece that seems to be missing is to believe. I know this to be true. I need to tap into belief in myself and my own powers, belief that I can survive on my own, belief that I don't really need anything from anyone else, that I am enough. It is, after all, my own dream.

"It was a good effort last night," Chuck says, "and the fact that you did not sleep clamped between the train tracks is major, but you still need to believe."

"I can do it," I say. "I can power myself up and away, fly out of the darkness, get away from the control of those beings in the train yard. What I really need, if I am to advance, doesn't exist there."

The train yard is a prison, a place of torture, a dark place controlled by armed guards. It's a place of rules and routine and I am electing to break the rules and routines, represented by the rails, electing to get away from the torture and safety of habits that I am no longer interested in engaging in. It's a concentration camp and I have indeed survived it. "I survived," I said to myself. "I am a survivor. I am not a prisoner any longer." From my new vantage point in the hovering pod in last night's dream, I could see that I have indeed been in a concentration camp, but the war is over now. I can leave now. I can let go of PTSD and OCD, and all the routines of old. No one will try to catch me when I leave. The suffering is over now; no more hands touching me, no more hands hurting me, no more torture. I must put on my wings and fly away. I can do it. I can free myself. I just have to believe strongly enough. Believe, Neo, believe!

Even as I write this and yearn to believe, I am pulled back down to that dark place. Why? Why can't I get away? Why does the darkness still feel so safe? Is it because it's so familiar? Is that it, just that it's totally familiar?

"Leave; just leave. Don't turn back," says Jeanne. *"You have those girls in your heart; they are all with you. You aren't leaving anything behind, except your own terror and you don't want that terror. You certainly don't want that terror. You know how strong you are. You have had glimpses of the new you, and you also know from your past just how incredibly strong you have always been. You survived the abuse because you are incredibly strong. There is no one with your strengths. Remember that. Take that strength. Leave the terror. Believe. You are going to a beautiful and safe place. Believe in yourself. Trust and believe. Trusting and believing don't have to be so difficult and so painful. In fact, they are the means out of the pain."*

"What am I trusting and believing in?"

"Yourself, and the whole universe."

My spiritual advisors are right here. Whenever I look for them they are here, waiting for me to just open my eyes and see them. I go quiet inside to hear what they tell me. They know everything about me; there is no explaining to do. I just have to listen, trust, and believe in myself.

"Please stay with me," I pray to them. "I need you all, now more than ever. This is the end of the darkness and it is always darkest just before the dawn."

I realize that the inner voice, a soothing voice that I hear when I sit quietly, has always been with me. It's not Jeanne's voice, but another more ancient voice. I've noticed it a lot more lately because I've been consciously paying attention to it, learning to listen more deeply to what is inside me, taught by Jeanne to really listen and trust what I hear. As I have begun to really pay attention, I am able to clearly identify it as always having been present, warning me, prompting me, helping and guiding me throughout my life. I always knew I wasn't alone. I always heard that voice. And now I realize that it has been speaking to me from the very beginning, from the earliest days of life. I remember hearing it and understanding it long before I could even speak myself.

The kids and I spend the afternoon visiting with friends in Massachusetts, with the woman in the leopard skin dress of my dream of a few nights ago, my childhood friend and her family. They don't offer us anything to eat except a bowl of popcorn, though we are visiting for hours. I know the kids must be hungry but they barely eat any of it. I nibble a little, drink some water, but otherwise go the whole day without food. We stop at a restaurant on the way home and I make sure the kids eat.

While driving back on the Massachusetts Turnpike I drive into one of those cosmic tunnel experiences like I had on the bridge. I pull out of it immediately. It's not a good time and I'm on unfamiliar ground. Besides, it's raining, and I'm going seventy miles an hour and I have my kids with me, not a good situation. I beg out of it and am able to stay out of it, calling upon Jeanne and all of my guides to keep me present and alert and get us home safely. No cocoons of nothingness on this night, please!

I find the trip exhausting, especially the long drive home in the rainy darkness, the experience of the old friends less than pleasant, from an old world I no longer live in. The visit was torturous, almost like being strapped to those train tracks of my dream! I have so little in common with people I used to know, so little to talk about, and that childhood friend, once so special to me, no longer holds a special place in my life. I see that now. Childhood and the old life have long been over. In fact, the whole visit felt unreal. At least I felt unreal, like I wasn't really there. The old me felt obligated to do the right thing, to visit my old friends when asked, thought it was necessary and good to do, *for them.* The new me really just wanted to say, "look, I am too emotionally and physically drained to make the trip." The old me made the trip. The new me went along for the ride but barely surfaced.

December 31, 2003

All night I dream that I'm skiing through snowy dark woods looking for lost children. I collect as many as I can find in the darkness and lead them out of the woods. I do this over and over again, until I am exhausted. The job never seems to be done. I feel such a commitment to finding them and even though I'm exhausted I won't stop looking, worried that I've missed some of them. I know there are more out there and I'm concerned about leaving them behind in the cold dark snowy woods. Even though I have no energy left, I am determined to find them all. I cannot leave them to suffer or be destroyed by their circumstances, it just doesn't feel right. I take everyone home with me and try to give them advice about what to do with their lives. I get on the phone and call around trying to find places for all of them to stay, try to find them jobs, get them into schools, and get them settled in new safe and stable circumstances.

I wake up so disappointed. I couldn't do it! I couldn't do what I wanted to do in my dream last night. I didn't fly out of the train rails. I am back in a negative place, back in the darkness, my legs stiff with pain. Maybe now that I've gotten everyone else safely settled I can fly tonight. I'll rest up and prepare myself. I have to admit, the need to take care of everything and everyone else before I move on is great. Am I causing more anxiety by trying so hard, expecting too much? Chuck told me to not get discouraged, to keep the intent. The truth is, I have to stop rescuing and caring for others and shift all that energy to caring for myself now.

I take the kids to the mall to spend some of the money they got for Christmas. My daughter gets her ears pierced, sitting very bravely, her eyes scrunched tightly closed as the piercing tool stabs through her small pink ear lobes. My son buys a movie and a book, they both buy headphones. Then I drop them off to celebrate New Year's Eve with some friends.

I watch movies while the kids are away. No wine. No champagne. I didn't buy any. It would just add to my mental edginess and unhappiness, stir the already flaring emotional fire. I'm depressed. I hate my life! I absolutely hate it! How can I change it? It might be better to wait until I'm in a better frame of mind before even thinking about it. Haven't I changed enough already this year? Then why so depressed? Self-despair and self-hatred, my sad old companions, cozy up to me, delivering their old negative messages until I feel like crying. They are not whom I want to end the year with!

As a new year comes, what will it bring? What decisions, changes, and circumstances will I encounter? Who will I interact with? As I stand here on the cusp of the unknown, I feel fragile; as thin as fine porcelain, breakable as glass. I feel like I could fall to the floor and shatter into a million pieces and all that would be left of me would be tiny shards of glass glittering in the light, like droplets of bitter tears. Step on me then and grind me back into sand, smear me into dust so that I no longer feel the pain, until I am wiped into the cracks in the floor, swished down into gritty darkness. Blow me off the bottom of your shoes then too, and bury me in the garden among the spring daffodils, the hyacinths and tulips. Think of me there, happy at last, among the flowers and scents I once loved in real life. This is how I feel on the last day of the year, boringly alone and sad, planning my own funeral. Yuck! A big part of me doesn't care at all that a new year is about to begin. Another part of me hopes, just *hopes* for something to spark me back into life again. And hope is enough to start with.

Empty-Sad, Empty-Sad, Empty-Sad. I know I should be writing Full-Happy after several years of recapitulation, but it would be a lie, and more than anything I don't intend to lie to myself ever again. No more denial. I am being truthful at last about how I feel. I am a vessel full of unshed tears, sadness in my throat burning to be released, an ache in my heart that needs bursting, but I still hold it all in. The alchemical fire burns on unabated. Why can't I release the heat and the pressure? Here I am, acknowledging my pain, but to whom? Myself again, as usual, and this brings up another truth: I am lonely and yearning for someone who doesn't even exist.

The kids are home now. We're all turning in. It's been a lonely and depressing evening and now I just want to sleep, roll into a ball and sleep. I'm not going to intend any dreams tonight, it's too disappointing if they don't work out. I don't care if the old feelings take over. I know I'm just feeling sorry for myself, but I just need to sleep, to find a little comfort for my body and soul. I don't even care about dreaming anymore. I don't care about anything. I don't care what Chuck says, I'm not Neo.

My New Year's resolution: I'm not going to do anything for anyone except myself, at least for a few days, just take care of me. Then I intend to do what the voice inside tells me to do, the ancient voice that I have been reconnecting with. I have to get out of this rut, so I will listen to it very carefully. And not to just what comes from inside me, but to what comes from outside of me too, from all around me, because messages don't just come from inside. I am sure that if I open up and listen very carefully, I will receive the messages I need to hear.

I will stay open. That is my only intention for now. I will rest mentally and physically over the next few days, so I can do my life, live the life I am meant to live. I am an evolving being. I will follow my path and see where it leads, listening to my heart as I go, the voice of my own spirit. I intend to listen very carefully. And if my heart feels shattered and broken I must let it express that. Perhaps that's where I'm stuck, in not allowing my heart to express the emotions it needs to express. Until I do, there is no room for new life or new strength or new powers. There is only the pain and heat of the alchemical fire within me, flaring up, scorching me with its need for release.

"Stop holding, open up, let it flow," says Jeanne. *"Let the river of emotion flow. Let those dream figures in and let them show you all the sorrow they have been holding for you. They are here because they are done with holding. All the little girls are done with holding in and only you can free them so they can move on. Allow them permission to express their pain and in so doing your own pain will flow out too."*

"Take care of yourself, Jan, and that means allowing yourself the release you need. Allow yourself the expression of pain and sorrow, of sadness and empty loneliness that you hold so tightly locked inside. Let the New Year begin with a flood. It will be okay. And then you will know what to do next. Make room for what you need to do next. Make room in your heart."

"Oh, and by the way, Happy New Year!"

"Happy New Year to you too."

And then I realize that I did get out of the train yard in my dream last night! How else could I have skied all over the darned place collecting all those lost kids? Somehow I turned the train tracks into skis and went on a rescue mission. A brilliant solution! Belief in myself worked! Go, Neo! And once freed, I did the only thing that makes sense to me, that has ever made sense to me; I went on a rescue mission, searching for all my lost inner children. There's no way I can move on without taking everyone with me! And, just as Jeanne kept insisting, I hadn't left them behind in the old crumbling brownstone. I didn't leave anything back there. They were in the woods, and appropriately so, for where else would they wait for me but right where they knew I would find them. Boy, it sure took me long enough to figure that out! Luckily, my unconscious was on top of it.

I think we are all going to finally move into that new modern house on the other side of the River of Letting Go before this night is over, together again at last. It's a matter of the heart, after all, as Jeanne says. For the heart, the real place of no pity, is only a place of love. And as this New Year begins, I must make room in my heart for what matters most: myself, all of me!

I've been steeped in my own darkness, and appropriately so, for it is my own darkness that has been my worst enemy, not my past, not my abuser, but my own defenses. With all my strength and willpower, I created the concentration camp and kept it running according to my own schedule. And it sure ran like clockwork! I have indeed been my own jailer. My darkness has also been the means to my salvation, to discovering myself, to loving myself, for I cannot deny that only in going through the darkness have I been able to achieve the light.

I have come through the darkest darkness now and I find myself standing on the cusp of a new dawn, shaking like a leaf as I peer into the light of a brand new day, a brand new year, and a brand new phase. How could it be otherwise? For I am about to leap into the great unknown, yet again. You'd think I'd be used to it, and in a lot of ways I am, but at the same time I am just a frightened being facing the truth that I really have no control over anything, and I have no idea where I'm going, where I'll end up, or even if I'll survive, but going I am.

Happy New Year, indeed!

About the Author

J. E. Ketchel is a writer, artist, and psychic. In 2001 she began a life-changing journey, a soul retrieval journey that she documented during the course of a three-year period of intense inner work. She shares her intimate experiences of that journey in *The Recapitulation Diaries*.

Messages of guidance from her spirit guide Jeanne can be found on her website: www.riverwalkerpress.com.

Books by J. E. Ketchel, published by Riverwalker Press in both paperback and e-book format are available for purchase through www.amazon.com:

The Man in the Woods
The Recapitulation Diaries: Volume 1

The Edge of the Abyss
The Recapitulation Diaries: Volume 2

Into the Vast Nothingness
The Recapitulation Diaries: Volume 3

Place of No Pity
The Recapitulation Diaries: Volume 4

The Book of Us
with Chuck Ketchel

***

Coming next, the final book in the recapitulation series:

Dreaming All the Time
The Recapitulation Diaries: Volume 5